MW00669137

The Early Imperial Republic

EARLY AMERICAN STUDIES

Series Editors
Kathleen M. Brown, Roquinaldo Ferreira,
Emma Hart, and Daniel K. Richter

Exploring neglected aspects of our colonial, revolutionary, and early
national history and culture, Early American Studies reinterprets
familiar themes and events in fresh ways. Interdisciplinary in character,
and with a special emphasis on the period from about 1600 to 1850, the
series is published in partnership with the McNeil Center for Early
American Studies.

A complete list of books in the series is available from the publisher.

THE EARLY
IMPERIAL REPUBLIC

From the American Revolution
to the U.S.–Mexican War

Edited by Michael A. Blaakman,
Emily Conroy-Krutz, and Noelani Arista

PENN

UNIVERSITY OF PENNSYLVANIA PRESS

PHILADELPHIA

Copyright © 2023 University of Pennsylvania Press

All rights reserved.
Except for brief quotations used for purposes of review or scholarly
citation, none of this book may be reproduced in any form by any
means without written permission from the publisher.

Published by
University of Pennsylvania Press
Philadelphia, Pennsylvania 19104-4112
www.upenn.edu/pennpress

Printed in the United States of America on acid-free paper
10 9 8 7 6 5 4 3 2 1

Hardcover ISBN: 978-0-8122-5278-1
eBook ISBN: 978-0-8122-9775-1
A Cataloging-in-Publication record is available from the
Library of Congress

CONTENTS

INTRODUCTION

MICHAEL A. BLAAKMAN AND EMILY CONROY-KRUTZ

The United States, Thomas Hutchins marveled in 1784, would soon be a more "potent empire" than any "that ever existed." Its dominion, he calculated, would stretch further "than the Persian and Roman empires together."[1] The first and last geographer to the United States, Hutchins made this pronouncement in his *Historical Narrative and Topographical Description of Louisiana and West-Florida*, a prospectus for U.S. expansion that compiled the expertise he had gained during twenty-eight years in the service of another empire—the British one—as a cartographer, Indian agent, and military engineer. Hutchins had shown no concern for colonial protests or patriot ideology during the 1760s and 1770s. In 1776, when his native New Jersey severed ties with Britain, Hutchins was in London, petitioning the ministry for a large land grant in West Florida and for an appointment that would place him closer to the property he already owned there. He cast his lot with the rebel republic only in 1780, after a securities scheme gone bad and a brief imprisonment dashed his hopes for British land grants and glory. Within months of returning to North America, he joined Congress's employ.

Hutchins published his *Topographical Description* amid a busy schedule charting paths for U.S. incursions into new regions. He drew maps, delineated state boundary lines, scouted canal routes, surveyed unceded Native lands northwest of the Ohio River, and at one point pondered an expedition to the Pacific. But the Gulf Coast was Hutchins's true passion, and by 1788 he had concluded that the infant empire was either uninterested in the region or impotent to acquire it. Even while holding national office, he spent the final year of his life making overtures to "become a Spanish Subject" and "geographer to His Spanish Majesty," who had gained claim to West Florida in the 1783 Treaty of Paris.[2]

Clearly, Hutchins was a creature of empire—or rather, of many empires, his allegiance and exuberance often chasing opportunity. So perhaps his premature paean to American empire should come as no surprise. And yet during the 1780s, Hutchins was not alone in trumpeting the United States as an imperial parvenu. John Filson, a surveyor and booster of Kentucky lands, described the Ohio Valley as eligibly "situated in the central part of the extensive American empire," while Thomas Jefferson imagined an unfurling "Empire of liberty."[3] In speeches and letters to domestic and foreign audiences alike, George Washington began calling the United States a "rising empire" even before the Treaty of Paris was signed.[4] During the revolutionary and early national eras, Americans referred to the United States as an empire repeatedly, in numerous contexts, and almost as soon as they started calling it a republic. What did they mean? Such language was not without its contradictions. For many of Hutchins's contemporaries, the lessons of classical history taught that empire spelled the end of a republic, and some wondered whether the idea of an expansive republic was a contradiction in terms.

In recent years, historians have begun looking to empire, imperialism, and colonialism as frameworks for thinking about U.S. history from independence to the U.S.–Mexican War. They have shown how the United States added its own imperial ambitions to a long Atlantic and North American history of competition and conflict among European and Indigenous polities. For years, the fledgling seaboard confederation struggled even to project power over the Appalachian crest. Yet within seven decades, it transformed itself into an imperial juggernaut with aspirations to rule a continent and beyond. By the 1850s, the United States had sharpened its tools for dispossessing Native peoples and expanding a political economy grounded in Black enslavement. White Americans had conquered an immense amount of territory and claimed the Pacific Ocean as their western boundary, while setting their imperial sights upon regions, people, and resources much further afield.

The language of Hutchins and others in the early republic opens a trove of interpretive questions about the character of the new nation and the meaning of empire, then and now. When we speak of empire, do we mean a political form? Something formal, or informal? A set of practices? A set of processes? A set of ideas, visions, and ambitions? We might ask how Americans reconciled the United States' simultaneous development as both a republic and an empire, and what kind of empire it was. We might look at the geography of the early republic to ask *where* the early United States was an empire, and how North American developments connected to U.S. efforts to project power in other parts of the globe.

These questions are at the center of this volume. *The Early Imperial Republic* draws together historians investigating the origins of U.S. imperialism from an array of vantage points. The essays gathered here do not advance one single definition of empire. But they fruitfully use an imperial lens to bring into focus patterns of continuity and change from the prerevolutionary period to the mid-nineteenth century. They are attentive to multiple forms and registers of imperial power—politics, culture, economy, and imaginaries—as well as their limits, vulnerabilities, unevenness, and failures. They examine white settlers, free and enslaved Black people, Native Americans, politicians, merchants, missionaries, and more on an even analytical footing, probing their interrelationships across evolving systems of power, sovereignty, and exchange. This volume does not aspire to present a comprehensive history of the origins of U.S. empire. Rather, it provides a series of snapshots of how early U.S. imperial claims, ambitions, and conflicts emerged in their local contexts. Taken together, its chapters illuminate how an imperial approach to the early republic opens new possibilities for understanding a polity that was simultaneously a republic and an empire, and for integrating the history of the early imperial republic with that of the larger world.

* * *

Although it is increasingly difficult to find scholars who would deny that the United States became an empire, diplomatic historians have traditionally marked 1898 as the beginning of the republic's imperial era. It was in that year that the United States went to war with Spain purportedly to liberate Cuba and the Philippines from Spanish rule. By year's end, Puerto Rico, Hawaiʻi, the Philippines, and Guam were U.S. territories. The liberating rhetoric of the American war was belied by the many years of brutal warfare it took to make the Philippines an American colony. As Rudyard Kipling's poetry urged the United States to take up the "white man's burden" of civilizing empire, the wars of 1898 saw a surge of both pro- and anti-imperialist fervor in the United States that asked, among other things, what kind of country the United States had been and would become on the world stage.[5]

These conversations were especially loaded because the possession of an overseas colony seemed to make the United States look more like the European empires that many Americans had spent decades defining their country against. What did it mean for Americans' national identity to have the United States stepping into this role? To resolve this apparent tension, pro-imperial Americans in the late nineteenth century emphasized continuity over change. The United States, they argued, would remain a different sort of power from oppressive European empires. In its new geographic reach, they claimed, the United States would spread the benefits of modern civilization. It was the anti-imperialists who emphasized change, insisting that the new colonial possessions overseas marked a turning point in American history—a break with long-standing American values like liberty and republican governance. Historian William Appleman Williams described this era as one of an American "anti-colonial imperialism," a seeming contradiction in terms that is a helpful reminder of the multiple forms that imperialism and anti-imperialism have taken.[6] For the imperialists of the 1890s, it was entirely possible to critique certain forms of empire while embracing others. Indeed, this sort of argument was a key to American imperialism throughout its history.

Just as the political debates of the 1890s were predicated on differences in terminology and definitions of what, exactly, constituted empire, so, too, is the historiography of U.S. empire. Scholars aim for specificity in our terminology, and "empire" has proven to be a vexing word for many Americanists seeking a definition that is neither too narrow nor too capacious. Too broad, and the word loses its specific analytical value; too narrow, and we miss important imperial dynamics. To designate 1898 as the beginning of an American imperial era, for instance, requires a particular definition of "empire." For the diplomatic historians' traditional chronology to make sense, "empire" must be defined narrowly as the assertion of colonizing political sovereignty over noncontiguous territory and the people who inhabit it. By contrast, broader definitions of the term have gained currency in global histories of empire, including the "new imperial history" of the British empire, the cultural analysis of American studies, and settler colonial and Indigenous studies. Since the 1990s, insights from these fields have in turn transformed the ways that scholars describe the longer arc of U.S. empire.[7]

"Empire," "imperialism," "colonialism," and "settler colonialism" all appear in these pages. In identifying imperial moments and dynamics in the history of the early American republic, the authors in this volume adopt a number of definitions of empire. They approach this question from multiple subfields, each of which has deployed the language of empire in this era slightly differently. Rather than insist upon a singular model of empire, we argue that a history of empire must emphasize local variation within a broad framework. We utilize "imperialism" as the most general term to describe unequal power dynamics between a government (or its representatives) and a foreign body that it is seeking to control. In this regard, we borrow from Jane Burbank and Frederick Cooper's observation that empires as distinct as the Ottoman, Russian, Spanish, and British all utilized the "politics of difference" and cultural intermediaries to rule.[8] It is these core characteristics that make imperialism distinctive and legible. But within that capacious definition of imperialism, American empire could look quite different in different locations and from different perspectives.

As the essays in this volume demonstrate, attention to these different forms of imperialism reveals a complex image of American power. Such complexity can be challenging if we seek to survey the history of the early United States. Locations and historical agents that do not easily conform to a clear narrative tend to drop away from view. But in order to understand the nature of U.S. power in this era, its implications for later periods in American history, and the way it shaped U.S. relations with other peoples and polities, we must contend with the multifaceted nature of American empire in the era of the early republic.

The evolution of British imperial historiography can be instructive here. The traditional division of "first" and "second" British empires, divided by the American Revolution in their chronology, geography, and governance, makes clear that it is possible to talk about multiple forms within the same imperial history. The scholars who distinguished between these two eras were attempting to capture real historical transformations in imperial practice and form, including a shift away from relying on settler colonialism and toward colonial rule over large populations of non-white subjects.[9] More recently, historians of the British empire have questioned this clear categorical division. They have noted important continuities, arguing that settler-colonial structures and rule over non-white subjects describe British imperial projects of both eras.[10] Yet the impulse to differentiate between two eras of British empire should sound familiar to historians of the United States, who have puzzled over how to describe the breaks and continuities across the history of American imperialism.

This is especially true for those Americanists who study the era of the early republic. In the years after the American Revolution, the United States emerged as a new nation out of a collection of colonies. It was not a dominant force on the international stage. Yet by the decades leading up to the Civil War, it had more than doubled its size, stretching its geographic footprint across the North American continent from coast to coast and claiming sovereignty over Indigenous people and their lands. It had sent merchants and missionaries around the globe. Private citizens had established a colony on the western coast of Africa and undertaken filibustering raids into Latin America. The United States was, in other words, an imperial republic. But only recently have scholars begun to call it that. Even as historians of later U.S. empire have pushed their accounts of its origins earlier into the nineteenth century, their focus has primarily been on the years after the U.S.–Mexican War, implying a stark historical departure from the earlier United States, including the revolutionary era's self-proclaimed empire builders.[11]

Historians' long-standing ambivalence toward understanding the early republic as an empire has stemmed from at least four sources.[12] First and foremost is American exceptionalism: a tendency to cleave off U.S. history as distinct, a unique political project in a world of empires. Though consciously rejected and critically dismantled by the vast majority of U.S. historians, exceptionalism retains a foothold in the historiography of the early United States through some of its organizing categories. Concepts such as national expansion, Manifest Destiny, and the American frontier originated in Whiggish narratives of the nation's past, and they have often served as obfuscating euphemisms for American imperialism. Even when shorn of their overt triumphalism, they tend to cast the history of U.S. power beyond comparison and to sever the history of the early republic from what came before and what would follow.[13]

The second source of scholarly unease about imperial approaches to the early republic is the fact that the young United States was weak. From a traditional foreign relations perspective, the new republic was a minor power, unable to assert its will overseas. From the standpoint of sociology and political science, meanwhile, the early United States was characterized by a small national state, bureaucratically anemic by design. More recently, scholars have begun to dispel the "myth" of the small or weak U.S. state, proposing new formulations—"out of sight," "light and inconspicuous"—to capture its peculiar character. Still, if the idea of empire has often stood as a synonym for top-down rule imposed from afar by a robust central state, then the early American republic hardly fits the bill.[14]

The third reason scholars have been hesitant to see the new republic as an empire lies in two entrenched distinctions: between empires and nation-states, on the one hand, and empires and republics, on the other, as antithetical political forms. The former dichotomy stems from nineteenth-century nationalist and colonial independence movements. The latter originated with eighteenth-century republican thinkers; despite many white Americans' embrace of the word "empire" to describe their revolutionary project, republican anxieties about centralized power's tendency toward tyranny could also brand empire as liberty's opposite. During the nineteenth and twentieth centuries, both diametrical pairs became calcified in the national origin story of a republic founded in anti-imperial rebellion. As historian Daniel Immerwahr has described, these distinctions have long served a crucial role in Americans' historical and ongoing efforts to "hide" their empire. The notion that empires are distinct from republics and nations has obscured the parallels between U.S. approaches to projecting power across vast distances and the political repertoires of other empires, enabling Americans to see the United States as anticolonial and to believe that its exertions of power have been typically benign.[15]

Constructs of American mythmaking, the empire/nation and empire/republic dichotomies have deeply shaped American historical scholarship. Casting continental conquests in North America as "national expansion," not empire, for example, enabled generations of historians to uncritically accept U.S. territorial claims to Indigenous homelands and to discount Native sovereignty.[16] The bifurcation of imperial and national history has also artificially segregated encounters and conflict in North America from the United States' place in global histories. As historian Rosemarie Zagarri has noted, it is no coincidence that scholarship on the founding and early national eras, a field that has taken nation-building as its defining historical problem, made the transnational turn quite slowly.[17]

At the most fundamental level, the dichotomy separating empires from nation-states has structured a key metanarrative of early American historiography, serving not just as a static dyad but as a plot: *from* a continent of competing empires *to* the early republic and the U.S. nation-state. Historian Johann Neem observes that over the last few decades, early American historians have framed their interpretations around this rupture. They have portrayed European empires as hierarchical but inclusive entities, defined on their peripheries by the fluid exchange of cultures, ideas, identities, people, and goods among diverse groups and across porous borders. This literature emphasizes how the drive to extend authority over contested territories required early modern empires to accommodate legal and constitutional pluralism, fragmented jurisdictions, and negotiated power. In this context, imperial borderlands were places where, despite violence and exploitation, Native people and polities as well as free and enslaved Africans and African-descended people could leverage European competition and exchange to chart advantageous paths for themselves. This scholarship contrasts empires with nation-states, portraying the latter as unitary legal spaces committed to border-making, territorial forms of sovereignty and jurisdiction, political and cultural uniformity, and racial exclusion. From this historiographical vantage, the birth of an American nation-state spelled the death knell for an eighteenth-century world of imperial exchange, mobility, and negotiation.[18] But what becomes of this narrative plot if we cease to understand empires and nations as mutually exclusive entities, and if we take seriously the claims of many eighteenth- and nineteenth-century contemporaries, both within and beyond the United States, that the new republic was also an empire?

The fourth factor obscuring our view of the imperial dimensions of the early republic is the organization of the historiography itself, which has tended to pull the study of U.S. imperialism's various regions and registers into separate methodologies and subfields. Before the Omohundro Institute began promoting a "vast" conception of early American history, the tension between Atlantic and continental frameworks—the one occasionally accused of being Eurocentric, the other considered teleological by some—drew scholarly attention toward one geography or another.[19] Thematic specialties have proven no less of an obstacle. Legal historians, military historians, diplomatic historians, religious historians, and intellectual historians each have developed rich approaches to the study of empire. Histories of borderlands, capitalism, gender, migration, Native America, slavery, and the state have all provided valuable insights into the form and function of American imperialism. Yet these various contributions have too often been siloed in the subfields that produce them.

Consider, for instance, two bodies of theory that different groups of specialists have recently deployed to situate the United States comparatively and to assess continuities from the prerevolutionary era to the early republic. During the past decade or so, early American and Native American and Indigenous studies scholars have seized on the theory of settler colonialism, which describes a model of empire typified by a "logic of elimination" as settlers claim occupied lands, remove Indigenous residents, and establish new communities in their place. Settler-colonial theory has proven useful for analyzing methods of dispossession, for drawing comparisons across settler regimes established by different imperial powers, and for highlighting common patterns of culture, rhetoric, and law.[20] But scholars have also noted that the concept tends to flatten variation across space and minimize change over time. Some point out that settler colonialism's focus on "structures" risks diminishing the contingency of settler expansion and the significance of Indigenous resistance, and that its emphases relegate to the background nonsettler forms of colonialism as well as other, interrelated expressions of imperial power.[21]

Historians seeking to evaluate the position of the United States in the world beyond North America have turned to a different framework: postcolonial theory. Seeing the United States as a postcolonial nation helps to explain its continued dependence long after 1776 on European goods and allies. From a comparative perspective, Ann Laura Stoler has argued that postcolonialism can also illuminate the role of intimate relations in the development of racial categories in the United States.[22] Yet if settler-colonial theory risks suggesting too much strength for the early United States, postcolonial theory does the opposite. The white founders who were anxious about their inferiority in the face of European powers were hardly subalterns in their interactions with Indigenous people.

In short, while both concepts offer important insights, they are also, in some ways, at odds. Moreover, they each present significant blind spots that render the two frameworks, combined, insufficient to explain the character of the new republic and its role in the world. For example, neither settler colonialism nor postcolonialism can fully describe the presence of white Americans in spaces defined by Native power or ruled by Indigenous empires. Neither can easily account for the experiences of the African Americans enslaved by Native Americans who were violently removed from their ancestral lands by the United States, or of eastern Native nations forcibly resettled on western lands that belonged to other Indigenous polities. Neither framework offers a conceptual language for analyzing the ordeal of emancipated African Americans establishing a colony on the western coast of Africa or the U.S. quest to possess uninhabitable guano islands in the 1850s. Though scholarly specialization serves many purposes, in these instances and many others it has had the effect of unraveling empire's warp and weft, making the early republic's broader imperial patterns difficult to apprehend.[23]

And yet recent scholarship has also made the imperial dimensions of the early republic impossible to ignore. Heeding Rosemarie Zagarri's call to the "global turn" for the study of the early United States, the latest histories of the early republic have embraced transnational questions and methods. This turn to the global has found Americans in European colonial spaces and revealed the extent to which Americans, too, had imperial ambitions on a global scale.[24] For instance, while it would not become a territory of the United States until 1898, Hawaiʻi had been an important target of American empire long before that point. American Protestant missionaries first arrived on the islands in 1820, and they enjoyed unusually good relations with Indigenous leaders as they went about their work of "civilizing" and Christianizing.[25] Liberia, too, holds a crucial position in the history of American empire. Established by the American Colonization Society (ACS) but largely funded by the U.S. government, Liberia was not part of Jefferson's "empire of liberty." It was never intended to become a state of the union, nor was it to become an overseas colony of the government. It operated in practice as a sphere of U.S. influence, but was intended, instead, as a home for formerly enslaved people to create a new country outside of the bounds of the United States.[26] The United States, in short, was never isolated from the rest of the world. Commerce, religion, the slave trade, and colonization all brought Americans out of the North American continent during the era of the early republic. To be sure, not all global encounters are imperial, and the United States remained a comparatively weak power in global affairs through much of this period.[27] Yet many of these encounters revealed the imperial ambitions and anxieties of state and nonstate actors alike.

If the global turn has directed scholarly attention to overseas spaces of American imperialism, the flourishing field of Indigenous history has reframed our understanding of the North American past. This scholarship emphasizes Native perspectives, centers Indigenous power in stories of early America, and adopts long chronological parameters within which Native communities saw various European and European-descended peoples come and go over the *longue durée*. The early republic, in this burgeoning literature, appears less like an exceptional nation-state and more like an entrant into a world of many empires, both Native and European. With this framing, the relative weakness of the United States does not signal the impossibility of empire. After all, as scholars of other empires have recently emphasized, fragility and failure have been imperial hallmarks throughout history.[28] Instead, the fledgling republic's imperial ambitions, shortcomings, and successes invite new questions for the study of American history.

* * *

Featured on countless book covers and glossy inserts, John Gast's *American Progress* (Figure I.1) is a familiar image to the student of nineteenth-century

Figure I.1. John Gast, *American Progress*, oil on canvas, 1872. Autry Museum, Los Angeles, 92.126.1.

America. The 1872 painting, an allegory for the nation's precipitous expansion in the preceding decades, highlights many of the themes that animate discussions of American empire, then and now. White male settlers move from the light of the east to the dark of the west, traveling alongside innovations of technology and transportation. In the shaded western region, Native men, women, and children flee with the buffalo. At the center of all of this is the ethereal figure of progress, a white woman clad in classical robes, crowned with a star, and holding aloft the twin symbols of civilization: the schoolbook and the telegraph wire.

Some thirty years earlier, members of the Missionary Society of the Methodist Episcopal Church would have seen a strikingly similar image illustrating their membership certificates (Figure I.2). Here, the otherworldly female figure holds not the schoolbook, but the Holy Bible. Under her feet, the world is similarly transformed. A missionary preaches to a group of rapt Native

Figure I.2. Membership certificate to the Methodist Episcopal Missionary Society, lithograph, ca. 1835. The Library Company of Philadelphia.

Americans, sitting together in front of their tepees, while an African family kneels in the front of the scene, broken chains by their feet and arms lifted up in pleading—a position that echoes that of the abolitionist "Am I Not a Man and a Brother?" emblem. Meanwhile, the left side of the scene reveals the conquering path of progress. Temples and columns crumble while the ungodly cower in terror.

Both of these allegories draw on a shared visual vocabulary. Figures are clustered and arranged so as to reify racial hierarchies. Symbols of white womanhood, hovering above the fray, herald the triumph of what the creators of these images understood to be "civilization." And both images deploy light and motion to suggest that the transformations they champion are somehow foreordained. But if their formal elements seem remarkably similar at first glance, upon further inspection these two images convey sharply contrasting visions of the nature, purpose, and future of American power. Gast's canvas envisions a continent purged of Indigenous people and devoid of African Americans. The settler-colonial process he evoked stretched back long before U.S. independence and had been a founding principle of the American republic, captured in revolutionary-era maps that erased Native presence and projected fanciful ambitions of an expansive republic domesticating allegedly vacant space (Figure I.3). The Missionary Society's iconography, however, posits a very different view of American power. With its allusions to African, European, Native American, and Asian architecture, the frame is not continental but global. And although couched in white supremacy, the plate centers Native and African people as part of an American Protestant future, rather than an extinguished non-Christian past. Despite their divergent messages, these illustrations of hierarchy, dramatic transformation, and varied ambitions each look like images of empire. Combined, they evoke this volume's contributions to the study of early U.S. imperialism.[29]

By analyzing the early United States as an empire, the essays in this volume reframe scholarly understandings of the new republic in three major ways. First, they bring the study of early U.S. imperialism down to earth. If the most recent work in global history and Indigenous studies has led historians to intuit that the early republic was indeed an empire, the authors in this volume show in detail *where* and *how* it was an empire. Historian Paul Kramer has urged scholars to expend less energy debating what empire is (and thus, whether or not the United States fits any particular definition at any particular point in its history), and to focus instead on what empire does.[30] Responding to this charge, the essays collected here catalog a

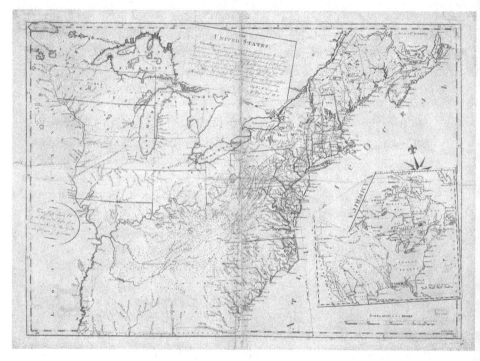

Figure I.3. William McMurray, "The United States According to the Definitive Treaty of Peace Signed at Paris," 1784. Library of Congress, Geography and Map Division. McMurray, a former assistant to Thomas Hutchins, omitted Native communities and polities from his map; the hand-colored lines represent the proposed boundaries of future American states under the Ordinance of 1784.

wide range of strategies for governing diverse peoples, calibrating different forms and levels of sovereignty, and projecting—and accommodating or resisting—U.S. power across vast distances. The timeworn notion of "national expansion" conjures images of a democratic and anticolonial nation folding new regions, imagined as blank territorial slates, into its uniform polity. But the contributors to this volume instead reveal a republican empire with many different faces. They encourage us to see the exertion of U.S. power on the ground as variegated, negotiated, and improvised—a process that both drew upon the example of its imperial predecessors and competitors and was forced to grapple with their legacies.

Second, the volume places the young republic in global context. Like the two allegories' separate geographic settings, scholars of the early republic have typically studied the United States' roles on the continent and overseas in isolation from each other. The notion of the continent that continues to influence the historiography in this regard was itself constructed by white Americans of the early republic, who deployed it to naturalize their quest to expropriate Native lands from Atlantic to Pacific.[31] The persistence of these geographical parameters only inhibits our ability to see U.S. empire in all its forms and spaces. As a whole, this volume advocates using the category of empire to bring continental and global histories of the United States into a single frame of analysis. It depicts white Americans' efforts to colonize Indigenous people and lands as an essential element in the history of U.S. empire, rather than a separate story.[32] Illuminating U.S. presence far beyond North America, its chapters reveal important connections between territorial conquests on the continent and the early republic's imperial incursions around the globe.

Third, with these approaches in hand, this volume challenges American historians' standard schema for periodizing the history of U.S. power and peripheries. The histories told here show that the 1898 turn to Cuba and the Philippines, the 1840s rise of Manifest Destiny, the constitutional reforms of the late 1780s, and even—in some ways—U.S. independence in 1776 were not stark ruptures from earlier eras. Rather than imperial turning points, they were moments of imperial acceleration, when prior patterns expanded in scale and when long-standing ambitions, settler-colonial and otherwise, became material realities. In pointing to these continuities over time, the volume collectively argues that American empire was never confined to one era, but is instead a thread throughout U.S. history.

*   *   *

The chapters that follow are organized into three parts that invite reflection on the different ways that thinking with and about empire transforms our understanding of the history of the early republic. The authors in Part I focus on problems of sovereignty and governance on the ground in North America. Jettisoning the dichotomies that have traditionally shaped scholarship on the early United States, they investigate multiple permutations of empire, state, and nation in the era of the early republic. In doing so, they illuminate telling comparisons and linkages between the United States and its imperial predecessors and competitors.

Robert Lee's essay, for instance, charts how British imperial frameworks resurfaced in the new nation's constitutional fabric. U.S. policymakers revived and reformulated the British empire's Indian boundary line, carving North America into legally distinct zones of imperial administration where—at least temporarily—different kinds of sovereignty would apply. To manage this system, the federal government reestablished the British imperial office of Indian superintendents. But in the U.S. context, Lee argues, these poorly paid bureaucrats were more accountable to the interests of local settlers than they were to the federal state or to the Native communities whose land rights they were charged with protecting.

Susan Gaunt Stearns turns our focus to merchants, long understood as agents of early modern empire. In the Mississippi Valley during the era of the early republic, Gaunt Stearns shows, imperialism rode on the back of private ambition and enterprise. Merchants not only bound the central state to the borderland periphery but also forged mutually beneficial economic ties between settlers and soldiers engaged in the work of territorial conquest. Conduits for both commerce and capital, merchants and their families were crucial to the young republic's efforts to project markets, military might, and state authority across its vast imperial claims. Investigating the institutional and personal ligaments that connected the national state to zones of imperial expansion, both Lee and Gaunt Stearns suggest what difference it made that the United States was a republican empire, not a monarchical one. By necessity rather than intention, early modern empires were fueled and steered by agents on the peripheries at least as much as they were directed from the metropole. These two essays suggest that the young United States transformed this de facto reality of imperial systems into a feature of its republican design.

Other contributors to Part I foreground historical continuities between the United States and other empires by investigating how groups that were partially or entirely external to the new republic interacted with it. Kathleen DuVal investigates the failed movements for Native confederacies promoted by Tecumseh, Tenskwatawa, and others in the early nineteenth century. Turning early American historiography's traditional empire-to-nation narrative on its head, she argues that these radical plans failed to take hold in Indian country because many Native people remained staunchly committed to their own separate nationhood—political forms and distinct identities that had guided prior interactions with European empires and that many Native people believed should remain the foundation of their stance toward a new republican empire. This Indigenous opposition to multinational confederations, DuVal suggests, helps explain the persistence of Native sovereignty in

North America from the prerevolutionary era through the long storm of U.S. invasion. Nation was a powerful weapon Indigenous people wielded against the imperial republic.

Brooke Bauer is similarly interested in how Native responses to the early imperial republic were rooted in Indigenous pasts. She investigates how Catawba people handled the incursions of South Carolina settlers under both British and U.S. imperial regimes. Bauer argues that Catawbas appropriated and adapted the idea of leasing Native lands to white settlers, a proposal first advanced by elite colonists as a thinly veiled strategy of dispossession and personal emolument under the British empire. After the Revolution, Catawbas drew on this prior experience with settler notions of property. They deeded some of their land to Catawba women and leased much of the rest to white settlers on their own terms, a dual strategy for retaining their land base and generating income, which quickly came into conflict with the political significance of freehold tenure for white U.S. citizens. Across both regimes, Bauer emphasizes the leading role of Catawba women in cultivating the land and making political decisions about how best to defend it. By the early nineteenth century, she shows, women were deeding property, inheriting it, and managing settlers' rents on behalf of the Catawba Nation—an adaptive continuation of their traditional role as stewards of the land.

The final chapters of Part I investigate how the early imperial republic extended its sovereignty and influence through the negotiated construction of property regimes on the ground. Julia Lewandoski explores how the republic incorporated preexisting land claims in Louisiana into its territorial sovereignty. If leaders in Washington envisioned folding the region into a tidy and uniform national land system, U.S. agents in the Territory of Orleans encountered a much messier situation. Land titles dating from the era of French and Spanish colonialism were vaguely delineated and often originated in the private purchase of Native title, a practice formally prohibited by federal law. Retrofitting these claims into U.S. systems of land tenure required federal officials to improvise around local understandings of property inherited from the French and Spanish eras. In doing so, they developed flexible notions of Native proprietorship and ensured that the legal remnants of prior imperial powers, less committed to Native dispossession, would remain a layered presence within the U.S. regime. In other words, national expansion, in practice, became a process of imperial accommodation—one that enabled the Chitimachas, Tunicas, Biloxis, and other Petites Nations to use land rights that had previously been recognized by the Spanish empire as a basis for asserting political sovereignty within an imperial United States.

Nakia Parker turns to antebellum Indian Territory, where, for some Cherokees, Creeks, Choctaws, Chickasaws, and Seminoles, slave ownership was a measure of political and economic success despite the violence and dislocation of Indian removal. A contested borderland, the southern plains offered strategic opportunities for Native leaders of the five "civilized tribes" as well as the people they enslaved. Native elites in diaspora worked to preserve their sovereignty and to economically benefit by playing competing powers—the Comanches, Mexico, the United States, and the Texas Republic—against each other, while enslaved people sought freedom among the region's preexisting Native communities or by fleeing to Mexico. Federal officials, eager to fend off Mexican influence and assert the United States' sovereign claims, cultivated the allegiance of Native leaders in Indian Territory by mobilizing the power of the national state to secure their property in slaves. Parker reveals that white southerners eagerly supported these efforts and came to see Indian Territory as "a slave state in embryo": a strategic colonial foothold, where the "domestic dependent nations" would serve as client states for expanding Black slavery into a new region, helping, in turn, to secure the institution's longevity in the southeastern homelands from which they had so recently been expelled.

Taken together, the essays in Part I suggest that if national leaders imagined that U.S. expansion would be defined by clear borders, uniform territorial sovereignty, white agency, Black exclusion, and Indigenous disappearance, what played out in practice was quite different. Tenuous, uneven, delegated, and negotiated, the construction and exertion of U.S. power in North America was recognizably imperial. When faced with challenges to the extension of their republic, U.S. officials consistently reached for solutions in familiar imperial forms and practices—fragmented sovereignty, public/private governance, legal pluralism, accommodation, and clientelage, among others—calling upon a political repertoire common to European empires. Meanwhile, Native people similarly drew on prior experiences, adapting the methods they had long used to deal with other empires, both Indigenous and European, in determining how to confront U.S. agents and citizens; at times, the new republic stepped into the role of an empire because that was how others perceived it and what they demanded of it. Emphasizing these historical continuities—the persistence and retention of imperial practices as the republic integrated new peoples and regions, often the pieces of older empires—the scholars in Part I remind us that the history of U.S. expansion was not written on a blank slate. Instead, they encourage us to see it as a process of accretion and to consider the early imperial republic as both the inheritor and the effect of other empires.

The volume's second part, "Continent and Globe," explores how American imperialism extended beyond the continent and out into the larger world, even in these early decades. The authors in Part II encourage us to see U.S. empire not only in the contiguous accumulation of territorial jurisdiction but also in networks of "corridors and enclaves," as Lauren Benton has put it: the establishment of outposts, channels, and spheres of influence in distant places.[33] Hawai'i, Liberia, and the Caribbean were all key sites for the history of early American empire and race, as these authors show. In these spaces, American individuals and organizations built upon earlier imperial practices and set the stage for future forms of U.S. empire.

As Tom Smith reveals in his essay, the imperialism of the American Protestant mission to Hawai'i was complicated to the point of paradox, incorporating both an embrace of Indigenous sovereignty and a racialized understanding of governance. This dynamic is clear in the ways that Protestant missionaries wrote about the Hawaiian expulsion of French and Irish Catholic priests for American audiences. Although the priests' banishment clashed with the supposed American value of religious liberty, Protestant missionaries asserted its legitimacy by emphasizing the sovereign power of Native Hawaiian leaders, such as the queen regent Ka'ahumanu. They insisted to American readers that the Hawaiian monarchy had the right, like all sovereign powers, to determine which foreigners could or could not reside within their territory. In so doing, the missionary writers differentiated between U.S. respect for Indigenous sovereignty (as they saw it) and the imperialist overreach of the French, whom they accused of attempting to force Catholicism upon an unwilling people. Yet as missionaries supported the actions of Indigenous leaders, they also embraced a different type of racial imperialism that would prove quite influential later in the century. Most Hawaiians, the missionaries argued, were not yet capable of identifying for themselves the "falsehood" of Catholic doctrine due to their "heathenism." Accordingly, they were not yet ready for the kind of religious freedom that existed within the United States and needed the intervention of Indigenous leaders to keep Catholics out.

The racist logic behind missionary thinking in Hawai'i also shaped the colonization movement. As Eric Burin discusses, racial governance was a key question as the American Colonization Society began planning its settlement in West Africa. African American settlers in Liberia would, on paper, be led by white colonial agents and governors. But in practice, the settlers often governed themselves due to the frequent deaths and departures of white agents. The governance of Liberia, unsurprisingly then, became a point of contention between the African American settlers and the white agents of the ACS and U.S. government in the first years of the settlement. In 1823, settlers protested their situation when conflicts over land allotments and low provisions became unbearable. The result, Burin argues, was a new and mutually acceptable definition of Black freedom in the colony's 1824 constitution, which granted African Americans in Liberia considerably more rights than those enjoyed by people of African descent in the Americas.

Race, slavery, and freedom are at the center of Scott Heerman's essay, as well. The imperial history of slavery's expansion in the early nineteenth century is clear: it involved the seizure of Native lands and the removal of Native peoples to make space for white-owned plantations worked by enslaved people of color. By 1846, it would be a major factor inspiring the United States' war with Mexico for still more territory. Focusing on the Atlantic politics of slavery and abolition, Heerman reveals the importance of interimperial entanglements and competition to this story. He chronicles the kidnapping of free British subjects in the Caribbean into slavery in Texas—a borderland that functioned as a key entrepôt for illegal slave imports into the United States after the closing of the Atlantic slave trade. These illegal traders appreciated the jurisdictional fuzziness of the Texas borderlands, which made it possible to break American and British laws against the Atlantic slave trade in the service of expanding the U.S. "slave empire." The traffic, in turn, offered a vector for U.S. enslavers to exert authority and influence in extraterritorial zones. And when those who were kidnapped into Texas slavery were free British subjects, Heerman shows, their stories raised questions about the value of membership in the British empire and the sovereignty of the empire over its subjects.

Ousmane Power-Greene returns our attention to the imperial dimensions of the colonization movement with a different lens. He explores how Black thinkers understood the political means and ends of emigration across the first half of the nineteenth century, from the movement's origins into the era of abolition and slave-trade suppression. The racism at the root of the colonization movement was evident to Black Americans, many of whom objected to the premise that in order to enjoy freedom and rights, they must remove themselves from the nation. But for some, emigration appeared to offer real possibilities. Figures like Paul Cuffe and Martin Delany turned to African colonization as an opportunity not just to escape racial discrimination in the United States but also to pursue a broader political agenda abroad. Both sought to establish a strong emigrationist polity in Africa, which would oppose the slave trade and Euro-American oppression while promoting trade, commerce, Christianity, and democratic values. Neither Cuffe nor Delany considered themselves imperialists. Yet their plans for colonization were unmistakably imperial, advocating a settlement that they hoped would regenerate Africans and African Americans alike.

Together, the essays in this section draw a wide geography of early U.S. empire, demonstrating that it was shaped in conversation and conflict with other world empires. The British served as a model and a collaborator in West Africa, but a competitor in the Caribbean. In Hawai'i, the French emerged as a foil for white Americans to define themselves against. The United States, far weaker than either Britain or France in these years, moved in a world dominated by European colonialism. But American individuals and organizations—including missionaries and the American Board of Commissioners for Foreign Missions (ABCFM), settlers and the ACS, and slave traders—set out to create a new role for the United States. They embraced visions of the new republic as a civilizing power and a slave power—contradictory roles that suggest the range of ideas nongovernment actors could have about what form American empire should take. Each of these visions, though, was defined by ideas about racial and civilization status, which enabled some groups to claim sovereignty and self-governance but curtailed or denied that right and ability to others.

In Part III, "The Ideologies of Empire," essays by Nicholas Guyatt, Margot Minardi, and Amy Greenberg explore how Americans understood, described, and promoted or contested notions of empire and colonialism during the era of the early republic.[34] As Guyatt discusses, fluid notions of empire in the late eighteenth century meant that white Americans were far more comfortable describing their country as an empire than the historians of subsequent generations have been. American revolutionaries were particularly keen on the notion of federative empire: a vision for liberal imperialism, forged in response to the imperial crisis of the 1760s and 1770s, which would champion equality and uplift over domination and exploitation. Along with an apprehension toward foreign entanglements, Guyatt argues, these aspirations explain why white Americans were slow to denounce the idea of empire.

Federative empire, to the republic's founders, represented an improvement on the British model as well as a solution to the problem of race. Plans to establish dependent polities in distant lands for Native people and Black people offered a way to square revolutionary notions of equality and the "empire of liberty" with racism and white supremacy at home. But these racialized visions for a federative empire of liberty were also rife with internal contradictions—which were plainly exposed by Black critics of colonization, whom Guyatt sees as "among the first genuinely anti-imperial thinkers in American history."

Minardi and Greenberg find ambivalence and even opposition toward U.S. imperialism among some of the early republic's white citizens. Minardi investigates peace reformers, an understudied movement within the antebellum era of social reform. Though peace reformers advocated an end to war, Minardi shows that their rejection of violence and conquest did not necessarily extend to a rejection of empire. In debates over the First Seminole War and the U.S. invasion of Mexico, some championed the incorporation of people and territory within the republic's orbit through a more benevolent approach, arguing that nonviolent imperialism would advance equality, justice, the "civilizing" mission, and the expansion of Protestant Christianity. Peaceful means, they believed, could better serve empire's ends.

Greenberg turns our focus from moral crusaders to military ones. Parsing patterns of belief, behavior, and violence among officers and enlisted men in the Second Seminole War and the U.S.–Mexican War, she finds that soldiers were far less enthusiastic about Manifest Destiny than the settlers in whose name they fought—and that at least some articulated anti-imperial sentiments. Many soldiers disdained the campaigns in Florida and Mexico for self-interested reasons, decrying the dangerous and disease-ridden environments to which they were subjected. But others opposed these conquests on ethical grounds. Sympathizing with Seminoles or denouncing the invasion of a sovereign neighbor in Mexico, they came to see wars of plunder as unjust, unlawful, and unchristian. When disabused of the glorifying ideologies of republican empire, soldiers were left only with what Greenberg calls "mercenary ambivalence."

These three chapters offer an additional perspective on what difference it made that this empire was a republican one. Republican ideologies and federative approaches to divided sovereignty furnished U.S. citizens with a conceptual tool kit for improving (as many of them saw it) on European models of empire. The goal was not to abandon the imperial form, but rather to perfect it. Yet these ambitions met scores of critics—many of whom likewise drew on republican rhetoric in leveling their protests. Black emigrationists insisted on self-rule, not colonial dependence, as a condition for resettlement. Peace reformers denounced the invasion of a "sister republic" as a tyrannical act, unbefitting an enlightened and liberal government. As soldiers waged wars of conquest in Mexico and Seminole territory, their disillusionment often sprang from the creeping suspicion that the United States was not so different from the oppressive and monarchical empires of Europe, after all. Those who were skeptical or ambivalent about U.S. empire neither shared a single rationale for their critiques, nor were they consistent in the specific means and ends of American power that they opposed. But by drawing on a republican idiom, such critiques pushed many nineteenth-century Americans to increasingly distance themselves from the *idea* of empire—to ideologically camouflage the republic's imperial dimensions, even as, in practice and on the ground, U.S. empire grew into its own.

* * *

The imperial framework that these chapters adopt affects the geography, chronology, and the very language that scholars use to describe the early United States. It asks us to look at parts of the continent and the world beyond that too rarely appear in histories of the young republic. It enables us to see Catawba territory and Havana, Cape Mesurado and Prophetstown, Natchez and Hawai'i as part of a single story. It invites us to make connections across political periodizations back to the colonial era and forward to the late nineteenth and even to the twentieth centuries. It compels us to debate the nature of American governance at the scales of the local, the regional, the national, and the global. It draws together methods and approaches often siloed among scholarly subfields that too rarely intersect. It brings forward a new cast of characters to the history of American power, with sutlers, missionaries, disaffected soldiers, formerly enslaved people, and Native women playing significant roles. And it helps us to situate the early republic in the global context its contemporaries understood—connecting the history of the United States to that of other polities, both on the North American continent and around the world.

By focusing on local dynamics while placing the United States in its global context, the chapters that follow collectively argue that the American republic was always imperial, and that this matters for our understanding of the political, social, and cultural history of the United States. They explore the tensions and resonances of an imperial republic's dual identities. Created in a world of empires, the United States of America was to be something new: an expansive republic, proclaiming commitments to liberty and equality but eager to extend its territory and influence. Yet from the moment of its creation, Native powers, free and enslaved Black people, and foreign subjects perceived, interacted with, and resisted the young republic as if it were merely another empire under the sun. Over time, the young United States did not simply emulate but also adapted many of the imperial practices that defined prerevolutionary North America, fashioning them into new tools for accomplishing different types of expansion, extraction, and sovereignty across continents and oceans.

Further investigation into these problems can offer keys for explaining the astonishing rise of U.S. power and the ultimate success of its founders' aspirations: how in the span of a single lifetime, the United States claimed a continent that European empires had struggled and mostly failed for centuries to dominate, and how the new nation's imperial ambitions stretched in global directions precisely as the Age of Revolutions, for a time, put many of the world's older empires in retreat.

PART I

Empires, Nations, and States

CHAPTER 1

The Indian Boundary Line and the
Imperialization of U.S.–Indian Affairs

ROBERT LEE

Crack open any American history textbook and you can probably learn that the Royal Proclamation of 1763 forbid settlement on Indigenous lands beyond the crest of the Appalachians. You might even be treated to a handy map of the proclamation line. Flip forward a few pages and you will just as likely find nothing about the proclamation's second coming under the Trade and Intercourse Act of 1796, which similarly restricted access beyond Indian country's "boundary line."[1] Given the relative impact of British and American efforts to impose order on the colonization process, the disparity is odd. Both laws projected a border cutting across settler jurisdictions, configured as the movable spine of a centralized system of land expropriation. Neither could close the gap between the aspiration and the application of its vision. But only one of these boundaries' dislocations charted the most expansive burst of dispossession in North America in the last five hundred years. The other was the Royal Proclamation line.

The Indian boundary line conjured in 1796 remained a feature of U.S. law for nearly eighty years, until a major reorientation in the administration of Indian affairs in the 1870s. In 1871, Congress ceased ratifying treaties with Indigenous polities as independent nations. Next, in 1874, it quietly dropped the Indian boundary from the revised statutes. Finally, in 1878, the executive branch eliminated the regional superintendencies used to regulate trade and treaty relations since the 1790s.[2] The end of formal treaty-making, the erasure of the Indian boundary, and the liquidation of the superintendencies— three foundational pillars of U.S.–Indian affairs—signaled a pivot off a footing for colonization that U.S. policymakers borrowed from British reforms made in the decades preceding the American Revolution.

Historians have regularly described the reforms that culminated with the Royal Proclamation as a form of *imperialization*, that is, an effort to central-ize control over matters of law and commerce in the Crown's dominion abroad. Whereas provincial officials in the colonies had previously managed diplomatic affairs pertaining to Indigenous trade, treaty-making, and settler expansion separately and with little external oversight, the Board of Trade began to more aggressively intervene in the eighteenth century. By the 1750s, these efforts manifested in attempts to consolidate treaty-making, launch re-gional superintendencies, and declare a settlement boundary line. These ad-ministrative changes sought to impose a coherent intercolonial Indian policy controlled from London that contemporaries would have recognized as im-perial. In the parlance of modern scholarship, they constituted "formal" strat-egies of empire building, as opposed to the indirect techniques associated with "informal" empires.[3] Historians have had no difficulty recognizing them as such. They were components of the "imperialization of Indian relations," key features of the "imperialization of British Indian policy," part of an at-tempt to "bring the mainland territories into a regulated imperial system."[4]

The young United States long escaped similar treatment despite its trans-parent emulation of British designs. Most of the scholarship that filled out our understanding of what Francis Paul Prucha called the British "imperial experiment" was written by twentieth-century historians who were reluctant to cast the United States as imperial. The word disappears from Prucha's two-volume magnum opus *The Great Father* (1984), which remains the standard overview of U.S.–Indian affairs, after its coverage of British policy concludes, and it is likewise missing from other foundational studies of early U.S. pol-icy. As a result, the Revolutionary War became a breakpoint rather than a bridge in narratives of the formation of U.S. Indian policy. In the most com-mon telling, the triumphant Confederation Congress used victory against the British as a pretext to unilaterally declare tribal nations conquered. When those nations refused to buy into the fantasy, they forced the first Washing-ton administration to embrace Secretary of War Henry Knox's more subdued proposals for expansion by treaty through the "civilization plan."[5] From there, U.S. Indian policy metastasized in response to various events on the ground as it lurched through a series of ad hoc developments from the factory sys-tem through removal and into the reservation era. This approach was useful for capturing the dizzying, violent, and contradictory array of U.S. relations with hundreds of tribal nations across the continent, but it clouded the big picture, pushing the United States' sine qua non of converting Indigenous-controlled territory into vendable public property into the background.

Recent historians of Indian affairs have become more attuned to that larger picture and less shy about calling it imperial.[6] What they have not yet done is reconstruct the origins of U.S. Indian policy as a British inheritance with a long-lasting imperial coherence. To chart that development, this chapter offers a new narrative of the emergence of the foundational structures of Indian affairs administration in the United States, one that builds on efforts to recover continuities amid the ruptures of the revolutionary era.[7] It shows how, in addition to embracing the centralized treaty-making practice advocated by prerevolutionary British policymakers, the United States reconfigured the British empire's superintendency system and reconstructed its vision of an Indian boundary line cutting across settler jurisdictions. In this telling, the imperialization of Indian policy in North America did not culminate with the Proclamation of 1763 then recede in the wake of the Revolution, as the story is often told. Rather, it reached a climax with the creation of the U.S.-Indian boundary line in 1796 and enabled the aggressive expansion of the United States that followed. This account not only helps explain how U.S.-Indian affairs became imperial, it draws out the key structures that underpinned a distinct epoch, a period lasting into the 1870s in which U.S. officials sought to project rule over Indigenous communities as haltingly subordinated foreign nations hemmed in by a rapidly growing U.S. public domain. The goal of this chapter is to sketch the origins of this epoch. If it contributes to a new synthesis of the United States as always already imperial, perhaps the Trade and Intercourse line of 1796 will warrant a mention. It might even get a map (Figure 1.1).

* * *

British efforts to centralize control over Indian policy in the colonies started slowly, then ratcheted up in 1750s. Until the mid-eighteenth century, provincial authorities generally took the lead in managing Indian affairs. But that did not mean officials in London were completely disconnected. The Board of Trade financially underwrote commercial and diplomatic efforts. It provided gifts for distribution to tribal nations, supported various forms

Indian Boundary Line, 1796

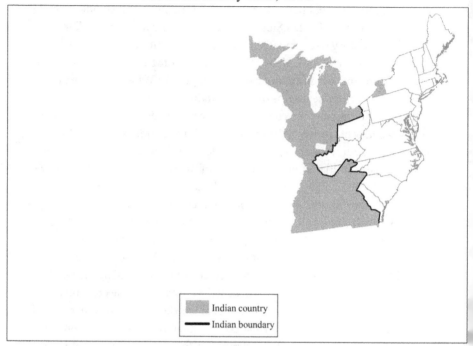

Figure 1.1. The Indian boundary described in Article 1 of "An Act to Regulate Trade and Intercourse with the Indian Tribes, and to Preserve Peace on the Frontiers" (1796). The described line excluded western New York, most of which was ceded the following year at the Treaty of Big Tree. Map by the author.

of colonial military defense, and occasionally hosted delegations in London. Generally, however, oversight was rather limited. This situation began to change gradually in the first half of the eighteenth century, occasioned by myriad conflicts that brought questions about the ultimate location of colonial authority into relief. In 1703, for instance, the Mohegan leader Oweneco petitioned the Crown to rescind Connecticut land grants that had usurped title to Mohegan lands, initiating a legal battle that stretched across the Atlantic and into the 1770s. The Mohegans ultimately lost most of the disputed land, but the lengthy case underscored two principles that would structure an increasingly interventionist stance among British leaders in the eighteenth century. First, authorities in London, not colonial governors abroad, had the final word over Indian policy, which most urgently concerned commercial practices and transfers of land titles. Second, tribal sovereignty placed Indigenous polities apart from the colonies and outside local laws.[8]

In other words, English leaders in Parliament and at the Board of Trade considered Indigenous nations part of the British imperial dominion and within its exclusive sphere of influence, which bumped up against similar French and Spanish domains. But they also cast tribal nations as jurisdictionally separate from the settler colonies whose boundaries appeared to swallow up Indigenous territories on maps. Efforts to realize these tenets led British leaders not just to recommend exerting more control over Indian policy *within* colonies but to align policy *across* them. The approach was, at root, reactive, made in response to Indigenous polities who acted independently, colonial leaders who pursued local interests as they exercised power under their charters, and imperial rivals who pursued their own North American agendas. It was also triggered by the dramatic expansion of English settlements on the eastern seaboard of North America, which had grown from tiny, precarious enclaves into firmly rooted settler societies. Between 1650 and 1700, English North America quintupled its population to about 250,000 inhabitants. By 1760, shortly before the Royal Proclamation, it sextupled again to nearly 1.6 million. With that growth came pressure on neighboring Indigenous polities and conflicts that spilled across colonial jurisdictions, which grabbed the attention of the Board of Trade and provoked responses that favored more robust forms of imperial administration.[9]

In the 1720s and 1730s, the Board of Trade began to more actively exercise authority from afar. Eager to diminish French influence on the continent, the board took steps to harmonize intercolonial Indian relations across the rapidly growing colonies of New York, Pennsylvania, and Massachusetts, all of which had connections with the militarily powerful and commercially influential Haudenosaunee, or Iroquois confederacy. The board started to scrutinize these colonies' trade regulations, weigh in on land disputes, and urge colonial officials to respond to Indian-related crises in other colonies. When the War of Austrian Succession jumped the Atlantic and spilled into the St. Lawrence River valley as King George's War (1744–48), Parliament faced a stress test for its loose push toward colonial unity as it sought to maintain an alliance with the Haudenosaunee. The results were less than encouraging. In the face of Iroquois determination to remain neutral until late in that conflict, provincial leaders in the colonies followed their own interests in different directions. While New York lobbied to enlist Iroquois aid against the French, Massachusetts sought continued neutrality. According to the legal scholar Robert B. Clinton, the war exposed the inadequacy of an uncoordinated colonial policy, setting the stage for major changes in the 1750s.[10]

By and large, efforts to maintain the Iroquois alliance formed the backdrop for a growing push to centralize intercolonial Indian affairs. When the Mohawk leader Hendrick threatened to sever the covenant chain with New York, citing fraudulent land sales and invasive settlers at a meeting at Albany in 1753, the Board of Trade directed New York's governor to arrange another conference to salvage the relationship. The result was the Albany Congress of 1754, which brought together commissioners from seven northeastern and middle colonies. The draft "Plan of Union" it produced proposed a "President General" from the colonies who would be empowered to direct Indian diplomacy for the common interest, enact Indian trade laws, purchase Indigenous land, and issue settlement grants in the Crown's name. The Albany Congress also produced a "Representation to the Crown" that decried the corrupting power of private interests in Indian affairs, denounced land frauds, and condemned the liquor trade.[11] The report recommended appointing Indian agents, making colonial governments the sole purchasers of Indian lands within their boundaries, and restricting those purchases to conspicuous public councils. As a vision to expand imperial control at the expense of local authority, full-scale implementation would have required fundamental changes to colonial charters, which doomed the proposal. Although the colonial assemblies rejected the Albany plan, it distilled a suite of ills that would only become more acute in the run-up to the Royal Proclamation a decade later.[12]

Among the contemplated cures, the prospect of a new administrative apparatus for managing Indian relations continually came to the fore. The idea first surfaced in a tract titled *The Importance of Gaining and Preserving the Friendship of the Indians to the British Interest, Considered* (1751), which argued for a new imperial post: "a *Superintendant of Indian Affairs*" that would expand the jurisdiction and consolidate the authority of the provincial secretaries of Indian affairs that already existed in several colonies.[13] In 1754, the Board of Trade issued a report on how to coordinate colonial Indian policy that embraced the notion of an Indian superintendent. Its "Plan of General Concert" urged the installation of a Crown official with sole authority over Indian affairs on the continent and access to the treasury to fund his duties. A separate report prepared by John Pownall, secretary of the Board of Trade, similarly advocated placing Indian affairs under a single agent. When the Albany plan reached London, the board highlighted how the proposed duties of the president general echoed the need for a superintendent. It recommended

William Johnson, who had served as the secretary of Indian Affairs for New York, for this new position.[14]

The outbreak of the Seven Years' War led to the unilateral installation of this superintendency system. Shortly after hostilities began, the board stripped authority over Indian affairs from the colonial legislatures. Next, General Edward Braddock, following the board's recommendation, placed William Johnson in charge of Indian affairs for the northern colonies, and ordered him to visit Indian country, distribute presents, address grievances, rein in traders, and report directly to London. His 1755 commission "to superintend and manage" relations with the Iroquois and their allies in the northern colonies marked a turning point in the imperialization of Indian relations on the continent.[15]

This novel post signaled a formal administrative restructuring designed to tighten the Board of Trade's ability to manage Indian policy across colonial jurisdictions. It took responsibilities previously delegated to governors and other provincial leadership and reinvested them in a new office attached to more expansive jurisdictions projected across colonial boundaries and answerable to officials in London. While the Board of Trade's ability to dictate terms on Indian lands within its putative dominion remained extremely limited, the pathway along which it aspired to exercise authority had shifted. The office of superintendent, responsible for the regional administration of Indian affairs and answerable to a distant central authority, would go through modifications, but it would remain a key intermediary in the piecemeal process through which Anglo empires in North America eventually translated fictions of imperial control into realities on the ground. Colonial leaders would claw back some authority during the imperial crisis of the late 1760s, but the superintendencies would remain. They would survive the Revolution as a part of the British administration of Canada and would find a place in the copycat apparatus put in place by the United States.[16]

The expansion of the superintendencies began the year after Johnson's appointment, when Edmond Atkin wrote his way into the position of the first superintendent for the southern colonies by furnishing the Board of Trade with a "34,000-word master plan for imperial control of the Indians."[17] Echoing a restructuring of Indian affairs that was already underway, Atkin's plan called for Parliament to vest two superintendents with exclusive authority over Indian relations, who would (with the aid of agents and a system of forts) negotiate treaties of allegiance and regulate trade, with an eye toward suppressing liquor traffic. Although their reach and effectiveness would never live up to Pownall's or Atkin's hopes, the British created these two superintendencies before the Revolution, one for the northern colonies and one for the southern colonies, and added a third for the middle colonies during the war in 1779.

The establishment of the northern and southern superintendencies created a new layer of authority that enhanced the Board of Trade's capacity to regulate the treaty-making process. In 1753, the board was already telling colonial governors to block private land sales and ensure that all purchases of Indian land "be made in his Majesty's name and at the publick charge."[18] But the power shift was neither complete nor uncontested. In one instance, Governor William Shirley of Massachusetts intimated to the Mohawks that Johnson was his subordinate. In another, Governor Charles Hardy of New York protested the dilution of his authority and argued Indian relations should run through him. Johnson in particular would complain to the board about colonial governors' land policies undercutting alliances and their proclamations undermining diplomatic efforts.[19] An uncoordinated Indian policy, pulled in different directions by the separate interests of the Crown and various colonies, would persist through the Seven Years' War and beyond. A similar tension over the relative authority of the states and federal government in Indian affairs would characterize the United States into the nineteenth century as state governments in New York and Georgia, in particular, sought to compel land cessions within their borders.[20]

This tension was on full display in negotiations with the Delawares in the late 1750s, which yielded the first steps toward the establishment of an intercolonial settlement boundary. At Easton in 1757, Pennsylvania authorities ignored orders not to engage in unilateral negotiations and came to terms of peace with Teedyuscung. The deal provided for a permanent Delaware settlement in the Wyoming Valley, but did not sync with Crown interests in cultivating Iroquois hegemony over neighboring tribes. Pennsylvania officials expected Johnson would support the agreement after the fact, but he refused. Instead, a new round of negotiations produced the 1758 Treaty of Easton, which retroceded lands west of the Appalachians (occupied by the Ohio Delawares) to the Iroquois. This new treaty evinced an emerging approach to competing Native-settler interests as a geographical problem that could be solved through imperial management of Indian boundaries. The line agreed to at Easton divested Pennsylvania of its claims "Westward of the Allegheny or Appalaccin Hills" and breathed life into an idea for a mountain boundary between colonists and Indigenous nations that the Board of Trade had discussed as early as the 1720s. In 1758, the board used this limited mountain boundary to reject a Virginia settlement plan farther south, a move that historian Max Edelson has argued raised the Easton Treaty "to the level of an international treaty that bound all colonies to respect Indian land rights."[21] A few years later, the Proclamation of 1763 would, in effect, take the Easton line and run with it, temporarily extending the mountain boundary down the back of the coastal colonies.

As the Seven Years' War wound down, proposals for the formal imposition of an intercolonial boundary ramped up. The line was envisioned as a tool for managing settlement patterns and economic activities to Britain's advantage. On the heels of the Treaty of Paris, Henry Ellis, who served successively as the governor of Georgia and Nova Scotia, penned a tract discussing how to govern the huge dominion relinquished by France. Ellis wanted to prevent settlers from moving freely. He proposed fixing "some Line for a Western Boundary" beyond which colonists would be not be permitted to settle in order to keep them within the effective reach of government and economically captive as markets for manufacturers. Indigenous lands beyond could be placed under the administration of military officers manning scattered posts, he suggested. William Knox, who had worked for both the Board of Trade and as the London agent for Georgia, likewise advocated placing "proper Limits" on American settlements. He argued that "no purchase of Lands from the Indians" should be allowed beyond their present reach so as to discourage outmigration from England from those interested in "getting Lands without purchase." William Johnson also wrote to the Board of Trade in support of establishing an Indian boundary line. Though his letter arrived too late to inform the Royal Proclamation, an earlier report had encouraged the Crown to "religiously" observe the "Bounds of our settlements toward the Indian Country" and expand the "Superintendancy" needed to oversee them.[22] For all, a prospective settlement boundary line was an administrative tool to manage distant populations, regulate trade, and protect the treasury.

The most influential recommendation for the Indian boundary line came in the Board of Trade's "Report on the Acquisitions in America," a plan to regulate North American colonization after the Seven Years' War. The board's report, prepared by Secretary Pownall and influenced by advisers who believed the colonial charters should be given up and imperial control over the colonies strengthened, imagined a border separating interior tribal nations from coastal British settlements, and even visualized it with a thick red line drawn onto on a copy of Emanuel Bowen's *An Accurate Map of North America*.

After outlining the advantages won by the enlargement of the British dominion, the report offered suggestions for how to subdivide it into jurisdictions.
It paid close attention to the challenges posed by rapid population growth,
which induced settlers to push into new lands "where they were exposed to
the Irruptions of the Indians as well as the Hostilities of the French." As a
result, it recommended strictly regulating settlement by designating a natural boundary west of the seaboard colonies. Pownall likewise outlined the
report in a letter to the king. His executive summary highlighted the proposed boundary along the Appalachian Mountains beyond which British
subjects might only conduct trade regulated by the Crown. To attend to
the Crown's interests in both keeping colonists accessible as consumers and
maintaining its alliances with tribal nations, he reiterated that the report argued that settlements "should not, for the present, extend beyond the source
of those rivers and waters which discharge themselves directly into the At-
lantick Ocean."[23]

The board's recommendations and Pownall's summary shaped the Royal
Proclamation issued in October 1763. The proclamation affirmed tribal possession of unceded lands, forbid colonial governors from parceling off ceded
Indigenous lands, reserved the sole right of purchase to the Crown or its
agents, outlined a trade licensing policy, and, most memorably, declared "it
to be Our Royal Will and Pleasure, for the present as aforesaid, to reserve
under our Sovereignty, Protection, and Dominion, for the use of the said Indians, all the Lands and Territories . . . lying to the Westward of the Sources
of the Rivers which fall into the Sea from the West and North West."[24] The
proclamation cinched together efforts to centralize the process of Indian
trade and dispossession, develop an intercolonial Indian policy, and separate
Indigenous and settler polities. In the process, it gave a legal footing to a vision of Indian country as a space of Indigenous nations beyond the reach of
the colonies' authority but within, and constrained by, the British empire in
North America.

The most important phrase in the description of the proclamation line
was "for the present."[25] Echoing Pownall's summary, the line was formulated
as a *temporary* expedient to more effective imperial control. It was never
meant to be permanent or fixed in place. Historians have periodically disputed popular conceptions to the contrary for over a century, but no one has
explored the instability of the line more fully than Max Edelson, whose recent study of the impact of the Board of Trade's "Report on the Acquisitions
in America" examines the surveys put in motion by the proclamation.[26] In

its immediate wake, the Board of Trade outlined an updated program for centralizing Indian affairs under the superintendencies. The convoluted forty-three point "Plan for the Future Management of Indian Affairs" was an aspirational fantasy of control over trade, diplomacy, and the distribution of land. It articulated what would have amounted to a full-fledged Indian department to be paid for by fur trade duties. Proposed after an expensive war and against the backdrop of a mounting crisis over taxation in the colonies, Parliament never signed off on the proposal and colonial legislatures continued to exercise authority in Indian affairs rooted in their charters.[27] But the management plan's official failure masks the extent to which it both reflected key changes in the administration of Indian affairs already underway and informally guided Indian policy in the 1760s and 1770s. William Johnson and John Stuart, the northern and southern superintendents, supported its tenets and received instructions to act on its program to the extent possible.[28]

When it came to administering the proclamation line, Johnson and Stuart used the management plan as a guide for ten major congresses and a host of minor ones prior to 1775. The plan's penultimate point called for surveying "the precise & exact boundary & Limits" of land reserved to tribal nations.[29] Figuring out where to lay the line quickly turned the temporary mountain boundary into a shifting treaty line, one that was adjusted by at least six additional land cessions between 1765 and 1774. Representatives of colonies continued to sign land cession and boundary-setting treaties in this period, but the push toward centralization manifested in the changing frequency of the officials taking the lead. In the first half of the eighteenth century virtually all non-Indigenous signatories of land cession treaties were representatives of provincial governments. Between 1755 and 1763, the ratio of provincial treaties fell to relative parity with Crown officials. Between 1763 and 1774, Crown officials within the new superintendency system framed around the new intercolonial Indian boundary signed four times as many treaties as provincial officials.[30]

This shift reflected yet another pillar of the British imperialization of Indian affairs: consolidating control over treaty-making itself. Imperial officials and colonial authorities frequently asserted an exclusive prerogative to control the acquisition of Indigenous land within their proclaimed borders. But the supposed right—legally theorized via analysis of Indian title, grasped at in myriad colonial statutes, and invoked in the eighteenth century as "a bare *Right of Preemption*"—was unevenly applied and irregularly enforced. Private purchases executed by colonists playing "the deed game" were legion, but they tended to erupt into the historical record only when they triggered conflicts. Tamping down on unauthorized purchases by individuals and reining in purchases by provincial authorities that might cause unintended consequences in neighboring colonies had motivated British Indian policy reform for decades when it gained formal expression in the Royal Proclamation's insistence that future Indigenous land purchases be made "in our Name, at some public Meeting." The 1764 management plan sharpened the vision by suggesting only the superintendents or their agents be empowered to make such purchases, except in cases where the Crown had previously vested those rights in corporations or colony proprietors, and called for making all such purchases at well-documented councils attended by recognized tribal leaders.[31]

By the time of the American Revolution, then, British imperial policy had shifted substantially from its footing in the early eighteenth century. It had projected an intercolonial Indian boundary line composed of the eastward-facing borders of interlocking Indigenous land cessions. That line could and did move with the pursuit of new treaties, to be made in the name of the Crown, under the watch of a new administrative class of regional superintendents and their agents. The Revolution did not destroy this system. The Proclamation of 1763 disappeared from U.S. history in 1783, but it persisted as North American law in Canada.[32] In the thirteen rebellious colonies, of course, independence cut off the Board of Trade's efforts to centralize Indian affairs, but it left behind a blueprint to follow, and an attractive one. The Revolution did little to change the conditions that had prompted the imperialization of British policy in the first place. Settler populations continued to boom. The prospect of states acting in their own interests continued to threaten to trigger costly conflicts. Imperial rivals continued to lurk to the north, south, and west.

The borrowing from British reforms began during the American Revolution itself and took off with its conclusion. In 1775, the Continental Congress created northern, middle, and southern Indian departments that mirrored the superintendencies, and it empowered its commissioners to negotiate "on behalf of the united colonies."[33] During the war years, however, advocates of giving Congress the exclusive power to maintain Indian alliances, purchase Indian lands, and regulate trade and boundaries lost ground in the process of ratifying the Articles of Confederation. Although the Articles of Confederation nominally gave Congress exclusive authority to regulate Indian affairs, seeming to resolve the tension between central and local authority in Indian affairs that frustrated British imperial reformers, they effectively hamstrung the provision by forbidding congressional agents from infringing on the legislative power of any state.[34] Even still, the Confederation Congress's first effort to exercise this power came just two and half weeks after the signing of the Treaty of Paris. Sometimes styled the "Proclamation of 1783," the resolution prohibited settlement in Indian country beyond the jurisdictions of states and outlawed private purchases of Indian land.[35]

As it was before the Revolution, the assertion of the sole right to make treaties would be contested by the colonies-turned-states. And as in that earlier period, there would be an unmistakable trend toward actual federal preeminence over the treaty process at the expense of individual states. Between 1775 and 1871, federal treaty commissioners signed five times as many land cession treaties as did state representatives (with 85 percent of the state-led treaties concentrated in New York, whose leadership clung to the preemption power delegated through its colonial charter).[36] Central to that development was a long-term effort by federal leaders in the United States to codify the so-called doctrine of discovery in U.S. law by statute, executive action, and through the courts. The effort extended into the early decades of the nineteenth century and reached its apogee in the Marshall court in the 1830s, which invented categories like domestic dependent nations and magnified concepts like preemption. As historians have recently pointed out, the manufacture of federal supremacy in Indian affairs was not an expression of actual power but a tactic of empire building designed to project U.S. authority into a dominion controlled by Indigenous polities.[37]

Such insights have emerged from perspectives that emphasize continuity over rupture in the revolutionary era. Once independent, the United States sought to join the "powers of the earth" with imperial interests in the Americas and used Indian relations to stake its claim.[38] It is well known that in the wake of the Revolution, the Confederation Congress's committee on Indian affairs took a hard line against Indigenous adversaries, insisting that victory against Britain meant Britain's Indian allies were vanquished by proxy.[39] Less well known is that embedded within this haughty and ultimately untenable stance lay a renewed effort to set the Indian boundary line that would survive the confederation era. While the committee on Indian affairs declared its claims to land by right of conquest, it simultaneously made clear its intentions to "establish a boundary line between them and us, beyond which we will restrain our citizens from hunting and settling, and within which the Indians shall not come but for the purposes of trading, treating, or other business."[40] The committee even articulated the exact geographic boundaries of the part of the line it sought to impose north of the Ohio River. Attempting to carry out this plan, Congress quite literally began investing in treaty-making at increasing rates. Despite massive war debt and without effective means to raise funds, the Confederation Congress's appropriation for Indian affairs nearly tripled between 1783 and 1784. In 1785, the appropriation nearly doubled again. In 1786, it more than tripled again.[41]

That year, the Confederation Congress also revived the superintendency system as part of its civil administration, at least on paper. An ordinance for the regulation of Indian affairs divided the United States into northern and southern districts at the Ohio River and authorized the appointment of a superintendent for each. The post was given a two-year term, with each superintendent able to hire two deputies. It required the superintendents to live at a location convenient to their work and report to the secretary of war. Their duties would include regulating Indian trade, monitoring and reporting hostilities, and keeping accounts. The same act restricted engagement in the Indian trade to U.S. citizens, required traders to have licenses from superintendents, and forbade the superintendents from participating in trade themselves. It demanded anyone wishing to travel "through the Indian nations" obtain permission from a superintendent. And it required the superintendents and their deputies to post a $6,000 bond to ensure the "faithful discharge of the duties of their office."[42] A set of instructions issued the following year added the distribution of presents, organization of Indigenous delegations to Congress, and holding of treaties to their responsibilities.[43] Implementation, however, would have to wait for ratification of the Constitution, which empowered Congress to regulate commerce with the Indians without kowtowing to state legislatures.[44]

Congress moved to develop a framework for the central administration of Indian affairs immediately. During its first session in 1789, it provided for a territorial governor of the western territory (that is, the Northwest Territory) whose responsibilities included "discharging the duties of the superintendent of Indian affairs in the northern department."[45] This was the first of thirty-nine superintendencies created by the United States, under which the U.S. Indian Office and Bureau of Indian Affairs would elaborate into sizable bureaucracies of superintendents, agents, interpreters, and various private contractors reporting east to the secretary of war, and later, the secretary of the interior.[46]

Unifying the office of territorial governor and Indian superintendent was perhaps the most significant innovation to the position made by the United

States.[47] Implemented as an economizing measure, the move instituted a conflict of interest between governors' duties to advance the settlement of their territories and protect Indigenous land rights, which almost invariably resolved itself in favor of the former.[48] William Henry Harrison, who served as one of the territorial governors/Indian superintendents, privately griped that his $800 salary "for my Services as Superintendent of Indian affairs" was "no compensation at all for the duties I perform." At that point—in 1804— he claimed to have issued four-fifths of the trade licenses given out by the United States, grumbled about entertaining Indigenous visitors "constantly," and noted that he was then engaged in "making a treaty" that would push back the Indian boundary line in present-day Missouri and Illinois.[49]

Indian superintendents' duties were even more wide ranging than Harrison's complaints suggested. They issued trade licenses, monitored movements into and out of Indian country, collected rumors of hostilities, sought to restore stolen property (especially horses), and investigated crimes committed by whites in Indian country and Indians in the civil jurisdiction of the United States. They hired personnel, like blacksmiths and interpreters, and contractors. They met with Indian delegations, heard complaints, distributed presents, and issued annuities. They attended councils, frequently taking the lead while doubling as treaty commissioners, and carried out treaty provisions. They would oversee agents assigned to tribes within their jurisdiction and, in some instances, manage the accounts and logistics from federal fur trade factories and forced removals. In short, their work revolved around managing connections, tensions, and obligations connected to a shifting Indian boundary line defined and redefined by a flurry of treaties.

Their authority came from the Indian Trade and Intercourse Acts, the first of which passed in 1790 and formally reintroduced the concept of "Indian country" into U.S. law. The act was renewed and enlarged four times before being made permanent in 1802, with the largest change arriving in 1796. Prompted by violations of federal authority along the border, "An Act to Regulate Trade and Intercourse with the Indian Tribes, and to Preserve Peace on the Frontiers" proclaimed a "boundary line, established by treaty between the United States and various Indian tribes" and described its path down rivers, past forts, over roads, and along mountain ridges from Ohio to Georgia. The description concluded by ensuring that if any new treaties should shift the boundary, then the provisions of the act would apply to the adjusted line.[50] Several decades later, after seeking input from two leading superintendents, the law would be revised one more time, reserving "Indian country" as land "not within any state to which the Indian title has not been extinguished" and charging the superintendents with regulating "their boundary."[51]

By the 1790s, the United States had adopted the basic features of midcentury British imperial reforms. It instituted superintendencies, committed itself to treaty-making, and laid down a mobile settlement boundary. Like their British imperial predecessors, federal officials insisted authorities in Washington, D.C., would have the final word over Indian policy in the dominion of the United States while placing tribal sovereignty apart from the colonies-turned-states and beyond local laws.[52] Its stance was less innovative than imitative, angled toward turning Indian country into settler property, and imperial from the beginning.

* * *

At root, the adoption of the Indian boundary line of 1796 was about asserting central authority over far-flung possessions, a lunge toward consolidating the power to determine how spaces could be used, occupied, and exploited. Laced into it were questions about who gets to live where, hunt where, fish where, farm where; who can own, alienate, exploit, or conserve land, water, and other natural resources; who can engage in trade or operate businesses where; who has the authority to impose civil or criminal penalties; who, in other words, makes the rules where. Whether it was setting up fur trade factories, targeting eastern nations for removal, or pressing for the safe passage of emigrants and railways across the continent, the United States spent most of its first century managing Indian affairs around this moving Indian boundary line, giving its imperial core a coherence that tends to get lost in accounts of early national Indian affairs as a series of policy experiments rather than a concerted effort to hold the reins in a breakneck process of settler colonial expansion.

Just as there was for the British in the 1760s, there was a wide gap between the aspirations and the reality of imperial control over the United States in the 1790s and beyond. Even still, the system of superintendents, imperfectly managing an Indian boundary moved by treaties, would shape the emerging United States by setting rules for trade and settlement that mattered even when they were broken. Legal settlers would use guidebooks and read newspapers that explained where the Indian boundary was and make choices about where to squat accordingly; illegal ones would sneak past the line, sometimes with permits to work as traders, then ask for, and nearly always win, clemency from superintendents. Superintendents would manage relations that produced hundreds of land cession treaties, carry out treaty provisions that forcibly relocated large Indigenous populations, and open up areas to land rushes that tilted the balance of territorial populations toward statehood.

This framework of managing Indian affairs would thread together a period when the United States sought to subordinate Indigenous communities as foreign nations within its expanding colonial domain. It was a time when the United States actively acquired preemption rights from other imperial claimants while simultaneously seeking to identify and reduce the boundaries of the Indigenous polities they contained, designated their inhabitants domestic dependent nations, eventually insisted they lived within the ambit of an Interior Department, and, finally, refused to treat with them as nations at all. As Brian DeLay has argued, the gradual subordination of Indigenous peoples into such categories was a product of imperialism, not evidence of its absence.[53]

Indian Boundary Line, 1874

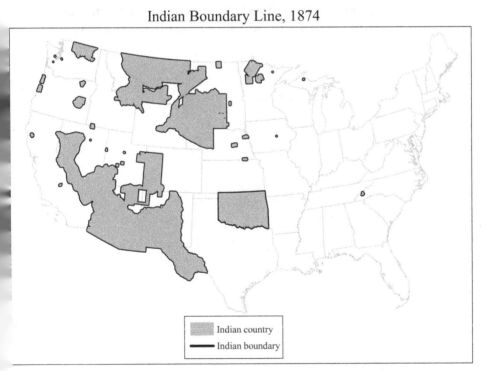

Figure 1.2. The Indian boundary line as it stood in 1874. Map by the author.

U.S. expansion into Indian country did not come easy or cheap. Between 1803 and 1867, the United States spent $53 million in nonmilitary expenditures to acquire its North American dominion from France, England, Spain, Mexico, and Russia.[54] In the same span of years, it appropriated more than double that amount—about $108 million—for nonmilitary expenditures on Indian affairs, money spent, one way or another, on the complex of activities putting dent after dent in the Indian boundary. In the 1850s, newly installed Indian superintendents began working the line eastward from the Pacific, peeling off sections of Indian country in Oregon by treaty and seizing California through a series of unratified treaties. The boundary then squeezed like a girdle, tightening around the continent until it broke through in 1868, opening a path of cleared Indian title across the Mountain West a year in advance of the completion of the first transcontinental railroad. By this time, the conquest was certainly not complete (see Figure 1.2).[55] Yet enough had changed by the 1870s for Congress to push back from an imperial program for managing Indian relations rooted in the eighteenth century. It ended treaty-making, erased the Indian boundary line, closed the superintendencies, and turned toward a new phase in the colonization of the continent.

CHAPTER 2

The Sutler's Empire

Frontier Merchants and Imperial Authority, 1790–1811

SUSAN GAUNT STEARNS

In June 1811, in Natchez, Mississippi, merchant Abijah Hunt was killed in a duel with territorial representative George Poindexter.[1] What inspired the duel is somewhat murky. Hunt, a staunch Federalist, had apparently offended Poindexter, a Democratic-Republican, leading to the challenge and a dawn appointment. While such behavior was not entirely unexpected from the flamboyant and frequently embattled Poindexter, the violence and sensation surrounding Abijah Hunt's death likely came as quite a shock to those who knew him. Hunt was a pillar of Mississippi's business community. He was a founding member of Mississippi's first bank; he owned perhaps as many as six plantations and several public cotton gins. He left behind a network of five stores and a cotton factorage business with interests that stretched from Natchez to New Orleans to Liverpool. His nephew, David Hunt, who inherited Abijah's estate, would parlay Abijah's already significant holdings into a small empire of his own: by 1850, David Hunt was, by some measures, the wealthiest man in the United States. At a time when there were only thirty-five millionaires in the country—twelve of whom resided in Natchez—David Hunt was worth over two million dollars; he owned over twenty-six planta-tions and controlled the earthly fates of nearly 1,700 enslaved men and women.[2]

In many ways, David Hunt's staggering wealth was the culmination of practices put into place by his uncle over the two decades following the na-tion's founding. Beginning in 1790, Abijah Hunt began to construct a network of businesses—each independent, yet all owned by members of the Hunt family—that expanded with the nation, collaborating both with the U.S. government and with western colonizers and, in the process, uniting the interests of the two.[3] Abijah Hunt's commercial empire can, in some ways, stand in as a microcosm of the early republic's imperial project writ large. As a sutler for the U.S. Army in the Ohio Valley during the 1790s, Hunt and merchants like him played a crucial role in the violent expulsion of Indigenous peoples from their lands by helping to make the project of western colonization profitable. In the early nineteenth century, after Hunt shifted his base of operations from Cincinnati to Natchez, he turned his mercantile attentions to the exportation of cotton abroad and the importation of enslaved people to the Deep South—building for himself a second commercial empire constructed on the basis of exploited labor and the oppression of peoples of color, once more greasing the cogs that allowed both the American state and American colonizers to occupy new territory. An empire in small places, Hunt's network of stores and agents sprawled across the landscape of the Ohio and Mississippi Valleys, tightening the bonds between the region and the emerging nation east of the Appalachians.

Abijah Hunt was a frontier entrepreneur, and as such, an examination of his life has much to offer both historians of borderlands and historians of the "new history of capitalism." In recent years, historians have demonstrated how diverse groups of people of European, Indigenous, and African descent negotiated and renegotiated their relationships with one another along the frontier. Many of these works document a region's transformation from Native territory to full incorporation into the American state, a shift, in the words of historians Jeremy Adelman and Stephen Aron, from borderlands into bordered lands.[4] Often, merchants were at the forefront of these transformations, creating the multicultural world of the frontier, a world that was subsequently transformed by the arrival of ever-greater numbers of American colonist-settlers and, with them, American authority. Men like Auguste and Pierre Chouteau, for instance, came to dominate cities like St. Louis through their careful cultivation of familial ties to the powerful Osages, who offered crucial access to local knowledge and were important trading partners. Such mercantile connections produced distinctive local communities that resisted Americanization until long after the Louisiana Purchase.[5] Yet while historians of frontiers have recognized the importance of western merchants, historians of the new history of capitalism largely have not.[6] In particular, historians interested in the "financial turn" have neglected the West as an arena of study. Perhaps this is not surprising. The region lacked the corporations, banks, and proximity to governmental authority that have fascinated historians interested in the relationship between the state and economic activity, and committed to untangling how financial relationships developed in the years of the early republic. Yet, as recent studies of the relationship between slavery and capitalism have shown, the absence of financial institutions is not indicative of the absence of entanglement in financial issues. Each zone of expansion—of slavery, of state power, of settlement and the accompanying expulsion of Native peoples—created its own unique set of financial issues.[7] The trans-Appalachian West developed within the shadow of the kinds of economic transformations that were emerging in the East.

This chapter makes two claims: first, that frontier merchants like Abijah Hunt were crucial agents in the construction of American empire; second, that the West matters in the study of early American political economy. Empire entails not just conquest and expansion, but the development of bonds that bind the metropole to the periphery. The Appalachians represented a bottleneck, beyond which it was difficult for the government to move either money or goods. By cultivating networks of merchants and government officials on both sides of the mountains, Abijah Hunt helped overcome these obstacles. He supplied the army with food that supplemented meager wages, ensured the payment of the troops, provided western colonizers with cash, and functioned as a crucial intermediary between East and West. Hunt and his activities illustrate the second key point: the first American West is a critical location for examining the development of the political economy of the American empire. Hunt operated first in the Ohio country and later in the Southwest, two laboratories of U.S. empire that were more closely aligned than they are usually portrayed. His career illustrates the interrelatedness of the conquest of Indigenous peoples, the expansion of enslavement, and the networks of commerce, finance, and family that created the bonds of empire.

As a merchant linking settlers and soldiers, Abijah Hunt helped to strengthen the bonds between the imperial periphery of the trans-Appalachian West and the nation's metropole in the East by moving federal money westward.[8] In the absence of a banking system, merchants like the Hunts performed the crucial role of facilitating the movement of money from the nation's capital to the empire's periphery—and back again—functioning informally as the branches of a national financial institution. Examining Abijah Hunt's role in the construction of an American empire underscores the crucial role that merchants played in facilitating both settler and state expansion, illustrating the importance of not only commerce but also finance in the U.S. government's ability to assert power over broad distances. Although Abijah Hunt may have operated on the edge of the nation, he nevertheless acted at the center of the empire.

Jesse, Jeremiah, and Abijah Hunt: Ohio Sutlers

In late 1789, Abijah Hunt moved west from his native New Jersey, joining his brother, Jesse Hunt, in the small village of Cincinnati. When Jesse Hunt arrived several months earlier, there were barely thirty residents of the village, but many were convinced of its future prospects, especially once the U.S. Army established nearby Fort Washington to serve as its base of operations in trans-Appalachia.[9] It did not take long before another brother, Jeremiah Hunt, joined Abijah and Jesse in Cincinnati. Over the next two decades, Jesse, Jeremiah, and Abijah Hunt would be joined in the West by their cousin John Wesley, and nephews David and Caleb Hunt, creating a network of businesses that would stretch across much of the continent.

When Jesse and Abijah Hunt moved to the Ohio country, they moved into a war zone. In 1786, after the failure of treaty negotiations between the Shawnees and U.S. commissioners, Shawnee, Cherokee, and Mingo war parties intensified attacks on Euro-American settlements in the Ohio Valley in response to increasing encroachment by thousands of white settler-colonists who chose to squat on Indian lands north of the Ohio—land that the federal government also claimed as part of the public domain.[10] The ratification of the Constitution and the subsequent deployment of federal troops to the frontier in 1790 changed the tenor of the war. This first expedition ended in a disaster known as Harmar's Defeat, when the U.S. government's two hundred regular troops and twelve hundred Kentucky militia were routed by Shawnee and Miami troops along the Wabash River.[11]

Whenever the army marched out of Fort Washington, Abijah Hunt went with it. Beginning in 1790, Hunt worked as a sutler, providing western troops with food and liquor.[12] As a sutler, Abijah Hunt was part of an ancient, if disreputable, tradition. Sutlers, according to historian David M. Delo, were "civilian peddlers who offered comestibles and small wares to men under arms . . . for a price."[13] Part of the inevitable body of camp followers so often denigrated by military officials, sutlers played a key role in the operation of premodern armies. While the Quartermaster Corps was responsible for the subsistence of soldiers, sutlers offered everything else necessary for soldiers' health and comfort. Sutlers supplemented government-issued rations of preserved meats by providing soldiers with fresh meat, often furnished in the form of cattle or pigs driven overland and slaughtered on site. By the mid-1790s, sutlers were licensed civilian merchants who had permission to do business in military camps. Throughout the first half of the decade, Abijah joined the army on a series of expeditions against the confederated Indigenous nations north of the Ohio. Based in the store he and his brothers ran in Cincinnati, yet traveling with the army, Hunt peddled necessities like cloth, thread, and soap, along with foods like sugar, cheese, coffee, chocolate, whiskey and seasonal vegetables, to the soldiers who composed the army of the republic.

Abijah Hunt had chosen a dangerous occupation. Sutlers were civilians, responsible for transporting their own goods to often inaccessible locations along the most exposed frontiers. "Wherever the army went," according to Delo, "so went the sutler; and whatever the army did, the sutler served as a witness, if not a participant."[14] If camps were attacked, so were the sutlers. Sutlers were particularly vulnerable while carting heavy supplies—hogsheads of bacon and whiskey, for instance, over primitive roads created by the troops as they hauled cannons and ordinance across the Ohio country. Yet, at the same time sutlers faced risk, they also stood to profit tremendously. Isolated several days' or even weeks' journey from Euro-American settlements, soldiers had little choice but to patronize a camp's sutlers. In villages like Cincinnati, frontier merchants competed with one another for the opportunity to supply the army. Sutling offered frontier merchants serious financial advantages, chief among them the fact that the soldiers were paid in cash. Although cash scarcity was a problem across the United States throughout the 1780s and 1790s, the problem was particularly acute in the trans-Appalachian West.[15] In 1784, Spain had closed the Mississippi River to American trade, reducing the region's ability to export farm produce to markets in the East, and thus restricting the amount of cash that flowed into the region.

Throughout the 1790s, the U.S. government, frustrated by repeated losses at the hands of the Indians, pumped an ever-increasing amount of money into the West, eventually tripling the U.S. Army's funding.[16] This investment bore fruit in 1794 when a new expedition, this time under the command of General Anthony Wayne, took shape in the West. The "Legion of the United States," as Wayne's army of three thousand regular troops was known, ultimately proved decisive in the battle against the Indigenous confederacy. On

August 20, at the Battle of Fallen Timbers, Wayne's army defeated a force of
five hundred Ottawas, Potawatomis, Shawnees, and Miamis.[17] As a sutler,
Abijah Hunt was likely close at hand.

Throughout the summer of 1795, Wayne had frequent need to intervene
in the activities of sutlers. While sutlers provided a necessary service, their
presence in a camp could be disruptive. On the one hand, rum, whiskey, and
other hard liquors were much in demand by soldiers and their provision was
necessary for troop morale. On the other hand, liquor posed a major threat
to military preparedness and to soldiers' comportment. Many sutlers violated
military orders relating to the sale of whiskey. In June of 1795, for instance,
sutler William Haverland was court-martialed for "Selling Liquor to a soldier . . . in Violation of the General Orders." Though Haverland pleaded "not
guilty," the court ordered him "to be Drummed out of the Cantonment with
Two Canteens or Bottles suspended about his Neck; and thence . . . out of the
Camp; and never to return in any Capacity."[18] The harshness of the punishment was likely warranted: by the early 1800s, half of all courts-martial involved drunkenness.[19] As Wayne prepared for the upcoming negotiation of
the Treaty of Greenville, he worried that sutlers and the whiskey they peddled might endanger the prospects of peace. One key aspect of the negotiations, Wayne knew, would be to control the behavior of both his soldiers and
the arriving Indians. That would mean titrating the amount of alcohol available to both groups. To that end, Wayne issued orders that, in order to "in-
sure Sobriety, Peace & harmony between the Troops and the Indians . . . all
and every Store keeper, trader and sutler" west of the Miami River was required to depart immediately. Abijah Hunt was one of only five sutlers allowed to remain in Indian country, assuring himself an ever-larger share of
the army's captive market.[20]

Abijah and John Wesley Hunt: Kentucky Merchants

Abijah Hunt was not in the Ohio country when Wayne issued his order. In
the spring of 1795, he had traveled east—in part to visit family, but also in
hopes of expanding his business. On April 29, 1795, Abijah met with his
cousin John Wesley Hunt to discuss the possibility of forming a partnership
to take advantage of emerging opportunities in the trans-Appalachian West
by establishing a retail store in Lexington, in the heart of Kentucky's fertile
Bluegrass region.[21] Although only twenty-two, John Wesley Hunt had much

to recommend him as a potential partner. John had already been a partner in one mercantile venture in Richmond and had served an apprenticeship in his father's store. Abraham Hunt, John's father, was Trenton, New Jersey's leading merchant; John's older brothers, Wilson and Pearson Hunt, had already gone into business for themselves as merchants in Philadelphia.[22] John Wesley Hunt's familial connections, as much as his personal accomplishments, made him an attractive partner to Abijah. Abijah proposed a simple partnership: he and John would each contribute one thousand pounds to the new venture. Abijah would do the buying, while John would "place [him]self behind the counter . . . where I know," Abijah assured his young cousin, "you will shine."[23]

A few days after Abijah and John W. signed a contract creating their new partnership, Abijah embarked on a buying spree in Philadelphia, purchasing an array of goods "well adapted to the Kentucky country."[24] According to James A. Ramage, biographer of John Wesley Hunt, between May 11 and May 30, "Abijah made purchases from at least twenty-four different wholesale firms in Philadelphia," laying in a supply of goods that he judged would appeal to a western market.[25] Abijah purchased dry goods, including fabric, hats, and other clothing items. From the firm of Taylor & Newbold he purchased "red morocco shoes," as well as a dozen silk gloves and five dozen satin lambskin gloves. From Whelan & Miller, he bought 542 pounds of coffee, as well as spices like pepper, allspice, brimstone, cloves, and cinnamon. He purchased knives, forks, inkstands, and brandy, along with one thousand flints—an essential component of frontier weaponry—and keg upon keg of bullets. Books, medicine, and even feathers rounded out his purchases.[26]

By far Abijah and John's largest purchase, though, was from John's brother Wilson, in whose shop the new firm purchased over a thousand pounds of goods—half of their total capital.[27] A relationship with the Philadelphia Hunts was a key component of how Abijah envisioned his and John's partnership playing out. John's brothers in Philadelphia would supply John and Abijah with imported and finished goods; because they were family, Abijah may have envisioned John's brothers, Wilson and Pearson, taking more care with the new firm's orders and perhaps extending them more generous credit than was typical (and, indeed, John and Abijah did take advantage of Wilson and Pearson by not repaying their debts to them as quickly as they did to other firms). Either way, Philadelphia-based Wilson and Pearson could act as agents for the western Hunt enterprises: sending remittances, forwarding invoices, and assembling future cargoes for transport west. John and Abijah's

first advertisement, which ran in the *Kentucky Gazette* in July of 1795, illustrated the important interconnections among the Hunt family traders. John
and Abijah promised their customers the lowest prices in the area, which,
they asserted, they were able to charge thanks to "the terms [the goods] were
laid in at in Philadelphia."[28]

On their departure from Philadelphia, Abijah and John hurried westward
with their shipment of goods. Army paymaster Caleb Swan, Abijah's "intimate acquaintance," had arrived in Philadelphia from the Ohio country just
as Abijah and John were negotiating their new business. Swan had informed
Abijah that the federal government was about to send an enormous payment
of "one hundred & sixty thousand dollars"—a substantial portion of the government's budget for that year—to Cincinnati to be distributed to the fifteen
hundred Kentucky volunteer militia who had fought in General Wayne's
campaign the previous year. Abijah believed that he and John would be able
to "take a proportion of [the] payment"—if they were able to time the arrival
of their goods in Kentucky with the arrival of the government's payment.
Having an abundant supply of goods on hand as the money was being distributed would assure John and Abijah their share of the custom of several
thousand militiamen with cash in their pockets.[29]

In Lexington, John and Abijah joined a bustling community of merchants.
When Abijah and John opened their doors, there were as many as twenty
mercantile establishments vying for the trade of Lexington.[30] Despite the lack
of market access caused by the closed Mississippi, Kentucky's settlers had already become increasingly enmeshed in an Atlantic world of consumer
goods, engaging in what historian Elizabeth Perkins has characterized as "a
remarkably sophisticated, international pattern of consumption [which] laid
a cultural base for American life."[31] From their post in the Kentucky Bluegrass, John W. and Abijah Hunt were merely the westernmost outpost of networks of credit and exchange that stretched across the Atlantic. In the
Hunts' case, the connections are clearer than most. East Coast merchants,
like Wilson and Pearson, placed orders with British merchants to import the
manufactured goods that filled the shelves of their Philadelphia stores. These
merchants then extended credit to their western counterparts like John and
Abijah, who hoped to repay their debts through sales of the merchandise.[32]

The lack of cash among the settlers of Kentucky and Ohio meant that re-
tailers like John and Abijah sold most of their goods either on credit or in
exchange for "country produce," often via convoluted and confusing delivery methods, which might involve obtaining payment from a third party who

was in debt to the initial purchaser.[33] As a result, the Hunts often charged consumers a higher price for goods exchanged in barter instead of cash. As Abraham Hunt assured his son John Wesley a year after the younger Hunt's departure to Kentucky, "taking goods to Kentucky is occasioned with a great deal of hard labor Trouble & Anxiety & a Person ought to get well paid for it."[34] After all, owning a great deal of flour or bacon in Kentucky was not particularly helpful for settling John and Abijah's own debts in Philadelphia. The closed Mississippi made it difficult for western merchants to settle their debts with their eastern creditors. Abijah Hunt's relationship with the army ultimately allowed him and his cousin to overcome this problem.

Abijah Hunt: Grand Sutler

In the winter of 1796, General Anthony Wayne grew frustrated with "the Extortions, Abuses & Excesses daily committed by the Swarm of Petty Traders & Smugglers who [creeped] into" the army's encampments. Thus on February 27, 1796, Wayne ordered his officers to select one individual who would serve as the army's "Grand Sutler"—a post frequently used by the British army—who would be responsible for providing the army with "a Competent supply of wholesome groceries & Provision," as well as a "suitable Assortment of Dry Goods." The grand sutler was to be responsible for licensing other merchants to act as "petty sutlers." Thus, one man would now be able to control the trade of the entire western army. Thanks to his six years working as a sutler in Ohio, as well as close personal friendships with army paymaster Caleb Swan and General James Wilkinson, the highest-ranking member of the army after General Wayne, Abijah Hunt was appointed to serve as the nation's first grand sutler.[35]

Abijah's appointment as grand sutler meant that the Cincinnati branch of the Hunt family enterprises would suddenly find itself in "want [of] much larger Supplies of Country Produce" than had previously been the case.[36] As grand sutler, he was responsible for supplying the goods that could slake the hunger of the two thousand men serving in the Legion of the United States. Abijah had found a ready market for all the flour, bacon, and whiskey John could acquire through trade at their Lexington store. In the Legion of the United States, Abijah had found an insatiable customer, which could consume almost everything John W. accumulated via barter from his post in Lexington. John and Abijah's store in Lexington would sell the country produce it accumulated to Abijah, Jeremiah, and Jesse's store in Cincinnati; Abijah would then broker the sale of that food to himself in his capacity as grand sutler, and then turn around and sell it all to the army.

On the eighteenth-century trans-Appalachian frontier, trade with the army offered something that was not available from almost any other outlets: cash. Most of this cash did not take the form of gold and silver, which would have been prohibitively difficult to transport to the northwest frontier. Instead, much of the money flowing into the West from the federal government came in the form of notes drawn on the Department of War.[37] Caleb Swan, the army's paymaster and Abijah's close friend, brought the government's bills west, where he advertised in the pages of the *Centinel of the North-Western Territory*, Cincinnati's first newspaper, that he had bills of exchange "at ten days sight, [drawn] on the secretary of War in Philadelphia," available.[38] Swan used the notes to pay local merchants for supplies for the troops; John Bartle, an early Cincinnati merchant, recalled that he would then take these drafts and "[cash] them in Lexington at a premium of two and a half percent. Whence they would be remitted to Phil[adelphia] to purchase goods for the new settlements of Kentucky."[39] Because the army's bills were a form of currency that could be used to settle western merchants' debts with their eastern counterparts, the bills held tremendous value on the cash-scarce Ohio frontier. As grand sutler, Abijah had secured for himself and his brothers and cousins a steady stream of currency they could remit to their creditors back east.

Yet the Hunts had another role to play, too, in the movement of money. Swan also used the drafts to gather money locally to pay the army. For the most part, bills drawn on the secretary of war were not issued directly to the troops. Army privates typically earned three dollars a month; negotiating a bill of exchange for such a small amount was not feasible, nor would it have been possible to have issued the thousands of such notes it would have required to pay the entire army. Instead, Swan turned to merchants like the Hunts. In June of 1796, for instance, a bill drawn on Secretary of War James McHenry was issued to the firm of Jeremiah and Abijah Hunt "for the sum of Three Thousand Dollars on account of the pay &c. Of the Army for two months."[40] Jeremiah and Abijah, along with other merchants, bought the army's bills in exchange for local currency—specie, bills of exchange, and occasionally banknotes—which was then distributed to the troops.[41] Unsurprisingly, much of that money would later find its way back into the Hunts' pockets: on payday, troops went on a spending spree, settling their debts acquired since their previous payday and exchanging their wages for coffee, sugar, bacon, brandy, and, of course, whiskey.[42]

The U.S. empire and the Hunts' trading empire expanded simultaneously and in conjunction with one another. By moving the government's money back and forth across the Appalachians, the Hunt family solved the crucial problem of how a distant government could pay and feed an army in the field. Meanwhile, the Hunts' ability to obtain bills drawn on the federal government allowed them to profitably extend their trade networks despite the cash-scarcity of trans-Appalachia. In the West, merchants like the Hunts played many of the same roles that the Bank of the United States played in eastern cities: the Hunts' dispersed geographic location allowed the brothers and cousins to move money and goods from branch to branch, ensuring that both the government and the Hunts had funds where they needed them.

At the end of 1796, the Hunt family was operating a veritable western empire of trade. Abijah spent much of his time traveling, either to Philadelphia to replenish goods for the western branches of the family or in the field with the army. Brothers Jeremiah and Jesse acted as the family's representatives in Cincinnati, facilitating the transfer of whiskey, flour, bacon, and other foodstuffs arriving from Kentucky and the movement of manufactured and imported goods from Philadelphia to John W. Hunt's store in Lexington. The Cincinnati branch exported shoe and saddle leather to Kentucky but far more importantly injected bills of exchange drawn on the army into the family's flow of goods. These bills traveled both to John, where they helped balance the trade between Cincinnati and the Bluegrass, and to Philadelphia, where they helped offset the debts of both branches of the family's trade. The family's trade had even begun to expand further: John and Abijah's partnership now operated stores in Danville and Frankfort, Kentucky, both of which offered better access to waterways than Lexington.[43]

Hunt's activities did not go unnoticed, nor unresented. On February 27, 1798, more than twenty Cincinnati merchants sent dual petitions to Congress and to the secretary of war, James McHenry, complaining of Abijah Hunt's conduct as grand sutler. According to the merchants, Abijah Hunt was abusing his power. As grand sutler, Hunt had the "Sole Power of Licensing all other Persons or Little Sutlers to Trade with the Army."[44] Apparently, he had chosen not to, preferring to make himself and his firm the sole providers of goods to the army. Following Hunt's appointment, "a number of sutlers of unblamable character, with large supplies of necessaries on hand, brought forth with great expence of transportation, ware suddenly oblig'd to shut up their shops, let their property perish, retransport it to the settlements or sell it to the person who had the exclusive privilege at his own price." Hunt had, according to the merchants, used his influence with General Wilkinson, acting commander of the U.S. Army, to become the sole sutler "at all the Posts from Fort Defiance to the Ohio . . . & likewise for Massac and the Posts on the Mississippi." Even where other sutlers had been allowed to remain, as at Fort Wayne, the troops had been "recommended . . . to trade with the Hunts." General Wilkinson's "predelection" in favor of the Hunts, the merchants complained, threatened to create a "complete monopoly."[45]

The Cincinnati merchants saw Wilkinson's decision to appoint Hunt grand sutler and Hunt's subsequent decision to deny other merchants licenses as threatening their own livelihoods, but also as threatening to "the Inhabitance of the western Country in General."[46] The merchants recognized the importance of the army to the western economy. "Since the first establishment in the Western Country," the merchants lamented, "the trade and intercourse with the army & military posts . . . has been a very considerable source from whence the means of remitence have been derived for the Merchandize brought from the Atlantic Ports." With the Mississippi closed, trade with the army had proved to be one of the central mechanisms by which westerners could hope to balance their debts with eastern merchants; if the Hunts alone had access to the military's money, the merchants worried, the result would be to "restrain & embarrass the internal commerce of the Western Country."[47] John and Abijah's success in feeding the troops with the produce of their central Kentucky stores illustrates just how much a western "internal commerce" was tied to sales to the army.

Western merchants were quick to point to yet another consequence of the Hunts' monopoly. In 1798, citizens of the United States' nascent settler empire in Kentucky and Ohio still found themselves with large surpluses of goods on hand and no way to export those goods to markets elsewhere. That this remained the case was somewhat embarrassing for the federal government. In 1795, American negotiators in Spain had concluded a decade-long fight to obtain access to New Orleans for American citizens. According to the terms of the Treaty of San Lorenzo, better known as Pinckney's Treaty, "the Citizens of the United States" now had permission "to deposit their merchandise and effects in the Port of New Orleans."[48] Yet, two years after the Senate had ratified the treaty, Ohio Valley merchants and farmers still lacked access to New Orleans as reluctant Spanish officials delayed the port's opening. The Cincinnati merchants were quick to remind Congress of this shortfall and of Congress's role in the situation. Trade with the army, they informed Congress, was the only available outlet for the produce of the West that had "in some measure compensated for the embarrassments of our Commerce down the Mississippi."[49] With the Hunt family monopolizing the army's trade, there was nothing left for other western merchants.

Even as the merchants wrote, however, a profound change in the federal government's role in the West was taking form. The defeat of the Northwest Confederacy in 1794 had reshaped the United States' Indian affairs north of the Ohio. No longer an aggressor in a protracted war, the U.S. Congress, often loath to fund an army in the first place, reduced the number of troops in the field, shrinking the army from 5,120 men to 3,359 men.[50] Moreover, those troops were more scattered than ever before. In the summer of 1796, the terms of Jay's Treaty between the United States and Britain had finally been carried into effect, and Britain's remaining forts south of the Great Lakes had been handed over to American forces. New outposts at Michilimackinac, Detroit, and Niagara suddenly formed the northernmost edge of the United States' military presence. Although merchants in Cincinnati and Kentucky would provide some of the supplies to these forts, preexisting communities in places like Detroit, as well as Canadian merchants, who were far closer to hand, were better suited to meeting the needs of this new northern army.[51] Furthermore, American diplomatic efforts had also borne fruit in another arena. In 1795, the United States had concluded the aforementioned Pinckney's Treaty with Spain. The treaty had settled a disputed boundary between the United States and Spain, and in the process had transferred several Spanish military forts to American control.

The simultaneous spread and diminution of the American army transformed the role of the federal government in the Ohio country and in the trans-Appalachian West more broadly. The Hunt family's advantageous location in Cincinnati no longer functioned as the central way station in trade between the settlers of Kentucky and a captive military market. Moreover, in 1798, the U.S. Army reorganized how it supplied its troops, dividing the forts of the trans-Appalachian West into six districts, each one of which merchants could bid to supply. Soldiers, of course, had no choice in where they were transferred. Sutlers like Abijah found themselves in a similar position. When the army was subdivided, many of the soldiers and officers indebted to the Hunts departed for the Natchez district, which the United States had just acquired from Spain. With their primary source of income marching off, Abijah proposed to Jesse that they should send "a quantity of goods" downriver, "for the purpose of trading with the army."[52] Although Jesse opposed the move, Abijah decided to open a new branch of the store, this time in Natchez. The timing seemed fortuitous: John W. Hunt had grown frustrated with sharing his profits with a partner who was seldom present, and he and Abijah were preparing to amicably part when news of the troops' transfer arrived. At the same time, General James Wilkinson, Abijah Hunt's patron in the Ohio country, had, with the death of Anthony Wayne, acceded to the head of the U.S. Army. When Wilkinson departed for the Lower Mississippi in the summer of 1798, Abijah Hunt followed close behind.

By December of 1798, Abijah had once more resumed his strategy of being as useful as possible to American government officials. That December, Abijah fronted Winthrop Sargent, the first governor of the Mississippi Territory, four hundred dollars to purchase trade goods for the Choctaws; when the Department of State repaid the money, it used Abijah as the intermediary for transferring a thousand dollars to Sargent to serve as a "Contingent Fund."[53] But this amount was small in comparison to the scale of Abijah's total business with the government. Between 1798 and 1800, Abijah received over thirty thousand dollars in drafts drawn on the U.S. government for his services supplying the army with food, horses, liquor, and cash.[54] Abijah also established a second government contract, serving as the first postmaster for the newly created postal route between Natchez and Nashville.[55] As postmaster, Hunt became directly responsible for linking officials in Natchez, at the furthest edges of the American empire, to the central government in the East.

Abijah Hunt: Slave Trader

At Natchez, Hunt established a store, where he sold, in the words of one historian of early Mississippi, "white hats and ladies' 'delicate shoes.'"[56] But it was not selling millinery that would make Abijah a fortune. In 1800, Abijah turned to selling what was, for him, a new commodity: enslaved people. In February of 1800, he wrote to John in Lexington. "Negroes are in demand & will Sell well," Hunt informed his cousin. While flour and tobacco were currently "dull," whiskey and enslaved men and women would, Abijah assured John, "command money."[57]

By 1800, the Americanization of Natchez was fully complete. The small community had undergone a sea change in the previous five years, transforming from a Spanish outpost, dependent on government subsidies to produce tobacco and indigo, into an American outpost consumed with the production of cotton. In 1795, the planters of Natchez had produced their first crop of cotton, and by 1800, their output was well over a million pounds of cotton a year.[58] As early as 1797, the shift to cotton had created an explosion of demand for the labor of enslaved people. That year William Dunbar, appointed as Spain's commissioner for surveying the boundary between the United States and Spain, had been uncertain if he could find the number of enslaved men he regarded as necessary to carry the expedition's heavy surveying chains: the labor of the enslaved men and women of Natchez was all employed in planting cotton.[59]

It was not long after the popularization of the cotton gin that the domestic slave trade began to take shape, fueled by enslavers' demand for more and more captive laborers. In 1800, when John and Abijah first ventured into bringing enslaved people from Kentucky to Mississippi, such a trade was still in its infancy, and lacked both the infrastructure and the accepted practices that would become commonplace in the 1820s, when the phrase "sold down the river" would encapsulate the experiences of hundreds of thousands of enslaved people.[60] Nevertheless, the brutal logic that underscored the domestic slave trade was already in place. When Abijah first wrote to John asking him to gather a cargo of enslaved people, enslaved African American men of prime working age were trading for an average of $303 in Kentucky; in Natchez, in contrast, enslaved men sold for an average of $500.[61] Moreover, enslaved people, unlike general merchandise, could be sold almost immediately for cash—a factor that was frequently at the front of Abijah's mind. In Ohio, Abijah had carefully structured his relationship with the army to supply the cash that kept his family's businesses running; in Natchez he found an even more lucrative avenue to financial liquidity in selling captive bodies. From 1800 onward, Abijah Hunt's businesses operated along two divergent business models, one predicated on the expulsion of American Indians and one based on the expansion of slavery.

In 1800 and 1801, John, Abijah, Jesse, and Jeremiah Hunt joined together in the slave trade. Abijah once more assessed the marketplace and fronted the money; in the fall of 1800, he sent Jeremiah $3,000 and instructions to purchase enslaved people in Kentucky for the Natchez market.[62] John helped Jeremiah find slave owners who might be willing to sell, and by December 17, 1800, Jeremiah Hunt had purchased five women, four men, and four children, all of whom would be sent downriver once the weather improved.[63] On February 14, John dispatched the thirteen enslaved people from a point just east of Cincinnati in the care of Captain Philip Buckner, a wealthy Kentuckian who was embarking on a slave-trading journey of his own.[64] On February 23rd, when the boat touched at Louisville to portage around the Falls of the Ohio, Buckner took on board more merchandise for the firm of A & J Hunt—this time consisting of candles, nails, 147 gallons of peach brandy, and 357 gallons of whiskey.[65] The records of the journey reinforce the logic of the slave trade. We know exactly how many barrels of brandy and gallons of whiskey were transported to Natchez, but the name of just one of the enslaved individuals who, together with the liquor, composed the cargo: Little Robin, who was small enough that on February 10 he got a kernel of corn stuck in his ear.

Abijah Hunt's slave-trading venture directly benefited from his ongoing relationship with the federal government. By 1801, the U.S. Army had established several posts along the eastern side of the Mississippi River, which lowered the risks involved in engaging in river trade. But Abijah's army connections retained a central role in his activities: at Chickasaw Bluffs, the site of modern Memphis and the location of the newly established Fort Pickering, Buckner landed his boats to deliver 207 gallons of whiskey and 300 pounds of bacon to Abijah's agent at the fort. For Abijah Hunt, a single venture could serve the army and help to establish the downriver trade in enslaved people.[66]

By 1803, Abijah Hunt's new trading network was firmly established. He remained a partner in the Cincinnati firm of Hunt & Co., which he operated with his brothers Jeremiah and Jesse. Now this business was primarily concerned with importing finished goods from the East to be sold to the population of the newly created state of Ohio. They also regularly shipped goods downriver to Abijah in Natchez, charging him a premium of 15 percent for the transportation of the goods.[67] John remained in Kentucky, and although he and Abijah were no longer business partners, they continued to collaborate on various ventures. The trade through New Orleans had proved so lucrative that, in the three years between 1798 and 1801, John and Abijah had been able to clear all of their outstanding debt—although Abijah had not yet settled his own accounts with John.[68] Abijah himself operated primarily out of Natchez, but his new mercantile ventures extended further: trading with the army at Loftus Heights and Fort Pickering and operating retail stores in Natchez and the outlying communities of Washington, Greenville, Port Gibson, and Big Black.[69]

Once more, Abijah operated his stores through a mixture of barter and cash, only now the commodity he received in barter was almost exclusively cotton. In exchange for manufactured goods imported from Philadelphia, Abijah received thousands of pounds of cotton; however, once more, Abijah developed a business model that stretched far beyond the doorsteps of his stores. In Natchez, Abijah had again branched out: each one of his stores was accompanied by a cotton gin. Planters could bring their crops to Abijah's gins to have their cotton cleaned and baled; Abijah would receive 10 percent of the cotton in exchange for the use of his machines. As a gin owner, he was instrumental in issuing the ginning receipts that functioned as money in territorial Mississippi.[70] However, his business extended even further: he also acted as a cotton factor, brokering deals for Mississippi cotton with merchants in New Orleans, eventually going so far as to dispatch his brother Jeremiah to England to oversee the sale of the cotton, and acquiring a $30,000 line of credit with Barclay's of London.[71]

In this new venture, Abijah once more reached out to family, employing his nephews Caleb and David within the firm and partnering once more with John W. Hunt in Lexington.[72] Beginning in 1803, John W. Hunt decided to invest the profits he had made working with Abijah into one of the West's first ropewalks. In his factory, enslaved people worked transforming hemp fiber into both rope and a second, more lucrative product: cotton bagging—the rough, canvas-like material that was used to bind together the circular bales of cotton produced in the first decade of the nineteenth century. When John first proposed developing a hemp manufactory, Abijah had greeted the idea with enthusiasm. Manufacturing cotton bagging, he informed his cousin, would be "more productive than any other business yet established in your country as there is, and ever will be, a very great Consumption of that article in this lower Country, and it will always command money."[73] Abijah proved correct, and over the next decade, John W. Hunt's business would explode, as would his dependence on enslaved workers. By 1809, his factory relied on the labor of seventy-seven enslaved people, the majority of them—forty-five— boys under sixteen. At his death in 1849, John Wesley Hunt was widely regarded as the West's first millionaire.[74]

By the time Abijah Hunt died in 1811, he had created two intertwined trading networks. Capitalizing on his relationships with brothers, cousins, nephews, and uncles, Abijah formed the hub of an extensive network that made him rich and his successors phenomenally wealthy. Partnerships with the U.S. government were instrumental to this process. As a merchant and a sutler, Abijah acted as the go-between between the U.S. Army and the settler population. By cashing government checks in the West and transporting government bills of exchange eastward, Abijah Hunt provided a necessary financial glue that was essential to binding the edges of the United States to the central core.

When Abijah died in the feud with Poindexter, he did so in large part as a Federalist partisan. Because dueling was illegal in Mississippi, the two men crossed the river to Louisiana, where Abijah, like Alexander Hamilton before him, succumbed to his injuries. In life, Abijah Hunt had profited from close relationships with a powerful central government embodied in the U.S. Army, and from a reliance on networks of patronage and exchange. He moved around the money that made it possible for farmers to pay their taxes, to remit them eastward, only to be sent back westward once more as pay for the army. He profited from the expulsion of Indigenous peoples and the expansion of slavery. The death of Abijah Hunt reminds us of something important: when Thomas Jefferson characterized the American republic as an "empire of liberty"—one in the hands of white, yeoman farmers who would spread across the countryside—he in many ways elided the importance of a shadow financial empire that would need to accompany it. That was Abijah Hunt's West: a world dominated by commerce and finance harnessed to create not only an American empire but also his own.

CHAPTER 3

How Native Nations Survived
the Imperial Republic

KATHLEEN DUVAL

In the fall of 1811, an Osage crowd assembled to listen to the Shawnee speaker Tecumseh convey the message that he and his brother, the prophet Tenskwatawa, were spreading across central and eastern North America. The speech went something like this: "*Brothers*—We must be united; we must smoke the same pipe; we must fight each other's battles; and more than all, we must love the Great Spirit: he is for us; he will destroy our enemies, and make all his red children happy."[1] What Native Americans could resist such an argument in 1811, as the juggernaut of the imperial republic threatened to destroy them all?

Well, the Osages could. They told Tecumseh that his fight was not their fight. In fact, one of the many fights the Osages were engaged in was against Potawatomis, Sauks, and Illinois peoples, many of whom were known to be part of Tecumseh and Tenskwatawa's movement. And the foremost of Tecumseh's battles—against the United States—was not one that Osages in 1811 saw reason to join. With the benefit of hindsight, of course, it is easy to see Tecumseh's point. If the Osages and other powerful people in the West had decided in 1811 that the battles in the Ohio Valley were their battles, the course of history might have been different. If more Native Americans had followed the Shawnee brothers' advice to identify and act as a unified people, a continent wide movement might have lessened land losses and carved out some of the continent as permanent Indigenous space.

The Osage listeners in 1811 might not have agreed even with that hindsight-inflected argument. It is possible that nothing was going to stop U.S. settler colonialism by the nineteenth century. Even more important, decisions like those of the Osages in 1811 are part of the reason that there is an Osage Nation today, two centuries later.

Not only have Native Americans survived repeated predictions of their demise, as well as concerted efforts to make those genocidal predictions come true, they have remained nations, with separate sovereignties, identities, land bases, languages, art, beliefs, rituals, histories, and methods of dealing with federal, state, city, and other tribal governments. It was the insistence by Osages—as well as Chickasaws, Caddos, Tuscaroras, Occaneechis, Catawbas, Pamunkeys, and hundreds of other Native nations, including most Shawnees—that they were not and should not be all the same that enabled Native people to remain nations through the horrors of the nineteenth and twentieth centuries.

For historians of pre-nineteenth-century North America, Native power is clear. Native Americans were most of the continent's population into the eighteenth century and held most of its land for another century after that. But it is remarkable that Native nations survived the period of removal through allotment, boarding schools, and termination in the twentieth century. It is remarkable that well over five hundred separate Native nations still remain today within the bounds of the United States, and many more throughout the rest of the Americas. The expansion of the United States from the Atlantic to the Pacific and beyond was in no way inevitable. There were many other ways the continent's future might have gone. But one of those many historical possibilities was that Native nations would cease to exist as separate sovereignties, either being absorbed into the white or free people of color populations or becoming a generalized American Indian minority within the United States.

Decisions made by the men and women of Native nations in the nineteenth and twentieth centuries prevented that possible future from coming to pass. Most of the challenges to Native nationhood came from the imperial republic, but some came from Nativists like Tenskwatawa and Tecumseh, who believed unity was the solution to the astounding dangers posed by the United States. Like threats from the United States, these efforts inspired urgent debates within Native communities about who they were and who they should be. Sometimes people purposefully rejected amalgamation and assimilation, but more often it was shorter-term reasons that worked against the kind of unity Tenskwatawa and Tecumseh called for. Those reasons might be Native rivalries, such as that between the Osages and the Potawatomis.

Sometimes people worried about the conflict that might break out if some people joined the movement and others did not. And sometimes people specifically rejected the prescriptions and proscriptions of Tenskwatawa and Tecumseh, which could seem sanctimonious, self-serving, or simply not correct.[2]

A Shawnee Debate

In 1775, a baby boy was born in a Shawnee town on the Mad River. His father was Shawnee, and so he inherited a Shawnee patrilineal family and division. His mother had grown up in the Shawnee settlement in Upper Muscogee (Creek) country. She probably was Shawnee, but if she was Muscogee, her children also were fully Muscogee and part of her matrilineage. The baby would become the prophet Tenskwatawa. One of his older brothers was seven-year-old Tecumseh. Their father had died at the Battle of Point Pleasant a few months before Tenskwatawa's birth, so it was their older brothers who taught the younger boys how to hunt and led them on raids against squatters in Kentucky. Both boys were at the Battle of Fallen Timbers, where the last of their older brothers was killed.[3]

It was ten years later, in the spring of 1805, when Tenskwatawa had the vision that would direct his path thereafter, give him the name Tenskwatawa (The Open Door), and put that name in the histories of Shawnees and all their neighbors. In Tenskwatawa's vision, the Master of Life told Shawnees to return to older ways of clothing and economics and give up alcohol, goods manufactured in Europe, polygamy, private property, and violence against one another. Tenskwatawa's vision appealed to many Shawnees. Their world had changed fast, and the change was hard to comprehend. In just the thirty years since Tenskwatawa had been born, hunting and trade had shrunk, tens of thousands of white Americans had moved into the Ohio Valley, and the U.S. military and its squatters had forced Shawnees off more of their lands.[4]

Like most people, Shawnees put themselves at the center of the world and the center of the Creator's designs. An earlier Shawnee speechmaker explained two years before Tenskwatawa's vision, "the Master of Life . . . made the Shawaneese [Shawnees] before any others of the human race" and "gave them all the knowledge which he himself possessed." Indeed, that Shawnee explained, "all the other red people were descended from the Shawaneese," and "the Shawaneese for many ages continued to be masters of the continent, using the knowledge which they had received."[5] Only a bit more modestly, George Bluejacket said in 1829, "We were a great people. Our men were great warriors. They fought many tribes and always beat them."[6]

Shawnees had long been at the center of intertribal organizing, so it is no surprise that, within a few months, by December 1805, there were Delawares and reportedly some Ottawas, Wendats, and Ohio Senecas among the Shawnees listening to the prophet Tenskwatawa tell how the Master of Life "had shown him" that the game had not disappeared as they feared it had. The deer were merely "half a tree's length under the ground." If they did as the Master of Life said, he would turn the earth over, and the deer "would soon appear again." In parallel, the Master of Life had promised the prophet, "If you Indians will do everything I tell you I will turn over the land so that the white people are covered and you alone shall possess the land."[7]

Shawnees were hardly alone in looking to overturn the past few decades of history. While the independence of the United States would not affect the Navajos or the Kiowas or other western nations for another couple of generations, Native people east of the Appalachians already knew its threat intimately. By 1810, the number of white and Black Americans west of the Appalachians had passed one million, so now the hundred thousand Native people living between the Appalachians and the Mississippi River were looking urgently for new explanations and ways to make it stop.[8]

Between the Ohio Valley and the Great Lakes, a large number of peoples were living in closer proximity than in the past. Wendats, Delawares, Shawnees, and other Iroquoian and Algonquian refugees from eastern wars against the English and the Haudenosaunee (Iroquois) had resettled in the West, many of them at the invitation of the Anishinaabe nations. Shawnees had lived in the Ohio Valley in the early seventeenth century, dispersed as they fled violence there in the 1660s and 1670s, and returned in the eighteenth century. Moving was a long-standing tradition in North America. A town or band or nation could remain a coherent group even in a new place, even with a changed name. These resettlements in the Ohio Valley had required a tremendous amount of diplomacy and continuing coordination among the newcomers and older residents, the kind of intricate, alliance-building, kinship-building diplomacy that the United States did not do when its people came to the Ohio Valley.[9]

In 1829, looking back, Shawnee George Bluejacket recalled the Native migrations as a success. "North of the Great *Se-pe*" (the "Great River," the Ohio River), he said, "Here we were given much land by our brothers, the Wyandots. We built many towns and lived . . . in peace."[10] Still, George Bluejacket's grandparents and parents remained Shawnees. Indeed, throughout many migrations and dispersals, Shawnees maintained and developed a Shawnee identity through shared culture and language, through careful cultivation of ties across their scattered communities, and as diplomats and network-builders in the places where they went.[11]

But being Shawnee did not mean being unified politically. Even as leaders at times tried to create a centralized leadership, Shawnees continued to identify primarily as smaller political groups, as towns and families. Historian Stephen Warren observes that both intertribal organizers like Tenskwatawa and Tecumseh and also their opponents like the Shawnee leader Black Hoof who were trying to build more of a national Shawnee politics wanted more political centralization than most Shawnee men and women probably wanted. And historian Susan Sleeper-Smith has shown that Native women in the Ohio Valley created multiethnic regions, towns, and families that shaped Native lives, probably more than the efforts of either nationalist or Nativist male leaders.[12]

By 1806, Tenskwatawa was urging his followers to leave their Shawnee, Wendat, or Delaware towns to move to a location on Greenville Creek, a northern tributary of the Ohio River. There they built a new town, and Tenskwatawa preached a universal message. In addition to Delawares and Wendats, some Ottawas pilgrimaged from the north, and Sauks traveled from the Rock River on the Upper Mississippi. Miamis, Potawatomis, and Ho-Chunks came from the west around Lake Michigan. In a 5,000-square-foot council house, Tenskwatawa preached, and celebrants danced. Some settled in to stay. Women planted corn, beans, and pumpkins. Men cut down trees to build houses: fifty, sixty, and counting. The camp-meeting atmosphere would have been recognizable to contemporary Americans as a religious community in the making.[13]

Some people who came to Greenville Creek went home to evangelize. In May of 1807, an Ottawa man called "the Trout" was back home four hundred miles north of Greenville Creek, at L'Arbre Croche, near where Lake Michigan and Lake Huron meet. Speaking to an open council of men, women, and children, he conveyed Tenskwatawa's message, along with eight strings of wampum, four white and four blue, that the prophet had sent.[14]

Following Tenskwatawa's call, the Trout's sermon was not just about the Shawnees or just about the Ottawas. He told how the Creator had seen that "my *Red Children* . . . had become scattered and miserable." Through prophets like Tenskwatawa and the Trout, the Creator gave them the solution: "You are to have very little intercourse with the Whites. . . . The Whites I placed on the other side of the Great Lake [the Atlantic], that they might be a separate people." His "Red Children" could play ball against one another, but "you are however *never to go to War against each other* But to cultivate peace between your different Tribes that they may become one great people."[15]

Separate creations was not a new or even particularly radical idea in 1807. The belief that the Creator had made Native Americans, Europeans, and Africans separately went back at least as far as Neolin and Pontiac in the 1760s. And historian Gregory Evans Dowd points out that Black Hoof basically agreed with Tenskwatawa and The Trout on that much. Black Hoof, Miami leader Little Turtle, and other nationalizing leaders who opposed Tenskwatawa's movement had long worked to implement new kinds of coordination across their nations, including not selling land unless all of them agreed. What was radical in 1807 (although not completely new either) was the Creator's wish that Native Americans "become one great people."[16]

You can hear how far Tenskwatawa had developed the idea by a speech the following year: "The Religion which I have established for the last three years, has been attended to by the different tribes of Indians in this part of the world. Those Indians were once different people; they are now but one; they are all determined to practice what I have communicated to them, that has come immediately from the Great Spirit through me."[17] When Little Turtle challenged his plan to move his settlement to lands the Miamis considered theirs, Tenskwatawa replied that he would not change his plans, "which had been laid by all the Indians in America."[18]

By 1808, becoming and being "one people" was self-evident to Tenskwatawa and his brother Tecumseh, who carried the message far and wide. Their confidence and rhetorical power persuaded some people of their day, and ever since, of their message's self-evident truth. But there were many who did not see the world Tenskwatawa's way, who did not agree that Native peoples "are now but one."[19]

The movement of Tenskwatawa and Tecumseh was largely aimed at men, even though Shawnee women's support would be necessary for it to succeed. As in most Native American societies, Shawnee women were the farmers, and so every time Shawnee towns moved, women had to plan and prepare new fields and raise crops in new places with new soil and water conditions to learn. Unfortunately, the sources that survive pay little attention to women's decisions, and there certainly were some women at the town on Greenville Creek and later at Prophetstown, including Tenskwatawa's wife. Still, most Shawnee women stayed where they were, and it is easy to imagine that moving again to live and farm alongside non-Shawnee women, without metal hoes or other tools that Shawnee women had used for generations, had drawbacks that outweighed any religious and political appeal. There are differing accounts of whether Tenskwatawa required casting away current multiple wives. If he did, following his teachings would tear apart existing families. There were more women than men in the war-torn Ohio Valley, and widows and younger sisters often married into existing households and added to their agricultural production. Even if Shawnees only stopped making *new* polygynous marriages, there would be serious disruptions in women's familial and work lives and, as a result, the Shawnee economy. The prophet's requirement that "all Indian women who were living with White men" had to be "brought home to their friends and relations, and their Children to be left with their Fathers, so that the Nations might become genuine Indians" would force the immediate rupture of families. Tenskwatawa's path was a hard sell if it required becoming "one people" with foreigners while abandoning sisters and children.[20]

While women's reactions are harder to see, it is clear that Black Hoof rejected Tenskwatawa's message in favor of his own vision of Shawnee nationhood and his own leadership of it. Before the disruptions of the Seven Years' War, Pontiac's War, and the American Revolution, Shawnee towns had each belonged to one of five patrilineal divisions, each of which had its own responsibilities. Each town had autonomy over matters within the town, and each had its own peace chief and chose its own war chiefs in time of war. But dispersal had shifted towns and roles and resulted in some towns of people from multiple divisions. In addition, during the decades of near constant war, war chiefs whose authority would traditionally have been temporary became permanent. Black Hoof was a successful war leader and town chief but did not have a hereditary right to become a chief or spokesperson for the Shawnees beyond his own town.[21]

Yet since the 1790s, Black Hoof had been working to centralize Shawnee political leadership and to implement economic changes, both of which he believed would help Shawnees firm up their position in the Ohio Valley. At Black Hoof's town of Wapakoneta, Shawnees had started raising cattle and selling meat and dairy products and growing cash crops to sell. They built a blacksmith forge, a gristmill, and a sawmill and tried to establish a salt processing business with Delawares. They leased out tribal land, thereby embedding their land title in the kind of paperwork that they hoped would hold up in U.S. courts. To finance these efforts, Black Hoof made use of U.S. resources, including the annuities paid for land cessions starting at the 1795 Treaty of Greenville, and invited Quaker missionary William Kirk to help them break into new markets.[22]

Sometimes these kinds of efforts are portrayed as knuckling under to the U.S. "civilization program," but leaders like Black Hoof and countless Shawnee women and men whose names did not make it into historical documents were in no way attempting to assimilate into white America or just doing what U.S. politicians and agents told them to. They were trying to lead their people into a new future, a Shawnee future. At the same time, most Shawnee effort went into supporting neither Tenskwatawa's nor Black Hoof's efforts but the work of farms, households, and towns. Still, importantly, Black Hoof's changes fit better with older social and economic patterns. Shawnee women at Wapakoneta continued to farm, while adding new crops and markets and accepting the help of Shawnee men with clearing and perhaps plowing. Shawnee men substituted the declining fur trade with livestock raising and other economic pursuits but, despite U.S. pressure, for the most part did not do the women's work of growing and harvesting the crops.

Tenskwatawa would not agree with that interpretation of what was happening at Wapakoneta and other Shawnee towns in the Ohio Valley. He charged that Black Hoof and leaders like him had "abandoned the Interests of their . . . nations and sold all the Indians Land to the United States and [had] requested the President to . . . appoint masters over" the Indians. To Tenskwatawa, Black Hoof was allowing the United States to make Shawnees into slaves and into "women" by giving up men's traditional work of hunting and war. How to explain these leaders' treachery? They must be witches.[23]

The witch hunts inspired by Tenskwatawa were not simply attacks on political opponents; they were deeply religious. The witch hunts' major target was religious leaders who rejected Tenskwatawa's demand that they give up their medicine bags and their specifically Shawnee or Delaware ceremonies. Tenskwatawa's followers killed two Shawnee men for religious reasons—"bad Medisin"—and accused Black Hoof of being a witch. They also targeted Native leaders who had converted to Christianity and allied themselves with Christian missionaries.[24]

Right in the midst of this early stage of Tenskwatawa's evangelism, in September 1809, Miami leader Little Turtle and other Miami, Delaware, and

Potawatomi leaders signed the Treaty of Fort Wayne, in which they ceded over three million acres to the United States. Frustrated, new people came to Tenskwatawa's camp, including some Wendats and Ohio Senecas who considered the treaty a violation of earlier agreements not to sell land without the consent of all. Tenskwatawa and Tecumseh agreed with them and threatened to kill the chiefs who had signed it. The following summer, Tecumseh traveled to Vincennes to tell William Henry Harrison (in the version that Harrison wrote down) that "it was the object of his brother and himself from the commencement to form a combination of all the Indian Tribes in this quarter to put a stop to the encroachments of the white people." Past efforts had not worked, and "the Americans had driven them from the sea coast, and would shortly if not stopped, push them into the Lakes." Therefore, "they were determined to make a stand, where they were," to establish and defend the "principle that the lands should be considered common property and none sold without the consent of all." For some, the Treaty of Fort Wayne proved that Native nations needed more than agreements not to sell land but to make all Native land "common property."[25]

Tecumseh also told Harrison that it was the movement's "intention to put to death all the chiefs who were parties to the late Treaty, and never more to suffer any village chiefs to manage the affairs of the Indians, but that everything should be put into the hands of the warriors." Village chiefs like Black Hoof were part of the Shawnee political structure that Tecumseh and Tenskwatawa hoped to destroy, to meld into their larger polity of all Native people. Tecumseh told Harrison, "we have endeavoured to level all distinctions to destroy village chiefs by whom all the mischief is done; it is they who sell our land to the Americans." From now on, Tecumseh said, Harrison should negotiate through him because "I am authorised by all the tribes to do so" because "I am at the head of them all."[26]

That was not true. It was not just leaders like Black Hoof and Little Turtle who had no desire to yield political authority over their towns, divisions, and nations to Tecumseh and Tenskwatawa; even many ordinary Shawnees deduced from the troubles since the American Revolution that it was time to stop fighting and rebuild. They had fought hard for their previous lands but had lost again and again. With the Treaty of Greenville in 1795, many decided it might be best to try to get along with everyone, including Americans. Some of them changed their minds because of the brothers' preaching, but still, in the coming battles against the United States in 1812 and 1813, there were Shawnees who fought or spied for the Americans, and most Shawnees stayed out of the fighting entirely. Of the around 1,800 Shawnees, only a few families—perhaps forty fighting-age men—joined the movement.[27]

By the end of the eighteenth century, most Shawnees had already moved west of the Mississippi, and their decision not to return east to join Tenskwatawa's movement would be one of the brothers' great disappointments. While around 800 Shawnees lived in the East, a full 1,000 had moved to what is now Missouri, including some of the brothers' kin. They already were fighting a war against the Osages, on whose former lands they had settled. They were focusing their diplomatic efforts on building a military alliance against the Osages with Cherokees, Delawares, Miamis, and Kickapoos who also moved west of the Mississippi, with Quapaws already living there, with Potawatomis who had long fought the Osages on both sides of the Mississippi, and (most troubling for Tenskwatawa's movement) with French Louisianans, who themselves had long been hemmed in by the Osages and were delighted to have powerful new Native allies.[28]

On at least two visits and possibly more, Tecumseh tried to persuade the Shawnees west of the Mississippi to stop fighting the Osages. During his 1810 visit, an Osage war party had just killed two Shawnees. One of the dead was related to Tecumseh and Tenskwatawa, so his words urging unity and forgetting past offenses carried particular weight as a relative. Yet the Shawnees in the West were not persuaded, and their war against the Osages continued.[29]

The Shawnee debates over Tenskwatawa and Tecumseh's movement reveal both that their concerns and solutions were rooted in specifically Shawnee history and institutions and that, as ardently as they differed, they shared some basic beliefs about the Shawnee future. As historian Bethel Saler has pointed out, neither revivalists nor Native Christians nor advocates of Black Hoof's kind of economic and political change accepted white Americans' categorization of them as subordinate, deficient, and doomed. And even Nativists did not see themselves solely as general Native Americans. Historian Stephen Warren observes that when Black Hoof and Tenskwatawa were interviewed in the 1820s, both of them pointed to family and town as their primary allegiances.[30]

The North

Tenskwatawa and Tecumseh would have to look beyond Shawnees for their greatest support. Tecumseh and other emissaries carried the vision far from home. Harrison marveled in 1811 that "for Four years he has been in constant motion. You see him today on the Wabash and in a short time you hear of him on the shores of Lake Erie or Michigan, on the banks of the Mississippi, and wherever he goes he makes an impression favorable to his purposes."[31] As people gathered and listened to the increasingly famous speaker, local history, conditions, needs, beliefs, and power structures affected how they responded.

The message found no enthusiasm in Haudenosaunee country. As scholars Alyssa Mt. Pleasant and Lisa Brooks have shown, after the American Revolution, Haudenosaunee people focused on repairing the damage the war had done to their Great League of Peace. Some members of the Haudenosaunee League had joined Shawnees and others in large military and diplomatic efforts in the past, and the Haudenosaunee had found themselves pulled into the fighting on both sides of the American Revolution. Now they turned inward to rededicate themselves to their Great Law of Peace and its ability to restore the relationships among the Six Nations. And they worked together to promote Haudenosaunee independence through peace and diplomacy. They nearly universally stayed out of Tenskwatawa and Tecumseh's movement, to the frustration of many within that movement.[32]

Seneca leader Young King explained to a U.S. official who, like Tenskwatawa, tried to draw the Haudenosaunee into renewed conflict: "you must listen, and hear what is the full determination of all the sachems and warriors of the Six Nations. . . . We are neither on the one side, or on the other . . . we desire to be still, and to be at peace with both." Young King insisted that they were unified—perhaps a prescriptive message directed at his Haudenosaunee audience as much as a declaration of truth to the outside recruiter: "you have heard the sense of the Six Nations, . . . for, amongst us, there is not one deficient."[33]

Young King exaggerated Haudenosaunee unity, but his intense insistence on inward-looking work—on being "still"—helps to explain Haudenosaunee reticence toward war, no matter who was calling for it. The Seneca prophet Handsome Lake beginning in 1799 preached a similarly inward-looking prophecy, advising Haudenosaunee to resist both war and land sales and work on their spiritual health within the longhouse. The Haudenosaunee League was already an ancient, spiritual as well as political, coming-together of nations that still retained their separate identities. And the Haudenosaunee succeeded. They rebuilt their league as well as their separate nations and, unlike so many others, held onto land in the East.

Some Native people explicitly rejected Tecumseh and Tenskwatawa's religious message. The Christian Mahican leader Hendrick Aupaumut called Tenskwatawa a "false prophet." Aupaumut found blasphemous Tenskwatawa's claims to be able "to change the course of nature" and "to take down the sun and moon." Tenskwatawa's claim, according to Aupaumut, that within four years, "if the different nations should not obey his commandments ... then he shall cause the day of Judgement to come" and "all the unbelievers shall be utterly destroyed" was unpersuasive both theologically and politically, as well as soon proved untrue.[34]

The message found more recruits on the upper Mississippi River than in the northeast. In the summer of 1810, Tecumseh had a successful northern tour. Potawatomis, who had been traveling to the Ohio Valley to hear Tenskwatawa's word since at least 1808, were especially enthusiastic. Tecumseh kept going, to Peoria towns on the Illinois River, Ho-Chunks on Rock River, and Menominees at Green Bay. He spoke to diverse people gathered at the post of Prairie du Chien, then descended the Mississippi River to the Sauks and Foxes.[35]

Some of their greatest converts were here. Potawatomi prophet Main Poc became one of Tenskwatawa's firmest allies. It was apparently Main Poc's idea to move Tenskwatawa's Prophetstown to the Tippecanoe River, closer to Potawatomi towns so that Potawatomi women could feed them until their first season of crops were ready and on the site of a former agricultural town that had been destroyed in 1791 by Kentucky militiamen. But Main Poc modified the message, making it more palatable to Potawatomis. Tenskwatawa not only declared that "all medicine bags, and all kind of medicine dances and songs were to exist no more," people were to gather and publicly destroy their medicine bags. Main Poc's version, in contrast, encouraged Potawatomi traditions and practices. As historian Jonathan Hancock puts it, Main Poc ultimately "refused to cede spiritual and political authority to the Shawnee brothers."[36]

For some converts, the religious message helped to unite their cause even more than land protection or opposition to the United States, yet calls to discard tribally specific religion pushed more people away. A Sauk man named Wennebea told an American, "we always carry medicine bags about us ... we take them when we go to war ... we administer of their contents to our relations when sick. . . . They have been transmitted to us by our forefathers, who received them at the hands of the Great Master of Life himself." And yet, Wennebea recalled, speaking in the 1820s, "some of us did, at one time, at the instigation of the Shawnee prophet, . . . throw them away." Wennebea remembered that Tenskwatawa and his emissaries had told them "that the medicine in our bags, which had been good in its time, had lost its efficacy," so "many of our chiefs cast away their bags." "But this proved to us the source of many heavy calamities[;] it brought on the death of all who parted with their bags."[37] Wennebea was looking back, after military defeats, and he found answers in the religious beliefs and practices of Sauk forefathers.

In contrast to Haudenosaunee who spoke of staying "still," there was some military support here, but usually the answer that interested people gave Tecumseh was an enthusiastic if vague statement of future support with an explanation that they would need to finish an ongoing war with Native enemies before they could send military assistance. Main Poc insisted that the Osages were an exception to the unification of all Native people. He told Tenskwatawa, "the Great Spirit always told him that . . . he must war (upon other Indians), otherwise his medicine would become weak and of no effect, and would be inferior to many Indians of the Nation."[38] Right after he met with Tenskwatawa for the first time at Greenville Creek in the fall of 1807, Main Poc went back west with two objectives that Tenskwatawa would have found contradictory: to spread the word of Tenskwatawa's vision and to muster fighters to go against the Osages.[39] And things were even a little muddy at Prophetstown. Some Kickapoos there in 1810 told a Frenchman that they knew the prophet intended to lead them to war, but they were not quite sure "whether he designed to attack the United States or the Osage nation."[40]

While these wars posed practical problems—military effort was directed away from the common U.S. enemy and against potential allies, and resources focused on western wars meant less food supply for Prophetstown and its armed forces—they even more importantly completely undercut the message of being one people. This was a problem that Nativist military leaders always faced. Generic unity and opposition to U.S. expansion sounded good to a lot of people. Actually working together with enemies against a less immediately threatening enemy was quite a different matter. Over a generation earlier, Pontiac's attempts ran up against people who wanted to unite but demanded huge exceptions for Native enemies. A Sauk war leader in the 1760s, for example, was certain that the "perpetual war" that the Sauks were waging against the Illinois would "endure as long as the sun, moon and stars." If "our bones should meet after death, they would fight together 'till they would be broke to pieces."[41] Native men and women set their own priorities and followed their own values, even when they were receptive to much of what Nativists preached.

The South

Tecumseh and Tenskwatawa were most optimistic about recruiting in Muscogee towns. The Shawnee families who had moved to Muscogee country more than a century earlier had built strong connections. While most had moved back to the Ohio Valley or west of the Mississippi by the early 1800s, Shawnees still regularly traveled to Muscogee country. The brothers' mother and possibly their father were born in or near the Shawnee settlement on the Tallapoosa River, and they still had kin there. Muscogees had fought alongside Shawnees in the raids and battles of the long war against the States from the 1770s into the 1790s, in both the Ohio Valley and Cherokee country. Shawnee emissaries regularly came south to recruit Muscogees and Cherokees and to join in their battles, including the Muscogee fight against Georgia in the 1780s. Tecumseh himself may have fought in Chickamauga Cherokee country with other Shawnees and Muscogees.[42]

So, in August 1811, Tecumseh and a delegation including Shawnees as well as Kickapoos, Ho-Chunks, Sauks, and Muscogees traveled south with high hopes. One of their party was Seekaboo, a man related to the brothers and to the Shawnee settlement in Muscogee country. He may have previously traveled south to recruit. Certainly Muscogees and Cherokees had traveled north to hear what was happening and to report back home, seeing large new U.S. settlements on their trip through Tennessee that provided proof of the urgency to act. By the spring of 1810, there were a reported twenty to thirty Muscogees at Prophetstown (perhaps counting Shawnees from Muscogee country) and some Cherokees as well.[43]

The purpose of Tecumseh's 1811 mission was to recruit not only Muscogees but also Cherokees, Chickasaws, and Choctaws. These four nations together had well over 10,000 trained fighting men, and they seemed likely to want a united war. With the exception of the Cherokees, they had not suffered any major defeats at the hands of the United States, yet they knew from the experience of the Cherokees and, in the case of Muscogees and Chickasaws, seeing squatters appear on their own land for a generation that the United States was a threat. Muscogees had already fought Georgia, and all suspected that more conflict was to come.

Muscogee country had its own history of trying to organize the very kind of consolidation of not just military effort but also identity that Tenskwatawa and Tecumseh were attempting. It was here in the 1780s—a generation before Tecumseh—that Muscogee leader Alexander McGillivray began to build a "Southern Confederacy," modeled on and in coordination with the "Northern Confederacy" centered in the Ohio Valley. By the time that Tenskwatawa had his vision, McGillivray was dead and the Southern Confederacy with him, and Southeastern peoples' memory of that attempt would affect their decisions as they listened to this new invitation.[44]

Muscogees received Tecumseh well in 1811. In countless towns for at least a month, he gave his religious, historical, and political speech, smoked the calumet, and taught Tenskwatawa's new war songs and dances. Seekaboo, who had trained with Tenskwatawa, followed up with a more explicitly religious message. Seekaboo could speak Muscogee fluently in addition to Shawnee and some Choctaw and English, so he was able to speak without an interpreter, using Muscogee religious words and concepts.[45]

Tecumseh also visited Choctaw and perhaps Chickasaw towns, where he urged everyone to come to the Muscogee town of Tukabatchee that fall for the annual Muscogee National Council, where he was to give a great speech. Muscogees from the upper and lower towns, Alabamas and Seminoles (both loosely part of the Muscogee Confederacy), Cherokees, Choctaws, and Chickasaws showed up. According to later accounts, there were hundreds, quite likely thousands, assembled by the time Tecumseh spoke, which he waited to do until after the U.S. representatives had left. In Tukabatchee's town square, according to accounts given later by listeners, Tecumseh, with Seekaboo interpreting, "talked much of conversations with God on Indian affairs." He detailed U.S. aggression, spoke of the long history of Shawnee-Muscogee cohesion, and outlined the plan "for all the Indian tribes on the continent to hold their lands in one common stock." He promised that they "could recover all the country that the whites had taken from them" if northern and southern peoples unified to expel white Americans and their ways and throw over any local leaders who stood in their way. Some people said they thought Tecumseh was a *harjo* (crazy man) or a liar or both, but many found his vision just what they were looking for.[46]

Tecumseh left Muscogee country promising to send messengers when the war was imminent. As in the North, some converts left with him, including Josiah Francis, an Alabama who would become known as "Francis the prophet" and also "Heles Harjo" ("Crazy Medicine"). Tecumseh and Francis headed west across the Mississippi River, while others of the party rode directly to Prophetstown. Seekaboo remained in Muscogee country to continue to spread the word in this fertile ground, converting Muscogees and Alabamas. He, Francis, and other prophets who arose in the Muscogee Confederacy combined Muscogee religious traditions with Tenskwatawa's prophecies and prescriptions. Thus the movement that they created—the Red Sticks—became much more Muscogee-centered than the kind of universalist Nativism that Tenskwatawa and Tecumseh preached.[47]

Putting Muscogees at the center of his organizing efforts was logical, but it hurt Tecumseh's chances with the Chickasaws and Choctaws, who still had bitter memories of McGillivray's Muscogee-centered attempts to build a Southern Confederacy in the 1780s. In letters to his Spanish and British contacts, McGillivray had claimed that he was "head of a Numerous brave Nation, and of a Confederacy of the other Nations" and that the Muscogees were the "head and principal" of the southern branch of the "Nations in Confederacy against the Americans."[48] The problem back in the 1780s was not that multitribal movements were controversial among the Chickasaws and Choctaws. On the contrary, starting in the 1750s, Choctaws and Chickasaws had devoted tremendous diplomatic effort to ending decades-long wars, first between themselves—the Chickasaws and Choctaws—and then throughout the region, with Muscogees, Cherokees, Catawbas, and Quapaws.[49] And for over a year in the early 1780s, Chickasaw headmen and warriors formed part of a delegation with Shawnees, Delawares, and Cherokees traveling to visit, in their estimation, one hundred large and small nations east of the Mississippi and south of the Ohio to discuss peace among themselves, no matter what happened in the Revolutionary War.[50] After the war, in the summer of 1784, Chickasaws and Choctaws led a delegation of more than one hundred Shawnees, Cherokees, and Haudenosaunee to seal an alliance with the Spanish at St. Louis.[51]

The problem for the Chickasaws and Choctaws in the 1780s was that McGillivray's Southern Confederacy threatened their sovereignty and the peace they had worked hard to build. In 1787, Chickasaw leader Piomingo and his council decided to grant the United States some of their more distant lands to get rid of squatters who had set up camp only a half day's journey from a Chickasaw town, and they approved a U.S. trading post on Chickasaw land. In response, McGillivray accused Piomingo of ceding land "which belongs to my Nation," and a war party of Muscogees rode in to Chickasaw country. These Muscogees rode up to where a group of Americans was building the trading post and, not bothering to speak to the Chickasaws, killed seven of the Americans and put the rest to flight. The Muscogee party made a point of riding through Chickasaw towns on the way home, displaying the seven scalps. Chickasaws were shocked at this Muscogee violence on their own land and other Muscogee and Cherokee attacks on Chickasaws and Choctaws who went to meet or trade with Americans. A few years later, in 1794, Chickasaws considered joining the northern confederated forces, but when a group of Chickasaws arrived at a joint war camp, they immediately clashed with their Kickapoo enemies there. Instead, some Chickasaws fought at Fallen Timbers on the side of the United States, against the Northern Confederacy. Not all Chickasaws agreed with that decision, but they knew that history by the time Tecumseh arrived in 1811.[52]

When Chickasaws and Choctaws listened to Tecumseh speak, there was much that rang true. The United States was a new threat that clearly required new solutions. Tecumseh's talk of declining game surely struck a chord. But there were many ways to respond. McGillivray's vision of "one Nation" had threatened the regional peace that southern Native nations had worked to build, and this new Shawnee vision of "one people" seemed likely to do the same. They listened and discussed, but, almost universally, Choctaws and Chickasaws declined to join.[53]

As for the Muscogees, few of them would fight in the North. Instead, inspired by both Shawnee and Muscogee prophets, including Seekaboo and Francis, the Red Sticks fought not only the United States but also other Muscogees, for similar reasons as in the North. Chickasaws and Choctaws were right in their worries that their pan-Native peace would fall apart. As one Red Stick tellingly explained, "the war was to be against the whites and not between Indians themselves,—that all they wanted was to kill those who had taken the talk of the whites, viz.: the Big Warrior, Alex. Cornells, Capt. Isaac, Wm. McIntosh, the Mad Dragon's son, the little Prince, Spoko Kange and Tallasee Thicksico"—all prominent Muscogees. In other words, the Red Stick War would definitely be "between Indians themselves."[54] It was the worst possible outcome. Over 1,500 Muscogees, Chickasaws, Choctaws, and Cherokees fought against the Red Sticks along with U.S. regular army and militia. Similarly, in the North, Shawnees, Delawares, and Wendats were part of the forces fighting Tecumseh. Native people fighting one another was the exact opposite of what McGillivray or Tecumseh had hoped, although a possibility that others predicted.[55]

The West

From Muscogee country, Tecumseh and Francis, the Alabama prophet, crossed the Mississippi. They made another attempt to recruit the western Shawnees, Delawares, Miamis, and Kickapoos. Some Kickapoos did move back east to Prophetstown. And Francis and probably Tecumseh went to speak to the Osages. The Osages were a strong and militarily successful people, and their thousands of fighting men could make a significant difference if war came. Also, Tecumseh and Tenskwatawa may have seen recruiting the Osages as the ultimate proof of their movement's truth. Wars against the Osages were serious and long-standing, and truly being "one people" would require ending these old animosities. In turn, ending those animosities would reveal the rightness of their teachings.[56]

So it was that in the fall of 1811, a large Osage crowd listened to the invitation to take a new path. The much-later recollections of John Dunn Hunter, who witnessed the speech as a young man, are the only account of what was said that day, but his account seems in line with what Tecumseh said to other crowds:

> *Brothers*—We all belong to one family, we are all children of the Great Spirit; we walk in the same path; slake our thirst at the same spring; and now affairs of the greatest concern, lead us to smoke the pipe around the same council fire! . . .
> *Brothers*—My people are brave and numerous, but the white people are too strong for them alone. I wish you to take up the tomahawk with them. If we all unite, we will cause the rivers to stain the great waters with their blood.
> *Brothers*—If you do not unite with us, they will first destroy us, and then you will fall an easy prey to them. They have destroyed many nations of red men, because they were not united, because they were not friends to each other.[57]

To the Osages in 1811, though, these threats of destruction rang hollow. Osage history over the past century stood in stark contrast to Tecumseh's history lesson. The Osages had militarily expanded, conquering, expelling, or controlling everyone in their way, including Europeans. Of course, Tecumseh's history was right, and by the end of the nineteenth century, the United States would dominate the continent and, in the next century, the world. But for now the Osages still had the upper hand in interactions with outsiders. People feared them. Osage men shaved most of their hair to exaggerate their commanding height, with a five-inch roach, often of porcupine quills or an eagle feather to stand straight up, bringing their total height often to seven feet. Thomas Jefferson, no shorty at six feet two, referred to the Osages as "certainly the most gigantic men we have ever seen."[58]

To the Osages, the Shawnees, Delawares, and Cherokees who had moved west were the problem. They were the ones squatting on Osage land. In 1805, a delegation of Osages had signed a peace treaty at St. Louis with some of these rivals, because the United States promised to keep the peace and provide the hosting and presents required for ongoing diplomacy. But the peace had not held, and Osages blamed the Potawatomis for breaking it and for capturing more than thirty Osage women and children who were still held captive in Kickapoo, Sauk, and Fox towns east of the Mississippi, even as Tecumseh spoke.[59]

Still, it may have been the religious message even more than the political one that the Osages rejected. In Hunter's recollection, even though Pawhuska and the other Osage leaders ultimately turned down the request, they were impressed by "Tecumseh's eloquence," and they did discuss his military and diplomatic advice in council.[60] The Osage reaction was quite different to the more explicitly religious speech given by the prophet Josiah Francis. His sermon, Hunter recalled, "enlarged considerably more on the power and disposition of the Great Spirit." Hunter believed that Francis's words did "more injury than benefit, to the cause he undertook to espouse." In 1811, Osages may have been willing to start to consider new military and diplomatic alliances, but they were not at all interested in this movement's call to give up specifically Osage ways for beliefs and practices that to them probably seemed more Muscogee and Shawnee, and perhaps more Christian, inflected as they were by Shawnees' interactions with Christianity for generations.[61]

The emissaries went home disappointed and would fight their coming war against the United States without the Osages or the western Shawnees and Delawares. Francis would return to Muscogee country and help to lead the Red Sticks and coordinate Spanish and British assistance. In 1813, he wrote to a Spanish contact that "we have given our talk out to the nations," and the "whole Creek nation is united and taken up the red stick."[62] It was a large and determined movement, but it was not the "whole Creek nation," as their bloody civil war would prove.[63]

Conclusion

The imperial republic did tremendous damage, and continues to do so, in the face of alternatives that Native people have always identified. Yet despite centuries of pressure to assimilate—to one another or to white America or to a general category of people of color—Native people throughout the Americas have done something very different from that. They did not vanish, or become white Americans, or become a single Native American identity. In the early decades of the American republic, debates were urgent and deadly serious over how to forge a future in this changed and changing world as so much power was lost. Some people envisioned a united Native America, one people together against foreign invaders. Others hoped family, clan, or town would remain the center of power and identity and struggled against the centralizing efforts of both Nativists and nationalists. And some worked to strengthen and save the Native nations that today are the site of Native sovereignty and identity and are having a renaissance in language, culture, art, and economics. In the 1810s, and still today, there have been non-Native Americans who saw no future for Native Americans, who believed that, as individuals and as nations, they would cease to exist. One belief that Tenskwatawa and Tecumseh shared with all of their Native audiences, even the most skeptical, was that there would be a Native future.

CHAPTER 4

Catawba Women and Imperial Land Encroachment

BROOKE BAUER

In the late eighteenth and early nineteenth centuries, the Catawbas of South Carolina responded in various ways to the effects of settler colonialism, a form of colonialism where a powerful imperial authority sought to establish a dominant settler society that drove Natives from their land. In South Carolina, the English, Scots-Irish, Scots, and Germans began settling on Catawba land as early as 1750, creating a space of British imperial control in what they called the backcountry. In the wake of the American Revolution, as settler encroachments continued, Catawbas found that they had to contend with not one imperial authority but two: the new United States, and the sovereign state of South Carolina. South Carolina legislators, aware of the weak powers the Articles of Confederation conferred to Congress, had their own agenda, which focused on expanding the state's power into the backcountry. These leaders even considered inviting European immigrants to settle that region of the state, on land that belonged to the Catawba Nation. As Colin G. Calloway writes, "individual states made their own treaties with Indians, often in defiance of federal wishes, and sometimes challenged the authority of the federal government to conduct Indian affairs."[1] Even though Catawba men had served as American allies during the Revolution, the infant empire's expansionist philosophy had critical consequences for Catawbas, especially when it came to the part that South Carolina played in territorial growth.

This essay examines how Catawba Indians confronted empire-building in South Carolina from 1783 to 1840. It reveals how Catawbas strategically adapted Anglo-American property practices and legal instruments of land tenure, melding them with Catawba customs to carve out a zone of local authority and autonomy amid the shifting landscape of competing imperial regimes: British, U.S., and South Carolinian. In the 1780s, acting as legal landholders with documents that proved their possession, Catawbas responded to the influx of white settlers by establishing their own lease system.[2] Self-interested South Carolinians had proposed to lease Catawba lands before, but failed to ever implement their plans. By launching such a system themselves, Catawbas sought the control to decide who settled on their land and the ability to legitimize their land tenure in the eyes of Euro-American colonizers. However, Catawbas confronted overwhelming odds in the late 1700s and early 1800s. By the 1790s, the flood of white settlers content to rent Catawba land affected the natural environment in ways that threatened Catawba well-being. To preserve their dwindling access to a share of their own territory, Catawbas turned to another tool in the Anglo-American legal kit—the deed—conveying a tract of land to themselves, on terms that reflected long-standing traditions. At the same time, however, the Catawbas' white tenants began petitioning the state to acquire Catawba land and turn renters into freeholders. The shift from leasehold to fee simple title would provide these citizens with the right to vote and enable them to run for office. Thus, Catawbas still found themselves fighting to hold onto their land. In the end, leasing land was not the best solution to settler encroachment, but the practice delayed dispossession for a time.

Catawba women were central actors in this story. Although narratives of Native resistance to settler colonialism often focus on what men did, Catawba women were mothers of new generations and stewards of the land, and their opinions mattered when issues arose concerning Catawba land. Extant sources about late eighteenth-century Catawba women are few. But important evidence can be drawn from the scraps that survive, including in the county courthouses of South Carolina. Moreover, it is possible to discuss the significance and influence of Catawba women by analyzing documented interactions between white and Catawba men within the historical context of Catawba culture and gender roles—seeing women's actions between the lines of sources that do not mention them. Through both these methods, this essay explores Catawbas' strategies against land encroachment and dispossession while centering Catawba women in the story.[3]

After the American Revolution, British authority shifted into the hands of the new republic, which George Washington called a "rising" or "infant" empire. Several years later, James Madison referred to the republic as "one great, respectable, and flourishing empire." Even before the war's end, Thomas Jefferson wrote of the future United States as an "Empire of liberty" that would creep into the western frontier on "extensive and fertile Country," land that belonged to Native Americans, who certainly did not see the white settlers' world as one of liberty. The narrative of settler encroachment on Native land that immediately followed the American Revolution generally centers on Indigenous groups of the Ohio Valley, who fought the infant empire to retain their land. This story unintentionally excludes what was happening to Native people in the Carolina backcountry during the same period. The Catawba Nation of South Carolina is not often thought of when discussing Native nations in the Southeast—historians tend to focus on larger groups like the Cherokees and Creeks—and few scholars have examined Catawbas' interaction with the new republic. Approaching this story from a Catawba perspective, where "imperial" refers to the white settlement that forced Native people from their homeland, and "empire" implies a regional authority that used military, political, or economic power to dispossess the minority, can explain much about Catawba women's role in thwarting America's designs (via South Carolina) at the dispossession of Catawba land.[4]

Catawbas' settler problem grew to a crisis level as British control shifted to the new U.S. government in the late-1700s. In 1777, the Second Continental Congress drafted the Articles of Confederation, a document that established some functions of a national government of the original thirteen colonies, now states. The lack of a centralized government under the Articles of Confederation (1781–89) provided South Carolina with the power to take full advantage of its sovereignty to expand its territory and authority to regions the state claimed as its backcountry. In South Carolina, as in other southern states, white men based their liberty on acquiring land and expanding an agrarian society. As wave after wave of landless Americans flooded the region because of the cheap, fertile soil, white men of all economic statuses viewed landownership as the only way to climb the social ladder. White migration into the backcountry of South Carolina led to the rise of a yeoman class determined to express their freedom through landownership. Thus, as South Carolina's population and authority expanded, the new American republic expanded its sovereignty into the foothills of the Blue Ridge Mountains, on land that belonged to the Catawbas.[5]

Catawbas' thoughts about landownership and mobility conflicted with European and Anglo-American definitions. Catawbas' concept of landownership was akin to the "use" of land that encompassed towns, burial grounds, agricultural fields, and hunting grounds. Their expansive territory accommodated practices like hunting and farming, and it provided Catawbas with space to relocate their towns when natural resources grew scarce. They had already moved their towns several times before the American Revolution for this reason and many others. Because of the spiritual connection to their ancestors, they sometimes returned to previously occupied land; so, from their perspective, they belonged to the land. They were born of the land, lived off the land, and returned to the land at death. This type of land control, management, and knowledge was foreign to Anglo-American men, who viewed landownership in a capitalistic manner that called for making improvements to the land, building homes, felling trees, fencing property, and farming. Thus, non-Native men's prejudiced notions about the lack of Catawba land improvements and proper housing left Catawba land open to white settlement from the 1750s into the 1840s. Yet, Catawbas maintained some control over their land and determined who had access to it via a land leasing system.[6]

To understand how Catawbas began leasing large plots of land to landless white settlers, we must first step back to the decades before 1783. Paradoxically, the idea of land leasing began not as a Catawba attempt to protect their land, but rather as a colonial effort to swindle Catawbas out of it. In the decades before the American Revolution, Catawba landholders leased some land, but they did not consider these early leases (and later leases) as land sales that extinguished Catawba landownership. Instead, they considered the leases assigned before 1774 as only surface use agreements negotiated verbally and settled with a handshake. At this time, the 1763 Treaty of Augusta promised the Catawbas ownership of 144,000 acres in the Piedmont region of South Carolina through an official land survey (Figure 4.1).[7] The survey would prove critical in creating land boundaries and a legal paper trail for Catawba landholders. As settler encroachment swelled, though, Catawbas found it increasingly difficult to prevent squatters from settling on and taking their land. They complained about the problem to South Carolina leaders time and again, but received little assistance from the colony.

In this context, William Henry Drayton, a young land speculator and member of the South Carolina Royal Council, eyed the potential of a financial windfall. In January of 1772, probably on a freezing winter day, Drayton met with the Catawbas and offered them a proposal to lease their land. Everyone from the town would have been in attendance, both women and men. Although Drayton came from a wealthy planter family that lived in Charlestown, South Carolina, he was destitute from years of gambling and thought

Figure 4.1. Detail of the Catawba Nation, 1775. The square represents the 1764
survey of Catawba land boundaries guaranteed by the 1763 Treaty of Augusta.
From Henry Mouzon, *An Accurate Map of North and South Carolina, with Their
Indian Frontier . . .* , 1775. Library of Congress, Geography and Map Division.

to get himself back on his feet by leasing all of the Catawbas' land.[8] However,
he had to get the land scheme past John Stuart, the British southern superintendent of Indian affairs, a man Drayton viewed as the problem to South
Carolina's authority, especially in regard to taking Indian land. Drayton apparently believed that Catawbas would readily agree to the lease proposal as
the best solution to the encroachment problem, providing him with the authority to sublease the land to other settlers.

However, Drayton was not truthful to Catawbas about his proposal, and
his scheme soon fell apart. By early January 1773, John Stuart learned about
Drayton's plan via a letter sent to the Catawbas' local agent. The contents of

the letter alerted Stuart to the fact that the Catawbas "did not understand that [Drayton] was to Settle the whole of the Land." Stuart went before the South Carolina Council to state his opposition to the Drayton land scheme, arguing that the 1763 Royal Proclamation prohibited such negotiations between individual colonists and Indians. Indeed, only representatives appointed by the Crown (such as Stuart) could negotiate Indian land transfers. Although the estrangement between the colonies and the Crown was growing, South Carolina, like other colonies, did not yet see a complete dissolution of their relationship with the British government in 1773. As such, the council prudently withdrew its support of Drayton's plan. South Carolina's royal governor, Charles Greville Montagu, responded to Stuart that the land lease was "an improper and impolitic measure" that could result in "bad consequences," such as another Indian war. Catawbas, who were apparently alarmed that Drayton planned to lease all of their land, told council leaders via an interpreter that "they [Catawbas] would not part with their Land to any people whatsoever, that as long as any Indians remained the Land was to belong to them." Though it failed, Drayton's scheme under the British empire set the stage for the Catawbas' land crisis under the emergence of an independent U.S. republic bent on building an empire of its own.[9]

Several years into the American Revolution, the Southern Campaign battles came to the Catawbas' backdoor, dragging them into warfare they preferred to avoid. Nonetheless, Catawbas joined the war because they perceived that siding with the American patriots was the only way to protect their land. So, in May 1780, Catawbas, like many Native nations, became embroiled in a contest of land, freedom, and wealth in the South. The same year, South Carolina patriot leader General Thomas Sumter and five hundred starving men encamped near the Catawba Old Town. General Richard Winn referred to this camp in his memoir, writing that "after the fall of Charleston we often Encamped on their land for days together. Those friendly Indians drove to us Beef from their Own Stocks, and Several times brought Out their whole force and Encamped near us." Catawbas had demonstrated their allegiance to the American cause over the past three years (1777–80) not only through men's service but also with Catawba women providing local non-Native families with corn until they had no more to spare. However, they still had cattle, which Catawba men drove to the patriot camp, where a few Catawba women most likely butchered the cattle and cooked the meat for Sumter and his men. Although the record mentions "Indians" in general as helping the American men, it was Catawba women who managed the homes,

fields, and livestock. Thus, they would have the final word about what happened to the crops and domesticated animals, while the men were responsible for driving the cattle.[10] Such aid often placed women in the heat of battle,
a fact that Catawba men tried to prevent from happening because women's
productive and reproductive labor was crucial to the survival of their people.

In truth, the realities of war are often glossed over or erased when con-
sidering Catawba women, who experienced the loss of their fathers, uncles,
husbands, sons, and brothers. The deaths of Catawba men meant that women
had to take on duties that typically fell to men, like burying the dead. They
also experienced violence at the hands of non-Native men, brutality that went
beyond physical abuse. In June 1780, the British army destroyed many homes,
fields, barns, and mills in the backcountry, including the Catawba towns and
farming areas. When the British approached, they threatened the lives of Catawba women and children if the men refused to ally with the British. In
response, Catawba men of fighting age guided their women and children
north, away from the wartime violence. In October 1781, returning Catawbas were met with the burnt remains of houses and cornfields. They realized
their agricultural economy was in ruins as they struggled to rebuild homes
and recultivate fields. Farming in late fall was not only ill-advised but an impossible time to cultivate a crop. Retreating British troops had confiscated
any stored corn and sweet potatoes held in granaries and seized or killed the
livestock, leaving nothing behind. It is easy to imagine Catawba women
standing in the center of what was once a small town, looking at the terrible
aftermath of destruction. Homes where they raised children and cared for
their family were gone. Catawba women most likely worried about feeding
their families because of the absence of crops and stored foodstuff. The dev-
astation to their town may have seemed hopeless as everything was razed to
the ground. Yet they responded as their ancestors had, picking up the broken pieces left in the wake of imperial contest, to begin again. Indeed, resil-
iency provided Catawba people with the coping skills that helped them
respond to chronic adversity, whether it was war, poverty, or land loss.[11]

Catawba men's martial support of the American cause did not protect
their land against further encroachment. In fact, the Catawbas' settler problem only escalated after the American Revolution. By the 1780s, sharp population decline left the Catawbas with less than four hundred people. Because
of the low population, Catawbas' diminishing military power hindered them
from preventing squatters and land speculators from invading their land. On
November 2, 1782, the Congress of the Confederation met with two Catawba

diplomats in Philadelphia. The two men appealed to Congress to protect "certain tracts of land reserved for their use in the State of South Carolina, which they wish may be so secured to their tribe as not to be intruded into by force, nor alienated even with their own consent." The concern the men expressed suggests that Catawbas' relationships with squatters had led them to distrust South Carolina's commitment to preventing encroachment on Catawba land. But Congress responded by punting the matter of Catawba land rights back to the state, informing the men that the state legislature should "take such measures for the satisfaction and security of the said tribe, as the said Legislature shall in their wisdom think fit." South Carolina leaders were, of course, aware that Congress would defer to them under the Articles of Confederation, and they took advantage of the opportunity to expand the state's control into the Piedmont region, on Catawba land.[12] State leaders wasted no time in this expansion policy because, after all, they believed that South Carolina's Piedmont boundary extended west to the Mississippi.[13]

Under the Articles of Confederation, Congress had few powers while state legislatures acted autonomously, especially when it came to making decisions about debt and tax relief. Congress looked at the western lands that extended to the Mississippi River as more than enough land to pay the government's war debt. For example, Congress turned to selling western lands in the Ohio Valley region to American settlers to pay debts. However, many Native groups held the Ohio territory near the Great Lakes in common, insisting the land could not be sold without their consent. In January 1785, U.S. commissioners met with delegates from the Wyandot, Anishinaabeg, Delaware, and Ottawa, reminding them that they were a defeated people who had aligned themselves with the enemy and thus had no power in land cession negotiations.[14] To the south, the Treaty of Hopewell (1785–86) reaffirmed Cherokee, Choctaw, and Chickasaw boundaries, but the treaty did not halt settler encroachment. South Carolina also looked to its western lands to settle the state's war debts, and, in 1785, its governor, William Moultrie, eyed Catawba land as the ideal place to grow revenue.

That same year, Catawbas heard that Governor Moultrie pushed the General Assembly to develop a Catawba land leasing system. When explaining his plans to the legislature, Moultrie referenced the 1763 Congress of Augusta treaty that guaranteed Catawbas a tract of territory of fifteen miles by fifteen miles (225 square miles, or 144,000 acres). He told the South Carolina House of Representatives that the Catawba Indians had "a large tract of rich, fertile lands," and that little of it "is made any use of either by their Occupancy or

Cultivation." To him, this assessment justified taking Catawba land. Moultrie's was a common perspective among Anglo-American settlers who viewed occupancy and "improvements"—like European-style fields, homes, and churches—as features of so-called authentic landownership. The state-controlled land tenure system was what set Moultrie's plan apart from Drayton's earlier leasing scheme. Drayton would have leased Catawba land as a private individual if such an exchange was legal under British law. Subleasing smaller parcels of land to landless settlers would have made him immensely wealthy, and Catawbas would receive no compensation. Moultrie's plan, by contrast, would have been entirely state-controlled and supported by the General Assembly. Theoretically, the lease payments collected by the state would "be applied Solely to their [Catawba] Maintanence [sic] and Support."[15]

Moultrie considered the leasing plan central to improving South Carolina's stagnant postwar economy. The revolution had left South Carolina with a war debt higher than other states except for Massachusetts. Unlike Congress's plans for the territory it claimed northwest of the Ohio River, however, Moultrie's goal was not to raise revenue through land sales further west. Rather, he hoped Catawba lands would help stanch the decline of the state's white male population, enabling South Carolina to bounce back from the brink of financial ruin by attracting new settlers. The governor explained to the representatives that his leasing plan would open allegedly vacant Catawba land to upward of seven hundred white families. A population increase of this magnitude would boost the economy by introducing more agricultural production and skilled labor for the state, generating more tax revenues for the long haul. And although Moultrie's plan to lease Catawba land to white renters fell short of the fee-simple ideal at the heart of Jefferson's vision for an "Empire of liberty," it still entailed providing white citizens with a modicum of economic opportunity by taking Indigenous land.[16]

Although Catawba women's voices during this time are absent from American records, one can imagine that they verbalized their concerns about Catawba land dispossession, loss that would limit women's ability to move villages and fields every few decades if necessary. Moultrie stipulated that for the leasing proposal to be effective, the Catawbas had to approve of it. As with past decisions that focused on Catawba homeland, the agreement would have necessitated the support of a majority of Catawba men and women. Moultrie added that if the representatives failed to implement the proposal, and Catawbas were "Suffered to live in their present Ignorant uncivilized manner," they would become "a burthen to the State, and the land [would] remain un-cultivated, and an useless Forest for many years." But South Carolina repre-sentatives discovered that Catawbas had in fact not requested any form of leasing system. They shelved Moultrie's plan, deeming it "inexpedient at pre-sent to take any Steps Concerning it." Although their reasons for doing so are not entirely clear, their choice of words—"inexpedient at present"—suggests that they approved of the plan's outlines but simply believed the time was not yet convenient.[17]

But Catawbas quickly took the logic of Moultrie's leasing system and ap-propriated it for their own ends. In late 1785, mere months after the legisla-ture put Moultrie's plan on a temporary hold, Catawbas began leasing their territory on their own accord. Perhaps they thought it was better to initiate a leasing system of their own than to be coerced by the state. By taking this initiative, Catawbas could determine the terms of the leases, including to whom they would rent land, how much land would be rented, and what the terms of the rent would be. Taking control of the land leases also enabled them to establish a paper trail as landholders, which temporarily safeguarded their lands. The first documented lease that Catawbas initiated was to Sam-uel Knox, who had first migrated to the region in the 1750s. The 1785 lease agreement began, "This indenture made this fifteen day of November in the year of our Lord, one thousand seven hundred & eighty five, Between John Col. Airs, Major Brown, Major John Thompson, Capt. Squash and Pine Tree George, with the consent of Genl New river chiefs of the Catawba Indians. And Samuel Knox of the County of Mecklenburg and State of North Caro-lina." Catawbas set a term of twenty-five years on the lease, and during that time Knox was to pay the tribe ten silver dollars, three horses, and a rifle for an unknown amount of acreage. The lease could be extended by Knox's heirs if they paid ten silver dollars annually. Although the lease shows only the names of Catawba men, based on Catawba political practices before and after this document, they could not lease the land without the consent of most of the tribe. However, the Knox lease started a flurry of people migrating onto inexpensive, fertile Catawba land.[18]

Meanwhile, the rhetoric of equal representation and liberty continued to fill the South Carolina statehouse chambers. Many of the Lowcountry state representatives had fought in the Revolutionary War, as did their backcoun-try counterparts. Veteran soldiers from the backcountry believed the ideol-ogy of liberty and equal representation that Lowcountry statesmen claimed applied to them as well. This discourse excluded Catawbas. And resting as it did on the political rights attached to fee-simple landownership, it also posed problems for the Catawbas' new strategy of leasing their land to white renters. In February 1791, a group of 152 backcountry petitioners, who leased land from the Catawbas, wrote to the House about the 1790 state constitution. They pointed out that article 1, sections 4–8, prevented tenants from participating in the government by restricting their voting rights and preventing them from running for office. An excerpt from the petition read, "Your Petitioners well know that [a]s the law now stands that leasehold Estate[,] however the sum may be[,] is less than a Estate least [*sic*] for the life of one Man, but at the same time humbly [Pr]esume that it is in the Power of the legislature to consider the leases of your Petitioners which are all for ninety nine years to be such Estate as would Constitute them Electors qualified to vote for members to both Houses of the legislature." At issue here was the notion of independence. Voter eligibility and running for office were based on landownership, because as white Americans understood it, private property made republican citizens politically independent—free from the whims of a master or a landlord. Though tenants, the petitioners did not conceive themselves dependent on the Catawbas. In fact, they argued, their ninety-nine-year leases were as good as fee-simple deeds, which, as they shrewdly put it, endowed an individual with landownership only as long as he lived. In short, the petitioners were content to lease Catawba lands; it was the political rules that needed changing. Among other things, their disenfranchisement had implications for the regional balance of electoral power. Catawba leases in the backcountry helped Lowcountry elites to maintain political control in the state.[19]

Catawbas, who were excluded from the Anglo-American ideals of freedom due to settler notions of race, responded to the renters' petition with a set of their own grievances in a 1792 petition by the Catawba leader General New River and thirty Catawba men. Based on three hundred years of Catawba political tradition, it is likely that Catawbas discussed the petition as a political body and made a near-consensus-oriented decision to send the petition to the General Assembly.[20] Women, who managed the land through kinship, no doubt would have been instrumental to the discussion. In the petition, General New River referred to the 1763 Augusta treaty that resulted in a documented land survey in 1764, reminding the assembly that the Catawba Nation had "free possession" of the 144,000-acre tract. Simply put, Catawbas possessed legal ownership of the land. Thus, they claimed Catawba territory through the matrilineal tradition and by using the American legal system, which required documented proof of landownership. New River reminded the assembly that "We Were Necessiated [*sic*] to Rent out of our land for the Suply [*sic*] of our Wants which we Sustained by the Distress of the War." Catawbas had, "With deliberation," agreed that this strategy was "Just and Right," and they affirmed their "Desir[e] to Stand to our bargains and Contracts." But problems had arisen with their tenants. Even as they pressed for political equality, many of the settlers who rented land from the Catawbas proved conniving or unreliable. Some partitioned the land they leased, subleasing it to other Anglo-Americans, immediate and extended families, for an increased rent rate, pocketing the profit. On several occasions, renters refused to make their annual lease payment. As the Catawbas' petition put it, "What We do Desire of those Who have Sold part of the Lands we have leased to them is to pay their Contracts." General New River appealed to South Carolina officials to do their duty to compel the leaseholders to honor their agreements and provide adequate compensation, especially if they had subleased the land.[21]

New River also went further, touching on a topic that among his people would have been under the purview of Catawba women. Taking natural resources by force or coercion was a fact of American empire building, environmental colonialism, and capitalism. When Europeans initially arrived in South Carolina, they sought wealth by extracting natural resources. This practice remained unchanged during the era of the new republic. As white migration into Catawba territory swelled, the overharvesting of timber or deforestation for home building, field clearing, and ship making destroyed the backcountry forests. One traveler to the South remarked that Americans "attack[ed] all the timber around their houses with such an undistinguishable rage, as not to leave themselves . . . a tree within sight." This type of excessive deforestation caused considerable flooding and significant change to the climate. Drastic ecological change had a detrimental effect on the availability of natural resources upon which Catawbas had always depended. Waterways shrank, rerouted, or disappeared, while seasonal temperatures changed. Winters grew colder, summers became hotter, and drought and flooding became a common effect of extensive timbering. The post-settler environmental change caused a decline in the animal population, especially bears and deer, upon which Catawbas still relied for meat and clothing. As the backcountry's plantation economy grew in the late 1700s, so did the spread of tobacco, cotton, hemp, and wheat fields in the region, crops that exhausted the soil and triggered additional ecological damage.[22]

Extensive farming caused considerable soil exhaustion, so much so that New River feared the expanding agrarian economy "may Distroy [sic] our land to have so many Improvements thereon." Catawbas did not practice the same kind of extractive agriculture that Euro-Americans did, clearing hundreds of acres of forest to build homes and cultivate fields, nor did they view the custom of deforestation as "improvement." From the Catawba perspective, deforestation would have signaled destruction of the land. Instead, Catawba land use traditions meant that women and men applied a type of nature conservancy; they never used or took more than was needed, whether land, plants, or wildlife. For example, Catawba women collected herbs from the forest for medicinal treatments, but always made sure to leave enough of the plant for later use. However, with deforestation, Catawba women had less access to these plants, and men's hunting grounds were reduced. In this "distroy[ed]" environment, Catawba women found it increasingly difficult to move their towns to rich land where harvest yields would be higher, and the lack of fertile soil meant they were always in need of corn to feed their families.[23]

In short, the continuing influx of white settlers meant that the leasing system had gone from a strategy that might protect Catawba land to one that threatened their ability to access or use any of it. A unique source housed at the Lancaster County Courthouse reveals that, by 1796, Catawba people realized they had to do something to prevent further encroachment. Although the document itself—a deed—is rendered in legalese and spare of detail, the historical context of Catawba governance and gender roles enables us to postulate why and how it was created. Responding to land encroachment and dispossession, Catawba Indians probably met in council, as they always had to discuss issues of great import. General New River and several headmen from notable Catawba families would have called their people together, holding a meeting like those practiced by their ancestors and still practiced by their descendants. The Catawba council would have gathered in a log house with a central fireplace for such proceedings. The men would sit circling the interior on cane-constructed benches, while women stood or sat behind the men. New River would have reminded the Catawbas that renters and squatters had taken most of the 144,000 acres. He would have told the men and women gathered that they could not move beyond the 500 acres on which their fields, towns, and homes currently stood. New River, yę miigrá?hare (lead headman or chief), did not have absolute power and probably knew going into the gathering that he needed a majority vote of adult Catawbas when deciding how to protect their land. The decision was not his alone to make.

The council meeting probably transpired with men and women asking questions and discussing probable solutions, as has been the practice for hundreds of years. Because of Catawba women's spiritual tie to the land, their opinions mattered when significant decisions about the land were made. One can imagine the meeting proceeded with Catawba men and women speaking quietly to one another, contemplating the options open to them. Catawba women, caretakers of the land, must have asked: what would happen when the soil was exhausted? Would they be able to feed their children? Would they be able to provide for the elderly and infirmed? They still had the clay holes and could harvest clay to make pots to sell or barter, but the manufacture of pots barely supplemented Catawbas' needs. Men, debating among themselves, must have wondered about their hunting domain, a territory in which they harvested wild game for their families.[24]

Catawbas would have conferred with one another about their options for several days. They commonly held lengthy deliberations when making such weighty decisions. As the document housed in the Lancaster County courthouse demonstrates, they finally agreed to deed the remaining five hundred unleased acres of their 144,000-acre tract to Catawba women. The five hundred acres, named after the leaders buried in the land, is known as King's Bottom. New River and other headmen made their marks on a land deed that legally bestowed the acreage to their women, following the Catawba custom of women controlling land. The deed explicitly named Sally New River and "other women of the said Nation" as receiving the parcel of land "for and in consideration of Divers good causes unto them done by her this said Sally New River." The good causes could have included bearing and caring for Catawba children, cultivating and harvesting crops, and providing town upkeep. What is clear is that conveying the land to Sally demonstrated that the council and community held her in high esteem. The Catawba headmen made their marks on the document and pledged their acknowledgment of women's landownership. Furthermore, the men promised to defend the land for all time and vowed that "her [Sally's] heirs" would receive the land, which reinforced the matrilineal custom in which a woman passed her control of the land to her female heirs.[25]

The land deed provides us with a rare glance into eighteenth-century Catawba politics and social structure, particularly the lives of Catawba women.

Sally was General New River's wife, which placed her higher in rank than other Catawba women. The land indenture shows the authority and respect that Catawbas bestowed on women. By naming Sally New River specifically, Catawbas spoke loudly about the trust and reverence they imparted to her. One can imagine Catawbas hoped that conveying the land to Sally and other Catawba women would prevent further leasing of the remaining land. With the deed, they had the legal authority to do so. Arguably, Catawbas' land indenture decision served as an impenetrable wall that thwarted, for a time, South Carolina's imperial land encroachment.

By 1800, Catawbas had leased most of their territory to landless Americans. Parcels of land within the 144,000 acres guaranteed to them in 1763, excluding the five hundred acres held by Sally and other women, were allotted to individual Catawba men and women, though how and who assigned these allotments remains unknown. Catawbas also leased tracts ranging from hundreds to thousands of acres of land to white settlers for a term of ninety-nine years, collecting annual payments that ranged from fifty cents to ten dollars. As we have seen, the leasing strategy came with mixed results. On the one hand, the settlers it attracted changed the landscape in ways that challenged Catawba relationships to their land and resources. On the other hand, Catawba women and men used the land leases as legal documents that proved their landownership and self-governance. The decision to lease their land helped Catawbas maintain some control of their territory, unlike Drayton's and Moultrie's proposals, which would have reserved control for settlers— and most of the profits as well. The paper trail of the 1763 Treaty of Augusta, the 1764 land survey, the 1796 land deed, and the lease documents served as irrefutable proof of Catawbas' land tenure.[26]

Such documents do more than illustrate boundaries, acreage, property improvements, and neighboring renters. They also reveal how Catawbas appropriated Anglo-American forms of land tenure for their own purposes, and, in doing so, creatively fused them with Catawba culture and customary practices. A Catawba plat and rent book, kept from 1810 to 1825 and housed now in the South Carolina Department of Archives and History, shows rental accounts that include the names of white tenants and, most importantly, Catawba landholders. Catawba names listed on the book's rent payment pages are especially significant in demonstrating that Catawbas still held the land communally, a factor that pushed back against the American ideal of land as a commodity. A close analysis of the rent payments shows Catawba family members collected rent for one another, thus maintaining the kinship ties that bound them to the land. Rental payments for land leased from Sally New River illustrate this perfectly. As a landholder, Sally collected rent for at least eleven leases. She leased 340 acres of land to James Spratt in September 1810 for five dollars per year over ninety-nine years. She received payments until she died in 1821. Upon her death, the Spratt lease changed hands to her niece Betsy Ayers, later going to other relatives, with each collecting rent from Spratt. Other Catawba women collected rent payments for orphans and shared annual payments with their people. The business of leasing reinforced rather than diminished communal landholding, and it sustained the kinship bonds created by early agricultural practices and hunting. [27]

The lease book reveals how Catawbas fought against imperial land encroachment by using the American legal system of documented proof of ownership, while at the same time preserving women's roles as land stewards. Three wills transcribed in the book show that Catawba landholders named individual family members as heirs who continued collecting rent for certain leaseholds, land that remained in Catawba hands. Although Catawba women and men collected rent for a somewhat equal portion of Catawba land, the wills illustrate the endurance of Catawba matrilineal traditions. The wills list women as the heirs of real property, a continuation of women's role as custodians of the land. The wills provide snapshots of information on Catawba kinship. For example, William "Billy" Ayres bestowed the rent collected from Benjamin Patterson's lease to his daughter Polly and left her all future payments from two additional leases. Billy's younger daughter, Anny, inherited a different lease, from which she collected rent "everafter this time." Billy's will is just one example that highlights how Catawba families took care of one another, as their ancestors had for hundreds of years. The rent book shows that Catawbas remained resistant to losing their homeland.[28]

But frustrated petitions from the Catawbas' South Carolina tenants grew in the early 1800s, placing a bull's-eye on Catawba landholding. Between 1800 and 1808, settlers' pressure on Catawba landholders hit a breaking point. Backcountry land-leasing Anglo-Americans again appealed for voting and office-holding rights within the state government. Before 1800, previous South Carolina state constitutions required that white male voters and officeholders followed strict qualifications that included fee simple title of a specific acreage of land clear of any debt. Consequently, elite Lowcountry officeholders managed to keep control of the state government by maintaining strict eligibility requirements. Eventually some backcountry white yeoman farmers became prosperous planters who wanted to serve in the state legislature.

They needed the votes of their neighbors who rented land from Catawbas, and who themselves continued to demand enfranchisement and the ability to run for office. This growing group of men eventually convinced the state to purchase Catawba land through a land cession treaty held near the Nation Ford river crossing in 1840.[29]

The 1840 Nation Ford Treaty ended Catawbas' legal ownership of 144,000 acres of land. Although Catawba families dispersed to other parts of the South, some remained near their ancestral homeland. Within ten years of the treaty, many Catawbas returned to their homeland, where women reestablished homes, raised their children, and shared cultural knowledge. The tribe continued following a matrilineal kinship system until the early 1900s when ancestry shifted to tracing lineage through a Catawba mother or father.[30] Although this story seems to imply that South Carolina's imperial encroachment and dispossession of Catawba land was successful, it was not. In 1976, the Catawba Nation leaders sued the federal and state governments for violating the Indian Non-Intercourse Act of 1790, which prohibited states and individuals from purchasing Indian land. The Nation settled with both governments in 1993 and regained federal recognition and land rights.[31] In spite of settler colonialism and imperialistic agendas, my people are still here and live on the Catawba Nation, where women and men still fight the state to hold onto ancestral land.

CHAPTER 5

An Empire of Indian Titles

Private Land Claims in Early American Louisiana, 1803–40

JULIA LEWANDOSKI

The Louisiana Purchase was a milestone in the escalation of U.S. empire. But the paper acquisition of some 800,000 square miles west of the Mississippi River was not really a land purchase. What the United States bought from France, recently reacquired from Spain, was a preemption right to territories controlled by hundreds of Indigenous nations. The United States purchased the exclusive privilege among other empires of negotiating with Indigenous peoples over land within the vast and undefined Louisiana Purchase territory.[1]

The United States aspired to construct its empire through an orderly process. First, U.S. officials would extinguish what they defined as aboriginal title, or "original Indian title": the authority that Native nations held over their territories through their own sovereignty. U.S. leaders believed they could legally extinguish original Indian title by purchasing land through federal treaties or seizing it by violent conquest. Native nations would supposedly remove farther westward, live in confinement on reservations, or disappear. The federal government would map and divide that land using the Public Land Survey System (PLSS) and distribute it to settlers to be held as individual titles.

This process was to solidify federal control over both Indigenous and settler lands and peoples. Settlers were prohibited from directly purchasing Indigenous land, thus removing Native sovereignty as a source of any settler's title. By making itself the only authority that could guarantee land titles, the U.S. empire would secure the loyalty of its settlers. And landowning settlers would secure the territorial existence of the empire itself through their physical occupation of land.[2]

Such an orderly process could only be aspirational. The realities of Indigenous diversity and resistance, and of federal disorder, corruption, and inertia, assured that empire building would remain disorganized and contested. But in the Lower Mississippi Valley, after 1803 called the Territory of Orleans, and today the state of Louisiana, the United States encountered a distinctive set of challenges: the lingering eighteenth-century land tenure patterns and legal regimes of the French and Spanish empires.

U.S. officials hoped that the Territory of Orleans would be the easiest, swiftest place to create U.S. land tenure. They assumed—falsely—that the French and Spanish empires, during their century-long occupation, had already completed the first step: extinguishing the original Indian title of the dozens of small polities in Louisiana, which the French called the "Petites Nations." All that was left to do, as mandated in the Purchase Treaty, was to confirm and incorporate French- and Spanish-era land titles into the PLSS. Rather than sending Indian agents to negotiate treaties ceding Petites Nations territories, federal leaders appointed land commissioners to evaluate thousands of individual land claims.[3]

Land commissioners, most of them southerners with experience in land surveying and speculation, knew they would have to grapple with foreign legal and measurement practices. But as they translated arpents into acres and attempted to affix Spanish "floating grants" to geometric meridians, they confronted the difficult reality that the French and Spanish had not systematically extinguished the original Indian title of any Louisiana Native polities. France and Spain had never drawn clear boundaries between Indigenous and colonial territories on land or on paper. Nor had they restricted settler subjects from engaging in land negotiations with Petites Nations peoples.[4] Tunicas, Ishak/Atakapas, Pascagoulas, Chitimachas, Apalachees, Biloxis, and other polities had engaged in all sorts of land negotiations with individual settlers, trading companies, and colonial governments. These interchanges often blended diplomacy, economic exchange, and resource sharing arrangements, and they drew on French, Spanish, Choctaw, and Petites Nations sovereignty as sources of authority. They did not fit into the clear categories— imperial land cession treaty or individual settler land purchase—that the United States hoped to impose.

This reality was everywhere in the piles of documents that commissioners sifted through. Settlers filed more than sixty land claims that originated in negotiations with Ishak/Atakapas, Chitimachas, Colapissas, Pascagoulas, Caddos, Choctaws, Tunicas, Biloxis, Natchitoches, Tensas and Apalachees. Deeming them valid U.S. titles required much more than determining compliance with French or Spanish law by reading the *Coutume de Paris* and the *Siete Partidas*. Land commissioners had to transform histories of complex negotiations over well-known but unmeasured places into narrative chains of title that showed clearly bounded properties and individual owners. To achieve this, they invoked an imagined likeness of Spanish authority, conjuring a form of imperial sovereignty that could legitimate the U.S. land titles they created.

Petites Nations peoples, too, mobilized an embellished Spanish past to carve out futures for themselves under U.S. occupation. Houma, Biloxi, and Chitimacha leaders also submitted private land claims alongside settlers. They shaped their interactions with imperial officials and settlers into stories of title that positioned them as landowning nations well recognized by Spanish authorities and demanded that the United States follow suit. Long after Spanish commandants had packed up their land registers and departed for Cuba, the imperial past continued to influence how the U.S. settler empire would grow and be challenged in Louisiana (Figure 5.1).

The adjudication of "Indian title" claims in early American Louisiana offers an exceptional window into the development of U.S. empire at ground level. It reveals the dilemmas produced by the U.S. fixation on individual landownership as central to territorial expansion. Incorporating French and Spanish land titles was not a minor administrative detail. It was central to achieving sovereignty over the Lower Mississippi Valley. Because they understood landownership as extending across imperial jurisdictions under the Law of Nations, land commissioners went to great lengths to transform French- and Spanish-era landholdings into U.S. titles. But this commitment to property collided with another central U.S. tenet: the need to extinguish original Indian title and thereafter exclude Indigenous peoples from their empire of landownership. "Indian title" claims reveal the limits of U.S. interimperial flexibility as it was interpreted and expressed by the dispersed, delegated authorities who adjudicated claims and constituted much of the federal presence in Louisiana. Land commissioners were willing to transform settler titles created under Indigenous sovereignty into U.S. titles by invoking a myth of Spanish authority. But would they uphold claims from Petites Nations peoples who demanded to be recognized as proprietors and nations?

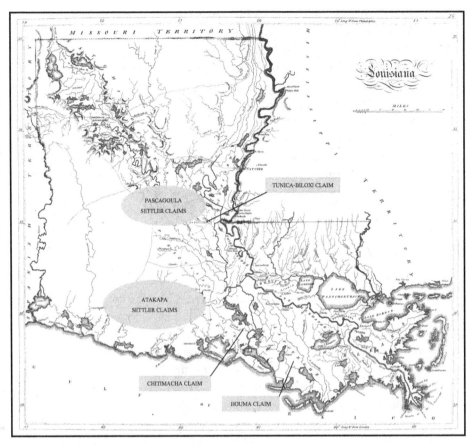

Figure 5.1. Matthew Carey, *Louisiana*, Atlas Map, 1814, David Rumsey Map Collection. Labels created by author. Locations of claims are approximate.

Private land claims also demonstrate the creativity and legal skill with which Petites Nations peoples negotiated the transition from Spanish to U.S. occupation in Louisiana, deepening our understandings of Indigenous survival across multiple colonizing regimes. The Louisiana Purchase narrowed the diplomatic opportunities available to many nations in the Lower Mississippi Valley. Petites Nations peoples could no longer strategically manipulate multiple imperial relationships to maintain their independence. But their legal options remained somewhat more fluid. Decades after Spain lost Louisiana, they still invoked Spanish law to carve out a space for themselves within a hardening American jurisdiction.[5]

Histories of U.S. relations with Indigenous peoples in the early republic often focus on the development of the federal treaty process, or paradigmatic legal decisions like *Johnson v. M'Intosh*, a sweeping 1823 Supreme Court decision defining all original Indian title as weak occupancy rights.[6] But these frames do not capture the experience of many Native polities, like the Petites Nations, who never made federal treaties. Because they had already been colonized, U.S. officials saw the Petites Nations as already conquered and made no efforts to negotiate. In response, some of these polities defended land and asserted their existence in the only diplomatic arena available to them: the private land claims process. Their savvy and creative legal actions demonstrate that the heightened chaos and flexibility of imperial transitions provided opportunities not just for land-hungry settlers but for Native nations defending territory under U.S. settler colonialism.

*   *   *

In 1803, at least thirty-five Native nations lived in the Territory of Orleans, from powerful polities like the Choctaws and Caddos to the dozens of Petites Nations. These included the long-term inhabitants of southwestern bayous and prairies like the Ishak/Atakapas and the Chitimachas, as well as refugees from the southeast, like the nations of Mobile Bay—the Chatots, Biloxis, and Pascagoulas, among others—who had moved into Spanish Louisiana after 1763, fleeing Choctaw and British aggression.[7]

U.S. leaders were aware of both the presence and the territorial holdings of these nations. Thomas Jefferson noted that many held "delightful lands," and were "aboriginal of the [part] they live in," a clear recognition that U.S. appropriation would require treaty negotiations.[8] But the president's direct acknowledgment did not lead to action. William C. C. Claiborne, the first governor of the Territory of Orleans, directed local officials to "speak of the Friendly disposition of the President of the United States, to his *Red Children* and his great desire to see them happy." But he privately expressed to Jefferson that he anticipated "very little difficulty" with the Petites Nations.[9]

Claiborne did not even respond to a direct appeal. In 1808, Alabama leaders had approached a local official, expressing "great distress" because they had "no claim to any Land in the Country." They asked for a "permanent" title to "Lands of the United States" to establish a village. Claiborne arranged to grant a "donation" of land for them, whom he described as "poor wanderers" and "exiles from the country of their ancestors."[10] He mused that other small nations might also "receive from Congress a small grant of Lands to reside on."[11] But Claiborne failed to follow through on the creation of even the Alabama land grant.[12]

Most likely, federal officials hoped that the Petites Nations, who already had small populations, would simply disappear. John Sibley, who was sent to the Territory of Orleans as an Indian agent in 1805, described Petites Nations peoples on the Red River as "gradually diminishing," with some already "extinct," though he admitted that the Alabamas were "said to be increasing a little."[13] But the 1806 Freeman and Custis expedition described Petites Nations peoples as thriving. The Apalachees on the Red River, they noted, "possess horses, cattle and hogs" and "dress better than Indians generally do."[14]

Clearly, extinguishing Petites Nations original titles or recognizing and protecting their land bases were not federal priorities. But dividing up Louisiana land to create U.S. titles clearly was. In 1805, Secretary of the Treasury Albert Gallatin directed Surveyor General Isaac Briggs to begin laying out meridians, cautioning him to inform "both the white inhabitants and several small tribes of Indians, who are scattered through that territory, that the running of such lines will not in the least affect their rightful claims."[15] Without diplomatic agreements that clarified these "rightful claims," these assurances were empty promises. But Briggs could not lay out PLSS lands anyway, because of French and Spanish titles. As Treasury Secretary George Graham put the problem to Congress in the 1820s, the surveys of public lands "cannot be completed . . . until *all* the private claims are located and surveyed." This was because the "only salable lands" were "interspersed among" the many private claims.[16]

Private claim adjudication had been underway since Congress established a process in 1803. Appointed land commissioners were to establish local offices where they would evaluate claims, take testimony, and submit recommendations for final confirmation or denial to Congress. To the western district, headquartered at the Opelousas Land Office, Jefferson sent Levin Wailes, Gideon Fitz, and William Garrard, all southerners with land or legal experience. Wailes had first surveyed for Robert Morris's North American Land Company in Georgia in the 1790s, and in 1805 surveyed the boundaries with the Choctaw Nation created by the Treaty of Mount Dexter. Gideon Fitz, from Virginia, had been a deputy surveyor. Garrard, also a Virginian, had become a judge in Kentucky.[17]

These men were familiar with the Public Land Survey System, with land speculation, with treaty-based Indian removals, and with U.S. law. But claimants in the Territory of Orleans immediately made it clear to them that they needed to adjudicate claims in the context of French and Spanish land law and custom. The brand-new Orleans Territory House of Representatives sent an 1805 petition arguing for such an approach. Many French and Spanish titles, they explained, might appear incomplete: lacking final plats, approval by officials, or even original grants. This, they argued, was actually a good thing. "The former Governments," they explained, "did not consider the vacant lands as a source from which revenue was to be derived." Incomplete titles were a virtue, reflecting the lack of "a disposition to speculate in lands."[18]

Many petitioners were long-term inhabitants from French- and Spanish-era families. But a significant number were U.S. immigrants who had moved west of the Mississippi in the 1790s to obtain land under Spain's generous terms: after swearing an oath of allegiance, settlers could essentially locate and choose their own land grant.[19] Their 1805 advocacy was clearly in the service of seeing their own land claims confirmed. But they were correct that French and Spanish land distribution had been chaotic and many titles were incomplete. Since planting their colony in 1699, French administrators had struggled to establish a settler population. They established land grants unevenly along major watercourses, typically laid out in long, narrow lots extending perpendicularly from both sides. After they took power in the 1760s, Spanish officials upheld the highly informal land titles held by French inhabitants and made generous grants to new immigrants under even more casual terms.[20] French administrators typically sent officials to lay out land grants and orient them to a river, but the Spanish issued "floating grants." These allowed petitioners to locate their own landholdings and did not require them to be oriented to any landmark or line.[21]

Now, in 1805, these proprietors demanded that the United States respect the slapdash Spanish process. Given "the injustice of changing the tenure," they argued, the United States should not also "make the titles of the citizens of this Territory depend upon conditions not known to them at the time of acquiring their property."[22] In general, their demands were accommodated, with Congress loosening land claim regulations the next year. Petitions for further accommodations continued for decades as the process dragged on, and Congress continued to loosen regulations until it approved the final claims in 1897, nearly a century later.[23]

Many land claims relied on originating French and Spanish government grants, on purchases made from French- and Spanish-era settlers, and on evidence of occupation, settlement, and improvement. But at least sixty settlers made claims based on "Indian titles." These claimants reflected the range of Territory of Orleans claimants, from recent U.S. immigrants to long-term residents of Francophone descent. Most were white, but a few were free people of color, and while most were men, a few women made claims.

Land commissioners lacked federal guidance for adjudicating these claims. In U.S. jurisdictions, Indian land purchases had been prohibited since the 1790s. In Louisiana, they intended to evaluate them under French and Spanish criteria. In doing so, they faced not just different bodies of law but different legal categories. Specifically, Spain lacked the clear distinctions that U.S. law hoped to make between collective Indigenous territory and individual settler property. The United States assumed that a claim should recount a history of economic transactions between individuals, leading back to an original title created by a sovereign empire, or, in these special cases, a purchase from a Native nation clearly sanctioned by imperial authorities.

But most "Indian title" claims originated in a more complex array of negotiations. Some nations had sold land to settlers without involving Spanish authorities at all. And others participated in land negotiations that involved multiple parties, including individual and corporate buyers, Spanish officials, and other Indigenous peoples. These exchanges were hardly dispassionate economic transactions. In several cases, Petites Nations peoples were defrauded from their lands by traders who manufactured imagined debts and then proposed land cessions as debt repayment, with the willing collaboration of local Spanish officials. In other cases, Petites Nations peoples leased lands or made usufruct agreements exchanging pasturage for cattle, which settlers then repackaged as sales. And some granted small parcels of land to settlers as a strategy to control encroachment or as part of long-standing patterns of migration and multinational settlement.[24] In none of these cases were they acting as individual economic agents exchanging a commodity under Spanish sovereignty. They were negotiating as nations who participated in a web of complex relationships with small and large Indigenous polities, with settlers, and with the Spanish empire.

Some of the largest "Indian title" claims were in Rapides Parish, on the Red River and its tributary bayous in the center of the state. Settler Joseph Gilliard submitted a claim for nearly 10,000 acres on the Red River. Gilliard had purchased the land from another settler, who had purchased it from the Pascagoulas in 1795. But claim documents and witness testimony revealed something more complex than a straightforward chain of title. Gilliard's title was the product of the complex relationships and diplomatic negotiations that had defined the Spanish era for Petites Nations peoples.

At least 180 Pascagoulas had emigrated onto the Red River in the 1780s, alongside several hundred members of other Petites Nations, including Apalachees, Alabamas, and Tensas.[25] Gilliard's claim included a copy of a 1787 letter of permission from a Spanish post commandant, allowing the Pascagoulas to "form a settlement" on the Red River, "until it shall please the Governor" to "grant them the title of possession." A local official had given them permission to stay there, but had not granted them a specific piece of land. After they immigrated, the Pascagoulas established themselves on the Red River just above two Appalachee and Tensa bands, also recent immigrants. They did so with Apalachee and Tensa permission and under the custom of Petites Nations land tenure. As the local commandant Valentine Layssard described, "the Indians settled themselves in different places, and cleared land and raised corn on the north and east side of the Red river, and extended their settlements or villages with little intervals." The Pascagoulas had clearly chosen the fertile lands on the river, ignoring the places that were "poor pine and swamp land."[26]

Their dispersal and occupation of fertile alluvial lands made them an obstacle. Natchitoches post commandant Louis de Blanc complained that this pattern of "scatter[ing] their Indians along the shore with their habitations considerable distance apart" would "ruin the lands of this river" by "abandoning them and taking others after raising two or three crops." Especially as settlers continued to arrive from the United States, de Blanc worried that they would "find the best land occupied or ruined by this sort of people."[27]

Rather than granting them the "title of possession" promised in 1787, Spanish Governor Francisco Luis Hector, Baron de Carondelet hoped to move the Pascagoulas farther northwest. In 1795, he instructed Layssard to "assemble" the Pascagoulas "to elect a chief" to whom he would grant a medal and commission, and to "engage them to establish an only village" farther north, where they would "receive annual presents more considerable than heretofore." A month later, de Blanc and Layssard presided over the sale of the Pascagoulas' Red River lands to a settler for $250. Soon after, Carondelet ratified the transaction in New Orleans. A local witness testified that Carondelet had approved the sale because of "the frequent complaints made by the white people against the Indians, who were said to do considerable mischief to the inhabitants."[28] Was this settler purchase part of an enticement for the Pascagoulas to move northwest? Or did the Pascagoulas negotiate the sale after Layssard informed them they would have to move?

The claim's clear origins in diplomatic negotiations were evident throughout the claim testimony. But Wailes, Garrard, and Fitz recommended it for confirmation, because Spanish authorities had explicitly approved the sale. Still, they had work to do to create a land title. The original Spanish "concession" to the Pascagoulas, they acknowledged, was just a letter permitting them to settle in the Red River region in general. Thus, the tract had "no determinate boundaries." They decided to apply what they saw as "the general usage of the Spanish Government," and delineate a square "the depth of forty arpents on each side of the river."[29] This practice referred to a French unit of measurement—the arpent—and the French technique of measuring forty arpents perpendicular on either side of a river, a custom still followed by some Spanish authorities in Louisiana.[30] Commissioners drew a rough square around the Pascagoulas' village and created a land title to 9,300 acres.

Wailes, Garrard, and Fitz applied the same creative method when approving other neighboring claims based on purchases from the Apalachees and Tensas. They also used it to complete another title based on a Pascagoula purchase. After they sold their Red River lands in 1795, the Pascagoulas asked the Yowanis, a band of Choctaws, for permission to settle on the lands they held on Bayou Boeuf, a Red River tributary. There, they joined some three hundred Yowanis, Biloxis, and Chatots.[31] In 1802, all of these nations sold their Bayou Boeuf lands to the U.S. trading firm Miller and Fulton. Ten years later, Miller and Fulton submitted a land claim for an enormous tract of more than forty-six thousand arpents.[32]

Much like the Red River claims, the Bayou Boeuf claim was based in a complex history of negotiations. The Pascagoulas had obtained their land on Bayou Boeuf under Choctaw, not Spanish, authority. Claim testimony revealed the extent of Yowani Choctaw control over Bayou Boeuf. One witness testified that the Yowanis had allowed two white men to settle "a small piece of land" that was "lent them by the Choctaws, on the express condition" that they "should repair and keep in order the guns of the said Choctaws." Other than this, they "uniformly refused to admit any settlers within their boundaries."[33]

When Miller and Fulton purchased their lands in 1802, they involved Spanish authorities. Layssard, the Rapides post commandant, facilitated the transaction, and the sale was approved by Juan Manuel de Salcedo, the last

Spanish governor. But other evidence submitted with the claim cast doubt on the purchase. Miller and Fulton claimed that the land was in exchange for trading debts that the Bayou Boeuf nations owed to their firm. But Indian agent John Sibley reported that a Biloxi leader had told him that "neither himself nor any of his people had any knowledge of the debt being contracted." The deed itself was signed after Fulton arrived with "thirty bottles of Taffia, and made many of his people drunk," and then "produced a paper and requested him to sign it." Rather than stopping this coercive transaction, Layssard had told the Biloxi chief that "they had better all move off into the Spanish country, for the Americans would soon drive them off and take their land from them."[34]

Sibley's claim testimony suggested Spanish and corporate collusion to enact a fraudulent sale. But Wailes, Garrard, and Fitz nevertheless recommended the exceptionally large claim for confirmation. Spain had never prohibited "Indians from holding and selling lands" in Louisiana, they reasoned, and, most important, Miller and Fulton had obtained "ratification of the sales by the Governor."[35]

Again, they had to create the rest of the title. The 1802 land sale had been made "without specifying any quantity" of land, other than for "the portion of land which had been granted them by the Baron de Carondelet for their villages and fields of culture." But even they acknowledged that Carondelet had never directly granted land to nations on Bayou Boeuf. That "grant" had been a "letter of office," approving "the conduct of the commandant in putting the Indians in possession of the lands which they occupied."[36] Claim evidence made clear that what Miller and Fulton held up as an originating Spanish grant was better described as a general recognition by Spanish officials that these nations were already living and farming on Bayou Boeuf under Yowani Choctaw authority.

As they had on the Red River, Wailes, Garrard, and Fitz drew a rectangle stretching "forty arpents in depth on each side of the bayou," because such a layout would "comport with the general usages of the Spanish Government."[37] They knew that there never was a specific Spanish land grant, but if there *had* been one, it might have taken such a form. They created a U.S. title by applying an approximation of French land tenure to a record of diplomatic communications between Indigenous nations and Spanish officials.

Wailes, Fitz, and Garrard were clearly willing not just to apply a generous interpretation of Spanish law to land claims. They actively created U.S. titles by transforming evidence of motley diplomatic negotiations into chains of title and, more important, assigning geographic locations and physical amounts of land. One reason for their willingness to make these efforts was certainly that their own interests were frequently involved. Gideon Fitz confirmed a 143-acre tract to himself in Opelousas in 1811, while Levin Wailes, who had a history as a land speculator, may have been an investor in Miller and Fulton's considerable trade and land interests on the Red River.[38] William Garrard, who continued on for years as land register in Opelousas, was sued by the federal government in 1825 for defrauding the U.S. Treasury of $27,230. Like many land registers during this era, Garrard had simply been collecting the money from settler land sales and keeping it.[39]

But these commissioners did not uniformly approve all Indian title claims. A few years later, Wailes and Garrard evaluated another cluster of claims and denied almost all of them. Nearly forty of these claims were based in land negotiations with the Ishak/Atakapas, a Petites Nations people still living on their ancestral territories in southwestern Louisiana. The Ishak/Atakapas had been drawn into eighteenth-century trade networks with the French, but their relative isolation across the perilously swampy Atchafalaya Basin from New Orleans minimized the involvement of imperial authorities in their affairs.[40] Unlike the migrant nations on the Red River, they had never asked for or been granted Spanish permission to live in their own territories.

As settlers moved into their territories, they had leased and sold portions of their lands as a strategy to control and contain encroachment. The settler claims resulting from these negotiations lacked evidence of meaningful involvement from Spanish authorities. Instead, claim evidence reflected how these properties were carved out of Ishak/Atakapa territories under their sovereignty. One such claim was premised on a purchase from Ishak/Atakapa leader Kanimo in 1760. While the sale had been "passed before" the governor of Louisiana, the boundaries of the claim described it in the terms of its relationship to Indigenous territory. It was of two leagues of land "at the Attakapas, running from north to south from the actual settlement of the said Kanimo."[41] The tract could only be located through the social landscape of the Ishak/Atakapas.

After American settlers moved into Ishak/Atakapas territories in the 1790s, land sales increased. On the Nementou (Mermentau) River, settlers made a cluster of purchases in 1803. The claimants located their tracts by their relationship to the Ishak/Atakapa village there. One was adjacent to "the land reserved by the Indians," while another began "above the village which was inhabited by the Indians."[42] Though these purchases were made after the

Louisiana Purchase, they were transacted under the authority of a local Spanish commandant who had navigated the transition to U.S. rule, commissioners noted, by "styling himself 'Commandant for the United States of America'" of the Attakapas post.[43]

On Bayou Vermillion, another cluster of Ishak/Atakapa claims revealed the complex origins of settler claims in a spectrum of land arrangements. In claim testimony, settler Thomas Nickelson recounted how he had occupied Ishak/Atakapa land without their permission. He had been warned off the land by a local Spanish official after "the Indians had made their complaint." The Ishak/Atakapas had later acquiesced, selling him land for "a valuable consideration," but had attempted to attach restrictions to the title, specifying that his tract would be "of use only for the wintering of cattle."[44] In Nickelson's account, they had sold him the tract. But if the commissioners had taken Ishak/Atakapa testimony in the claim, they might have framed the arrangement as a less permanent, usufruct agreement.

Commissioners had been able to evaluate the few large Red River Indian title claims on an individual basis. Yet there were so many small claims based on Ishak/Atakapas purchases that Garrard and Wailes penned an extended treatise on "Indian title" claims known as the "Opelousas Report," in which they attempted to develop a general legal rubric. They reasoned that while Petites Nations peoples had been allowed to sell lands under Spanish law, such sales "could only vest in a purchaser the kind of title which the Indians held," which they defined as a "right of occupancy *which they held at the will of the Government*." This definition of Indian title would be formalized in U.S. law in *Johnson v. M'Intosh* (1823), casting all ancestral Indigenous title as mere rights of occupancy.[45]

Garrard and Wailes made an important exception. If a Spanish governor had ratified an Indian land sale, the title would be transformed from weak occupancy to complete fee simple. As they clearly knew from the copious claim evidence they themselves evaluated, Spanish governors had not specifically done this. Spain simply had not seen land negotiations in the same terms that the United States did. It was land commissioners in the present, not Spanish authorities in the past, who were transforming diverse negotiations into complete U.S. titles. But Garrard and Wailes attributed this transformative authority to Spanish governors, not themselves, and located it in the past, not the present.

Garrard and Wailes quoted U.S. statutes and opined on Spain and its orientation toward "Indians not denominated Christians." But the Opelousas

Report was a hodgepodge of legal assumptions designed to solve their own highly local problem: a large number of "Indian title" claims without any federal guidance for adjudicating them. The simplicity of their criteria—a Spanish governor's stamp—would allow quick and easy decisions. Using their homemade framework, Garrard and Wailes rejected nearly all the Ishak/ Atakapa title claims because they had never received a governor's stamp in distant New Orleans.[46]

The small, delineated settler claims based on Ishak/Atakapa purchases looked much more like French and Spanish land grants and U.S. settler titles than the huge, undefined locations on the Red River rooted in so much complex diplomacy. But approving Ishak/Atakapa claims would have been an affirmation of Ishak/Atakapa sovereignty beyond the reach of Spanish rule. On the Red River, the fact that the Pascagoulas and others were recent immigrants enabled land commissioners to rely on a delicate premise that the titles to these huge claims originated in Spanish land grants. In Ishak/ Atakapa territory, they were selling pieces of their ancestral territories in ways that suggested that they had the power to shape how land would be divided, even under intensifying settler pressure.

Garrard and Wailes applied considerable imagination to their evaluation of claims and the creation of their rubric. But despite all the time they spent thinking through questions of "Indian title," they neglected to imagine that Petites Nations peoples could play any role in the process other than as sellers or losers of land. But the many small nations of Louisiana had already spent decades entangled in settler land negotiations. Many had used their considerable diplomatic skills to secure or recover land during the Spanish era as they migrated, resettled, and took in refugees after conflicts.[47] Now, under U.S. occupation, several nations made land claims for portions of their own territories.

In fact, almost immediately after they penned the Opelousas Report, Wailes and Garrard evaluated a Petites Nations claim. In 1816, a claimant identified as "Bosra, an Indian" sought approval for "301 superficial acres" of land on Avoyelles Prairie, in Rapides Parish. As evidence, Bosra included an 1808 survey plat that displayed the small tract's boundaries, and a certified copy of a 1786 letter from the Spanish governor Esteban Miró to a local post commandant, instructing the official to tell two settlers "to look out for some other part to place themselves, as the lands they demand belong to the Indians, and that they cannot have them but by a formal sale, as the Indians have known rights that ought to be respected."[48] The Indians that Miró referred to on Avoyelles Prairie in the 1780s were the Tunicas, Biloxis, and Ofos, who had moved there early in that decade, where they joined with the Avoyelles, the prairie's original inhabitants.[49]

Wailes and Garrard reasoned that Bosra had "a valid title in the claim" based on his survey plat. But they saddled his confirmed title with "the restriction imposed on other Indian titles within the limits of the United States." By this they meant that Bosra's title would be a weak occupancy title, restricting him from being able to sell the land.[50] Did this decision fit within the rubric they had just created? Bosra claimed land as an individual, but his claim relied on a history of collective Indigenous territorial possession. Of course, so did many settler claims. In Bosra's case, there had been no Spanish government sanction of a land sale, but Spanish approval of their on-going possession and invocation of the necessity of "a formal sale" to transfer title in general. Wailes and Garrard had been more than willing to transform Indigenous "occupancy" into settler property on the Red River, even when it required extensive manipulation. But because Bosra identified himself as "an Indian," they chose to limit the rights attached to his title.

Other Louisiana land commissioners would evaluate Petites Nations claims with even less consistency. In 1817, the "Homas tribe of Indians" filed a claim for a tract of land "containing twelve sections" on Black Bayou, in the eastern district of Louisiana. Just as settler claimants referenced Spanish letters of permission for the Pascagoulas to settle on the Red River, the Houmas referenced their own Spanish-era permission to settle on Black Bayou in the 1780s.[51] Eastern district commissioners Samuel Harper and Alfred Lorrain were apparently unfamiliar with the creative work and reasoning that Wailes, Garrard, and Fitz had done in the western district. They rejected the Houma claim, explaining that they "[knew] of no law of the United States by which a tribe of Indians have a right to claim lands as a donation."[52] The Houmas were not requesting a "donation" of land on Black Bayou. They were making a claim based on Spanish approval and long-term occupation, just as settlers did.

Like their western district counterparts, Harper and Lorrain had been willing to approve vague and unsupported settler claims. They had approved a nearby settler claim based on a Spanish grant, even though it lacked "evidence [of] when the original possession commenced." Harper and Lorrain wrote that they "know of no law by which the claimant is entitled to this land"—using the same phrasing that justified their rejection of the Houma claim—but recommended it for confirmation nonetheless, because it had "been in a state of cultivation when the claimant purchased it, and from its being in an old settled part of the country."[53] A settler could rely on vague understandings of a "settled" location to obtain a complete title. But the Houmas were rejected outright—not because of lack of evidence, but because they claimed as a Native nation.

A few years later, two Chitimacha men filed a claim in the western district. They identified themselves as "John Louis and Gros Pierre," but made it clear that they were "acting as the representatives and two principal men of the Chetimaches Indians," and making the claim on "behalf of the said nation." They sought title to a tract of "about one league" on Bayou Teche, which the Chitimacha had "occupied and cultivated for more than fifty years." As evidence, they included documents that established Spanish recognition of the Chitimacha as a nation in general, and of their lands on Bayou Teche in particular. These included a 1767 French letter that "recognized the Chetimaches nation," and a 1777 Spanish act instructing settlers to "respect the rights of the said Indians in the lands which they occupied." They also included testimony from local settler witnesses, one of whom declared that "from his earliest recollection the Chetimache Indians have resided on the river Teché, at the place where they have claimed," and that "the rights of the Indians in that situation . . . have always been respected by the Spanish government." Finally, they included evidence of several land sales made to settlers for parts of their original claim, "made in good faith, and for full and valuable considerations."[54]

Wailes and Garrard had moved on from the western district, and this claim was evaluated by the succeeding Opelousas land register, Valentine King. King found their evidence highly compelling. In 1826, he declared the claim to be "equal to the highest order of grants," and recommended its confirmation. He arrived at this enthusiastic and unconditional recommendation by referring to the Opelousas Report, which he quoted at length. But while Wailes and Garrard had argued that Indigenous peoples could only hold occupancy rights, King apparently read the report and came to a different conclusion. He argued that the Chitimachas had "an absolute right to the soil." Under Spanish sovereignty, he wrote, "the claims of Indians were always recognized by the Spanish government, and no act thereof was ever considered necessary to their validity." He saw no inherent restriction on title tied to Indian identity, and no need for a Spanish-sanctioned sale to create a complete title. Just as Wailes and Garrard had completed settler titles by creating boundaries, King did the same for the Chitimachas. He drew an eighty-arpent-long square on either side of Bayou Teche, following the French style, and recommended that a complete title be issued to the Chitimachas.[55]

These highly uneven responses to "Indian title" claims demonstrate how flexible the Spanish imperial past could be. Spain's approach toward Indigenous lands, in which they neither explicitly extinguished, upheld, or defined them, allowed considerable perimeters within which claimants and commissioners could improvise. But the stakes and consequences of the land claims process were starkly different for settlers and Petites Nations peoples. Settler claimants simply sought land, and if one claim was denied, they might claim again on another pretext or in another place. Land claims had no dramatic impact on their political identities. But Petites Nations claimants sought titles to protect important places and, in some cases, to resist complete dispossession and removal from their territories. And while the United States refused to treat with them as polities, the private land claims process was one of their only avenues to defend land and defend themselves as nations.

*   *   *

As the United States continued to conquer and seize lands for its territorial empire, land officials labored through land claims processes continuously from the 1780s into the twentieth century. As Gregory Ablavsky has argued for the early Northwest and Southwest Territories, some private land claims processes bolstered federal sovereignty. By resolving claims created under overlapping imperial and Indigenous sovereignties, the United States became the sovereign arbiter over how land would be distributed between property-owning settlers and Indigenous nations.[56] But in Louisiana, rather than decisively establishing U.S. law, land commissioners turned to interpretations of Spanish law to adjudicate their claims. Making U.S. sovereignty was a process of invoking the authority of other empires.

For Petites Nations peoples, the failure of U.S. federal entities to recognize or clarify the status of their Louisiana lands pushed some to use land claims processes. But land commissioners failed to establish a consistent approach to Petites Nations territories. They denied one claim, approved the second with conditions, and fully confirmed a third. While unintentional, the inconsistency of these decisions was also an extension of Louisiana's Spanish past, in that they prolonged Spanish-era ambiguities between property and territory, diplomacy and economic transactions, and individuals and nations in negotiations over Indigenous land.

For Petites Nations claimants, land claims were not a radical break from past strategies demanded by a new imperial regime. They were part of a larger and longer pattern of strategic negotiation with imperial officials, individual settlers, and other Petites Nations. Petites Nations peoples had already spent decades involved in relationships conducted in the languages of landownership, diplomacy, and territorial negotiation. These relationships had generated an archival paper trail of written documents that they continued to invoke in ongoing claims.

Favorable or not, land claims decisions did not mark the end of land negotiations for Petites Nations peoples either. U.S. land titles could not bestow the sovereignty so clearly reflected in claim evidence. And confirmed titles only conferred a limited security to Petites Nations peoples living under U.S. colonialism. Titles lacked the legal standing of a federal treaty. Instead, they placed both Petites Nations peoples and their lands into legal limbo: as treatyless landowners during an era in which Indigenous peoples were increasingly defined by their treaties, their reservations, and their exclusion from landownership. This unresolved status guaranteed that confirmed claims would only spur further claims and counterclaims as these nations continued to seek both land and sovereignty.

The Chitimachas on Bayou Teche continued to make claims. In 1846, they sued the federal government, taking their case all the way to the Supreme Court to confirm title to their Bayou Teche lands. In 1916 these lands were finally taken into trust by the federal government, and the Chitimachas became one of only four contemporary Louisiana nations with federal tribal status.[57] The Tunica-Biloxis on Avoyelles Prairie brought land suits against settler neighbors beginning in the 1820s. In 1848, they secured title to 130 acres of land in an out-of-court settlement. This land was recognized by the federal government as a reservation in the 1980s.[58] After the Houmas' 1817 claim denial, many moved into southern swamplands that remained unsurveyed until the 1870s. While this continued existence beyond the reach of the Land Office may have facilitated their survival, it has proved challenging for contemporary efforts to gain federal recognition.[59] In their contemporary legal and political efforts, Petites Nations peoples invoke their ancestral claims to their territories. But they also continue to mobilize the ambiguous documents accreted across empires and over centuries of colonialism to support their ongoing sovereignty and survival, just as they did in their early nineteenth-century "Indian title" claims.

CHAPTER 6

"A Slave State in Embryo"

Indian Territory, Native Sovereignty, and the Expansion of Slavery's Empire

NAKIA D. PARKER

On November 21, 1850, the New York newspaper the *Evening Post* republished an article from the *Fort Smith Herald* in Arkansas with the provocative title "A Slave State in Embryo." The piece addressed the sectional crisis over slavery, a hotly debated issue in the months after the passage of the Compromise of 1850, and the westward expansion of slavery in Indian Territory (now Oklahoma). The federal government had already expelled five Native nations—the Creek, Cherokee, Choctaw, Chickasaw, and Seminole—to Indian Territory from their original homelands in the Southeast. Now, the writer expected that they "will again, in a short time, too, be surrounded with States, and be hedged in with a dense white population."[1] The writer envisioned that Indian Territory, designed as a sovereign space for the Native nations forced from the Southeast so that slaveholding whites could settle on their land, would quickly be surrounded by American states thronged with white enslavers.

The author of "A Slave State in Embryo" expected that Indian Territory would eventually be turned into a "territorial government and then be admitted into the United States, as a slave state."[2] After all, these nations possessed "a large number of slaves, negroes," just as their white American neighbors did. The enslaved arrived in the area a number of ways, whether their enslavers brought them to Indian Territory or purchased them when settled there through the domestic slave trade or through natural increase.[3] While the writer predicted that the addition of Indian Territory as another slave state might outrage abolitionists, he believed that this future was "inevitable, so you may just make up your minds to grin and bear it."[4]

Why did Indian Territory, with fewer than nine thousand enslaved people (14 percent of the total population of the five slaveholding nations), preoccupy the minds of land-hungry white enslavers and politicians during the antebellum era? Why did they identify this region as "a slave state in embryo," a potential site of explosive growth and permanent establishment for the institution of chattel slavery?[5] The politicians and citizens of the antebellum period understood the strategic importance of Indian Territory in the political struggles and contests of power within the United States and in the U.S./Mexico borderlands. The creation and subsequent settlement of the territory led to a contest of power between the Five Nations, the United States, the Republic (later state) of Texas, and Mexico over the related issues of white settler expansionism and the spread of chattel slavery in the years leading up to the Civil War. As southern slaveholders set their sights on making a "vast southern empire" by establishing and protecting the institution in places like Nicaragua, Brazil, and Cuba, they also eyed a "new" location within the continental United States: Indian Territory.[6]

The formation of Indian Territory as a space for expelled nations from the Southeast was part of the same imperialist project the federal government began with the Louisiana Purchase: eliminating multiple European empires from the continent and consolidating the diverse groups that lived in that region under the control of the United States. The expulsion of Native southerners facilitated the explosive growth of chattel slavery in the "cotton kingdom"—but also brought the institution westward. Native slaveholders forcibly took enslaved laborers with them to their new homeland to recreate the plantations and lifestyles they left behind when white settlers stole their land. Ironically, Native people's economic and political success put Indian Territory in the crosshairs of the expansionist desires of their neighbors and white counterparts farther east.

In fact, almost immediately after they resettled in Indian Territory, Native nations found themselves in the middle of power struggles between the Republic of Texas and Mexico. When the United States annexed the Republic of Texas and made it a state, enslavers in the Chickasaw Nation confronted a new threat: white Texans who disrespected Native autonomy and property rights by invading their nation to steal enslaved people to sell them in the domestic slave trade. By the 1850s, Native leaders had to wrestle with yet another affront to their sovereignty as white enslavers eyed Indian Territory as a site to extend slavery's economic and political influence. This placed Native nations in the middle of sectional issues between the northern and southern states, a predicament they wanted no part of. Indeed, as white American enslavers envisioned an "empire" for slavery across the hemisphere, they also turned their covetous eye toward Indian Territory—an extension of their decades-long quest for more land for slavery, and part and parcel of their efforts to consolidate domestic power within a republic perilously divided over the question of slavery's limits.

Creating Indian Territory

The creation of a physical space that came to be known as "Indian Territory" began to germinate at the dawn of the American republic. Secretary of War Henry Knox defined the approach that Washington's administration adopted for dealing with Indigenous polities—a strategy that scholars have dubbed "expansion with honor," for it involved making treaties, not warfare, to acquire land.[7] Even though the new country had just fought to free itself from a colonial power, leaders such as Knox and Washington had no qualms about exercising authority over Indian nations or obtaining their land. Beginning soon after the Revolutionary War, white American leaders harbored aspirations of a vast American empire on Native soil, despite the insistence of Indigenous peoples that they receive the same diplomatic and political treatment as European sovereign nations like Britain, Spain, and France.

The imposition of white norms was a form of cultural imperialism exercised by the U.S. government over Indigenous societies as evidenced by the "Civilization Program," a state-sanctioned plan to "assimilate" American Indians into white society. Leaders like Thomas Jefferson believed that if they could get Indians to accept and practice some economic and social mores of white Americans, they would need less room to hunt and would cede the excess land to the United States.[8] Missionaries worked in tandem with government agents and went into Indian country to convert Native individuals to Christianity. They built schools and churches and taught Indigenous people to read and write English. Missionaries also encouraged Native people to adopt white concepts of gender roles. Thus, instead of cultivating the fields, Native women were directed to do domestic work, like spinning and weaving. Instead of respecting the fact that in Indigenous societies women wielded political and social power, missionaries advocated a patriarchal structure that mirrored white American culture.

The five nations in the Southeast seemed receptive to some, though not all, of these tenets of the Civilization Program. In part, this was a strategy to placate the aggressive expansionism of the federal government. They hoped that by accepting white American definitions of civilization, they might move U.S. politicians to treat them as sovereign nations. In 1827, the Cherokee Nation took the radical step of restructuring their traditional forms of governance by adopting a republican style of government that resembled the United States, complete with three branches of authority and a written constitution. Like the U.S. Constitution, this document tacitly condoned the institution of slavery and deemed Blackness as incompatible with citizenship and belonging, as evidenced by its provisions that prohibited the descendants of Black women from obtaining citizenship and voting and denied the right of anyone with "negro or mulatto parentage" to hold office.[9] In the 1830s, the constitutions of the Choctaw and Chickasaw Nations created similar legal restrictions on enslaved and free Black persons.[10] In response, whites referred to these nations as three of the "Five Civilized Tribes."[11]

Race-based chattel slavery was another colonialist practice that some Native people embraced. Earlier forms of Indigenous captivity practices did not make enslaved or free status heritable or mark an individual or group as racially inferior. Chattel slavery in the Native South, however, looked almost identical to slavery among white southerners, with its slave codes, labeling people of African descent as "property," and equating Blackness with enslavement.[12]

The Civilization Program was not the only factor shaping federal Indian policy: westward expansion and a growing sense of American nationalism were equally important, especially with regard to the five southern Indian nations. When Thomas Jefferson acquired the Louisiana Purchase in 1803, he envisioned this region partially as a place for expelled Indigenous groups to reside away from white Americans. Less than twenty years later, the Monroe administration passed policies that fed the insatiable desires of white settlers for mobility and wealth in southern Indian country.[13] John Calhoun, Monroe's secretary of war, reformed the superintendencies of Indian affairs, which handled policy and relations and reported to the War Department.[14] He also articulated a new kind of relationship between the federal government and Native polities. Long before Supreme Court Justice John Marshall labeled Native nations "domestic dependent nations" and declared that Indian

Territory should "compose part of the United States" in *Cherokee Nation v. Georgia* (1831), Calhoun believed that the relationship between the United States and Indigenous communities should be that of a ward/guardian. In 1818, he reflected that "they neither are, in fact, nor ought to be, considered as independent nations. Our views of their interests, and not their own, ought to govern them."[15] Calhoun's words reveal the imperialist overtones and strategies that remain a hallmark of relations between the United States and Native peoples.

White settlers desirous of the fertile lands of the Native South rejoiced with the election of Andrew Jackson. As a settler raised in the frontier lands of Tennessee, Jackson believed that the westward expansion of the nation was integral to its survival. As a slaveholder, he desired land for cotton. As a white supremacist, he believed that Native people were incapable of becoming American citizens or being incorporated into the body politic. Therefore, when he assumed the presidency, he made expulsion of the southern Indian nations a top priority of his administration. In May 1830, after fiery political debates and after vociferous protests from Native people and white anti-removal activists, Congress passed the Indian Removal Act, which authorized the president to negotiate with Native nations to "exchange" their homelands east of the Mississippi River for land in the West, "Indian Territory." The government settled the Native nations of the Southeast in this region without regard for the Native people already there, including Caddos, Comanches, and the many other smaller groups to whom the region had long belonged. As the federal government expelled more and more Native nations from their ancestral homelands, they compelled them to settle in this already settled space, compounding the tragedy of Native expulsion with the appropriation of more Native land.

Treaties that resulted from the passage of the Indian Removal Act outlined the legal and political aspects of the relationship between the expelled nations and the federal government in the West. They set the stage for the battles that ensued between Native leaders and the U.S. government over how sovereignty would be established, defended, and disrespected after resettlement. For instance, the Choctaw treaty, the Treaty of Dancing Creek (1831), stated that the Choctaws had the right to "live under their own laws in peace" in Indian Territory and that the land in the West would be granted to the Choctaws and their descendants "while they still exist as a nation and live on it."[16] This wording gave tacit acknowledgment to Choctaw demands for the United States to respect their right to govern their own affairs in the West while at the same time implying that their continuance as a nation was not assured—even after being promised by U.S. politicians that expulsion to Indian Territory was the only way to avoid extermination. Moreover, the treaty decreed that "no Territory or State shall ever have a right to pass laws for the government of the Choctaw Nation," but also stipulated that the federal government must provide protection to the Choctaw Nation "from domestic strife and from foreign enemies on the same principles that the citizens of the United States are protected."[17] By permitting the Choctaws to control their internal governmental affairs while simultaneously assuming control of the protection and defense of the nation, the United States essentially made the Choctaw Nation a protectorate of its growing empire.

Almost immediately after receiving word that the Indian Removal Act had become a reality, white settlers flooded onto Indian lands, squatting illegally and setting up claims on Creek, Cherokee, Choctaw, and Chickasaw land. A popular song of the time highlights how some white settlers viewed this manifestation of settler colonialism:

All I want in this Creation
Is a pretty little wife and a big plantation
A-way up yonder in the Cherokee Nation.[18]

In the minds of enslavers and those who aspired to be enslavers, the future of slavery's empire rested on Native lands. By 1860, thirty years after the Indian Removal Act, the homelands of the expelled southeastern nations contained the highest concentrations of enslaved African Americans.[19]

Slavery in Indian Territory

When they arrived in Indian Territory, Native individuals began the task of rebuilding their lives, and Native leaders set about the work of reconstructing their nations politically. In Indian Territory, leaders in the Choctaw, Chickasaw, and Cherokee Nations adopted forms of republican government with executive, legislative, and judicial branches and written constitutions similar to the United States, as they had done east of the Mississippi. But republican government was not the only institution brought westward by the southern Indian nations because of an imperialist and expanding United States. Some Native individuals brought chattel slavery practices, too. With the aid of enslaved labor, they hoped to regain some of the wealth stolen from them by white settlers. In fact, the move to Indian Territory prompted some Native individuals who had not previously enslaved anyone to purchase enslaved individuals for the first time.

Bob Shields, for example, recognized the value of investing in enslaved people during the removal period. He was a Choctaw man preparing to migrate west who owned land in Mississippi. Financially, it made sense for him to sell property he could not take with him (land) for movable human property (enslaved people) he could bring to Indian Territory. And so he sold his land to Greenwood Leflore, a prominent Choctaw leader and a wealthy enslaver. In exchange for the land, Shields received several enslaved workers.[20] Leflore decided to stay in Mississippi and became a U.S. citizen. He eventually acquired over fifteen thousand acres of land and enslaved four hundred people.[21]

White politicians tried to justify removal by extolling the physical virtues of Indian Territory and its economic potential for the Five Tribes. In 1836, Choctaw land was considered "particularly fitted for raising stock" and "destined to be a fine cotton-growing country. . . . It is estimated that about five hundred bales will go down Red river, from the Choctaws, this year."[22] Although Cherokee land was not as "advantageously" suited "for the cultivation of cotton" as that of the Choctaws, a federal agent noted that they still "raised corn, beef, pork, sheep, &c. to a considerable extent."[23] With regard to the Creeks, he wrote that they "have a rich county, and those of them that emigrated . . . have been engaged busily in making corn; they usually have a large surplus, as high some years as thirty thousand bushels, besides stock of every description."[24] Agents pointed to the agricultural possibilities of Indian Territory and the opportunities to advance to more "civilized" pursuits as excuses to downplay the trauma and injustice of removal. Enslaved labor made it possible for each of these industries—raising cattle and pigs, cultivating cotton, corn, and wheat—to become commercial enterprises.

White settlers traveling through Indian Territory en route to western destinations like California noticed how the labor of enslaved people helped some Native individuals prosper in Indian Territory. In 1858, a traveler on the Butterfield Overland Mail stagecoach trail, Waterman L. Ormsby, commented that "many of them [Choctaws] are quite wealthy, their property consisting chiefly in cattle and negroes" and that "their ownership of slaves is quite common."[25] Native slaveholders used enslaved labor to engage in other profitable industries besides agriculture. Ormsby also wrote about Chickasaw Benjamin Franklin Colbert, a "young man—not quite 30," and "of great sagacity and business tact," who, in addition to growing plentiful corn crops each year, operated a ferry that provided transport on the Red River between Indian Territory and Texas.[26] Colbert, as a shrewd businessperson, let the stagecoaches of the Butterfield Overland Mail cross on the ferry without a fee in anticipation of receiving more business from whites for this consideration to the company. Colbert also used his enslaved labor to take care of the surrounding roads to make travel easier. Ormsby saw "a large gang of slaves at work on the banks of the river, cutting away the sand, so as to make the ascent easy."[27] Colbert's ferry, operating because of enslaved labor, was a form of conveyance that linked people to Indian Territory, bringing them into and through the region, giving removed Indians more contact with the white settlers. Arguably, Colbert's ferry and other businesses impressed white slaveholders who might have been surprised to see the makings of a slave society just a little over twenty years after the Chickasaw Trail of Tears began in 1837.

To keep this profitable business running, Colbert enslaved twenty-five individuals. Ormsby noted that Colbert "says he considers them about the best stock there is, as his increase is about four per year."[28] Indeed, Native slaveholders as well as white ones often described enslaved peoples' reproductive labor in the same terms they used for cattle. Lycurgus Pitchlynn, a Choctaw slaveholder, wrote to his father to inform him that "the stock in negroes are doing and increasing finally . . . our horses, hogs, and negroes look the fattest and sleekest of all the horses and negroes in the country."[29] In the kinds of businesses they were involved in and in how they referred to their enslaved people as stock that could be bred and that would increase their wealth, some Native enslavers were adopting the characteristics and practices of capitalist white slaveholders.

Federal agents also remarked on the variety of commercial industries present in Indian Territory, many of them worked by enslaved people. The operation of saltworks was another business Native individuals developed to resounding success. In 1839, William Armstrong, the head of the Choctaw Agency, noted that the manufacturing of salt opened up financial opportunities for business-minded Choctaws. One such person was David Folsom, who came from a prominent slaveholding family. Armstrong described Folsom as "enterprising," and so successful at his salt works that he produced enough "for both Choctaws and Chickasaws in that part of the nation, as well as Texians, who have only Red river to cross and travel twenty miles to the works."[30] The agent's words reveal that the saltworks business afforded opportunities for Native people to have economic ties with white settlers in surrounding areas like Texas. Far from being an unconnected territory isolated from other parts of the United States, Indian Territory played a role in the growing nineteenth-century market economy of the expanding nation.

All the removed tribes from the Southeast, except the Seminoles, operated saltworks. Given the capital, expense, and labor power needed to run a profitable saltworks, wealthy slaveholders like David Folsom dominated this industry in Indian Territory. Eliza Hardrick, enslaved by Cherokees before the Civil War, recalled how some enslaved people arrived in the Cherokee Nation because of the intensive labor needed for this enterprise: "My grandfather told me that it was about 1838 that Louis Ross chartered a boat and shipped five hundred slaves from Georgia to Indian Territory. He said . . . that Louis Ross had come on ahead and had settled on a plantation in Saline District. He said Louis Ross met the boat with an armed guard of full-blood Indians and ox wagons and took them to his plantation in Saline District. Here a lot of the slaves were sold to other Cherokees in the nation, and a lot of them he kept to farm and run the salt works, which he operated."[31]

Hardrick's account demonstrates multiple forced migrations. Ross was expelled from Georgia in the infamous Cherokee Trail of Tears. Making room for slavery in Georgia for Ross meant loss of land and family—but also the movement of slavery westward to Indian Territory. The five hundred slaves that Ross supposedly sent by boat were also affected by the imperialist aims of the United States and its greedy desire for Native land. Perhaps some of these enslaved people arrived in Georgia by means of the domestic slave trade and then experienced another forced migration to Indian Territory to labor in Ross's saltworks, a physically exhausting and dangerous place to work. Settler colonialism and dispossession of Native lands fueled the westward expansion of slavery to the outer fringes of the cotton kingdom and beyond.

Indian Territory, Texas, and Mexico

Neither residence in Indian Territory nor economic success shielded Indigenous nations from the constant encroachment of white settlers. The expelled southern Indian nations had to defend their new homelands and establish their political autonomy from the expansionist goals of white settlers almost immediately after arriving in the West in the early 1830s. The white American settlers who poured into the neighboring region of Mexican Texas in the

1820s, for example, came from southern states like North Carolina, Tennessee, and Kentucky, looking to find fortune in the planting of cotton. In 1836, the conflict between Texas and Mexico over slavery and Texan sovereignty left some U.S. military personnel worried that Indian Territory, located directly to the north, would be drawn into the fray, possibly lending Mexico the support it needed to defeat the Texan insurgents.

In 1836, U.S. general E. P. Gaines wrote to two military men who oversaw forts in the region, Arbuckle and Vose, to inform them of overtures by the Mexican government to involve Indigenous nations in Indian Territory into its conflict over independence with Texas. Gaines reported that the Mexican government had commissioned a Tejano Indian trader named Manuel Flores "for the purpose of enticing the Indians in the Western Prairies, on our side of the line, to join the Mexicans as auxiliaries in their war of extermination in which they are now approaching the above mentioned boundary, and that with this view he has lately passed up the valley of Red River."[32] Flores's efforts to join Native nations in Indian Territory to the Mexican cause originally focused on the Plains Indian group the Caddo.[33] Flores tried to convince Indians to join Mexico by telling them that the United States was preparing to attack these nations and destroy them. Knowing the history of expulsion and extermination that marked U.S. relations with the groups in Indian Territory, Flores and the Mexican government probably assumed that Native peoples would find it plausible that the United States was preparing for future attacks. Gaines warned the American military men to be on the lookout for Flores to arrest him.[34] Seven years later, Flores was still working in the employ of the Mexican government to fight against Texas, now an independent republic, when he was apprehended in the Creek Nation. The U.S. government charged him with residing in Indian Territory without a pass, which came with a hefty fine of one thousand dollars. He disappeared before he could be brought to Fort Gibson for trial.[35]

The efforts by the Mexican government to enlist Indigenous help in its wars with Texas partly succeeded. In 1838, two years after Manuel Flores began his campaign, William Armstrong, a U.S. Indian agent stationed at the Choctaw Agency, heard rumors that the Mexican government offered land to individuals among the Cherokees, Creeks, and Choctaws who would agree to fight against Texas.[36] Armstrong feared that leaders of these Indian nations would side with Mexico. At the very least, he worried, they might turn a blind eye to some of their people agreeing to join the Mexican army, or they might allow other Indigenous and removed groups in the area, such as the Comanches and the Delawares, to raid Texas on Mexico's behalf and then take refuge in Indian Territory. Armstrong sent Captain John Stuart to inquire about the intentions of the Cherokees, Creeks, and Choctaws in the ongoing conflict between Mexico and Texas. Stuart reported back that although the Cherokees could be counted upon to remain neutral, he was worried about the Creeks, particularly those who were not of the economic and social elite and are "generally of the number who were robbed by speculators east of the Mississippi."[37] In his opinion, "that portion of the Creeks, it is supposed, would join Mexico, or would resort to any other expedient by which to be enabled to gain a subsistence."[38] Why precisely Stuart believed Creeks to be more likely than Cherokees to ally with Mexico is unknown (perhaps he referred to the "Red Sticks" faction of the Creek Nation, who sided with the British in the War of 1812 and who fought Andrew Jackson in the Battle of Horseshoe Bend). Nevertheless, Stuart's anxiety about a possible alliance between Mexico and the Creek Nation indicates that the imperial aggressions of the land hungry American republic had wider, transnational repercussions.

Mexican promises of land also struck a chord with certain Choctaws. Some Choctaw men left for Mexico when emissaries arrived in Choctaw country and offered land to anyone willing to join the Mexican army.[39] For some individuals, Mexico seemed to offer a solution to the ongoing frustrations with Texas: the encroachments of white Texans on Native land, the theft of resources, the disrespect of Choctaw sovereignty without repercussions. Nevertheless, the issues between Texas and Mexico also exacerbated political tensions in a nation already trying to piece itself together after the trauma of removal.

An incident in the fall of 1838 highlights how the internal struggles in the Choctaw Nation and the institution of chattel slavery in Indian Territory collided with struggles over empire in the Texas-Mexico borderlands. In July 1838, Pierre Juzan defeated Nitakechi for the position of district chief in the Choctaw Nation. Both men were respected Choctaw leaders. Juzan, however, belonged to an influential family of French and Choctaw heritage, possessed an American-style education, had closer relationships with Washington politicians, and was a wealthy slaveholder.[40] Juzan believed these connections, as well as his power among the Choctaws, fed Nitakechi's resentment of him, motivating Nitakechi to welcome Mexican envoys, who wanted to secure Choctaw support against Texas, to his home a few months later in the fall of 1838.[41] U.S. Indian agent William Armstrong was concerned about Mexico's influence in Choctaw affairs, and alarmed by the claims of Anson Jones, the

minister of Texas to the United States, that Mexicans were inciting Indigenous groups in the region to attack its citizens. In February 1839, Armstrong
went to investigate. He questioned Nitakechi about the purpose of the emissaries' visit. Nitakechi claimed that he had not extended an invitation to the
Mexicans; rather, another Choctaw had brought them to his house, and he
decided to hear what they had to say. Nitakechi said that the diplomats tried
to bribe him into supporting their cause, and, according to Armstrong, explained that they had "used great exertions to induce him with his warriors
to join the Mexicans against the Texans—they promised him money, goods,
& land if he would accompany or meet them against the Texans, that he refused to do so unless he could see me to know if it would be wrong to enter
the contest with the Mexicans."[42] It is unclear if the Mexican diplomats in
fact offered these gifts or not. What is clear from this account is that Nitakechi was skillful in diplomacy and playing both sides, courting Mexican support while assuring the U.S. officials of his deference to their authority and
to Indian policy.

Nitakechi's rival, Juzan, gave Armstrong a different explanation for how
the Mexican diplomats arrived in Choctaw country. Juzan claimed that Nitakechi had actively courted Mexican support against Texas. He informed
Armstrong that in May 1838, while he was still in the role of district chief,
Nitakechi had sent eleven Choctaw men to Mexico and gave one of the men,
Jim Kelly, gifts to offer the Mexican president, including tobacco and white
beads. The trip did not occur because of infighting among the eleven men.[43]
Nevertheless, the supposed diplomatic mission demonstrates the political
awareness of international events that Indian leaders possessed. Though
Choctaws wished for their sovereignty to be respected, they did not view their
nations as insulated from conflicts on the North American continent. In the
fall, the Mexican government, perhaps encouraged by Nitakechi's overtures,
sent ambassadors to Nitakechi in the Choctaw Nation.

Juzan's anger about the situation involved more than just a political ri-
valry with Nitakechi. After hearing the Mexicans were still residing in the
Choctaw Nation with the approval of Nitakechi a few months later, in February 1839, the U.S. government decided to act and ordered the arrests of the
diplomats. Before they made their escape, Juzan claimed that with Nitakechi's support the diplomats had had "several secret interviews" with his enslaved men at his rival's home and had promised the men freedom if they
left with them.[44] He accused the diplomats of courting Choctaws as well,
allegedly by promising great rewards if they joined the Mexican army:

"instead of receiving their four bits, as they called the U.S. Annuity, they could have dollars by the hundred, a plenty of rich land to cultivate, and healthy country to live in, each man a mule, a gun, ammunition, clothing."[45] A few nights later, the four enslaved men decided to liberate themselves and join the emissaries in the trek back to Mexico. According to Juzan, the men escaped with "four of my best horses, two guns, four saddles and bridles, and many other minor articles, leaving me completely destitute of help to make my crop."[46]

In a letter to Armstrong asking for the intervention of the U.S. government, Juzan tallied his losses. The enslaved men were "richly worth twelve hundred dollars each," and the four horses, "at the least calculation, worth six hundred dollars each."[47] He stressed the enormity of this financial blow, writing, "I am broken up. I cannot submit to such a loss. . . . I have worked hard to get property and now to have my property taken from me is too much. I hope you will lay the subject before the government."[48] Juzan also warned Armstrong that if the federal government did not take decisive action to retrieve his property, "I can muster my warriors and take satisfaction."[49] Fourteen months after the initial escape, Juzan was still actively searching for three out of the four enslaved men. He placed a runaway ad in the *Austin City Gazette*, offering a six-hundred-dollar reward for the capture of Billy, his brother Washington, and Hartwell, who "were seduced away by two renegade Mexicans."[50]

This convoluted case shows how the issue of slavery shaped conflicts between the Choctaw Nation, the Republic of Texas, and Mexico, and it demonstrates how enslaved people had an awareness of the geopolitical circumstances around them and took advantage of the power contests between nations to enact freedom strategies. The Juzan/Nitakechi account also emphasizes that in the struggle for supremacy between Mexico and Texas, Indian Territory was more than just a peripheral player. Both Texas and Mexico viewed the region as strategic (for Texas, a place to trade, acquire enslaved people, and expand the institution of slavery; for Mexico, a needed ally against Texas), and both nations coveted the support of its leaders. Just as Native leaders played European colonial powers off one another to their own advantage before the birth of the American republic, they continued to use these techniques after expulsion westward. And just like in the colonial era, Indigenous leaders had less of an interest in which foreign power came out victorious than in having their sovereignty respected. In speaking about the continued maneuvering for power between Texas and Mexico in 1842, Isaac

Folsom, a leader in the Choctaw Nation, reassured an Indian agent that the Choctaws "could not be induced . . . to take part in a war between such lawless and unprincipled nations, as Mexico and Texas." "Let them fight," Folsom declared, noting that his people "care not how much they fight" as long as "they leave us alone."[51]

In economic matters, however, some white Texans and Native people found common ground. The Choctaw and Chickasaw Nations bordered the northern Texas counties of Cooke, Grayson, and Fannin. This area, due to its strategic positioning between the Texas state border, the Choctaw and Chickasaw Nations, and Comanche and Kiowa territory, served as a key economic and trading center. While Native leaders insisted that the federal government and neighboring southern states must respect their political autonomy and sovereignty, they also realized that for their nations to survive, economic, political, and social ties had to be forged with some white people in the region.

Moreover, chattel slavery and the wealth it produced bound some Native and white families together. White settlers willing to live on the frontier made Cooke County their home and traded and socialized with Choctaw and Chickasaw slaveholders. A former resident of Cooke County, Texas, a Mrs. A. Y. Guenter, remembered camaraderie between white and Indian slaveholders. When anyone moved into the neighborhood, the surrounding families would welcome the new family by hosting "get acquainted parties." The festivities usually took place during Christmas week. "Everybody in Sivells Bend went," Guenter wrote of one such gathering in 1861. "The Murrells, Manions, and Bourlands came from the lower bends of the river, while the Overtons, Loves, and Gaines were among those present from Indian Territory. There were more than 100 persons present and an elaborate supper was served. We danced all night."[52] All the families who came from Indian Territory were prominent slaveholders. These social gatherings provided a time for relaxation as well as a time to conduct business. Slave hiring contracts typically lasted between the first of January and Christmas, confirming the temporal importance of these gatherings.[53] It is probable that Native and white slaveholders discussed the buying or hiring out of enslaved people at these affairs.

Despite this camaraderie, however, disputes also arose between Texans and Indigenous enslavers over slavery. The crime of "slave stealing," for instance, became a point of contention between Texas and the Choctaw and Chickasaw Nations. When Texas declared independence, it created a clear proslavery constitution that not only protected the institution but sought to expand it as well. Historian Andrew Torget aptly describes the Republic of Texas as "a dress rehearsal for the Confederacy" that embraced "a remarkable worldview of nineteenth-century American slaveholders and their hopes for building a cotton empire along the Gulf Coast of North America."[54] These desires for a cotton empire meant acquiring more slaves, and some white kidnappers in Texas, with no respect for Native sovereignty, saw Indian Territory as a prime location to abduct enslaved people and sell them and their labor to slaveholders in surrounding areas. The annexation of Texas by the United States in 1845 failed to stem white Texans' quest to capture enslaved people in Indian Territory. The next sixteen years represented a phenomenal growth rate in the state's enslaved population (more than 455 percent by the outbreak of the Civil War).[55]

An example of these tensions occurred in 1849 when John Guest and Overton "Sobe" Love, brothers-in-law and slaveholders in the Chickasaw Nation, petitioned the U.S. government for compensation for enslaved people taken by a raid by ten white men from Texas. Guest and Love filed this claim on the basis of a clause in the Intercourse Law of 1834, which declared that if a white person was convicted of stealing, harming, or destroying the property of "a friendly Indian," the criminal had to pay double the value of the property. If they did not have the funds to make restitution, the federal government would be required to compensate the loss. However, a Native person forfeited the right to restitution if "he, or any nation to which he belongs, shall have sought private revenge, or attempted to obtain any satisfaction by force or violence." Once again, the United States acknowledged the right of nations in Indian Territory to have their property claims upheld. Yet, like any imperialist power, the federal government dictated the terms of concession by reserving the right to decide what nations were considered "friendly" by the federal government and by creating a loophole to avoid paying restitution by forbidding the use of force to seek redress.[56]

The group of kidnappers who raided the Love plantation came from the Red River region of Texas. They stole four enslaved people: three women (Malinda, Lucinda, and Susan), and one man named Patrick. The claim reveals some of the ways that the Chickasaws adapted to U.S. patriarchal notions of property. Although it was Love's wife, Nancy Guest, who owned the enslaved, the family's best chance of compensation lay in making the claim in the husband's name. While the Chickasaws honored the wife's right to property, the federal government was less likely to do so. The raiders also kidnapped an enslaved woman and her infant Andy, from John Guest, "a minor and brother of Mrs. Love."[57]

The kidnappings, therefore, represented not only an affront to Chickasaw sovereignty but a loss of family property. They show how Native slaveholders bought and sold enslaved people from and to family members to perpetuate wealth. The case had first been taken to the federal agent in the Chickasaw Nation, A. J. Smith, who then sent it to the commissioner of Indian affairs. The commissioner decided the case was of utmost importance, since the Intercourse Law was involved, and he took it to the solicitor of the Treasury, who then instructed the district attorney of Texas to begin legal proceedings against the kidnappers in U.S. District Court. After bringing the case to trial, the district attorney declared the accused "irresponsible" of the crime, guessing that they were most likely either "dead or fled to California or Mexico, and beyond the reach of process." The enslaved individuals, moreover, could not be recovered, as they "were removed to parts unknown."[58]

Love and Guest, however, persisted in petitioning for compensation of the loss of their enslaved property. Following the Intercourse Law to the letter, they had "not only not resorted to any violence or retaliation, but have patiently awaited the result of tedious and ineffectual legal proceedings." They appealed to the federal government for payment, the value of four enslaved people for Love at $2,400 and the loss of the enslaved woman and her infant for Guest at $1,300.[59] Enslaved people were valuable commodities, and for young John Guest, the theft of an enslaved woman who could bear more enslaved people and as a result more property was a particularly acute loss. When it came to the issue of slavery and valuable enslaved people, the essential ingredient for creating their "empire for slavery," white Texans did not feel the need to respect Native boundaries and sovereignty.

Indian Territory and Sectional Tensions

As sectional tensions rose in the 1850s, Indian Territory was not immune from the controversy. Historian Barbara Krauthamer has written about how Choctaw and Chickasaw leaders in Indian Territory were keenly aware of the crisis between advocates of free labor and proslavery proponents, watching with concern to see if the conflicts would spill over into Indian Territory.[60] Native leaders in all five nations, however, had a reason for alarm. White southern slaveholders became increasingly invested in the westward expansion of slavery and set their sights on Indian Territory as another jewel to add to the crown of slavery's empire. Commenting about the provision in the Compromise of 1850 that took away a portion of territory claimed by Texas for the United States, an editorial in the *Texas State Gazette* declared that the boundary dispute involved not just Texas but the fate of slavery as a whole. "The territory proposed to be surrendered by Texas lies throughout its whole extent along the western frontier of the Indian Territory," the writer opined. "This is now a slaveholding country; and must be considered as part of the South."[61] The writer warned that if Indian Territory was surrounded by free states, Native enslavers would be incapable of maintaining the institution: "how long will the Indians be able to maintain the institution of slavery?"[62]

Due to its strategic position and the allowance of slavery, Indian Territory became a site of contestation and of expansion in the eyes of proslavery advocates. The writer of the opinion piece asserted that Indian Territory should even be considered "southern." Just thirty years before, the five nations in Indian Territory had their homelands in the South and were expelled to the West for the expansion of "slave country." And although the federal government decreed they would not be disturbed in their new homelands in the West, in 1850, with arguments over whether or not the United States would expand as a slave empire reaching a critical point, Native lands were targeted again due to their apparent success in establishing and maintaining the institution of chattel slavery.

Ironically, white southern enslavers justified absorbing Indian Territory as part of the South and deemed the region as fit for incorporation into a slaveholding empire precisely because of the resilience of the Cherokees, Creeks, Choctaws, Chickasaws, and Seminoles after removal—their social and economic ties with white counterparts, their success in reconstructing their nations after expulsion, and, perhaps most of all, their embrace of chattel slavery. As an 1857 editorial in the *Southern Intelligencer* put it:

> Nearly all that is valuable among them [the five southern Indian nations] in education, intellectual development, and the arts of civilization, is attributable to amalgamation and slavery. In other words: no tribe without slavery and the admixture of whites has thus advanced. . . . It is a question in which Texas and all the South has a deep interest. Slavery is already established there, by these "squatter sovereigns." The United States paid for the transportation of the slaves there. The country was part of the Louisiana Territory. . . . Humanity

would forbid expulsion; but the same humanity would invite them into the Union, and thus secure a Southern State.[63]

With the pejorative phrase "squatter sovereigns," the editorial conveyed a condescending view of Native autonomy and a patently false narrative of Indian expulsion. The term implied that Indigenous peoples were the illegal invaders of the territory of the United States, not the other way around, and gave credit to the government for paying to move enslaved people to the West. Decades earlier, proponents of expulsion argued that the process was humane because if Native people stayed in their homelands east of the Mississippi River among white people they would perish. In 1857, with sectional tensions rising and white slaveholders determined to expand slavery's reach, their twisted reasoning declared that the humanitarian choice was to make Indian Territory a part of the slave South.

Similarly, a December 1858 article in the New Orleans *Daily Picayune* called for the federal government to establish "a closer connection" between Indian Territory and the United States as "the next step of advance in our Indian policy." The writer claimed that the nations in Indian Territory wanted deeper social and political affiliations to the United States; they "desire to become white men" as evidenced by their dress and education, had "adopted the social institutions of the South," and looked forward to the day "when their descendants, at least, shall form part of that nation to whom the empire of this continent seems a destiny."[64] A similar allusion to American empire and Manifest Destiny with regard to Indian Territory appeared in the *Annapolis Gazette*: "The tide of population is steadily rolling West. These Indian states cannot exist when the Caucasian race presses upon them as independent states."[65] Again, the contradictory proslavery reasoning concerning Native nations' capacity for self-governance is evident in these two accounts. According to this opinion, Native nations would be unable to withstand the force of settler designs on Indigenous land for the expansion of slavery's empire without the guidance of, and eventual incorporation into, the United States.

Indigenous leaders, however, looked at this imperialist rhetoric and calls to formally territorialize Indian Territory as further proof that the federal government would never accept Native political autonomy. When seven southern states, including Texas, decided to secede from the Union and form the Confederate States of America, the Creek, Cherokee, Choctaw, Chickasaw, and Seminole Nations desired to stay neutral. But the sectional crisis of the previous years had already highlighted the strategic importance of the region, especially to white southern leaders. Confederate politicians made immediate overtures to win over the Five Nations to their cause for slavery. The Confederacy sent negotiators such as Douglas Cooper and Albert Pike, who had served in Indian Territory and were also slaveholders, to appeal to Native leaders on the basis of similar "ways of life." These emissaries played on resentment against the federal government because of removal, fraud, and failure to abide by treaty promises. "They have learned that the southern people are not only their friends," crowed an editorial in the *San Antonio Ledger*, "but are disposed not to treat them as infants who are incapable of self-government, but allow them all the privileges and immunities of intelligent white people."[66] Despite this rosy picture, Indigenous people had no illusions about how enduring "friendship" with white southerners could be, especially in political matters. Nevertheless, all five nations sided with the Confederacy, and all of the treaties contained language referring to "natural affections" and shared "social and domestic institutions"—a clear acknowledgment of how chattel slavery ultimately proved a uniting force between Indian Territory and the American South.[67]

* * *

In less than three decades, many white enslavers and advocates of expulsion went from viewing Native nations in the Southeast as a people on the verge of extinction to seeing them as an ally that could help overthrow the Union and solidify the place of chattel slavery in the western hemisphere. Southern whites coveted Indian lands east of the Mississippi, and Native leaders' efforts to protect their lands west of the Mississippi met the same avarice from white settlers and enslavers. Indian Territory was an important site in conversations about the sectional crisis and the westward expansion of slavery—a deeply consequential place in the political debates leading to the Civil War. Although Native nations insisted that the United States, Texas, and Mexico respect their sovereignty, the region was not an insular space or uninvolved on the national and global scene. Indeed, to reach a more complete understanding of the shape and scope of U.S. empire in the nineteenth century, conflicts over chattel slavery, sovereignty, and settler colonialism in Indian Territory cannot be ignored.

PART II

Continent and Globe

CHAPTER 7

American Protestant Missionaries, Native Hawaiian Authority, and Religious Freedom in Hawai'i, ca. 1827–50

TOM SMITH

The history of the Protestant mission of the American Board of Commissioners for Foreign Missions (ABCFM) to Hawai'i is inextricably linked with the story of how the islands became a U.S. territory in 1898. Scholars have described how ABCFM evangelists, first arriving in 1820, promulgated a "rhetoric of revulsion" about Native Hawaiians and unleashed a "religious imperialism" crucial to eroding Indigenous sovereignty and lifeways.[1] Others have viewed them as pioneering a settlement model for Protestant missions, unusually successful in Christianizing the Hawaiian people, and as thinking about the possibilities of U.S. "Christian imperialism" beyond continental boundaries even in the early republic.[2] Ultimately convinced of Native Hawaiians' inherent "licentiousness" and "morbidity," missionaries by the mid-nineteenth century "encouraged American colonization of the island nation and played a major role in its takeover."[3] Moreover, as missionaries raised children in the islands, they developed an economic agenda, encouraging their key converts and allies, the Native Hawaiian chiefs (or monarchy), to move toward a system of private landownership. This land reform in turn facilitated the growth of a sugar plantation economy from which missionaries heavily benefited.[4] In the hands of their children and grandchildren, ideas about missionaries' rights as settlers and about their racial superiority were translated into claims to sovereignty.[5]

These culminated in the Hawaiian monarchy's overthrow in 1893 and subsequent lobbying for U.S. annexation.

This essay, however, argues that during the ABCFM mission's early years, missionaries' relationship to the idea of imperial power was characterized by ambivalence; even if missionaries and their board hoped for a "Christian imperialism," they were not suggesting to U.S. audiences that Hawai'i was ripe for American dominance in any other sense. The chapter analyzes missionaries' correspondence with the ABCFM in Boston, exploring how this correspondence was reproduced and commentated upon for broader audiences in the ABCFM's flagship periodical, the *Missionary Herald*—a key source of information about the world for readers in the early republic. Reading dispatches from ABCFM workers in Hawai'i and the words of the board, Americans would have been struck by missionaries' continued dependence on Indigenous authority, their limited ability to spread the "liberal and tolerant institutions of their own native country," and their placement within a "deeply fractured" cultural field in which unusual alliances were formed and coherent national or imperial interests broke down.[6]

In particular, the essay focuses on Protestant responses to attempts by Roman Catholic evangelists to establish a foothold in Hawai'i in the early decades of the ABCFM mission. In these cases, Protestant Native Hawaiian chiefs conspicuously showed that they remained the authority whose word was law in the islands, moving to deny Catholic priests residency and to ban Catholic practice.[7] The Indigenous monarchy, suggests Lilikalā Kame'eleihiwa, overthrew their old religious system in 1819 and adopted Protestantism in the years after missionaries' arrival in 1820 for reasons in keeping with their traditional cosmological understandings. Rapid depopulation was proof that the reciprocal relationship expected between Native Hawaiians and the *akua* (gods) had broken down, making clear the need for a new system.[8] Recent scholarship has moreover emphasized that these Native Hawaiian leaders upheld traditional forms of governance in the early nineteenth century. Undoubtedly, Hawaiian politics was evolving in response to intensifying contacts with the European and American world. Most notably, the chief Kamehameha used weaponry and military expertise gained in exchanges with European traders in the late eighteenth century to embark upon a campaign, completed by 1809, to unify the islands under a single monarchy.[9] Nonetheless, the monarchy's authority continued to rest on traditional understandings and practices, characterized by deliberation among chiefs, oral legal proclamations, and swift discipline, responsive to specific challenges to societal balance.[10] By adopting written proclamations to amplify and reinforce their oral pronouncements, chiefs made clear that foreigners in the islands, especially "unruly" sailors, were also subject to their rule.[11] Catholics had to leave Hawai'i because they apparently flouted Indigenous authority, failing to seek permission to reside in the islands, ignoring chiefly proclamations, and challenging the Protestant cosmological order that was now seen to underpin chiefly power.[12]

As missionaries sent letters, reports, and journals to the ABCFM in Boston, and as the board in turn curated information for publication in the *Missionary Herald*, American audiences saw the importance of Indigenous authority in keeping Catholicism at bay and facilitating the mission's work. It was, in fact, in the ABCFM's interests to demonstrate the sovereign power of Native Hawaiian leaders in dealing with Catholics. This was because the highlighting of Indigenous authority offered a defense against the claims of American and British sailors and merchants in Hawai'i who supported the rights of French, Irish, and Native Hawaiian Catholics against American Congregationalists and Indigenous chiefs. These figures insisted that ABCFM missionaries themselves were ultimately responsible for the monarchy's religious intolerance, thus acting in ways antithetical to ostensible American values.[13] By emphasizing Native Hawaiian chiefs' authority and the limits of their own influence, missionaries rejected these assertions and reassured American Christians that their representatives were not inhibiting religious freedom in foreign climes. The ways in which the *Missionary Herald* edited missionaries' correspondence and framed their activity for American Christians' consumption suggested a particular concern to shield donors from the claims that the evangelists they supported had anything to do with religious repression.

David Sehat has argued that religious freedom in the early republic (and beyond) was a "myth." While the First Amendment reflected the desire of some of the Founding Fathers to disentangle church and state, federalism gave significant latitude to individual states, which inscribed specific and restrictive Protestant moral ideals in their constitutions and laws.[14] Nonetheless, missionaries' keenness to demonstrate that they were not violating religious freedom in Hawai'i shows the rhetorical currency it had as a "defining national ideal," in Tisa Wenger's words, marking out Americans abroad. Wenger argues that American imperialists used "religious freedom talk" to strengthen the case for U.S. overseas empire in the late nineteenth century, invoking religious freedom because it was emblematic of what they believed to be the superiority of white American values.[15] However, this essay focuses on a case in which white American Protestants' "religious freedom talk" displayed more ambivalence about U.S. empire. As missionaries in Hawai'i and the *Herald* in North America sought to square a desire to curb Catholic influence with a need to be seen as upholding supposed American constitutional freedoms, they talked about religious freedom in ways that emphasized not the desirability of American control but the limits of Americans' ability to impose themselves on Hawaiian systems of governance.

While demonstrating the viability of Indigenous authority, though, missionaries simultaneously expressed a heavily racialized ideology: when dealing with a people emerging from "heathenism" and subjected to a world of competition between foreign actors, American principles of religious freedom could not apply. The ABCFM assured Americans that missionaries themselves were not violating religious freedom, but concurrently asserted that Native Hawaiians' racial inferiority left them ill-equipped to discern Catholic "falsehood," necessitating the heavy-handed authority of the chiefs. In truth, Native Hawaiians exercised religious choice throughout the nineteenth century in ways far more complex than allowed for by missionaries' dichotomization of "enlightened" Protestant leaders and "low" Catholics. Many turned to Catholicism, Anglicanism, or Mormonism, seeing in each opportunities to protect traditional modes of living as missionary Protestantism became increasingly associated with the erosion of Native Hawaiian sovereignty.[16] Others clung to Protestantism, expressing their indigeneity and loyalty to the monarchy in sincere Christian terms, even as in their loyalism they found themselves increasingly at odds with the missionary community.[17] Little of this nuance mattered to white American missionaries, however. In their assertion that Native Hawaiians needed paternalistic guidance in spiritual matters, we see emerging a blueprint for Americans' imperialistic dealings with island peoples in the later nineteenth century, whereby Americans styled themselves as liberal and democratic, but also as best placed to determine what was right for racial others. By the 1890s, such racialized language would be turned against the Hawaiian monarchy itself.

The *Missionary Herald* as a Source of Intelligence

The ABCFM perceived the *Missionary Herald*'s wide distribution in America as "essential." Published monthly and amounting to four hundred dense

pages of "missionary intelligence" annually, it kept American Christians—
or at least the northeastern Congregationalists and Presbyterians who primarily constituted the ABCFM's membership—abreast of "the proceedings
of the Board and its Missionaries."[18] It curated missionary letters, journals,
and reports from across the ABCFM's wide field, adding editorial comment
spelling out American Christians' responsibilities. For an organization dependent on U.S. church congregants' donations, "some such means of making known readily its enterprises, successes and wants" was crucial.[19] While
there were various attempts to publish ABCFM intelligence in other forms,
the *Herald* remained a steady source.[20] Following on from the earlier Congregationalist periodical *The Panoplist*, the *Herald* was published from 1821
until 1934, when it merged with the *American Missionary*.

The board's grand designs for the *Herald* were accompanied by anxieties.
At the ABCFM's annual meeting in September 1841, David Greene, secretary
for Indian missions and the *Herald*'s editor, noted that the periodical was the
only "vehicle by which missionary information is systematically and widely
disseminated," and that its print run of 22,000 yielded only seven copies per
congregation among the 3,000 churches upon which the board relied for donations. While the *Herald*'s circulation was twice as large as that of any
other similar periodical in America or Britain, Greene believed that missionary intelligence still only reached a tenth of its target audience.[21] However,
the size of print runs was not necessarily a true measure of the *Herald*'s national impact. In 1828, the board noted that in an age of burgeoning religious
publishing, information from the *Herald* appeared in "almost every work on
practical religion that issues from the press," having a "considerable" effect
on "public sentiment."[22] By the mid-1840s, the board believed that even secular papers were "extensively becoming vehicles of intelligence on . . . missions," taking their material from the *Herald*'s "authentic sources."[23]

Despite anxieties, therefore, the board reaffirmed during one annual
meeting that the *Herald* was "one of the most valuable periodicals of its day."[24]
In its commitment to reporting on "the character, manners, and customs of
the various nations" and "whatever has a direct bearing on . . . Christian benevolence," it positioned itself as a key vehicle for American knowledge about
the world, during an age in which, Emily Conroy-Krutz has argued, missionaries were unusual among Americans in being "more concerned with events
across the globe than they were with those across the continent, and . . . open
to the possibilities of empire."[25] In choosing which missionary writings to
publish, and how to frame the actions of missionaries, local peoples, and other

foreigners, the *Herald* recognized itself to be significantly shaping U.S. Protestants' perceptions of American engagement with the world. As the *Herald* reported the Catholic controversy in Hawai'i (or the Sandwich Islands, as it was referred to in the first half of the nineteenth century), Americans saw missionaries' struggles to position and justify themselves as sympathetic white Americans in a complex world of Indigenous authority and foreign incursion.

Exhibiting Indigenous Authority

Two Catholic priests, one French and one Irish, accompanied by mechanics and agriculturalists, attempted to settle in Honolulu in July 1827, having set sail from Bordeaux eight months earlier.[26] They found themselves opposed by Protestant Hawaiian chiefs, notably the queen regent Ka'ahumanu, who demanded their departure, but welcomed by U.S. consul John Coffin Jones and the Native Hawaiian governor of the island of O'ahu, Boki, thus according them some protection from the opposition of the most powerful chiefs.[27] They remained to reportedly baptize sixty-five adults and seventeen children within two years, even as Ka'ahumanu toured the islands in 1829 commanding Native Hawaiians to have nothing to do with the priests and punishing those who attended Catholic worship.[28] The support from the U.S. consul for the priests might seem curious. After all, Jones represented the interests of a community of American traders in the islands who were predominantly Yankee Protestants, and thus whose counterparts in the United States simultaneously railed against Irish Catholic immigrants.[29] In the Catholics arriving in Hawai'i, however, Jones and the merchant community saw an opportunity to challenge ABCFM missionaries, whom they regarded as being more concerned with educating islanders in the Bible than with making them productive, and as driving Protestant chiefs' repressive moralism.[30]

ABCFM missionaries at Honolulu were concerned by the Catholic presence. Informed by what Kealani Cook refers to as their "rabid anti-Catholicism," they viewed the priests first warily, and increasingly with alarm.[31] But they also recognized the potential image problems for the mission in being associated with Ka'ahumanu's repression of Catholic worship, especially among American audiences.[32] Wanting the Catholics gone but not the responsibility for their removal, missionary Levi Chamberlain told the board that ABCFM workers were "afraid to open our lips . . . lest we should sanction persecution, or say something that should lead to the toleration of a delusion."[33] At their general meeting in January 1830, missionaries underscored their opposition to "all coercive measures of the civil authority to control religious opinions or practices." However, they would also not stand in the way if, as they clearly thought was likely, the Hawaiian chiefs attempted to remove the "deadly influence" of Catholics from the islands, preempting accusations of monarchical "persecution" by invoking this word only to deny its relevance. All the same, missionaries established distance by clearly defining themselves as spiritual advisers, rather than advocates of any particular course of governmental action.[34] In other words, they sought a way of sanctioning chiefly prerogative to remove the Catholics without offering ammunition to the traders who wanted to convince U.S. audiences of missionaries' active involvement in persecution. "The cry of persecution against the chiefs & missionaries has already been raised," noted missionary Ephraim Clark in November 1830, "& will probably soon be resounded in America."[35]

The board appeared to recognize the situation's sensitivity. To the missionaries' dismay, it refrained from offering concrete advice, despite repeated requests.[36] The *Missionary Herald* too initially held back from offering any opinion. Even in the periodical's report on the missionaries' 1830 general meeting, at which the issue of the priests had been discussed at length, any mention of a struggle with Catholicism was omitted.[37] The board, despite showing in the *Herald* that it was perturbed by Catholicism in other mission fields, perhaps did not want to risk fueling any impression among American audiences that their missionaries were driving religious intolerance in Hawai'i or embroiling themselves in local politics.[38] After all, the periodical had already, in September 1827, needed to counter claims made against ABCFM missionaries to the islands in the *Quarterly Review*—an influential British periodical reprinted for American audiences by Boston publisher Wells and Lilly.[39] The *Review*, drawing on the observations of British naval officers, argued, first, that Catholicism had in fact predated Protestantism in Hawai'i— Boki and another chief had been baptized by visiting French Catholics in the late 1810s.[40] It also charged that the arrival of American evangelists had led to Hawaiians' neglect of industry in favor of education, and thus to their desolation: "Nothing flourishes but the missionary school."[41]

The *Herald* had also found itself involved in two further controversies relating to Hawai'i in the late 1820s, which had prompted missionaries on the

ground to counsel greater "caution . . . in presenting . . . facts before the publick."[42] First, accusations made by missionary William Richards that William Buckle, captain of the British whaleship *Daniel*, had purchased a Native
Hawaiian woman, Leoiki, during a visit to Hawai'i in 1825 were disseminated
through the *Herald* of February 1827.[43] The British consul at the islands declared the *Herald*'s article to be libelous, and Richards was hauled before a
chiefly court.[44] Second, Ephraim Clark rebuked the *Herald* for publishing,
in January 1829, ABCFM missionaries' private complaints about conditions
aboard the *Parthian*, a ship that had carried some of them from New England
to the islands.[45] Perhaps unnerved by this recent flurry of controversy and
reproach, the *Herald* approached the issue of Catholic presence in Hawai'i
with caution.

The cue for the *Herald* to weigh in came after a major flash point in late
1831. Following Boki's death in 1830, Protestant chiefs intensified their efforts
to force the Catholic priests to leave Hawai'i. Having been rebuffed throughout 1831, in December they paid British sea captain William Sumner to take
the priests to California aboard the monarchy's brig.[46] Missionaries regarded
the priests' dismissal as an answer to prayer, and indeed had advocated it as
preferable to the punishment of Hawaiian Catholics themselves.[47] They were,
however, aware that an American "Christian public" might view the decision
as "ill timed, injudicious, or intolerant" and be uncomfortable with missionaries' failure to impress upon the chiefs the importance of religious toleration.[48] Preempting this discomfort, missionaries moved between denial,
justification, and obfuscation in their letters to the board. Hiram Bingham
simultaneously affirmed that missionaries had "endeavored to guard against
any infringement on the principles of religious and civil liberty," defended
the Hawaiian chiefs' right to remove foreign subjects, and reminded the board
that reports of missionaries' discussions of the Catholic controversy at general meetings were not for American public consumption—the missionaries
had, after all, affirmed in no uncertain terms their approval of the priests'
dismissal at their 1831 general meeting.[49] Another letter from a group of missionaries, dated January 17, 1832, suggested that they expected the board
would disapprove of their course, especially given that the ABCFM had itself run afoul of secular authority when expelled from India by the East India Company. Launching into a lengthy defense of the monarchy's rights,
missionaries noted the situation's "difficulties." "Lest it may perhaps be
thought we have been lookers on & suggested the chiefs . . . go headlong in a

course extremely wrong," they wrote, they believed it "proper to attempt some justification or palliation . . . which will . . . meet your inquiries, and . . . save ourselves from blame."[50]

When the *Herald* for November 1832 published this same letter, however, it offered a selective edit eliding the question of missionary responsibility.[51] It printed the parts that wrote of a desire to convey "some particulars of a providential character not immediately connected with our labors," framing missionaries as interested observers rather than as participants in an interreligious struggle. It omitted mention of missionaries' deep concern about the Catholic presence, affirming simply that it was the chiefs' decision to remove the priests.[52] The *Herald*'s own commentary continued in a similar vein. Although the timing of the periodical's intervention might well be explained by missionaries' fears that traders in Hawai'i would publish accounts asserting that missionaries were the architects of religious intolerance, it refused to dignify such accusations.[53] Protestant chiefs had their own reasons, it emphasized, for rejecting Catholicism. Catholic images and relics supposedly reminded them of "their former system of worship," which they had overthrown even before ABCFM missionaries arrived.[54] Moreover, in four years of Catholic residence, the chiefs had observed that Catholic practice was unscriptural, informed by their vernacular Bible and by missionaries' translation of a letter outlining Catholic activity in Syria. Finally, and perhaps most saliently, they resented the threat Catholicism represented to their authority. In the words of Kuakini, governor of Hawai'i island, "because their doings are different from ours, and because we cannot agree, therefore we send them away."[55]

Having established that Hawaiian chiefs were responsible for removing the priests, the *Herald* was also prepared to sanction this action, assuring that it was not, in fact, persecution. The Hawaiian government had not violated any of the priests' "natural or acquired rights" but rather, having been repeatedly disobeyed, had "exercised the right claimed by all civilized nations, of determining whether foreigners . . . shall remain."[56] The *Herald* did not offer a means of reading Indigenous voices on their own terms. In particular, it obscured the long-standing traditions of Native Hawaiian governance being exercised in the monarchy's approach to Catholicism, and instead framed chiefly authority in terms familiar to the board and to readers, finding negative analogues in "despotism" and positive ones in European monarchies. Nonetheless, by drawing analogies with monarchical leadership, the *Herald* did show American audiences that the authority of Native Hawaiian chiefs was sustained and rightful.

In Defense of Missionaries

In 1839, another flash point prompted the *Herald* to insist upon the salience of Hawaiian chiefly authority. The background was the Hawaiian chiefs' Ordinance Rejecting the Catholic Religion in December 1837, which banned outright the practice of Catholicism or the settlement of Catholic missionaries.[57] The Hawaiian king, Kauikeaouli (Kamehameha III), in fact revoked this ordinance in June 1839, fearing the exercise of French gunboat diplomacy as had recently occurred at Tahiti.[58] Nonetheless, the following month, Captain Laplace of the French naval frigate *L'Artemise* traveled to Hawai'i, threatening force if Kauikeaouli refused to "conform to the usages of civilized nations" by allowing liberty of worship and compensating Laplace for prior "insults." Kauikeaouli signed a treaty with Laplace on July 17.[59] The traders who opposed the Protestant chiefs and missionaries celebrated a major victory, having increasingly styled themselves across the 1830s as champions of religious liberty against ABCFM evangelists through their organ, the *Sandwich Island Gazette*.[60]

The *Herald* discussed Laplace's visit in March 1840, beginning with a report from the *Hawaiian Spectator*, a quarterly review printed by the mission press in Hawai'i.[61] As when reporting on the priests' removal in 1831, the first move was to establish missionaries' distance; the *Spectator* article was "not a communication from the missionaries, and does not relate directly to their operations."[62] The notion that ABCFM missionaries were not embroiled in the unfolding controversy was not easy to sustain indirectly on this occasion, however, given that Laplace had offered shelter from any violence to Americans in the islands, but deliberately excepted the missionaries—"individuals who, although born . . . in the United States, make a part of the protestant clergy of the chief of this archipelago, and are the true authors of the insults given by him to France. . . . They compose a part of the native population, and must undergo the unhappy consequences of a war which they shall have brought on this country."[63] Laplace's equation of missionaries with the Indigenous population spoke to fears that U.S. audiences might understand missionaries to have abandoned American norms in their dealings with

Catholics. Missionaries scrambled to offer their perspective to the board, and indeed to the U.S. Congress, recognizing that the inevitable circulation of Laplace's accusations in the press would make their donors "exceedingly distressed . . . with apprehensions that we had violated our neutrality."[64]

The *Herald* set about dismissing Laplace's allegations. ABCFM missionaries, it assured readers, were U.S. citizens, "commended to the friendly regard and protection of all other governments." They had done nothing other than "speak and print their views respecting what they deem religious error," as was done every day in America "by ministers and other men, from the pulpit, by the press, and in conversation."[65] The *Herald* also styled itself as a defender of Indigenous authority against imperialistic nations.[66] Just as it had when justifying the priests' removal, it argued that the Hawaiian government had done no more than any European nation in deciding "how far foreign priests may introduce . . . strange doctrines."[67] It accused Laplace of deception in suggesting that Hawaiian chiefs had violated "the usages of civilized nations," making the case that "not one government on the continent of Europe . . . permits any such toleration as he . . . was demanding." This was a formulation that simultaneously distanced the United States from illiberalism while equating the Hawaiian monarchy's authority with that of European governments. If Laplace really wanted to strike for religious toleration, the article continued, he should have taken on China, Japan, or Russia; perhaps his choice of Hawai'i had more to do with a desire to force the abstinent monarchy to accept imports of French alcohol—another provision of the final treaty—than with real concern for Catholicism. The *Herald* then followed its discussions of the Laplace affair with an "abstract of laws enacted by the king and chiefs" in the preceding decades, noting the inevitable continuity of chiefly ordinances with an "oppressive system . . . handed down from their heathen ancestors," while praising their overall effect. There was another clear assertion of distance between lawmaking and missionaries, who, it was said, had to a fault kept to their instructions "to abstain from . . . local and political interests."[68]

The November 1840 *Herald* reported further discussions of the affair at the ABCFM's annual meeting. The board's secretary for overseas work, Rufus Anderson, had read out a statement reaffirming the *Herald*'s editorial conclusions and underlining the board's belief that "missionaries are not otherwise the authors of the proceedings of the Sandwich Islands government towards the papists . . . than by having been the means of the general adoption . . . of the protestant evangelical religion." Anderson seemed more willing to label the Hawaiian monarchy's actions as persecutorial, stating that if missionaries were at fault, it was in not condemning persecution strongly enough "for fear of overstepping the bounds of propriety."[69] Either way, he again showed American audiences that proper authority in Hawai'i rested with the chiefs.

Nonetheless, Anderson feared that "multitudes . . . do really suppose that the missionaries at the Sandwich Islands have countenanced the native rulers in persecuting . . . the Romish religion."[70] Missionaries and their defenders alluded to a number of places from which Americans might have procured this idea: the French Catholic periodical *Annales de la Propagation de la Foi*, which was translated into English and republished in New York; a pamphlet supposedly authored by the former American consul John Coffin Jones; daily newspapers that repeated the accusations of missionaries' detractors; and U.S. naval surgeon William S. Ruschenberger's 1838 account of his voyage around the world.[71] To counteract such influences, the *Herald* reported the findings of a committee charged by the ABCFM with the task of ruling whether missionaries in Hawai'i were accountable for religious intolerance. This committee also concluded that missionaries had not "done any thing inconsistent with the spirit of our free institutions."[72]

In denying missionary authorship of "insults" toward Catholics and underscoring the propriety of chiefly prerogative, the *Herald* certainly sought to protect missionaries from accusations of religious intolerance. But it also conveyed an important truth to American audiences: that Hawai'i was not a blank canvas for imperial influence, but was governed by an Indigenous monarchy that arbitrated international and interreligious competition. Insofar as it demonstrated the viability of Native Hawaiian rule, the *Herald* provided a counterpoint to the suggestion by foreign merchants that the Indigenous government was in fact incapable of thinking for itself. Underpinning these merchants' certainty that missionaries were responsible for the repression of Catholics was a racialized conviction, expressed by the editor of the *Sandwich Island Gazette*, that the Hawaiian monarchy could be nothing more than a "misled child."[73] This idea that missionaries were obviously responsible for removing Catholic priests then filtered into twentieth-century Hawaiian histories by non-Natives.[74] The *Herald*'s denial of missionary responsibility, on the other hand, instead conveyed to American audiences that Hawaiian chiefs were sovereign in the islands. The understanding that the board showed of the traditions that underpinned Native Hawaiian spirituality and governance may have been limited, but nonetheless it pointed toward the idea that missionaries were taking a backseat to Indigenous authority.

The Racialization of Native Hawaiians

Although missionaries gave American audiences the opportunity to recognize the viability of Indigenous rule in Hawai'i, they simultaneously developed a pernicious idea about the need for heavy-handed monarchical authority. This idea originated with missionaries seeking to justify a forceful approach to Catholicism, arguing that "paternal guardianship" by Native Hawaiian chiefs was necessary because most Hawaiians could not make informed spiritual decisions.[75] Ephraim Clark, writing to the ABCFM in 1830, stated that while those in America, "a land of civil & religious liberty," might think that "moral weapons" were appropriate for combating Catholicism, "if we should tell the chiefs that they must use no coercive means to stop the progress of this evil, it would in effect be giving our assent to the spread of the evil." Those incapable of "investigating & thinking & deciding themselves" were not prepared for "true civil liberty," and evil would spread without "the strong arm of civil power."[76]

Across the 1830s, against the backdrop of numerous crackdowns against Native Hawaiian Catholics and several attempts to reintroduce Catholicism to the islands, the *Herald* distanced the ABCFM's missionaries from "despotic" governance and religious intolerance, but amplified missionaries' idea that illiberal means were necessary to protect "childlike" racial others from malign spiritual influences.[77] The ABCFM's celebration of Hawaiian chiefs' leadership might have counteracted other foreigners' characterization of the government as a "misled child," but it also cast the vast majority of Native Hawaiians as unable to make decisions for their own good: "If the common people are such children . . . , it is desirable for them to be under authority . . . much beyond the bounds which would be desirable for people of mature minds."[78] It was the responsibility of Hawai'i's "hereditary chiefs," of "a higher order than the common people," to decide what was best for them.[79]

In other words, as much as missionaries provided Americans with opportunities to understand that the monarchy's word was the law by which Hawaiians and foreigners alike had to abide, the overall impression given of Native Hawaiians was as depraved racial inferiors. While a February 1837 letter from missionary Titus Coan reprinted in the January 1838 *Herald* conceded

that there were "good figures . . . endowed with fine natural talents," this
was a glimpse amid descriptions of "torpid and sluggish" Native Hawaiians,
characterized by "unrighteousness," "grossness and intellectual stupidity,"
and "servility and sycophancy."[80] Another letter, from missionaries Asa
Thurston and Artemas Bishop, written in November 1835 and published in
the October 1836 *Herald*, agreed that "ignorance and depravity are the two
grand obstacles to the conversion of this people." Even when a Native Hawaiian "expresses his desire of being taught the truths of the Bible, it is extremely difficult to make him understand them." Moreover, continued
Thurston and Bishop, Hawaiians were beset by physical death.[81] Assertions
of the inevitability of Indigenous death were common across colonial contexts, and while they pointed to very real problems of disease and depopulation in Hawai'i, they also reinforced assessments of Native Hawaiians'
physical and moral inferiority.[82]

The missionaries' reminders of Hawaiians' apparent incapacity and morbidity served to temper the enthusiasm of American audiences who might
be led by reports of evangelistic success to believe that islanders were "further advanced in civilization and Christianity than they really are."[83] Certainly, reported the *Herald* in January 1833, it was true that "the most
distinguished and influential individuals of the nation, are professedly on the
side of truth and virtue," but "a relapse to idolatry" was possible, and there
was more work to be done.[84] Later that year, the periodical asked what, given
"the low walks" of Native Hawaiian life, the reader could "reasonably expect,
except the mere *essentials* of piety. . . . In knowledge, we ought to expect them
to be babes; in stability and decision of character, children; generally slow to
apprehend the spirituality and extent of God's law" rather than "quick to fly
to Christ."[85]

Laplace's threatened invasion in 1839 prompted the *Herald* to make this
argument with specific reference to Catholicism. While rejecting the charge
that missionaries were complicit in religious intolerance, the *Herald* also argued that the monarchy's heavy-handed authority was necessary, given Native Hawaiians' generally low condition: "The rulers of the islands supposed
themselves to have a right to protect their subjects . . . and to prevent their
minds, in their infantile and unenlightened state, from being distracted with
religious controversy; and . . . to preserve them from . . . the delusive influence of doctrines and ceremonies, the captivating power of which their own
remaining inclination to idolatrous rites would greatly enhance."[86] It was
irresponsible of Laplace to "forcibly . . . bind the papal yoke upon tribes just

emerged from heathenism."[87] The committee tasked by the board with defending the missionaries moreover reaffirmed through the November 1840 *Herald* that the Hawaiian government had acted in a manner "not inconsistent with the public welfare . . . among a people who . . . could have no correct ideas of the sacred principles of unrestrained religious toleration." Indeed, missionaries might have been forgiven for intervening, given that "they were laboring among a people just emerging from . . . heathen idolatry" among whom the introduction of new religious ideas could undo years of good work. But they had refrained from doing so.[88] Thus, the *Herald* assured readers that ABCFM missionaries had not done anything inconsistent with an American commitment to religious liberty, while also underscoring that this U.S. constitutional freedom was not suitable for Native Hawaiians.

In justifying Hawaiian chiefly power, the *Herald* reinforced racialized perceptions of Native Hawaiians in general. Even if missionaries and the board wanted to distance themselves from modes of rule that might be deemed "tyrannical" by American audiences, and indeed even if missionaries did lack power in a world governed by Indigenous authority, the *Herald*'s development of paternalistic ideas when describing the relationship between chiefs and commoners still rhetorically placed Americans on the ground as equipped to determine what was best for Indigenous people. In reiterating the need for chiefly authority, the *Herald* gave a platform to ideas that would later be used to strip Hawai'i's Indigenous people of their sovereignty altogether.

Confronting Catholicism in the 1840s

Missionaries, and in turn the *Missionary Herald*, discussed Catholicism in Hawai'i more frequently after Kauikeauoli's treaty with Laplace as they struggled against now unfettered Catholic influence. On the one hand, when publishing missionaries' comments on their dealings with Catholicism and adding its own observations, the *Herald* repeatedly assured Americans that Protestantism in Hawai'i was, on the whole, withstanding the Catholic onslaught. Supposedly, only certain types of Native Hawaiians were attracted to the priests' religion: those who wanted to revive "heathen" ways and resonated with Catholicism's idolatry and healing practices; those from "less enlightened districts" outside Protestant influence; those who wanted freedom from government and taxation; and "an ignorant, vicious, credulous, or unstable class" who found Protestantism's moral demands burdensome.[89] Native

Hawaiian Protestants, missionaries suggested, saw through Catholic "cunning and perseverance," and used biblical arguments to counteract it: "In their conversations with the priests," wrote missionary Lorrin Andrews in one 1840 letter appearing in the *Herald*, "the people manifest some knowledge of the word of God, and often give very apposite replies."[90]

On the other hand, missionary letters in the *Herald* continued to describe congregants as "partially enlightened," "babes in Christ," "sottish children," "foolish," "perverse," "fickle and wayward," unstable, and ill-equipped to counter spurious spiritual guidance.[91] Similarly, the periodical explained to American audiences the delay in building up a Native Hawaiian pastorate, on the grounds that "of our adult church members we can hardly say there are any who have so put off their former heathenish habits and acquired such an amount of intelligence, prudence, and maturity of Christian character, as to justify an attempt to train them to be pastors."[92] Evidence of Hawaiian Protestantism's ability to resist Catholic incursion, therefore, was tempered by continued assertions that Native Hawaiians were unable to decide what was best for them and that they needed a heavy guiding hand from those of a "higher order."

The Hawaiian monarchy's ability to provide that guiding hand appeared to be waning across the tumultuous 1840s as documented in the *Herald*, beginning with Laplace's treaty. There were further incursions by foreign powers—another French ship visited to make demands of the monarchy in September 1842, while the islands were held by the British naval officer Lord George Paulet for five months from February 1843 until another British delegation arrived and commanded him to give up his occupation.[93] Hawai'i's independence was formally recognized by the United States in December 1842, and by Britain and France in November 1843, yet still it was subjected to further invasion by French admiral Louis Tromelin in August 1849.[94] Such episodes gave the *Herald* a chance to favorably contrast the United States' respect for Hawaiian autonomy with British and French disregard, affirming America's allegedly exceptional refusal to engage in exploitative forms of imperialism.[95] In general, however, foreign incursions deeply concerned ABCFM missionaries whose letters appeared in the *Herald* and, as far as they saw it, were detrimental to political stability and morals.[96]

In their assertions of Native Hawaiians' inability to lead their own churches, and by showing how the Native Hawaiian monarchy was flagging in its ability to protect Hawaiian Protestantism, ABCFM missionaries increasingly positioned themselves as best placed to provide the paternalistic hand they believed that Hawaiian Christianity still needed. With questions of legal toleration of Catholicism and missionaries' complicity in illiberal practices largely put to bed, the ABCFM could reemploy the language it used in justifying the Hawaiian monarchy's approach to Catholicism to argue that the Hawaiian mission required ratcheting up, not winding down.[97] Native Hawaiian Protestants were still ultimately deemed too weak to face challenges without being subject to authority. In the 1850s, the ABCFM did in fact relinquish pecuniary responsibility for the mission, having found itself under pressure from abolitionists within the Hawaiian mission who accused the board of temporizing over the question of slavery.[98] Rufus Anderson argued that it was time to begin the transition to Native pastors, but missionaries themselves continued to express doubts about Hawaiians' racial capacity.[99] They and their descendants increasingly asserted themselves in politics and business, overwhelming Indigenous rule by the end of the century.

Conclusion

When referring to the Catholic controversy in Hawai'i, ABCFM missionaries, and in turn the *Missionary Herald*, offered evidence of Native Hawaiian leaders' agency in upholding Protestantism. Using empire as a category of analysis draws our attention to the fact that American missionaries in Hawai'i, often seen as the progenitors of U.S. empire in the islands, were ambivalent in the early decades of the mission about whether the subversion of Native Hawaiian authority by foreign powers, including the United States, was possible or desirable. Missionaries exercised a religious influence in the islands that has, with good reason, been seen as degrading Native Hawaiian lifeways and as intrinsic to colonialism. However, the continuation of a form of Indigenous governance that was not replaced by or incorporated into formal imperial structures of rule afforded missionaries opportunities to operate in a privileged position without openly betraying the myth of American religious freedom. In its particular concern to deflect ABCFM donors' attention away from criticism of the missionaries whom they supported, the *Missionary Herald* conveyed missionaries' ambivalence. In its pages, American audiences learned that missionaries, while seeking to spread a "Christian imperialism" with reference to American values, were both reliant on and subservient to Indigenous monarchical power as they fought for their religious interest. Meanwhile, foreign Catholics, traders, and naval officers, condemned by Protestant missionaries and by the *Herald*, used the language of religious freedom to justify Laplace's more nakedly imperialistic act of aggression. Undoubtedly, external threats such as that posed by Laplace prompted changes in Hawaiian law and governance, pushing chiefs to increasingly refashion themselves according to European and American norms.[100] But the ABCFM, at least until the early 1840s, presented the monarchy to American Christians as ultimate arbiters of the direction their island world took in response to outsiders. Missionaries and the *Herald* conveyed that this was a good thing, even if some of the methods employed were supposedly unpalatable to American ears.

On the other hand, we can also understand the ABCFM's sanctioning of the use of monarchical power to promote Protestantism and reject Catholicism as in itself imperial, giving voice to arguments about Native Hawaiian racial incapacity which would increasingly be deployed in efforts to undermine Indigenous authority as the nineteenth century wore on. Setting apart a few "enlightened" Indigenous people as exercising wise authority meant condemning the vast majority as childlike and in need of heavy-handed guidance, and demonstrating to American audiences what overseas empire might have to look like: the world could not straightforwardly be remade in the United States' image because not all were fit to enjoy its freedoms. As the Native Hawaiian monarchy seemed increasingly less able or inclined to privilege missionary Protestantism, the idea that Americans might themselves step in to offer paternalistic guidance became more compelling. By the end of the nineteenth century, the children and grandchildren of ABCFM missionaries, alongside other foreign businessmen, had turned the arguments used to justify Hawaiian chiefs' authority in the 1830s and the early 1840s against the Indigenous monarchy itself. Missionary son Nathaniel Emerson commented that "the ignorance of a child is no excuse for injustice, but it is good reason why the driving reins should be taken from its hand."[101] The American idea that paternalism rather than constitutional freedom was the key to good governance of "inferior" overseas populations also became evident elsewhere in the late nineteenth century, in the Philippines' "benevolent assimilation" and the designation of Puerto Rico as "unincorporated," or "foreign in a domestic sense."[102]

As missionaries and their U.S. audiences thought about the possibilities of overseas empire in Hawai'i earlier in the nineteenth century, however, they were led to see the benefits not of a totalizing missionary imperialism but of an Indigenous government that could promote the cause of Protestant civilization using methods that were supposedly anathema to Americans themselves. This was a pragmatic approach to foreign relations that allowed room for a thriving "Christian imperialism" while establishing rhetorical distance from knottier political questions surrounding interreligious competition and religious freedom, which also drew in traders and navies from multiple empires. Though it ultimately transpired that the American missionary community would tolerate Indigenous governance only for as long as it upheld their interests at the expense of other freedoms, the story across the 1820s and 1830s reveals the complex power relations that undergirded U.S. presence in Hawai'i and the rivalries that prompted Protestant missionaries to encourage monarchical power rather than to advocate for the wholesale export of American ideals and forms of governance.

CHAPTER 8

"The Colony Must Be Broken Up"

The Liberian Settler "Rebellion" of 1823–24

ERIC BURIN

Following the American Revolution, white Americans sometimes imagined that the United States becoming a racially segregated, federative empire, one in which they would enjoy liberty and equality within the metropole while Black Americans and Native Americans would do likewise elsewhere. This imperial arrangement, they reasoned, would be immensely advantageous: It would safeguard American republicanism from the corrosive effects of white supremacy, not by fostering racial egalitarianism domestically but by relocating people of color to some faraway place, where they would countenance U.S. interests in their new, liberal homelands.[1]

These ideas influenced white Americans' expectations for Liberia, which was founded in the early 1820s. To the leaders of the American Colonization Society (ACS), a white organization that played an important role in Liberia's establishment, the African settlement would be a refuge for persecuted and allegedly "degraded" free Black Americans and perhaps an asylum for their enslaved counterparts. To the white evangelicals who hoped to serve as the ACS's agents in Liberia and to the missionaries who imagined themselves proselytizing there, the tiny enclave would be a Christian seed planted in a heathen land. From the perspective of officials of the federal government, which ultimately supplied most of the funding for the enterprise, Liberia would be a landing place for "recaptured Africans" who had been rescued from the Atlantic slave trade. Some U.S. naval personnel imagined still grander things for Liberia, envisioning it as a strategically located base of operations, one well suited to combat human trafficking at its source and to provision U.S. vessels cruising the region. Indeed, the further one peered into the future, the more magnificent Liberia's prospects, for supportive white Americans expected that this extraterritorial enterprise would neither result in another state being added to the Union, nor permanently affix a colony to a nation that had none at the time. Instead, it would, after a sufficient period of white oversight, beget an independent country, a Black republic from which would germinate Africa's "redemption."[2] That was the theory anyway.

The reality of establishing a noncontiguous Black polity subject to white tutelage proved contentious. For starters, most African Americans insisted that the United States was their true home and decried the notion of a racially partitioned, federative empire. Moreover, those who were open to the idea usually insisted on self-rule for a prospective Black settlement. Consequently, ACS officials encountered substantial opposition among African Americans, and the individuals who were willing to move overseas often locked horns with the supercilious white agents who worked for the ACS and U.S. government in Liberia.

Such disputes bedeviled the Liberian enterprise from the get-go. They vexed the first pioneering party of Americans that sailed for West Africa in 1820 and perturbed subsequent expeditions, too. Yet the most noteworthy confrontation occurred in late 1823 and early 1824. At that juncture, the settlers and agents, having endured many conflicts and tribulations over the previous three and half years, had finally put Liberia on fairly secure footing at Cape Mesurado. That precarious stability was short-lived. Clashes between the agents and certain settlers over the distribution of land, withholding of rations, and other issues pushed the latter into open defiance, with the former essentially being run out of the settlement. The discord imperiled the entire enterprise, as ACS officials and settlers alike warned of Liberia's demise if their demands were not addressed. If the settlement disintegrated, if it collapsed on account of the disputes in 1823–24, all the vast expectations that its advocates harbored would likewise crumble with its demise.

To resolve the disagreements that jeopardized Liberia, the disputants would have to come to a mutually acceptable definition of Black freedom, one forged not only in the wake of strident settler resistance but also in the aftermath of striking instances of Black violence in other parts of the globe, such as Denmark Vesey's conspiracy in 1822 and the insurrection in Demerara in

1823. Otherwise, Liberia would be extinguished, as would its unique and important place in America's imperial history.

Founders

Founded in 1816, the ACS spent several years laying the groundwork for an African settlement. In late 1817, the organization sent two white evangelicals, Samuel J. Mills and Ebenezer Burgess, overseas on a "mission of inquiry." The pair stopped in England to discuss the project with potential allies, gathered additional information in the British colony of Sierra Leone, and then sailed seventy miles south to Sherbro Island. There, they met John Kizell, who had been born in the area around 1760, enslaved, and transported to South Carolina. Kizell secured his freedom during the American Revolution by escaping to British lines during the siege of Charleston, migrated to Nova Scotia when the war ended and then to Sierra Leone in 1792, and finally made his way back to Sherbro. Kizell urged Mills and Burgess to plant the Americans' would-be settlement at Sherbro, and the two agents agreed. During the voyage back to the United States, however, Mills perished. Even so, Burgess submitted their optimistic findings to the ACS Board of Managers in November 1818.[3]

Soon after Burgess filed his report, Representative Charles Fenton Mercer, a Virginian who had been instrumental in the ACS's founding, introduced in Congress a bill that would authorize the U.S. president to provide for the "safe keeping, support, and removal" of recaptured Africans, or "recaptives": enslaved Africans who had been rescued by the U.S. Navy as it enforced laws that prohibited Americans from participating in the Atlantic slave trade generally and from importing foreign bondspersons specifically. The measure also empowered the president to appoint a person "residing upon the coast of Africa, as agent," to receive the recaptives. Mercer's bill passed Congress on March 3, 1819, the last day of a session that bore the political wounds of the Missouri Crisis. President James Monroe, himself a longtime advocate of colonization, quickly signed it. Monroe subsequently interpreted the new law largely as Mercer had hoped, insisting that the statute empowered him to erect, provision, and defend an African station to which recaptives could be sent. Monroe assured Congress that his administration would "exercise no power founded on the principal of colonization," by which he meant it would not establish, in the words of his disapproving secretary of state John Quincy Adams, "a colonial system," a settlement "beyond the seas" over which the United States would claim sovereignty. Even so, as a practical matter, the money that Congress had appropriated under the 1819 Slave Trade Act would subsidize the ACS's activities abroad.[4]

As a case in point, consider the voyage of the *Elizabeth*, which embarked in February 1820 from New York City with one ACS agent, two U.S. agents, and eighty-six Black settlers, nearly all of whom were free residents of New York and Philadelphia. The ship was chartered by the federal government, provisioned with goods from a U.S. naval yard, and was to be escorted to Africa by the twenty-two-gun USS *Cyane*. Upon the party's arrival in Freetown, the agents realized that the three-hundred-ton *Elizabeth* could not satisfy the Americans' needs on the coast. The vessel was too large, and its charter would soon expire, so the head U.S. agent, Rev. Samuel Bacon, purchased a midsize schooner, the *Augusta*. The Americans then sailed for Sherbro Island, where Mills's and Burgess's former acquaintance John Kizell welcomed them. As the party optimistically negotiated with Indigenous leaders for land, a small party of *Cyane* seamen landed at Sherbro to assist the venture. By then, however, diseases had started ravaging the Americans' ranks. By mid-May, three of what would turn out to be seven of the *Cyane* sailors had died and all the agents had perished, too. As their demises approached, the agents transferred their powers to settler Daniel Coker, a forty-year-old minister from Baltimore who fancied himself an intermediary between the agents and the rest of the *Elizabeth* party. With the enterprise unraveling rapidly, some of the settlers, including Coker, took refuge in Sierra Leone. In late autumn, Coker, who at the time was esteemed by ACS leaders in Washington, briefly visited the *Elizabeth* survivors at Sherbro. He landed flanked by U.S. naval personnel from the USS *John Adams*, who were there partly to find out why seven of their comrades had died at Sherbro. Coker's pretentious sojourn exacerbated the ill will that other settlers harbored toward him, and he hastily retreated to Sierra Leone.[5]

In January 1821, thirty-three more settlers, along with two U.S. agents and two ACS agents, embarked for Africa aboard the *Nautilus*. Most of the settlers hailed from Richmond, Virginia, where four years earlier some Black residents had passed a resolution expressing interest in "being colonized," though instead of "being exiled to a foreign country," they preferred as a destination "the most remote corner of the land of our nativity," by which they meant North America. The *Nautilus* settlers, like their *Elizabeth* predecessors, journeyed to Africa in somewhat fractured familial units. Forty-two percent of them were under the age of eighteen, a figure that belied the government's claims that the African Americans on board were laborers tasked with building an overseas station for recaptured Africans. Among the adult settlers, men outnumbered women two to one, an imbalance not entirely uncommon among migrant groups. The *Nautilus* party's dominant figure was thirty-eight-year-old Lott Cary, a preacher who went out as an agent of the Baptist Board of Foreign Missions and was likely starting to see the world through a Pan-Africanist lens. As historian James Sidbury has observed, Cary's decision to become a missionary "on the continent probably reflected some preliminary engagement with a broader vision of African identity." After a seventy-six-day voyage, the *Nautilus* touched at Freetown, Sierra Leone, where it was greeted by *Elizabeth* survivors like Coker who had managed to escape the disaster at Sherbro Island.[6]

Also welcoming the newcomers were Sierra Leone officials. By this juncture, Sierra Leone had been a British crown colony for thirteen years. As such, it was regarded as an imperial asset, a tool with which Britain could advance its interests in the region. This made Sierra Leone distinct from the Americans' African enterprise, which would never enjoy the succor that came with being recognized as a U.S. colony. Britain's formally imperial relationship with Sierra Leone mitigated whatever sympathy the colony's officials may have felt for the Americans' venture in West Africa. They might offer aid, but never in a way that purposely undermined the empire.

What were Britain's interests in Africa? Sierra Leone's governor, Charles McCarthy, likely would have highlighted the colony's efforts to undermine slavery and promote "civilization." At the time, approximately 13,600 people lived in the colony—5,600 in Freetown and another 8,000 in the surrounding villages that recently had been founded for the "liberated Africans" whom the British navy had rescued from captured slavers. This village system strengthened Sierra Leone's territorial grip in the area, stimulated imports by creating an internal demand for foodstuffs, clothes, and other items, and provided the colony with a large and controllable labor force. In McCarthy's mind, this was not exploitation. Under the tutelage of the white missionaries who served as village superintendents, the liberated Africans were inculcated in Western ways—and for this, thought McCarthy, they ought to be grateful. In short, the village system was the cornerstone of the colony, the foundation upon which rested Britain's antislavery and civilizing agendas in Africa. Little wonder that McCarthy was determined to safeguard it and the colony it supported from outside threats, including any posed by Americans.[7]

Consequently, when the *Nautilus* docked at Freetown in March 1821, the Americans were received with measured warmth. Sierra Leone officers immediately explained to the ACS and U.S. agents on board that they were willing to help the Americans—they might allow them to land their cargo duty-free and could arrange for the rental of a farm at nearby Fourah Bay while the party planned its next step—but first the Americans needed to understand that they now opposed a settlement as close as Sherbro. The new agents quickly forswore any claims to Sherbro, and, as hoped, in short order the Americans signed a rental agreement at Fourah Bay and were soon landing their cargo duty-free.[8]

With Sherbro no longer an option for the Americans, two of the party's agents sailed 285 miles south to Grand Bassa, where they contracted for land. Upon their return to Sierra Leone, both agents revealed that they were going back to the United States and they advised the Black Americans they were leaving behind that they ought not to move to Grand Bassa until the rainy season ended, which would not be for another six months. Those two soon departed. As for the Black Americans, they hoped the worst was behind them. After all, a settlement in Grand Bassa appeared to be in the offing.[9]

In what would later be a source of contention, in late May 1821, while still at Fourah Bay, the head ACS agent, Rev. Joseph Andrus, drafted a town plan for the prospective settlement and held a lottery to distribute land parcels among the *Elizabeth* and *Nautilus* emigrants. Thereafter, over the course of the summer, the last *Elizabeth* survivors were transported from Sherbro to Fourah Bay. In July, agent Andrus succumbed to what was suspected to be yellow fever, leaving the perceptive but young white assistant agent Christian Wiltberger putatively in charge of the venture. However, in late October 1821, a new ACS head agent, Dr. Eli Ayres, who also carried the title of navy surgeon, arrived at Sierra Leone aboard the recently constructed USS *Shark*. Forty-two years old and from New Jersey, Ayres promptly informed the Americans that the ACS Board of Managers had rejected the Grand Bassa contract because the document prohibited the prospective settlement's residents from interfering with local slave trading (the board's decision made sense, given that the U.S. government was funding the enterprise under the general pretext of combating the Atlantic slave trade and that the restriction had also rankled the settlers). Twenty months had passed since the *Elizabeth*'s embarkation. During that time, a score or more of settlers had died, as had several white agents and over a half dozen U.S. seamen. All that suffering and sacrifice, and the Americans could not claim an inch of land in Africa. Yet the enterprise's fortunes suddenly revived with the appearance of another brand-new American ship, the USS *Alligator*, whose commander, Captain Robert Stockton, took Ayres and several male settlers 225 miles south to Cape Mesurado, where they struck a deal for land on December 15, 1821.[10]

The Mesurado contract raised thorny legal problems. Although the navy employed both Stockton and Ayres (with the latter doubling as the ACS's agent), the contract did not transfer land to the United States or the ACS. Instead, it indicated that certain "citizens" who desired to "establish themselves on the Western Coast of Africa" had invested Stockton and Ayres with the power to treat for land, which the two men would "hold . . . for the use of these said Citizens of America." Putting aside the contract's debatable description of Black Americans as U.S. citizens, the document's language implied that Stockton and Ayres would keep the land in trust until the settlers took possession. Once they did so, according to historian Charles Huberich, they would establish "a new political community possessing all the attributes of a state." If one accepts Huberich's argument, the Americans were on the cusp of creating not just a station for the United States or an outpost of the ACS. What beckoned was a free Black nation—though few if any contemporaries would acknowledge it as such.[11]

With the goal of securing land seemingly within reach, several leading settlers created the American African Union Society. The body would "regulate the conduct of the People" and as such would constitute an important affirmation of the settlers' collective autonomy. *Elizabeth* settler Daniel Coker, whose reputation had waned among ACS officials on account of his arguably injudicious decisions while serving as temporary agent, was the group's secretary. Another member was *Elizabeth* settler Elijah Johnson, a courageous New Yorker who previously had served in the U.S. military during the War of 1812 and reputedly retained anti-British sentiments. But the animating force behind the American African Union Society was Lott Cary, the bold Baptist preacher from Richmond who had voyaged to Africa aboard the *Nautilus* in March 1821. As president of the American African Union Society, Cary soon incurred the ire of Ayres, who disdained settler independence and said he "wanted to hear nothing more" about the organization. Laboring on, the Americans began moving to Mesurado in January 1822.[12]

A sizable number of the settlers (but not Ayres) were there in March 1822, when the Americans began a series of military actions against Indigenous people—four, by year's end. The first occurred when the settlers, who at the time were confined to a small, marshy island in the bay, attempted to secure fresh water. This act of self-preservation alarmed "King George," the Indigenous figure most opposed to the Americans settling at Mesurado, probably because their presence jeopardized his economic interests and valuable territorial claims (residing on the cape, King George had access to the Atlantic Ocean to his west and freshwater springs to his east). Felled in this exchange was twenty-two-year-old settler John Wiley, the venture's first military martyr. Soon thereafter, a second engagement erupted. This episode ensued after a British naval vessel, along with a slave ship it had captured, stopped at the cape to obtain drinking water. When the slaver beached under suspicious circumstances, the Americans fought alongside British sailors in an attempt to prevent a group of Indigenous residents (including some associated with King George) from plundering the vessel. The skirmish ended triumphantly for the settlers but at a high cost—during the fight, a British seaman accidently set the Americans' storehouse ablaze. About a month later, in April 1822, the last group of settlers arrived at Mesurado. Among those who stayed at Sierra Leone was Daniel Coker, who eventually moved to Hastings, an inland village for liberated Africans, where he became the patriarch of an influential family.[13]

Stuck on a brackish island in the bay, the Americans coveted the more elevated and better situated land on the cape. They got what they wanted in late April when an extended palaver concluded with Sao Boso, the head of the powerful Condo Confederacy who was intrigued by the prospect of Western trade goods flowing through Mesurado to his base inland, decreed that the Americans could occupy the cape because the coastal Indigenous leaders were not powerful enough to stop them. At that pivotal moment, Ayres, knowing that the rainy season would soon begin and fearing a replication of the disaster at Sherbro, suggested to the settlers that they lodge at Fourah Bay until the dry season returned. The party could leave some "useless trumpery" at Mesurado to signify their claims to the cape, Ayres assured his listeners. Lott Cary, who five months before had spearheaded the ill-fated American African Union Society proposal, objected to Ayres's plan and convinced most of his counterparts that they must not relinquish that which they had fought so hard to obtain. In response, Ayres essentially abandoned his post and sailed for the United States, one of the many instances in which the settlers, thanks to the death, incapacitation, or departure of the agents, were left to run their own affairs.[14]

As Ayres wrapped up his business in Africa, Navy Secretary Smith Thompson, knowing only that Ayres had helped secure a land contract in Africa and unaware that he was ditching the settlers at Cape Mesurado, picked

Ayres, who was already the society's head agent, to be the government's agent for recaptured Africans. In the meantime, ACS officials were anxious to send out additional settlers and consequently arranged for the embarkation of a third ship, the *Strong*. The federal government once again would be picking up most of the tab.[15]

The *Strong* embarked from Baltimore on June 20, 1822, and touched at Cape Mesurado fifty days later. On board were thirty-seven settlers (all Marylanders or Philadelphians), fifteen recaptives, and twenty-seven-year-old Jehudi Ashmun. Born in upstate New York, Ashmun was a white evangelical who previously had been an educator in Maine. A small scandal in which Ashmun had backed out of a relationship with one woman only to marry another expedited his departure from the state. He successively resided in Baltimore and Washington, publishing religious and pro-ACS works along the way. Those endeavors left Ashmun with a substantial debt, but they also convinced him that the Americans' African enterprise had considerable commercial potential, which, if properly managed, could benefit the settlement, the surrounding Indigenous population, and, of course, Ashmun himself. Ashmun's writings also brought him to the attention of ACS leaders, who tabbed him to head the *Strong* expedition. Accompanied to Africa by his wife, Ashmun expected to return to the United States immediately. But the society's instructions obliged him to remain in the colony as "acting agent" if the organization's previous agents had left the settlement or had died, as was the case at the time. (It was unclear whether Ashmun was the de facto U.S. agent, an uncertainty that would prove important when others, including creditors in London and federal officials in Washington, questioned his purchases on behalf of the African station.)[16]

After arriving in Africa, the *Strong* party, like its predecessors, was waylaid by tropical diseases. Ashmun fell gravely ill and his wife died. Almost miraculously, only one settler died. This group, though weakened, in November and December 1822, stood shoulder to shoulder with what remained of the *Elizabeth* and *Nautilus* settlers, thwarting with the help of U.S.-issued artillery two large Indigenous attacks on the settlement. Although Indigenous soldiers killed several settlers and one recaptive, and they kidnapped seven children as well, the attackers' ultimate objectives are unclear (did they aim to seize booty, annihilate the settlement, or something else?). But there is no doubt what individuals like Lott Cary were fighting for: Cary later compared the settlers' plight at that stage with that of the ancient Jews, declaring they had held a weapon in one hand while laboring with the other. There was never a moment, he added, not even when bullets were whizzing by his head, that he had wished himself back in America.[17]

In the aftermath of the December battle, an uneasy truce was effected by Alexander Gordon Laing, a British officer and explorer whose post-battle intervention exemplifies Britain's role in the establishment of the Americans' African settlement. Like Laing, British officials (and particularly those in Sierra Leone) usually assisted the Americans when they needed help. Sometimes doing so was very costly. When Laing left the cape aboard the HMS *Prince Regent*, for instance, twelve seamen from that vessel volunteered to stay, nine of whom died within a month. Nevertheless, British aid typically extended no further than that country's imperial interests. Had those interests veered wildly, had Britain suddenly thrown obstacles in the venture's way, it would have virtually incapacitated the Americans. For example, Britain could have barred vessels associated with the enterprise from docking at Freetown (an unlikely proposition given where the two nations stood in 1823, but it is worth remembering that only eight years earlier, the United States and England had been at war). In other words, stout British opposition would have profoundly affected the Americans' enterprise and might have thwarted their undertaking altogether.[18]

Liberia (which is what some in the settlement were now calling the place) was still limping along in mid-March 1823 when the USS *Cyane* sailed into Freetown, Sierra Leone. Now commanded by Captain Robert T. Spence, the ship had been on a Caribbean tour when it was dispatched to Africa. At Freetown, Spence found the *Augusta* in rough shape and heard that the Americans' situation at Cape Mesurado was rougher still. He consequently had the *Augusta* repaired, purchased supplies, and agreed to convey forty Kru (Indigenous migrant) workers to Mesurado with the expectation that they would labor on the Americans' defenses and then be transported in the *Augusta* farther south to Settra Kru. Two weeks later, in late March, the *Cyane* and *Augusta* touched at Liberia. Spence later wrote that he was certain that the local indigenous leaders harbored malevolent intentions and that they were biding their time, waiting for the right moment to crush the settlement. Spence reckoned that the moment might come within a month—once the rainy season commenced.[19]

This mindset convinced Spence that his timely arrival on the coast was providential. During Spence's stay at the cape, his signature accomplishment was overseeing the construction of a stone Martello tower, a substantial portion of which was finished within two weeks of the *Cyane*'s appearance at Liberia.

By then, however, Spence's crew was falling ill, exhibiting symptoms Spence associated with typhus and other diseases. The *Cyane* hastily left the cape in mid-April, only to drift amid the doldrums, alternately besieged by the sun's blazing equatorial heat and the Atlantic's bone-chilling dampness. Forty crew members perished by the time the vessel got to New York. His crew decimated and his ship quarantined, Spence was still sure that he had done the right thing, that his actions had probably saved the settlement. Little did Spence know that the Martello tower had collapsed soon after his departure from the cape. Although Spence overestimated his role in Liberia's creation, the navy certainly made critical contributions to the venture—there would have been no settlement if not for the tens of thousands of dollars' worth of provisions, trade goods, tools, and military wares that the navy supplied. (By contrast, the forty men that Spence lost, along with a handful of other U.S. seamen who had died assisting the Americans' African venture, were sacrificed without warrant, for in retrospect we can see that their deaths were hardly essential to Liberia's establishment.) In other words, the navy's contributions, and particularly the materiel it provided, were necessary for Liberia's founding. But they were not sufficient. Something more was needed.[20]

What the venture lacked the agents failed to supply. Over thirty-eight months had passed since the *Elizabeth*'s embarkation in February 1820, and during that span, there was no agent among the settlers for fifteen months. Even when one or more agents were present, they were often ill and sometimes inadvertently injurious to the enterprise. This does not mean that the agents lacked virtues or sacrificed nothing. Several died and those who survived suffered. For example, Jehudi Ashmun, who was still the ACS's acting agent in Liberia in April 1823, had been wracked by illness during his nine months at the cape, afflictions made more painful by watching in a leaky hut the tortured demise of his delirious, prostrate wife soon after their arrival at Mesurado. Nevertheless, even when Ashmun was physically and mentally able to fulfill his duties, he did nothing that was essential to the venture's success. His claim to fame was that he was the sole agent present when the Americans thwarted two Indigenous attacks in late 1822, and in his report to his superiors in Washington on the subject Ashmun gave himself a starring role in the settlement's defense. But victory on those occasions was a group effort, one that levied the ultimate price for several settlers. Perhaps it was fitting that when Spence departed Cape Mesurado in April 1823, Ashmun also briefly took leave of the place, sailing to Settra Kru with the Kru laborers, his absence an apt symbol of the modest contributions that the agents made to Liberia's establishment.[21]

Ashmun returned to Liberia a few weeks later, and soon thereafter, in late May 1823, the *Oswego* arrived at the cape. On board were sixty-five settlers and Eli Ayres, the man who had contracted for land at Cape Mesurado in December 1821 and subsequently helped superintend the settlers there, only to quit Africa immediately thereafter. While in America, Ayres had learned that he had been appointed the U.S. agent for recaptured Africans. Over the next nine months, he had counseled navy officials and ACS leaders about the African enterprise and oversaw preparations for the embarkation of the *Oswego* from Baltimore. Ayres being Ayres, with less than a week before the *Oswego*'s departure, he had doubted whether he would actually oversee the overseas journey. As historian Charles Huberich bluntly remarked, "indecision and lack of personal courage were prominent traits in Ayres' character." Those qualities, when combined with his opposition to settler autonomy, made Ayres an unwelcome sight among the *Elizabeth* and *Nautilus* survivors who recalled their previous experiences with him. Nor did Ayres bring Ashmun much relief, for the former bore unfortunate news. The ACS managers had questioned some of Ashmun's purchases (as had U.S. officials). It had refused to pay him for his previous services as acting agent. And, last, it had left his future compensation up to Ayres. Already prone to feeling underappreciated, Ashmun was doubly pained knowing that more than wounded feelings were at stake. Harried by indebtedness, Ashmun regarded being recompensed an urgent matter.[22]

As Ashmun watched Ayres and the *Oswego* settlers disembark, he no doubt would have been joined by others, including Lott Cary. The same Lott Cary who had run afoul of Ayres in December 1821 by proposing the creation of the American African Union Society; who had convinced his fellow settlers to occupy land at Cape Mesurado at the earliest possible moment when Ayres had counseled delay; who had established the first church in the settlement; who had tirelessly cared for the injured and ill after the Indigenous attacks in late 1822. The same Cary whom Ayres judged a nemesis.[23]

As the *Oswego* newcomers came ashore, Cary would have spotted a man with whom he had much in common. Like the forty-three-year-old Cary, twenty-eight-year-old Colston Waring was a well-respected minister from a Virginia port town—in Waring's case, Petersburg. A handful of settlers had previously lived in Petersburg, and if Waring reported favorably on the settlement, many more—hundreds, perhaps—of that city's Black residents were

expected to cast their lot with Liberia. Surveying his new surroundings, Waring liked what he saw.[24]

Also coming ashore was another man with whom Cary shared some qualities (even if he might have been reluctant to admit it). Twenty-one-year-old
Augustus Curtis was, like Waring, from Petersburg. While most of Petersburg's Black townsfolk had decided to wait for the report of the esteemed
Waring, Curtis had seized the initiative and set sail for Liberia with his
nineteen-year-old wife. Curtis, in other words, was not averse to risk or work,
just like the daring and indefatigable Cary. What differentiated the two men,
besides Curtis being half Cary's age, was their commitment to Liberia, for
Cary regarded it as a veritable homeland while Curtis saw it as one spot on a
larger canvas of opportunity.[25]

That spot was still modestly sized in the summer of 1823. In July, a small
trading packet, the *Fidelity*, arrived at Cape Mesurado with some supplies but
only five new settlers. All totaled, 221 Black Americans had moved to Africa
and a few more had been born since their arrival there, yet due to high rates
of mortality and out-migration, the settlement's population numbered just
122 souls. Most were familiar with port life—they largely hailed from New
York, Philadelphia, Richmond, and especially Petersburg (the former residence
of nearly one-quarter of Liberia's inhabitants in July 1823). Those 122 had
endured a great deal. The settlers' tribulations, thought Ashmun, had en-
deared their new home to them. "Harmony and a good degree of industry at
present prevail," he observed.[26]

Rebels

Ashmun's optimistic assessment was soon tested, as quarrels between the
agents and settlers grew more heated during the summer of 1823. Part of the
problem was that the relationship between the ACS and the settlers had always been murky and contentious. Initially, ACS leaders had put little thought
into the matter. Prior to the embarkation of the *Elizabeth* in 1820, they had
simply assumed that the settlers would dutifully obey the regulations established by the organization's board of managers and agents. But as specific disputes arose, the agents tended to improvise solutions, as was the case when
they produced the *Elizabeth* Compact, a now-lost document that created myriad government positions for the settlers but kept ultimate power in the so-

ciety's hands. Thereafter, the board of managers had issued the Constitution of 1820 and required all adult male settlers to affirm it. The document kept ACS officials nominally in control of the enterprise, but also guaranteed settlers "all such rights and privileges as are enjoyed by the citizens of the United States." Then there was Cary's and others' unsuccessful December 1821 proposal to create the American African Union Society. Interspersed throughout these episodes were periods in which the ACS agency had been temporarily placed in a settler's hands. (In addition to Daniel Coker's aforementioned stint as agent in 1820–21 following the *Elizabeth* debacle, Ayres, when he abandoned the settlement in the summer of 1822, designated as his successor settler Elijah Johnson.) As for the U.S. government, which was funding most of the project under the guise of combating the Atlantic slave trade, the Monroe administration continued to disavow any connection with colonization and contended that the Black Americans associated with the venture were merely laborers tasked with erecting a station in Africa to which recaptives could be sent. The modicum of stability that had been achieved in Liberia by mid-1823 did little to diminish, and may have intensified, the long-running power struggles between and among the agents and settlers.[27]

Disputes over the settlers' landholdings soon bedeviled the enterprise. Recall that when the Americans were still stuck at Fourah Bay in May 1821, they had drawn lots for their prospective settlement (which, at the time, they probably envisioned being at Grand Bassa). The ACS managers subsequently nixed the Grand Bassa deal, but Ayres and Stockton inked the Mesurado contract in December 1821. A few weeks later, the Americans began moving to the insalubrious island in the bay, but Ayres reported that "the land not being divided so that each one could work his own land, I found great difficulty in stimulating them to exertion." After the Americans relocated to the cape in April 1822, they had toiled tirelessly, but the Indigenous attacks later that year undid much of the progress they had made. Indeed, when Ayres had come ashore in mid-1823, he remarked that "not so much as a hill of beans" was growing in the colony. That was the situation in August 1823—provisions were dwindling and the rainy season had made farming impossible—when Ayres decreed that all previous land allotments were void. The *Elizabeth* and *Nautilus* settlers, along with some from the *Strong*, objected, becoming, in Ayres's words, "very turbulent." When ACS officials later investigated the matter, they decried the Black protesters, but they also found fault with Ashmun, remarking that he had erred in going unarmed and that he should have summarily fined, imprisoned, and even whipped those guilty of insolence, "contempt," and "abusive language."[28]

In truth, Ashmun was in no position to quash settler dissent. With his previous financial transactions in Africa still under scrutiny, Ashmun did not have the full confidence of the ACS managers or federal officials. Thus situated, Ashmun spent much of the late summer and early fall of 1823 reading books and berating himself for his spiritual shortcomings. As for his relationships with others, and particularly the settlers, Ashmun was not devoid of decency, but even his sympathizers described him as irritable and captious, especially when dealing with those he deemed inferior yet smug. "Ignorance," wrote Ashmun at the time, when accompanied with "swaggering pretensions either to knowledge or respect . . . merits equal share of the profoundest contempt and detestation." It is not hard to imagine that when Ashmun penned those words, he had certain settlers in mind.[29]

Discontent simmered through the autumn of 1823 as provisions ran lower still. The return of the *Fidelity* in November heightened tensions. The settlers, anxious to increase the number of laborers among them, resented the fact that the ten recaptives on board the ship were returned to their actual homes, which happened to be near Cape Mesurado. As for desperately needed supplies, the *Fidelity* brought a mere one hundred dollars' worth of goods to Cape Mesurado. Moreover, Ayres, who had abandoned the settlement once before, announced that he would be going back to America aboard the *Fidelity*. With some of Liberia's inhabitants questioning the ACS's commitment to the African enterprise, one of their number—most likely Lott Cary—proclaimed, according to one ACS official, "that he and his associates would not submit to Government twenty-four hours after the departure of the Fidelity."[30]

The protesters also drew up a "remonstrance" that enumerated their grievances. The document attests to the discontented settlers' legal acumen (for they enjoyed the right of petition under the 1820 constitution) and political savvy (for they understood that they could go over the agents' heads by appealing directly to the board of managers). Unsurprisingly, the first item on their list was the way lands had been distributed. They also maintained that orphans and widows ought to have a claim on the lands to which their deceased fathers and husbands were entitled. Regarding the improvement of landholdings, the petitioners maintained that, given their circumstances, it was unreasonable for the ACS to expect that they could clear two acres of land and erect a permanent dwelling in just two years. They further decried nearly all the agents that had been sent out. Finally, they were apprehensive that the society was on the verge of abandoning them. If the managers did not provide satisfactory answers, the petitioners averred they would leave Liberia.[31]

As the day of the *Fidelity*'s embarkation approached, Ayres issued his harshest proclamation yet. He decreed that if the settlers who had signed the remonstrance failed to cultivate their lands while the managers considered their case, they would be expelled from the settlement. (Interestingly, the agents and petitioners used the same threat if their demands were not met— that is, removal from the community.) Ayres further declared that all rations would cease in six months, except in cases of special necessity. In response, once the *Fidelity* set sail, Lott Cary and others, in the words of one ACS official, "cast off the restraints of authority" and attempted to "seduce others from obedience."[32]

Tensions escalated quickly. Cary and his cohorts refused to labor on public projects, and they vowed that they would leave the lands that had been assigned to them uncultivated until the managers had replied to their remonstrance. Ashmun warned that those who defied his authority would not receive provisions from the public store "till they earn them." The protesters remained unbowed. If anything, an ACS official later reflected, Ashmun's intractability prompted "the expression of more seditious sentiments and a bolder violation of the laws." Nevertheless, Ashmun refused to back down. Two weeks after the *Fidelity*'s departure, he made good on his threat, announcing that the "offending persons" would no longer receive rations. The next day, the same settlers gathered at Ashmun's house and attempted "by angry denunciations" to drive him "from his purpose." When Ashmun refused to reconsider the matter, they proceeded to the storehouse, where another settler, acting as commissary, was issuing the week's rations. The protesters seized "each a portion of the provisions" and "hastened to their respective homes." From Ashmun's perspective, the settlement verged on "rebellion."[33]

The appearance of the *Cyrus*, the venture's fifth vessel, in February 1824 meant that over one hundred new settlers—the enterprise's largest party yet— would be added to the fraught situation at Cape Mesurado. All of those on board were Virginians, including scores from Petersburg. Among them was Colston Waring, the minister who had scouted Liberia the year before and delivered a positive report upon his return to Virginia. Waring was now joined by his wife, Harriet, who as a young bride had reluctantly followed Waring from Norfolk to Petersburg and who had assented to another unhappy pilgrimage in moving with him to Liberia. In Harriet's care were her six children, who the twenty-eight year-old had borne in twelve years of marriage. Africa welcomed the Waring family as it did many newcomers from America, quickly killing two sons, ages five and one. Ten other children who migrated aboard the *Cyrus* also soon died, as did three adults who had journeyed with them. Lott Cary had frantically tended to those who were lost as well as the dozens of *Cyrus* settlers who clung to life. He also cared for Ashmun, who had once again been laid low and who later admitted that he would have perished if not for Cary's tireless ministrations.[34]

Cary did this even as the settlement trembled with material uncertainty. When Ayres had departed the previous December, stores were running low. The *Cyrus* had likely brought provisions to Liberia, but how many is unclear. In any case, the *Cyrus* party had hardly come to a land of milk and honey. That was one thing they shared with their predecessors. But in some respects, their experiences in Africa were distinctive and momentous. Even with the demise of fifteen of their number, the party increased Liberia's settler population by seventy percent. That influx occurred only two months before the start of the rainy season, at a time of unpredictable food supplies, and when there festered unresolved disputes over the distribution of lands and other issues. (The *Cyrus* had embarked before the ACS managers had even learned about the "rebellion" and remonstrance, much less formulated and sent a response.)

Those simmering disagreements boiled over within three weeks of the *Cyrus*'s arrival at Liberia. On March 15, 1824, Ashmun declared that settlers henceforth would receive only half-rations. Even with such parsimony, he added, supplies would last no more than five weeks. In response, some settlers were said to have "violently reproached the Agent in his presence." A few days later, Ashmun, lamenting that he could do no more than establish a "provisional Government" and insisting that he would not serve as agent "without the power to carry into effect a system of industry and other measures of vital importance," declared that he would be leaving Liberia. Given the condition of the settlement and his state of health, whether he would ever return was "a matter of much uncertainty." On April 1, 1824, he boarded the *Reporter* and set sail for America a worn and dispirited man.[35]

As fate would have it, during a stop at the Cape Verde Islands, Ashmun was stunned to see the ACS's secretary, twenty-seven-year-old Ralph Gurley, step ashore. Gurley, who had been commissioned by the society and the

U.S. government to examine the situation at Cape Mesurado and who carried with him the ACS managers' response to the settlers' "rebellion" and remonstrance, convinced Ashmun to return to Liberia, so that what they perceived to be a tottering settlement could be righted. Gurley and Ashmun did not arrive at the cape until early August. What transpired there while Ashmun was away is a mystery. When Ashmun had left the previous April, the settlers were said to be on the brink of starvation and the rainy season was about to start. Yet here they were four months later, toiling on. Few things better reflect the underappreciated importance of the settlers' efforts in establishing Liberia than the veil that hides what happened at the cape during Ashmun's absence in the perilous summer of 1824.[36]

The ACS managers had formulated their reply to the settlers' "rebellion" and remonstrance the previous March. From the managers' perspective, the discord's timing could not have been worse. The aborted slave uprising that Denmark Vesey had planned in South Carolina in 1822 and the actual insurrection that arose in Demerara in 1823 had left many white Americans on edge about Black violence. The "lawlessness" of some settlers and unwillingness of others to stop the "continuous riots," warned the ACS managers, would tank the African enterprise. "This is the very conduct repeatedly predicted by our opponents," they proclaimed. If the "riotous proceedings" continued, "the Colony must be broken up." Making this bleak vision all the more gloomy was the fact that the managers had thought that Liberia stood at the threshold of a brilliant future, for they had been planning on asking the federal government for additional aid. One leading colonizationist even hoped that Congress would "form a Government" for Liberia, explaining, "I do not wish to see in Africa a colonial government, permanently attached to the United States. I do not wish for the colonies to be held for use and made subservient: but I wish to see the paternal arm of authority stretched out for the protection of this colony, until it shall be able to manage its own affairs." The settlers' actions, inveighed the managers, had made even broaching the subject of federal assistance risky. Order, they insisted, had to be established. That meant the settlers had to recognize that the ACS could govern Liberia as it saw fit.[37]

Within that framework, however, there was room for compromise. To be sure, the ACS managers would not budge on some issues. For example, they backed Ayres regarding the dispute over land allotments. But otherwise, the managers tended to accommodate the settlers. In fact, when Gurley left the cape two weeks after his arrival, he had in his hands a new constitution for the settlement, one that gave the head agent the final say on nearly all public matters, but nevertheless granted the settlers exceptional opportunities to exercise political rights and to run Liberia's day-to-day affairs. The vice-agent, for instance, would be selected by the head agent from among settlers who had been nominated by their peers. In short, the 1824 constitution accorded the settlers rights that were routinely denied to people of color throughout the Atlantic world.[38]

As if to illustrate the point, Ashmun fell so ill after Gurley's departure that the newly elected vice-agent, Colston Waring, officially assumed Ashmun's responsibilities. Ashmun soon recovered, but four years later, in March 1828, he was once again so sick that he decided to leave Cape Mesurado for good. Upon his departure, vice-agent Lott Cary assumed Liberia's top spot, the onetime provocateur now cloaked, at least temporarily, with agency's considerable powers. Ashmun, it turned out, died on the voyage to the United States. Cary likewise was not long for this world. He perished the following November while inside an ammunition storehouse, preparing for an imminent attack on Indigenous slave traders. In a story rife with fitting symbolism, Cary's death topped them all, for this dynamic, unrelenting, and visionary figure left the settlement as he lived in it—explosively.[39]

By the time of Cary's demise in 1828, Liberia's roots had grown deeper and spread wider. It boasted a population of 638 distributed over several towns, plus a promising commercial economy. U.S. president Andrew Jackson, who had been elected the same month that Cary died, tried to pull the plug on the federal government's de facto subsidizing of the venture, but it was too late. Liberia was here to stay. The ACS managers picked white men to be their agents in Africa until 1841, when they appointed settler Joseph Jenkins Roberts, a free Black man from Petersburg who in 1829 had emigrated to Liberia at the age of twenty-one and whose family subsequently became entwined with those of Waring and others of comparable backgrounds. Soon after Roberts's appointment as governor, the United States and Britain signed the Webster-Ashburton Treaty, an agreement that led to the creation of the U.S. Navy's first-ever "African Squadron." An increased U.S. naval presence along the African coast was welcome news to Liberia's residents, who in 1843 numbered nearly 2,400 and who were divvied up among nine settlements, many of which were along the coast.[40]

These coastal enclaves were the sites of a brisk trading business, much to the benefit of commercially oriented figures like Roberts, who dominated Liberia even though manumittees—who had made up less than 1 percent of Liberia's population when the 1824 constitution was adopted—now, in 1843, constituted a substantial portion of its residents. Unlike Liberia's urbane traders, the manumittees tended to be tillers of the soil and hewers of wood, though some found niche work in Liberia's mercantile entrepots, and women, in particular, could come by employment opportunities in such an economy—as laundresses or seamstresses, for example, or, in Harriet Waring's case, as a milliner. The problem was that Britain balked at paying Liberia's commercial duties, insisting that those that were levied were illegitimate because Liberia was not a nation. Ever since the 1824 constitution's adoption, the settlers had been exacting more political power from the ACS managers, so a declaration of national independence on the former's part would have fit a larger evolutionary pattern. However, Liberia's ascent to official nationhood was not frictionless. White ACS leaders approached the matter with their characteristic imperiousness, while the settlers—or at least the merchant elite who dominated Liberian politics—were determined to imprint their own interpretation on this historic moment. In 1847, Liberia declared its independence, the second Black republic in a world suffused with Black bondage and white supremacy.[41]

Liberia's role in U.S. imperial history is thus emblematic and distinctive. Initiated when some white Americans hoped the United States would evolve into a racially segregated, federative empire, Liberia developed as one might expect: most African Americans refused to emigrate there and those that did sought self-determination. Eventually, in 1847, the settlers declared their national independence, but by then the federative imperial ideology that originally countenanced the enterprise was no longer prevalent. Consequently, the United States never replicated the project's unique model.

Even so, the Liberian enterprise was also influential, for subsequent U.S. ventures abroad bore the hallmarks of the Liberian experience. For starters, some of the people who had been involved in Liberia's creation were principal figures in later expansionist enterprises. Naval commanders Robert Stockton and Matthew Perry, for example, brought the lessons they had learned in West Africa to California and Japan, respectively. Moreover, as it had with Liberia, in the coming decades the United States poured resources into foreign locales with the expectation of achieving national goals while not explicitly claiming authority in those places. Likewise, the United States' relationship with post-independence Liberia, in which the former voiced support for the latter but stubbornly refused to grant it diplomatic recognition,

foreshadowed future instances in which Americans' affinity for republicanism elsewhere was undercut by its own racist practices at home and abroad.
Added to these legacies is another, arguably the most important one: Liberia's continued existence. None of this may have come to pass had not the
settlers, agents, and other parties arrived at a mutually agreeable definition
of Black freedom in the aftermath of the 1823–24 "rebellion."[42]

CHAPTER 9

Freedom in Chains

U.S. Empire and the Illegal Slave Trade

M. SCOTT HEERMAN

Charles Thomas spent the first part of 1857 working in the plantation districts of east Texas and suffering under the lash of his enslaver, like millions of other enslaved people in the Deep South. With planting season underway, the rituals of brutality had intensified, as owners and overseers across the cotton South sought to extort ever more labor out of their enslaved workers and reap ever more profit from the soil. It was May 1857 in Galveston, Texas, when Charles Thomas, "a young lad of colour," was "publickly whipped," and his enslaver then proceeded to "offer him for sale as a slave."[1] The season started like many others. Spectacles of violence were a key ingredient in the alchemy that would turn the blood of enslaved workers into fuel for the U.S. economy. Cases like these, that foreground violence in plantation economies, are a bedrock of the history of U.S. slavery and U.S. expansion. For years, scholars have pointed to these sorts of episodes in explaining the birth of a "slave empire" whereby "slave labor camps" metastasized across the U.S. South, forming one of the most profitable plantation sectors of the Americas.[2]

The spread of the plantation complex was an engine of U.S. empire, and it worked alongside an international set of slaving strategies that included the ongoing sale of captives from Africa and the Caribbean into mainland North America.[3] In fact, Thomas's case can help recast the story of slavery and U.S. expansion in the nineteenth century to include international dimensions. Like many of the enslaved people in the Deep South, Thomas had been trafficked into the region. Yet unlike most people working plantations, Thomas was not born in the United States and was not born into slavery. Rather, he was "native of the Island of St. Thomas" but could claim British subjecthood through his parents. He was born free, after British general emancipation during the 1830s, and was kidnapped into bondage. During the 1850s he "formed one of the crew of the American schooner 'Velasco'" and worked on voyages out of Port of Spain, Trinidad. He made landings in Pensacola and Galveston, and while in Texas he went ashore, and soon found himself destitute. Out of desperation he became an indentured servant for life, but soon his enslaver "exercised control over him as a master of a slave."[4] After his whipping, Thomas decided to act. He managed to track down the British consul in Galveston, where he applied for his freedom; the consul in turn filed a writ of habeas corpus to seek Thomas's emancipation. By the time his case concluded in late summer 1857, Texas's attorney general and governor would both become involved, and Thomas would again live in freedom.[5] This was only the latest instance where British subjects had been kidnapped into Texas. Looking back over these experiences in bondage reveals a connection between coerced international migration and U.S. imperial expansion that long predated Thomas's imprisonment.

The politics of slave trade suppression, the kidnapping of free people, and the creation of a U.S. slave empire all converged on Texas. The region had long been a landing site for the slave trade in North America, and for most of the first half of the nineteenth century British officials had worked to arrest the illegal sale of captives. Against this backdrop, a series of kidnappings in the 1830s and 1840s that brought free British subjects from the Caribbean, especially Barbados, into Texas alarmed officials at the highest level of the British government.[6] These cases in part provided a context for the conflicting British, U.S., and Mexican interests surrounding slavery's expansion to Texas, conflicts that in 1846 erupted into war. After Texas's annexation to the United States in 1845, and the war's end in 1848, the western march of the cotton complex continued seemingly uninterrupted. Situating the politics of Texas's annexation within a history of the slave trade reveals how the international trade in slaves supported U.S. imperial ambitions, and it can help move discussions of the U.S. slave empire beyond a focus on the plantation complex and the domestic slave trade to incorporate an international slave trade into the history of U.S. empire.[7] Rather than casting the politics over the U.S. slave empire in strictly national and sectional terms, incorporating the slave trade into the history of U.S. empire reveals how U.S. expansion was tied up with an interimperial politics of slavery and abolition in the Americas.

The slave trade to Texas exhibited many of the defining features of borderlands history where conflicting national and imperial interests jockeyed for power, often without resolution. While Texas had been a borderland for centuries, during the nineteenth century it took on new dimensions. The rise of free trade doctrines in the early nineteenth century enabled mariners and traders to cross in and out of a dizzying array of jurisdictions. Whereas eighteenth-century traders had to confront imperial borders and mercantilism, by the early nineteenth century, it would not be uncommon for a French vessel to move between British and Spanish colonies, only to stop in Danish ports along the way, before heading on to the United States. East Texas was a prime landing site for this trade. Controlling this promiscuous commerce was beyond any one empire's capacity for governance. Instead, the attempt to control the movement of people into Texas set the stage for conflict between various Indigenous nations and European empires within the wider conflict over slavery and the slave trade in the Atlantic world. While historians of the empires in North America during the eighteenth century have long talked about the importance of imperial competition, intercultural relations, and shifting identities, those factors have not had the same level of influence on scholars of nineteenth-century U.S. expansion into the Deep South.[8] Yet by foregrounding the imperial politics of the slave trade to Texas, a long history of imperial contestation, and of contests over drawing and crossing imperial boundaries, comes into focus as a key feature of the U.S. slave empire.

In several critical ways the slave trade of the nineteenth century played an important role in U.S. expansion and can help shed light on U.S. repertoires of empire.[9] First, in the nineteenth century, various empires helped erect a regime of slave trade abolition, but it scarcely worked. As a result, U.S. officials clashed with British and Spanish agents over who had the authority to stop and search suspected slavers on the high seas. Second, slave trade suppression was a key site of Atlantic politics. The migration of people across jurisdictions propelled imperial interests. Notably, ports of entry for illegal slavers—namely, Texas and northern Florida—were sites of U.S. imperial ambition. As slavers arrived on the margins of nominal U.S. boundaries and then crossed into U.S. territory to sell African captives, they helped U.S. planters gain a foothold in new parts of North America. Third, and combining the previous two forces, cases of kidnapping across jurisdictional boundaries raised profound questions about the sovereignty of empires over subjects. As imperial officials sought to regulate the movement of people, police the high seas for slavers, and protect their subjects from captivity, they began to set out what it meant to belong to an empire and what protections might be part of that subjecthood. After exploring these three key areas in turn, a case study in Texas will reveal the deep and lasting ties between the slave trade, kidnapping, and the contours of the U.S. empire in this period.

Abolition and the Reinvention of the Slave Trade

The era of slave trade abolition hardly looked like it. In the first half of the nineteenth century, economic forces encouraged a growing slave trade, and no effective police force existed. A variety of factors drove that increase, chiefly new business practices and new sailing technologies that made the trade astonishingly lucrative, as well the creation of new plantation economies in Cuba, Brazil, and the Deep South.[10] These changes collapsed both the time and distance between West Africa and New World plantations. Free trade policies also helped contribute to the rise of the slave trade by enabling ships of foreign flags to trade and travel around the Atlantic world. With vessels moving in and out of British, French, and Spanish colonies, the movement of people became ever more difficult to police. The aggregate data confirms what was known at the time: "the number carried into slavery" in the nineteenth century "so greatly increased" in part because of, as another report noted, "the enhanced price of the victims."[11] As one report on the trade put it, "the trade appears to be lucrative in proportion to its heinousness."[12]

This was all despite a long-running and well-organized campaign to abolish the slave trade. During the Age of Revolutions (1776–1804) the movement to abolish slavery and the slave trade matured into a robust, coordinated campaign. Around the Atlantic basin, a diverse constituency of activists sought to end slavery *and* to put an end to the coerced sale and trafficking of African captives, and the two campaigns were intertwined from the beginning.[13] However, the decade after U.S. independence saw an increase in the slave trade, with the 1790s standing out as one of the most prolific decades on record up to that point in the wider Atlantic world, and the early nineteenth century seeing a spike of importations into the United States. Within this context, abolitionists across the United States and Great Britain denounced the slave trade as legalized kidnapping, and they saw their efforts to suppress the slave trade as part of their wider antislavery agenda. While a full ban on the international slave trade was not possible in the United States before 1808, owing to a provision of the U.S. Constitution, other laws could curtail U.S. involvement in the slave trade. Congress took its first steps in 1794, when it outlawed the use of U.S. ports and shipyards for building or outfitting slave vessels. Legislators built on this act in 1800 when they banned U.S. citizens from participating in the slave trade, and U.S. sailors could be punished with hefty fines for violating this provision. Both of these laws offered substantial rewards to crew members and informants, thereby creating an incentive to turn in illegal slavers. Legislators in Congress debated imposing a tax on enslaved people, but failed to enact the measure, which would have cut into the profitability of the slave trade in these key years.[14] Still, antislavery activists looked at these laws as part of a "long antecedent" to total prohibition on the slave trade, a period when "congress legislated on the subject wherever its power extended, and endeavoured, by a system of rigorous penalties, to suppress this unnatural trade."[15]

Despite key legal victories for abolitionists, attempts to curtail U.S. involvement in the slave trade had a negligible effect in the wider Atlantic. Captains and owners of vessels could easily disguise the origin of their ships by creating false papers and manifests, clouding the nature of their commerce. Take, for instance, the 1805 case of the *Eliza*. While on a voyage to the British colony of Antigua, the crew off-loaded goods and took on board six enslaved children, who had "beads on their waists" and "did not speak english," suggesting they were African captives only recently landed in the British colony.[16] From there, the *Eliza* carried the children to Havana to be sold. The ship was captured and a trial ensued. When members of the Pennsylvania Abolition Society learned of this, they supported the case by gathering evidence, indicating how slave trade abolition was a key objective for this group of antislavery activists. But the trial went nowhere. The ship captain claimed the *Eliza* had French owners, the identity of the six children never came into focus, and there was never sufficient evidence to prove U.S. citizens violated the slave trade acts. It would seem the children lived out their days as slaves in Spanish Cuba. In countless other cases, ship owners created the pretense that their ship flew under a foreign flag in order to dodge U.S. laws. The early nineteenth century saw an "internationalization" of the slave trade that allowed slavers to evade detection, revealed the patchwork nature of slave trade abolition, and induced activists to push for more broad-scale victories.[17]

The movement to end the slave trade was, of course, also international, and in time a new Atlantic order emerged that outlawed slaving. While U.S. abolitionists lobbied Congress, British antislavery activists waged an unprecedented campaign against the slave trade. Over decades, a handful of devoted abolitionists won broad-scale acceptance for slave trade abolition, and by 1808 Parliament conceded to their pressure, banning the slave trade in the British empire.[18] At the same time, the U.S. Congress also outlawed the slave trade in absolute terms. British officials looked at these laws as merely first steps in an international campaign to stamp out the trade. By the 1810s, British officials had succeeded in pressuring other European powers into adopting an abolitionist policy, in part because the increasingly powerful British naval empire wrenched concessions from other powers. In 1815, at the Congress of Vienna that ended the Napoleonic Wars, the British delegation secured a statement from seven other European states that the slave trade was "repugnant to the principles of humanity and universal morality."[19]

As the legal landscape changed, so did the mechanics of the slave trade. Traders changed their business and relied on new tactics, which in time blunted the force of the new regulations.[20] Faster ships with larger holds, new methods of procuring and packing human cargo, surging demand, and declining costs of working the trade all reinvented this age-old business.[21] Whereas the slave trade in the eighteenth century had been a risky financial venture, by the nineteenth century the trade in human captives delivered more regular, high profits. Key technological changes facilitated this new reality. By the 1810s, faster ships, mostly built in Baltimore, came to dominate the trade, and they reduced the time of a slave voyage from a few months in the late eighteenth century to several weeks in the early nineteenth. New methods of loading, shipping, and selling captives also padded the bottom line. To facilitate faster loading, African captives were crammed into prisons on the small islands just off the African coast. Rather than slave vessels having to dock and ferry people from slave fortresses inland, Africans could be packed in quickly, drastically reducing the amount of time that ships spent docked on the West African coast, limiting the chances of detection. The ships also tended to have larger cargo holds, and traders increasingly turned to tight packing, which increased the number of enslaved people carried per voyage. As one observer in London noted, "the slave ships are now crowded to excess, and the mortality is dreadful."[22] Official reports in the British Foreign Office noted the commission of ever larger, ever faster ships, such as the

Venus, described as "one of the fastest sailing vessels ever built, and to be capable of carrying the enormous cargo of 1100 slaves."[23]

New business practices and sailing technologies helped to make the slave trade anew, and the booming plantation economies growing coffee, sugar, and cotton injected fresh capital into the trade. In Cuba and Puerto Rico, a new sugar economy took off and swallowed up bound workers as it ascended. Coffee and tobacco revolutions followed in Cuba's eastern districts in the middle of the nineteenth century. In Brazil sugar plantations modernized, the mining industry saw a second wave of production, and coffee plantations rapidly expanded. To thrive in all of these sectors, planters sought out fresh sources of enslaved labor, importing over a million captives into Brazil during the nineteenth century. In the United States, a cotton economy transformed the continent, bringing a modern, capital-intensive, and highly productive plantation economy to mainland North America.[24] Simultaneously, the goods needed to sustain the slave trade—from cowrie shells and cloth to trade in West Africa, irons and chains to shackle captives, and the meager provisions needed to keep those captives alive, if only just barely— became easier to acquire and at a lower coast. As one report concluded, "every article assorted for the Slave trade is now cheap."[25] In short, global economic trends, a reorganization of business practices, and faster sailing technologies made the nineteenth-century slave trade radically different from what had come before, which translated to steady, high profits. As one observer who had spent years working to suppress the slave trade noted, "the profits of the trade are certain and enormous."[26]

Limited resources and logistical obstacles, together with the circumscribed nature of the laws on the books, all conspired to prevent the effective arrest of suspected slavers. The shortcomings of U.S. law soon became apparent to almost any observer as a dispute over a suspected slaver made its way up the U.S. legal system, before eventually reaching the U.S. Supreme Court. The *Mary Ann* had an atypical itinerary for slavers in this period. Rather than transporting human captives from West Africa or the Caribbean, it departed with slaves from within U.S. soil. In 1818 it carried thirty-six captives to New Orleans, intending to sell them as slaves. It embarked from New Jersey with people who could not be legally transported out of the state or sold as slaves, as they were protected by the terms of the state's gradual emancipation law. Upon landing in Louisiana, the vessel was impounded, and proceedings began to confiscate the ship for violating slave trade suppression

laws. It might have seemed like a straightforward trial for an obviously illegal act, and at the local court the prosecutors won their case. Upon appeal,
however, the case became more complicated. Writing in 1823, Chief Justice
John Marshall found on a technicality that the *Mary Ann* could not be confiscated, due to specifics of how the ship's manifest was registered in compliance with the law. Moreover, the anti–slave trade statutes stipulated that only
vessels over forty tons could be forfeited for participating in the slave trade,
and the lower court had not established that the *Mary Ann* met that crite-
rion. On both questions, then, the chief justice reversed the lower court conviction on these narrow technicalities, despite his belief that the ship's captain
and crew had violated the anti–slave trade laws.[27] The decision underscored
the many loopholes enslavers could exploit and the difficulty in punishing
illegal slave traders.

The *Mary Ann* was a key test case of U.S. slave trade laws, but in the five
years between when the *Mary Ann* set sail and the Supreme Court ruled on
the case, the legal landscape changed significantly. Recognizing that the laws
outlawing the slave trade scarcely had their intended effect, various constit-
uencies in the United States mobilized to enact stricter legislation. Between
1818 and 1820, Congress passed laws that created a new system intended to
put an end to the slave trade. First, and most dramatically, it defined the slave
trade as piracy and made participation in the slave trade a capital offense. As
one commentator applauded, "the detestable crime of kidnapping the unof-
fending inhabitants of one country, and chaining them to slavery in another,
is marked with all the atrociousness of piracy; and, as such, it is stigmatized
and punishable by our own laws."[28] Next, Congress empowered the president
to use the U.S. Navy to suppress the slave trade, creating what was known as
the "Africa Squadron." Additionally, Congress set up a series of provisions
to free illegally enslaved people and return them to Liberia, a U.S. outpost
for freed people established by the American Colonization Society. Last, the
laws also changed the burden of evidence needed to convict individuals accused of slave trading and seize the vessels, like the *Eliza* or the *Mary Ann*.
Whereas before prosecutors had to prove the case against charged individuals or impounded vessels, now agents of suspected slavers and crewmembers
needed to prove they were not engaged in the slave trade. Together this series of laws passed in successive years increased the police powers of the national government to recapture, liberate, and repatriate enslaved men and
women, while also imposing stiff penalties for slaving.[29]

The move toward more effective laws came at roughly the same time that the British erected a world-class slave trade suppression force. The British empire assembled yet more power during the 1820s, through a series of bilateral treaties between the British and the French, Dutch, Spanish, and Portuguese empires. British officials could stop and search all ships suspected of slaving, and any vessels found in violation of the slave trade laws would be taken before the Mixed Commission Courts. These courts existed in cities around the Atlantic world as a series of international tribunals that would issue rulings in cases over suspected slave traders and be tasked with freeing the captives on board.[30] Yet, one key objective evaded the British government: a slave trade suppression treaty with the United States. In 1824, a provisional Anglo-U.S. slave trade convention that would allow for a limited right of search came up for ratification in the U.S. Senate. However, the body added several amendments that excluded U.S. coasts from the scope of the convention, effectively scuttling the pact. Some senators argued that the Constitution would not allow U.S. citizens to stand trial before an international court, and they pointed out that the lack of U.S. colonies in the Americas would deprive the United States of hosting a tribunal on its soil. Negotiations over a right of search would continue into the 1860s, and the United States rested on its commitments to police the high seas for illegal slavers without British aid.[31] In theory a U.S. and British police force could work in tandem, but in practice the British presence far outstripped its counterpart and the U.S. flag protected slavers from British police forces. A mere handful of U.S. vessels, in the early period mostly revenue cutters and later a modest naval detachment, bore the full weight of stopping illegal slavers using the U.S. flag.[32] This was a daunting prospect. Additionally, U.S. commitment to suppressing the trade was tepid at best, given the nation's ongoing dedication to human bondage, and the role slaveholders played in shaping U.S. foreign policy blunted the force of these laws.[33]

With such glaring exceptions in place, Spanish or Portuguese slavers would raise the Stars and Stripes, relying on this act of deception to all but remove the threat of being intercepted during their voyages. Slave trade suppressionists worried that the United States would provide both fast-sailing ships and protection under its flag, leading to ever more captives in bondage. Officials monitoring the slave trade routinely reported on vessels that had "hoisted an American flag" upon arriving in West Africa, before loading Africans into their cargo holds. With such easy evasion available, it was clear to any observer that the slave trade showed no sign of stopping. As one report from the 1820s on the illegal slave trade noted, "experience has proved the inefficacy of the various and rigorous laws which have been made in Europe, and in this country; it being a lamentable fact, that the disgraceful practice is even now carried on to a surprising extent."[34]

Migration and Jurisdiction on Slavery's Frontier

The familiar connection between expanding slavery and expanding U.S. borders played out not only when plantations pushed onto fresh soil but also when the slave trade brought U.S. interests into borderland regions. In the early nineteenth century, the United States received comparably very few slaves from Africa relative to its peer slave societies in Cuba and Brazil. Still, slavers did sell in mainland North America.[35] From the 1810s to the 1830s, two of the major landing sites for the slave trade sat on the borders of the United States, in northern Florida and in east Texas. As slavers sold their human cargo in these two regions, the traffic allowed U.S. planters to exert power in territory beyond U.S. borders. This coerced movement of people to Texas and Florida in turn helped set the stage for U.S. expansion into those regions and the making of plantation societies on Native lands.

Northern Florida, notably Amelia Island, served as a key spot for the transatlantic slave trade in mainland North America. Situated on the Eastern Seaboard, the Florida coast was well suited to receive transatlantic voyages. Moreover, northern Florida was a borderland, with Spanish, Seminole, and U.S. interests vying for control.[36] Starting in 1812, and again in later decades, warfare marked the region as would-be U.S. invaders waged war against the Indigenous Creeks and Seminoles. As the U.S. Army sought to cement this land grab, the invaders also had to contend with the long-standing Spanish colonial interests in the region. In 1812, a group of men from Georgia began a rebellion against Spanish rule. Starting first on Amelia Island, they in time occupied a strip of the Florida panhandle and ratified a constitution to establish the Republic of East Florida. The breakaway republic lasted scarcely a year. Still, across the first decades of the nineteenth century, identities within and allegiance to empires remained fluid and contested, with Spanish and U.S. settlers making and breaking alliances with the Seminole and Creek Nations.[37]

In such a setting, it would be a challenge to enforce U.S. laws, let alone those as complex as anti–slave trade provisions. Sitting just beyond nominal U.S. borders, slavers could avoid U.S. jurisdiction by landing at Amelia Island and then transporting their hostages to nearby Savannah, Georgia. This system exploited a loophole in U.S. law: before the 1820s, when U.S. officials captured illegal slavers, the captive Africans would be turned over to the governor of the state they were in, as if they were any other cargo. The governor of Georgia, then, could elect to auction off any slaves illegally brought to the state, effectively sidestepping the prohibition on importing new slaves.[38] Even if slavers were caught taking captives into Georgia, U.S. planters would still benefit from the trade, and U.S. interests in this border region would only grow stronger. With an approving nod from Washington, D.C., slave traders landed captives beyond U.S. borders and brought them into Georgia, one way or another, feeding the growing cotton revolution and expanding U.S. influence into Florida, if only partially.

Slavers not landing on the Eastern Seaboard tended toward east Texas as their depot.[39] Like Amelia Island, Galveston sat on the immediate borders of the United States and offered easy access to the major port at New Orleans. The area was also a borderland where no one polity could entirely control the flow of trade, with the Caddoan, Mexican, and U.S. people all attempting to carve out a sphere of influence. East Texas had long sat at the intersection of rival imperial interests, and in the nineteenth century those pressures only intensified. Spain had long claimed the region, but with the seat of Spanish colonial power so far to the south in Mexico City, their sovereignty had always been aspirational. Instead, the region belonged, however tenuously, to the Caddo Nation, which in response to expansionist pressure from U.S. colonizers and Comanche raiders centered their homes around the Brazos River in this period. By the 1820s, U.S. planters added themselves to this mix of nations vying for control over the region.[40]

U.S. slaveholders could accomplish this expansionist goal and extend their reach beyond the nation's borders thanks in part to the trade in enslaved people. Most typically, slave traders would land their human cargo in east Texas and from there carry them on to New Orleans, building a tie between U.S. slave interests and the east Texas borderlands. As one contemporary study of the slave trade concluded, "most of the goods carried to Galveston are introduced into the United States . . . the slaves, are smuggled in through the numerous inlets to the westward, where the people are but too much disposed to render them every possible assistance." As another observer noted of ships commonly landing "off the Sabine River; it is reported that attempts will be made to smuggle slaves into Louisiana, from Galveston, and the natural presumption is that they will attempt the Sabine or the Atchafalya rivers."[41] From there they would continue on to U.S. planters. Writing about a typical situation for the 1810s, an observer whose letter was republished in the annual report of the American Colonization Society noted that "several hundred slaves are now at Galveston, and persons have gone from New-Orleans to purchase them. Every exertion will be made to intercept them, but I have little hopes of success."[42]

Into the 1830s, Texas remained a hot spot for what Richard Madden, the British superintendent for liberated Africans in Havana, called the "diabolical trade" in African captives. As Joseph Crawford, British vice-consul in Mexico, observed, ships flying under U.S. colors could land "to the eastward of the Sabine, from whence the slaves were passed into Texas." From there, "slaves may be taken into that country over the Frontier of the United States."[43] In the mid-1830s Madden could "confidently assert" that "there are now upwards of 20 American slavers gone to the Coast of Africa, the greater part of whose cargoes are . . . contracted for and insured to be landed in the Province of Texas."[44] Transatlantic voyages may have been common, but traders also brought slaves to Texas from the Caribbean. For instance, Madden reported on hearing of "an American schooner [that] left the Havana destined for Texas, having on board a cargo of forty negro slaves."[45]

Like the British agent, the U.S. consul in Havana, Nicholas Trist, confirmed that a sizable trade in African captives ran between Cuba and east Texas. Trist undertook an investigation of the illegal slave trade and reported back to Washington, D.C., about the mechanics of the trade. First, he confirmed the British observations by reporting that "a branch of the African slave trade is at this moment in active operation and rapidly increasing . . . by the transportation of blacks from this Island to Texas."[46] He reported that "this traffic is carried on under the mask of contracts of apprenticeship, whereby blacks bought here for the Texas market" were signed onto contracts for a number of years. However, "these contracts are mere forms," he explained, and "the negroes are intended to be held, and they will be held, in perpetual slavery." As for the laws of Mexico, or any other jurisdiction purporting to prohibit the slave trade, they are "of no more value than a piece of an old newspaper."[47] To be sure, other U.S. agents in Havana dismissed reports of a large trade to Texas as mere rumor and hyperbole.[48] Uncertainty hovered over the scale of the illicit trade, but more than one U.S. State Department official reported on and worked to suppress the ongoing trade, whatever its true scale. The expanding plantation complex in east Texas, which drew at least some new captives from abroad during the 1830s, became an issue in international affairs because the ongoing slave trade attracted the interest and ire of agents in more than one empire.

If some U.S. agents questioned the scope of the trade, very few British officials did. The slave trade to east Texas, no matter its size, made slavery's expansion a critical issue in the imperial politics of the United States and Britain. British naval officials in particular were convinced that "a considerable traffick in slaves . . . is carrying on between the Island of Cuba and Texas."[49] In one instance in 1840, the *Industria*, a Spanish schooner bound for Galveston, made landing at Black River, on the south coast of Jamaica, with enslaved people on board. The customhouse official at Black River who first investigated the *Industria* believed "that the slaves were intended for sale in the American market," an opinion confirmed by Jamaica's attorney general, who agreed "there is much probable ground to suppose that the Slaves on board . . . [the] vessel were meant for sale at Texas or New Orleans."[50] As a result, local officials seized the ship, had the crew imprisoned, and had the captives "declared free, and set at liberty, on the ground that these were the necessary consequences of their having been brought into a British Port."[51] After interviewing the crew and the enslaved people, it became clear that the captain had "received convict slaves from the French Governor of Martinique" and taken them to "Vieques, and there converting them with the apparent permission of the Governor into Spanish slaves."[52] After extensive investigation, the British officials, from customhouse inspectors to the colonial governor of Jamaica, agreed that "the affair altogether indicates the probability that a Slave Trade in small Shipments of this description is carried on from the Foreign Colonies in this Quarter to the Continent of America."[53]

Sovereignty and Subjecthood in the Slave Trade

The rise of a disjointed antislavery order, and the resurgence of a second slavery, pitted empires against each other, especially when slavers kidnapped British subjects. Kidnapping cases emerged within the wider context of slave trade suppression, as various imperial officials worked through questions of what it meant to belong to an empire—questions of sovereignty, citizenship, and subjecthood. Slave trade suppression connected to the sovereignty of empires in several key ways, from defining the slave trade as a crime and creating international jurisdictions with the Mixed Commission Courts to regulating the movement of people across boundaries and creating a force to stop and search ships on the high seas. Kidnapping cases added yet more dimensions to these debates when cabinet officials, consuls, and statesmen tried to punish kidnappers and attempted to repatriate their subjects. No rights of repatriation, to return to a native land, existed, and imperial officials could not exercise control over citizens beyond their borders. As officeholders in the British empire looked for ways to return kidnapped subjects, they began to articulate what rights were fundamental to belonging in an empire and to search for avenues to exert power in realms beyond their borders.

Other kinds of captivity, including enslavement in the corsair states as well as naval impressment in the Atlantic world, also connected sovereignty, subjecthood, and unfreedom, making the slave trade suppression one venue of many where officials navigated this particular legal and political landscape. The problem of captivity had long animated debates over sovereignty in European nations, as well as in the Atlantic world. In an earlier era, people taken captive in the greater Mediterranean world had to be ransomed back, and sovereigns took a leading role in recruiting funds and sending delegations to redeem their subjects from bondage.[54] In more immediate contexts, the United States and Great Britain had a long-running set of disputes over naval impressment, its own kind of abduction and detention, that triggered sweeping political controversies over the sovereignty of each empire and the rights of their subjects abroad. At the turn of the nineteenth century, leaders in the United States tried to stop the practice of impressing U.S. citizens at sea into the British navy. They issued early forms of citizenship papers in an attempt to protect U.S. mariners, and they repeatedly lobbied for assurances from the British cabinet that it would end its impressment practices. These naval disputes fed into the outbreak of the War of 1812 between the two nations, and the conflict was ultimately resolved only when British naval officials abandoned their tactics in practice, if not in law.[55] Notably, no treaty provision protected the right of return for captive people, and so the issues of sovereignty, subjecthood, and kidnapping would continue to exist into the nineteenth century and inform the debates over slave trade suppression.

Kidnapping cases revealed how the United States' role in the slave trade affronted not only British principles but also Britain's sovereignty over its sub jects. Several kidnapping incidents occurred in this era, but the case of Joseph Bixby, a native of Carolina and U.S. citizen trading in Sierra Leone, is illustrative.[56] The case began in the 1810s, when a vessel leaving Sierra Leone shipwrecked not long after leaving port. Going on shore after the wreck, "two free boys that had assisted in navigating here, were seized . . . and sold at the Bissao for twenty dollars." There was perhaps little reason to anticipate that the two unnamed captives would ever see freedom again. Yet, when an official "learned they [the boys] were British subjects, he had them delivered" to Joseph Bixby, an American then on the coast of Africa "with a stipulation in writing from Bixby that he would restore them to their parents at Sierra Leone." But with the boys under his control, Bixby "carried them to America, and worked them on his plantation in Carolina, as slaves." These were not the only British people Bixby had working for him, having previously kidnapped "a free black boy to America, and made him work as a slave on his plantation." News of the boys' enslavement got back to their parents, and "the mother of one of these boys" lodged a "complaint against Bixby." The case worked its way up to the Colonial Office in London, where the colonial secretary decided "to request the American Minister would have the children restored to their country and family; and to make such remonstrances, against the conduct of the Americans." However, nothing seemed to have come of this request, and "the three boys, British subjects, and the children of British subjects, are suffered to this day to remain in slavery; and the moment for detaching the Americans from aiding the Slave trade, was neglected."[57]

These three kidnappings did not stand in isolation, and the rendition of free British subjects out of Sierra Leone continued as the slave trade intensified in West Africa. For instance, into the 1830s British officials confronted the reality that slavers were "in the habitual practice of kidnapping the liberated slaves of Sierra Leone for the purpose of reducing them again to slavery." Over these decades, several vessels staffed by U.S. crews had been stopped and searched, only to find Africans speaking fluent English, leading naval officers and British officials to the conclusion "that they also had been kidnapped from the British colony of Sierra Leone."[58] In time the British foreign secretary, Viscount Palmerston, became so alarmed he pushed for the "immediate adoption of such effectual measures for the future as shall prevent a recurrence of the atrocious practices."[59] As the foreign secretary stressed time and again, "it is impossible to permit British Subjects, *whatever their colour may be*, to be kidnapped into a foreign country, and there to be held in slavery."[60]

This articulation of the rights of British subjects, then, emerged directly from the politics of coerced migration in the Atlantic world.

The slave trade, and the kidnapping of British subjects, posed a series of challenges fundamental to empires. More than a criminal set of practices to be halted, the cases involved controlling the movement of people and goods in diverse jurisdictions and, more fundamentally, exerting the sovereignty of laws in far-flung lands. As one commentator noted, "to have tried Bixby at Sierra Leone, and to have punished him, to the utmost extent of the law, would have been useless." Even if they could imprison or execute Bixby for high crimes, British courts "could not have obliged him to restore the children to their parents, which was the principal object to be effected."[61] Kidnapping cases like these tested the authority of an empire over its subjects and laid bare the inability to exert power over such an extensive set of Atlantic spaces. British officials found they could not enforce their laws on U.S. citizens, control ships flying a foreign flag, or repatriate their subjects from captivity, which in turn set up a wide-ranging interimperial conflict over the slave trade and its suppression.

In the first half of the nineteenth century, the U.S. slave empire and the British antislavery empire increasingly were on a collision course, and the kidnapping of British subjects added explosive dimensions to the profound questions of sovereignty and slavery that played out around the Americas. By the 1830s, slavery's geography underwent a great reworking. In 1833, after intense public pressure, Great Britain abolished slavery in its empire by gradual, compensated means, to take full effect in 1838. For these years, provisionally freed slaves lived as apprentices, in what one scholar has dubbed "a half-way covenant" with freedom. For forty hours a week planters and workers maintained a relationship that was "much the same" as that between enslaver and enslaved people. Yet outside of those laboring periods, former slaves and former enslavers "were to assume their respective statuses of employer and employee freely negotiating conditions of work and wages."[62] In the post-emancipation period, conflicts between freed people and their former enslavers consumed islands around the Caribbean. A few years after emancipation, while discussing labor, tenancy, and rents to former enslavers, the colonial governor of Jamaica went so far as to remark on "the constant disputing which such a plan engenders."[63] To mediate these conflicts, in the early days of emancipation, the British government appointed hundreds of special magistrates to regulate the transition to freedom. Labor discipline no longer came from the enslaver's whip, and the commissioners possessed arbitration power over the division of land, labor discipline, and enforcing vagrancy statutes.[64] Although equal in the fiction of the law, former enslavers had an upper hand in conflicts with their former slaves, and before long a narrow vision of freedom, and a system of colonial repression, took hold across the Caribbean.[65] As one scholar of Barbados observed, this period became an era of "restrictions masquerading as freedom."[66]

With the slave trade growing, and plantation economies rapidly expanding, it is perhaps not surprising that formerly enslaved people were soon kidnapped into slave societies. Even before the period of apprenticeship ended, the British Foreign Office learned of possible kidnapping cases that acted as a powerful constraint on emancipation. These included instances of freed people being taken to Puerto Rico, Havana, and Guadeloupe. With these sorts of episodes in the background, the Foreign Office was on alert for any instances of kidnapping, when in the mid-1830s British officials learned that kidnappers had struck again. In the immediate aftermath of British emancipation, John Taylor, a U.S. citizen and slaver, carried a dozen apprentices from Barbados into slavery in Texas.[67] Interestingly, he carried them on the brig *Mary Ann*, possibly the same vessel at issue in the 1823 Supreme Court case.[68] When the British consul in New Orleans, John Crawford, became aware of these cases, he immediately began to investigate. After taking depositions, British officials concluded that John Taylor, a U.S. citizen and slaver, "actually contracted to deliver" to enslavers in the region "slaves or apprentices which he intended to bring to Texas."[69] Alarmed at the reports, British officials, under direct orders from Viscount Palmerston, then foreign secretary, tracked down some of Taylor's buyers. By 1839, Joseph Grisby and James Chessher, two Texas slaveholders, confirmed that the dozen trafficked people went to work in the burgeoning cotton economy. Writing from Jasper, Texas, one slaveholder reported that Taylor "imported twelve or thirteen Negroes from Barbados ten or twelve of which I saw myself including one woman and three children."[70] He detailed the purchases and identified their known whereabouts. In each case, their buyers "calculated to make slaves of those in their possession during life."[71]

More than isolated voyages, slave traders like Taylor planned to make a regular business out of selling human cargo. Chessher reported, "I proposed . . . to purchase some of the Negroes, his reply was that he had already disposed of them." Yet Taylor assured the prospective buyer that more would come. "He calculated to make a large shipment and that he would supply me with any number I wanted, for which I contracted to deliver him [illegible word] timber," reported the slaveholder.[72] Yet this does not appear to have happened, because in early 1840, Taylor stood trial "under a charge of slave trading." The colonial governor expected he would be convicted and barred from Barbados for "a breach of the Laws for the Abolition of Slavery."[73] The details of the trial, the kinds of evidence admitted, the communities that testified, and its outcome remain obscure in the colonial records.[74]

The mere report of Taylor's designs to continue trading in slaves alarmed British officials, and it led them to suspect a regular illicit commerce marked the region. This instance did not stand in isolation; the Foreign Office had evidence of other such kidnappings, which reduced British subjects to slavery in Virginia and Mobile, Alabama, to say nothing of the cases in Sierra Leone also taking place during the 1830s.[75] The foreign secretary weighed his options, and the British consul in New Orleans assured him, "there can be no doubt that most of these apprentices can be traced to their present abodes should Her Majesty's Government think proper to make a demand on that of Texas for their liberation."[76] Abolitionists in Pennsylvania also learned of these cases, and discussed if they might help free the captives from Texas, but ultimately decided they could not be of much help.[77] As emancipation dawned in the British Caribbean, slave traders appeared to have devised a plan for regular, albeit small-scale, traffic between West Indian islands and the cotton South.

Slavery and Empire in the Texas Borderlands

The ongoing slave trade to Texas, which at times ensnared British subjects, provided a context for simmering imperial disputes over slavery's expansion into the region. In the 1830s and 1840s, the British government found itself caught in tangled diplomacy with the United States over slavery's future in Texas. In 1836, leaders in Texas declared themselves part of an independent republic where slavery was legal. The Texan government quickly petitioned for annexation to the United States, but the Van Buren administration, along with the U.S. Senate, received the proposed annexation coolly. In another decade, the United States would annex the Texas republic (in 1845), and a subsequent war between Mexico and the United States erupted the following year. By 1848, a triumphant U.S. government would incorporate the vast region into its slave economy.[78] Between Texas's independence and the end of the war with Mexico, U.S. citizens relocated to the Texas republic and continued constructing a plantation economy. With cotton production taking off, settlers in the territory welcomed slavery's expansion with open arms. Importantly, U.S. influence grew both because of the expanding plantation economy and the ongoing slave trade. Seeing the writing on the wall, the British government worked to stop the push toward U.S. annexation.

While the U.S. war with Mexico cemented U.S. control over Texas, before the late 1840s authorities in Mexico tried to maintain their tenuous control over the northern regions of their nation by warding off U.S. influence. Slavery, and especially the importation of slaves, featured prominently in those political calculations. A standoff took hold in 1824, when officials in Mexico City banned the importation of slaves into Mexico, including its northern province, Texas. U.S. planters and Mexican slaveholders immediately converted all of the arriving slaves into lifelong servants, as a pretext to avoid this ban. The servitude system allowed slavery to continue, and it allowed free white migrants from the United States to stake a claim in the region much as they had before. When Mexican authorities debated various abolition provisions, and President Vicente Guerrero eventually passed an emancipation decree in 1829, planters in Texas blunted its impact in the short run and celebrated its eventual repeal a few months later when a coup toppled Guerrero's government. The servitude system came under fire in 1832, when authorities in Mexico City, undeterred and unwilling to allow planters in Texas to operate autonomously, voided all of the servitude contracts. A few years later, the revolution in Texas began, and leaders created an independent republic in 1835.[79]

The conflicts over slavery in northern Mexico and U.S. settlement in the region played out amid wider conflicts in the Americas between Britain's free-labor empire and the U.S. slave empire. As the two nations jockeyed for power in Texas, the Oregon Territory, and large swaths of Central America, slavery became a focal point of those disputes. In the Pacific Northwest, a boundary dispute in the Oregon Territory pitted the two empires against each other, setting the stage for a possible military conflict. In the East, long-running border disputes over the boundary with Canada, the rendition of British deserters out of the United States for trial in Canada, and reclaiming runaway slaves seeking safe haven north of the U.S. border all came to a head in this era. Two treaties, in 1842 and 1846, resolved the eastern boundary dispute with Canada and the western conflict over the Oregon issue, but those treaties left unresolved the question of returning deserters or recapturing self-emancipated slaves who crossed international borders.[80] With conflicts in diverse theaters, kidnapping from the West Indies to Texas crystallized the abstract issues surrounding the politics of slavery and U.S. expansion. From the perspective of British agents, expanding plantations in Texas threatened British free-soil principles and the freedom of their subjects. The captivity cases in part framed the macro-level foreign policy questions debated in, and between, London and Washington, D.C.

Throughout the 1830s and 1840s, the British government pursued two distinct approaches toward Texas. First, it hoped to see Texas exist as an independent republic, respected by Mexico and the United States. Second, it wanted to abolish slavery in Texas and create trade partnerships with its Caribbean colonies. Yet the situation in Texas made these two policies mutually exclusive. Abolition would require intervention that undermined Texas's strict independence. Simply allowing local actors to shape Texas's diplomatic course would let it slip into American hands. Before long, it seemed, the region would become part of the U.S. slave empire. Many in England hoped to avoid this course. Holding free labor as a touchstone of imperial order, many in British policymaking circles wanted bold action. In 1841, Thomas Morgan, an influential leader in antislavery circles, articulated this idea, saying it would be a "wise policy to Anglify Texas as much as possible."[81]

Abolishing slavery, at the risk of undermining Texas's independence, stood at the core of the so-called Anglifying process. Writing to the British foreign secretary, Viscount Palmerston, Morgan highlighted that effective abolition in Texas was both practicable and in line with long-standing British policy. "British antislavery mania affords an excellent opportunity to Anglify Texas by offering that Republic money (say 60,000£ *if* Parliament approves) to abolish slavery *for ever*," Morgan declared. He reminded Palmerston that the region "is more addicted to slavery than any other country."[82] Setting aside the questionable assumptions, Morgan's policy prescriptions were broadly in line with British foreign policy regarding slavery. The British foreign secretary declared his desire to see "the general abolition of slavery throughout the World." Even as he voiced his commitment to noninterference with an independent Texas, and cautioned against any antislavery agitation in the young republic, he also made plain that "the Slavery which now exists . . . we desire to see abolished in Texas."[83] Others agreed with this sentiment. Thomas Fowell Buxton, a leading parliamentary abolitionist, stated that "if the British Government did not interfere to prevent the Texian territory from falling into the hands of American slaveholders, in all probability a greater traffic in slaves would be carried on during the next fifty years than had ever before existed."[84]

With British designs to make a free-soil Texas taking shape, U.S. officials, notably John C. Calhoun, U.S. secretary of state from 1844 to 1845, took a keen interest in the situation. In particular, Calhoun suspected that abolition in Texas would spell doom for slavery in the Deep South. He, like other slaveholders, believed that the plantation economy had to expand to survive and that the contagion of abolition had to be combated at every turn. After meeting with Calhoun early in 1844, the British consul at Washington, D.C., signaled that U.S. annexation seemed inevitable. In the Caribbean, it had been a long-standing U.S. policy to keep British influence out of Cuba in order to protect the slave economy there, akin to the stance U.S. officials adopted toward the British in Texas.[85] "From the tenor of Mr. Calhoun's remarks," he wrote, "I infer . . . His strong opinions in favor of Slavery." This no doubt understated the situation. "He has been induced to become a Party to the measure of annexation," the British ambassador wrote, because abolition in Texas would "exercise an influence so fatal to the security of the Slave-holding States of the American Union, as to render the annexation of Texas a measure of self-defense which ought no longer to be postponed." Alarmed at the idea, and concerned that warfare would erupt with Mexico once Texas became part of the United States, the consulate asked that the U.S. and British governments, perhaps together with other powers such as France, "bind themselves to abstain from encroachment of any kind on the Independence of Texas." He reported with chagrin that "this remark was received by Mr. Calhoun with a smile, indicating how little such a proposition was in harmony with His present purpose."[86]

In two more years, Calhoun would come to oppose Texas annexation, but he was an outlier on this question. In a triumph for proslavery imperialists, the Texas republic became part of the United States in 1845—inaugurating a new chapter in the politics of slavery and imperial expansion, one where sectional conflict reached a fever pitch after the end to the war with Mexico in 1848.[87] Similarly, the international politics of kidnapping took on new dimensions. Rather than working with the fledging Republic of Texas and juggling the complicated relations between Mexico and the United States, British officials now had to challenge the United States head-on. Into the 1850s, the Foreign Office continued to confront cases of international kidnapping. According to the British consul in New Orleans, the "ports in the neighboring state of Texas afford the best opportunity for carrying on the crime without detection." Writing in the 1850s, he noted that he "received a letter . . . [from] Brazoria, Texas, stating that there were some negroes in that section claiming their freedom who said that they belong to the West Indies, and were brought from thence . . . about ten years ago."[88] The trade in captives was seen as one part of U.S. expansion into Texas, and the politics of slavery and empire had to contend with the ongoing forced migration of Afro-descended people, some of them British subjects, into the budding plantation complex.

Over many years, British officials from the local level to the cabinet objected to Texas's annexation to the United States and applied diplomatic pressure to abolish slavery in the newly minted republic. Slavery's expansion into the region did not just offend British ideals, it threatened the freedom of British subjects. Notably, British policy toward Texas came into being as apprentices and freed West Indians suffered re-enslavement.

Opposing this view, U.S. settlers and officeholders sought to extend their influence into the region, which built on a long history of slave trading. The trade in illegal captives from east Texas into the plantation South made relinquishing U.S. interests in the area almost unthinkable to advocates of the U.S. slave empire. Moreover, leaders like Calhoun believed that abolition in Texas would threaten slavery in the South.[89] The spread of plantations and the sale of African Americans from Virginia to Texas was undoubtedly a key component of U.S. expansion. Yet settlers and statesmen alike asserted their power over the region also in part due to an international slave trade into east Texas. Seen in this light, the U.S. slave empire was built in part through the illegal slave trade and had to contend with the interimperial politics of the greater Atlantic world.

Conclusion

A full accounting of how slavery supported the making of the U.S. empire requires including the illegal and international slave trade to the Americas in the wider discussion about the spread of the plantation complex into the Deep South. Recast in greater Caribbean and Atlantic contexts, the creation of the U.S. slave empire was bound up in the interimperial politics of the slave trade and its imperfect abolition. The most important ports of entry for slavers, northern Florida and eastern Texas, in time became focal points of U.S. expansion. When British subjects were kidnapped into plantation zones, it challenged the sovereignty of the British empire over its population, and tested the capacity of the British empire to enforce its laws on U.S. soil. As U.S. officials rebuffed British attempts to repatriate their subjects, they asserted an absolute right over the people in east Texas, which helped advance imperial ambitions over North America. Black migration—either in the form of the slave trade or under the auspices of emigration to Liberia—forged important contours of the Atlantic world. The kidnapping of free people stands out as a different kind of coerced mobility that sheds light on the fundamental forces of the Atlantic, no matter the relative scale of these migrations.[90] It is conventional to talk about the ways empires and imperial expansion used strategies of spatial control—the plantation complex and the reservation system, and in a later period internment camps and detention centers—but diasporic histories call for a fuller integration into the history of the U.S. slave empire.[91]

CHAPTER 10

An Empire of Illusions

Paul Cuffe, Martin Delany, and African American Benevolent Empire Building in Africa

OUSMANE K. POWER-GREENE

In July 1859, Martin R. Delany boarded the New York Colonization Society's ship the *Mendi* and left the United States for West Africa. By then, Delany was a national Black leader in the emigration movement that had been born in the shadow of the Fugitive Slave Law of 1850 and the racial violence in Kansas between those who wanted the state to remain "free soil" and those who defended the institution of slavery. A published author, journalist, newspaper editor, and revered orator, Delany considered himself a representative man who embraced his "Africanness" and called on free Blacks to emigrate from the United States to form a Black nation in opposition to United States, where racial caste and slavery defined the Black experience—both free and slave.[1] Yet, Delany believed emigrationism was more than a mere reaction to an ever increasingly hostile environment. It encompassed ideas rooted in biblical notions of racial destiny, as expressed in Psalm 68:31—"Princes shall come forth out of Egypt; Ethiopia shall soon stretch forth her hands unto God"—as well as Enlightenment ideals of liberty and democracy.[2] As a proto-Pan-Africanist, Martin Delany imagined building a Black nation in Africa that would include rather than exclude Indigenous African people and, by extension, would prevent further U.S. or European exploitation, enslavement, and the annihilation of African people who refused to submit.

Although Delany became one of the most well-known nineteenth-century champions of Black emigrationism, he was certainly not the first. Paul Cuffe, a Black ship captain and entrepreneur from Westport, Massachusetts, with back-to-Africa dreams, initiated an emigration movement to Africa in the 1810s. In fact, Cuffe had been interested in Black American emigration to Africa since the 1790s, shortly after Sierra Leone was established by British antislavery advocates and philanthropists. Like Delany, Cuffe came to believe African Americans had a distinct duty to uplift the African race by bringing Christianity, Western democratic traditions, and commerce to Africa.[3]

Recently, scholars such as Cassandra Mark-Thiesen, Moritz A. Mihatsch, and Brandon Mills have shown how American imperial ambitions reached beyond Jefferson's vision for a white, republican, and agrarian "empire of liberty" in North America. U.S. nation-building led not only to westward expansion, but also to the appropriation of Hawai'i and to proposals for colonizing Black Americans in the North American West or on the west coast of Africa. Meanwhile, the American notion of Manifest Destiny provided U.S. politicians and others with the intellectual justification for the genocidal march into the old Southwest against Native Americans in order to exploit virgin soil, while dragging enslaved Africans along the way. Delany's and Cuffe's emigrationism similarly embraced a notion of racial destiny—but they understood their movement as regenerative rather than exploitative. Through their efforts to promote legitimate trade and spread Christianity and modern medical practices and democratic virtues, they sought to undo two centuries of European-driven exploitation and destruction due to the Atlantic slave trade.[4]

Paul Cuffe and Martin Delany's imagined Black settlement, then, serves as a perfect site to explore how Black Americans understood a "benevolent empire" in Africa—one that would spread the virtues of American democracy and universal human rights as expressed in the Declaration of Independence and the French Declaration of the Rights of Man and Citizen. While Cuffe and Delany had no particular reverence for Thomas Jefferson, they did agree with the principles he wrote into the Declaration of Independence, as well as those expressed in the Bill of Rights. In fact, Black American emigrationists, as well as those who joined the colonization movement to Liberia, imagined extending these rights beyond the narrow racist framework that hampered the United States from achieving the destiny white founders claimed to seek.[5] African American emigrationists like Delany and Cuffe believed a colony of Black Americans in West Africa would strike the institution of slavery at the root by spreading U.S. democratic ideals and the virtues of Christianity in ways that mirrored the arguments Thomas Jefferson and the Founding Fathers used to justify independence and rehashed again and again each time the United States violated a treaty and extended its borders westward.[6]

This chapter compares Paul Cuffe's and Martin Delany's emigrationist programs from the 1810s to the 1850s within the context of American westward expansion, Atlantic world empire building, and British imperial ambitions abroad. It explores the similarities and differences between British philanthropists who helped establish Sierra Leone and those who supported Cuffe's and Delany's efforts in Africa.

The chapter begins by examining Paul Cuffe's emigration movement in the 1810s, which crashed against the British and American Atlantic world systems, and forced him to work within the U.S. political and philanthropic establishment to initiate his plan. Then, it shows how Martin Delany's emigration movement confronted similar obstacles thirty years later. Delany faced the additional burden of separating his movement from the American Colonization Society's efforts to promote Black American colonization in Liberia, which had been heavily maligned for its exploitative policies toward Indigenous Africans, such as the Vai, Day, Queah, Bassa, Kru, and Grebo who lived within its borders. Despite his criticism of Liberia in the early 1850s, though, Delany partnered with the colonizationists for his own emigrationist project by the end of the decade. While the circumstances surrounding Cuffe's and Delany's missions were different, they both offer clear examples of Black American emigrationists' attempts to use American and British empire in order to build an African nation based on democratic values and nonexploitative economic systems and social practices.[7]

The Origins of African American Emigrationism

It is impossible to examine the challenges Black emigrationists like Martin Delany faced within the British and American imperial network without placing his efforts in the 1850s within a longer historical arc, beginning with Cuffe in the 1810s. Like many African Americans struggling for equality in American society and frustrated by efforts to demonstrate that they deserved citizenship status, Paul Cuffe began pondering emigration to Africa as he witnessed the declining conditions of free Blacks living in Massachusetts during the first decade of the nineteenth century. Having witnessed slaver ships docked along the coastal ports throughout the South, despite the 1808 ban on slave trading, Cuffe had been inspired by the same antislavery zeal that led to the establishment of Sierra Leone in the 1780s.[8] Reflecting on his motives, Cuffe wrote: "I have for these many years past felt a lively interest in their behalf, wishing that the inhabitants of the colony might become established in the truth, and thereby be instrumental in its promotion amongst our African brethren."[9] Since the 1780s, activists had organized the African Institution, African Union Society, and other benevolent organizations for mutual aid and relief. The movement to create Black organizations and institutions illustrates African American agency and initiative, which fundamentally destabilized the assumptions about their inferiority that justified slavery and discriminatory laws and racist social practices. However, when faced with threats of violence and the political movement to deny them citizenship rights in cities, towns, and states in the North, African Americans considered leaving America to settle where they would be able to live peaceably.[10]

Cuffe had been inspired by African Americans in Newport, Rhode Island, who first advocated for emigration as an alternative to inequality in 1783. Leaders of the African Union Society sent correspondence to Providence and Philadelphia mutual aid societies to escape the stigma of race in their community. The African Americans Cuffe knew in Boston were especially responsive to the call for emigration, since several notable leaders petitioned the General Court of Massachusetts to pass legislation ending slavery.[11] Unlike Thomas Jefferson or Fernando Fairfax, a wealthy Virginia planter whose "Plan for liberating the negroes within the United States" promoted gradual abolition and Black colonization in Africa as a way to create a white nation-state, Cuffe understood Black emigration to Africa as a positive step toward racial uplift.[12] In fact, he did not seek to initiate a mass exodus of free Black Americans to West Africa. Rather, he hoped to start by settling a choice group of Black Americans there who would spread the Christian gospel to Africans and promote legitimate commerce rather than trade in slaves. This, he imagined, would provide West Africans with a source of income separate from the economy of the slave trade and the business of fitting slave ships with provisions for passage to the Caribbean and South America.[13]

Cuffe's interest in emigration became more pronounced when he learned of Thomas Clarkson and others' establishment of the African Institution in 1807. Sierra Leone became the priority of the British-based African Institution, which inspired Cuffe with a model for how to institutionalize his efforts in America.[14] This British colony did not seek to exploit Africans as an extension of broader British imperial ambitions. Instead, Sierra Leone provided a model British colony for the opposite reason: It sought to prevent the Atlantic slave trade by promoting liberty in Africa as a benevolent gesture on the part of the British Crown.

Cuffe planned on creating branches of the African Institution in the United States, and he even went so far as to reprint in his journal an epistle he found from members of the African Institution in Sierra Leone. According to Cuffe, the members affirmed that "we feel from an awful experience the distresses that many of our African brethren groan under. Therefore we feel our minds engaged to desire all the sain[t]s and professors in Christ, to diligently consider our cause, and to put our cause to the Christian query, whether it is agreeable to the testimony of Jesus Christ for one professor to make merchandise of another. We desire that this may be made manifest to all professors of all Christian denominations who have not abolished the holding of another."[15] It was this type of antislavery sentiment that assured Cuffe that he would find financial support in London for his emigration plan. First, however, he wanted to go to Sierra Leone to see if he could drum up support. In September 1810, Cuffe organized a meeting of Quakers in Westport, Massachusetts, to obtain official endorsements in the form of letters of recommendation. Such letters would offer him access to Quaker networks in England where abolition had become an important topic that united the various denominations. Although Cuffe regarded commerce as an important tool to combat the trade in human beings, he also viewed spreading the gospel as one of the pillars upon which he sought to base his movement. By January 2, 1811, Cuffe's ship, the *Traveller*, was on its way to Sierra Leone to examine the feasibility of using the British colony to encourage African commercial enterprise.[16]

Sierra Leone was a product of two imperatives that emerged during the Age of Revolutions. First, African Americans who fled to British lines during the American Revolutionary War landed in Canada and London, where neither social climate nor weather proved agreeable. Black loyalists transported to Nova Scotia arrived in a colony of twenty thousand former French-speaking Acadians, a handful of New Englanders, and only several hundred or so enslaved Africans and other British settlers. By 1783, over 16,000 refugees—Black and white—lived in Nova Scotia. Of those, 3,500 Black loyalists and several hundred enslaved Africans who came with their former masters transformed the British colony dramatically.[17] In less than a decade, racial violence from white settlers, unfulfilled promises of land, and few prospects for redress sent these Black refugees back into the British imperial network. They joined with some of the Black poor from London, and with Jamaican Maroons who negotiated a treaty with British officials for passage from the slave colony to Sierra Leone. Here, these Black British subjects meshed with the slave traders and military personnel stationed in Sierra Leone to protect the Crown's interests. With British abolition of the slave trade in 1807, Sierra Leone became the destination of those Africans seized aboard slave ships engaged in what was now an illegal trade.[18]

When Paul Cuffe arrived in Sierra Leone, white British authorities embraced him. Cuffe must have been impressed by those white and Black colonists in Sierra Leone who believed their efforts at Christian salvation were linked to the broader struggle against slavery. The more Cuffe observed the colony's commercial potential, the more he moved toward recruiting people there to his plan. Black refugees from Nova Scotia seemed the most enthusiastic about his idea, and even if he was concerned by some aspects of the colony—such as the use of alcohol and the continued importance of the slave trade to the economy, despite its ostensible prohibition—he felt confident the colony would work as a site for his emigration movement to West Africa.[19] In support, Black refugees from Nova Scotia signed a petition endorsing Cuffe's emigrationist plan and sent it to the governor.

Intent on finding financial backing for his cause, Cuffe sailed from Sierra Leone to London in May 1811 to meet with Thomas Clarkson and other members of the African Institution.[20] Although the British-based African Institution had been in recess, soon after Cuffe's arrival in London the group convened to hear him describe what he believed would be the most efficacious means to destroy the slave trade. Members of the African Institution in England listened to Cuffe explain the reasons he believed Sierra Leone, or another settlement in West Africa, could work to stimulate legitimate trade in raw materials and other goods between the United States, England, and West Africa. Thomas Clarkson and Prince William Frederick, Duke of Gloucester and Edinburgh, agreed to work with him in his colonization effort.[21] William Allen—a British abolitionist, close friend of William Wilberforce, and director of the African Institution—used his connections with British politicians to help Cuffe receive a license to trade in Sierra Leone.[22]

After visiting England, Cuffe returned to Sierra Leone on November 12. He spent three more months exploring the region's potential for economic development and establishing the Friendly Society of Sierra Leone with the aid of the Methodist congregation of Freetown. This society intended to aid

Blacks in the colony who were interested in independent trading, which did not rely on the European merchants who dominated the coast. Recognizing the importance of Black-run self-help ventures, Cuffe helped build the society into an organization that could challenge European traders who held a monopoly on commercial activities in the region. William Allen, the Englishman whom Cuffe befriended in Europe, funded the society with an initial donation of £70, while working with Thomas Clarkson in London to manage Sierra Leone's exports in Britain. Cuffe's next step was to recruit skilled and upstanding African Americans to emigrate to Sierra Leone. After offering advice, counsel, and the building blocks for the Black-owned cooperative venture, he set sail for the United States on February 11, 1812.[23]

When Cuffe arrived in the United States, he was optimistic about African American emigration and settlement. His optimism was disrupted when his ship was seized and accused of violating a ban on importing goods from a British colony. Frustrated and intent on reclaiming his ship and cargo, Cuffe traveled to Washington, D.C., to take the matter up with the secretary of the treasury and the president. Due to the great influence of several well-known friends, Cuffe was able to meet with the president about the seizure of his ship—an impressive feat for an African American during the nineteenth century. Albert Gallatin, the secretary of the treasury, received Cuffe as well, interviewing him about the circumstances that led to his ship being seized by federal officials. Gallatin, perhaps, was more intrigued by Cuffe's experiences in Africa than the matter of the ship. When President James Madison interviewed Cuffe, he also showed interest in Cuffe's trip to Africa and his plan for African American emigration. Although Madison did not endorse Cuffe's plan, he and Gallatin agreed that Cuffe did not intend on violating the federal mandate, and they promised to have his ship returned.[24] With this accomplished, Cuffe returned to the task of spreading the word about his emigration plan and sent letters to the heads of the African Union Society in Newport, Rhode Island, and Boston with hopes that they would assist him.

Initially, Cuffe envisioned that the pioneers of his new settlement would be Black American emigrants who were capable of utilizing their influence to help the development of Africa.[25] Writing to his friend James Forten, Cuffe explained, "I have suggested of settling 2 colonies, 1 in the United States, and the other in Africa."[26] Although Cuffe's primary goal was emigration to Africa, he recognized this required significant resources. In the meantime, Cuffe believed free Blacks living in the North would benefit from an alternative colony in the West. This would serve more as a refuge than a place where African Americans would exploit the land and dispossess Native Americans. In fact, although he identified as a "a man of color," Cuffe was of Native American and African descent. Cuffe figured that for those Black Americans who, for whatever reason, did not want to leave for Africa, a Black settlement in the West would provide an alternative. Cuffe's proposal paralleled Thomas Jefferson's evolving ideas about the Louisiana Purchase as a refuge for Indians. However, President Andrew Jackson had other plans for how best to remove Native Americans from within the United States to the periphery. The federal government under Jackson passed the Indian Removal Act of 1830, which provided official sanction for dispossession and relocation by the use of force. Such dispossession was rooted in the sorts of racist ideas Cuffe rejected. In fact, Cuffe's own biracial Native American and Black American upbringing showed the possibility of the two groups living harmoniously.[27]

Colonizing free and emancipated African Americans in Africa and inducing Native Americans to relocate in the West both jibed with the notion of the United States as an "empire of liberty" and revealed that concept's racialized limits. As historian Nicholas Guyatt has argued: "Before 1829 the debate over the fate of the eastern Indians proceeded along remarkably similar lines to the discussion of African colonization. Even after the passage of the Removal Act in the summer of 1830, many removal advocates clung to the idea that Indians were moving to a western colony and a civilized future."[28] While "border wars" in the Midwest forced Native Americans to move farther west of white settlements, anti-Black violence in cities, such as Cincinnati in 1829, drove Black Americans from the Midwest to settle in British Canada.[29] From planned military action to spontaneous acts conducted by white mobs, violence became a central mechanism to dispossess Native Americans and expel Black Americans from states in the Midwest—despite Jefferson's emphasis on the nation being an empire that promotes liberty.[30]

After two years of fundraising and recruiting, Paul Cuffe mailed letters to the president of the United States, the House of Representatives, and Congress, seeking permission to travel to Africa. Cuffe hoped to entice the U.S. government to embrace his emigration plan, which appealed to one important aspect of American empire building: spreading "civilization" and Christianity in Africa. He also explained that he believed an African American colony near Sierra Leone would work toward legitimate commerce, since slave trading in the Atlantic had been outlawed in 1808. Any goods gathered in Africa and brought back to the United States, Cuffe explained, would help alleviate the financial burden of the mission rather than boost his own individual wealth.

On January 7, 1814, the Senate voted 18–6 in favor of a bill in support of Cuffe's proposal. When the bill entered the House of Representatives, however, it had a much more difficult time passing. Serious discussion took place in the House over the bill, and supporters called attention to the benefits of free African American colonization in West Africa. When the opponents of the bill presented their case, they highlighted the fact that Cuffe could still act in behalf of his emigration plan without the approval of Congress. Why, they wondered, did he need to make his mission one that involved trading goods purchased in a British colony? The vote was close: 65 in favor the bill and 72 against it. Ultimately, it failed to pass in the House. This defeat did not prevent Cuffe from continuing his mission, and in December 1815, when hostilities between the United States and Britain died down, Cuffe set sail for Sierra Leone.[31]

Paul Cuffe arrived in Sierra Leone with thirty-eight African Americans, most in family units and two of whom were infants, as well as goods to trade to defer the cost of the trip.[32] The fifty-six-day voyage was one of the worst Cuffe had ever endured. A series of violent storms rocked the boat, causing virtually all the passengers—including the crew—to remain seasick for most of the journey. When Cuffe's emigrants finally arrived in Sierra Leone, British officials seemed indifferent or hostile toward them. Furthermore, Cuffe was forced to pay import duties even though he explained that he had paid out of pocket for the cost of the trip. All was not lost, however, and Cuffe soon learned that the Friendly Society he helped start had increased its funds from William Allen's initial donation of £70 to £1,200. When Cuffe left Sierra Leone in April 1816, he had lost nearly four thousand dollars, yet he remained optimistic about the possibilities of an extensive trading venture based on the success of the Friendly Society.[33]

While Cuffe hoped to sail to Sierra Leone once a year, he would never again set foot on African soil. He died nearly eighteen months later. But during those months, he joined with several white philanthropists to plan what would become the American Colonization Society (ACS). Cuffe's emigration movement set the stage for white clergy and politicians who founded the ACS in late 1816. Thus, the colonization movement to send free Blacks to Africa must be framed within the context of Cuffe's difficulty negotiating the U.S. and British imperial world. First, Cuffe confronted a British navy recently at war with the United States, which led to his ship being impounded. Second, he, like the initial Black Americans who traveled under the guidance and support of the ACS to Sherbro Island, depended on British officials and Black colonists in Sierra Leone to sanction Black American settlement. Otherwise, how would these Black colonists and white ACS officials buy land from African chiefs who lived in the area? Finally, like Cuffe, ACS board members believed the U.S. government was instrumental for the health of the colony.

To what degree was Paul Cuffe's project an extension of U.S. imperialism? Jefferson supported the deportation of free and newly manumitted Blacks, and his ideas influenced ACS members. But he did not make any claims that a Black American colony would work to create a U.S. imperial presence in Africa.[34] Cuffe, by contrast, in fact sought to extend Jefferson's notion of an "empire of liberty," both across the Atlantic Ocean to West Africa and beyond the white citizens who were Jefferson's focus. Cuffe believed a Black American settlement in Africa would offer the virtues of liberty to African Americans and Africans who continued to be victims of or willing participants in the Atlantic slave trade. For the next forty years, Black Americans who joined the colonization movement and settled in Liberia, as well as those like Martin Delany who initiated emigration movements to Africa, did so in opposition to U.S. slaveholding interests and with expansive political ambitions of their own. While ACS leaders claimed colonization in Liberia was a practical plan whose sole purpose was to gradually end slavery, African Americans, by and large, disagreed.

Martin Delany's Black Nationality in Africa, 1850–60

Between the Missouri Compromise in 1820 and the Compromise of 1850, U.S. and British politicians found themselves confronting an international campaign to end slavery. Free African Americans in the United States and those of African ancestry in Britain, West Africa, and the Caribbean joined with white philanthropists, politicians, and activists to form an interracial brotherhood rooted in the notion that slavery must be abolished immediately. These second-wave abolitionists, as historian Manisha Sinha has described them, pushed those who called for gradual emancipation and colonization in West Africa on their heels.[35] With pressure from enslaved Africans, who rose up in rebellion in places like Virginia and Jamaica and demonstrated their willingness to die for liberty, white MPs and congressmen in London and Washington found themselves ensnared in debates over the vitality of enslavement in an era when advocates of "free labor" and industrialization joined together with those who denied the ethics of slave labor to form new coalitions. This pressure from above and below took root in Britain, and by the mid-1830s, British politicians retreated from chattel slavery in the Caribbean. Meanwhile, American slaveholders regrouped and spread out into the old Southwest, in their march toward gobbling up any and all land available in the Mississippi Valley to build a cotton kingdom. Native Americans were forced farther west, or onto reservations, as American politicians did all in their power to ensure white settlers would thrive. Even those politicians who considered themselves gradualists or emancipationists found themselves between radical abolitionists and proslavery politicians, pulling in opposite directions.[36]

Within this context, African American abolitionists who were once colleagues with Paul Cuffe, such as Richard Allen and Thomas Paul, Jr., promoted emigration from the United States to various places within the Atlantic world: Haiti (1825), Canada (1829), and Trinidad (1840). Yet, it was a provision of the Compromise of 1850 known as the Fugitive Slave Law that inspired the greatest interest in an emigration movement from the United States abroad during the nineteenth century. Even Black Americans who had looked askance at the colonization in Liberia began to reconsider. By then, Liberia was an independent republic in Africa—the first on the west coast of Africa. In 1851, for example, Augustus Washington wrote to the ACS from Hartford, Connecticut, claiming that his inability to inspire an emigration movement into the West led him to reconsider Liberia as a more realistic place for Black Americans to settle.[37] Free Blacks in New York agreed with Washington, and some formed the Liberian Agricultural and Emigration Society in 1850, which cooperated with the ACS to send a group to Liberia in order to promote emigration from the Empire State.[38]

In Allegheny City, Pennsylvania, Martin Delany, the abolitionist and editor of the Pittsburgh newspaper the *Mystery*, told those gathered at an antislavery meeting in 1850: "Whatever ideas of liberty I may have, have been received from reading the lives of your revolutionary fathers." In his estimation, Delany claimed, it was his moral right to kill a slave hunter based on the revolutionary ideology Thomas Jefferson espoused.[39] Over the next two years, Delany emerged as a national leader in the emigration movement on par with Paul Cuffe in the 1810s. Delany's emigrationist treatise *The Condition, Elevation, Emigration, and Destiny of the Colored People of the United States* recognized Cuffe as a man as important as George Laws and Cornelius Vanderbilt—both of whom Delany considered instrumental to U.S. empire building in the Atlantic world. While Delany did not directly acknowledge Cuffe as his inspiration for his emigrationist ambitions, his passing reference to "Cuffy" as an "extensive trader and mariner" who "went to Africa" shows Delany did recognize Cuffe's importance to those who believed racial uplift required Black leaders to work within an Atlantic world context. Delany became one of those Black leaders who believed the time had come for Black people to leave the United States and form their own Black nation that could challenge U.S. slavery and racial discrimination.[40]

Delany, however, first looked toward Latin America as the most suitable place to establish a Black American settlement. This southern orientation probably came from a Black physician and boyhood friend, David Peck, who found himself negotiating the British and American imperial systems to his advantage within the context of the shattered Spanish empire. After the U.S. war with Mexico, ambitious Americans such as Peck arrived in the Nicaragua town of San Juan del Norte, known at the time as Greytown, which became an important path for American traders who sought passage to San Francisco on the West Coast. Peck chaired a gathering to figure out the specific structure of this new town and establish a democratic government in which the duly elected mayor would maintain power to control the military as well as the government. To Delany's surprise, he received a letter from Peck when he was in New York that claimed Delany had been elected mayor of Greytown. While such a letter was probably meant to recruit Delany rather than convey the results of an actual election, it signaled Delany's support among Black expatriates like Peck who seemed to thrive within this Atlantic world community.[41]

Like the African coast, the Central American coast had been important to British traders ever since the seventeenth century. By 1848, the British had seized San Juan del Norte in Nicaragua in the wake of the U.S. war with Mexico in order to maintain the Miskito Indians protectorate, which extended across the Honduran and Nicaraguan coasts. Having Belize under their authority, the British pushed back against American diplomats who complained that their presence violated the Monroe Doctrine and the U.S. efforts to allow the former Spanish colonies to become free and independent nations. Yet, it became clear to the British that U.S. commercial interests were the primary group who sought unencumbered access to Greytown for a path to the Pacific Ocean en route to California.[42]

Delany shifted his attention to Africa, perhaps, because of this lesson about U.S. imperial ambitions in Central America. While he continued to reject Liberia as a site for his movement to Africa, he considered East Africa as a possible site to establish a Black American nation, rather than West Africa where, in his opinion, Liberia represented the most negative aspects of U.S. cultural imperialism. Like Paul Cuffe, Delany regarded the British as more accommodating partners in his quest to create a Black homeland in Africa because they had already abolished slavery in the Caribbean and established Sierra Leone with the explicit intention of using the colony to thwart the slave trade. Delany believed Britain would stand behind his effort to establish a larger nation of Black Americans in the Niger Valley region, which had already been an important site for missionary work. "Certainly," Delany wrote, "what England and France would do for a little nation—mere nominal nation, of five thousand civilized Liberians, they would be willing and ready to do, for five millions." Of course, Delany had yet to prove he had the capacity to convince Black Americans to leave for Africa. Even Paul Cuffe had the experience and wealth to support those who chose to go with him.[43]

Why would Delany put such faith in European imperialists in his quest to establish an African republic that would work to regenerate Africa? Because Delany believed the modern world required the finance capital that Africa lacked, despite its past glories. Racial progress, Delany claimed, was about producing goods that others would pay for. "It is Commerce then that is ruling the world," he argued, and used as an example the cotton kings who dominated American politics. They borrowed capital from New York banks, enslaved Africans to pick cotton, and reaped the dividends by selling cotton to British cotton nabobs who made fortunes in northern England. Racial traits, or, as he called it, their "Anglo-Saxon blood," played no part in their success, Delany asserted.[44] All around the world, those who had the means to compel others to pick cotton or procure sugar made fortunes, whether they were from wealthy families or not. Delany noticed that British philanthropists who championed abolition had made a similar argument about the use of free-market capitalism as the means from which to build a free society. This had been the approach in the post-emancipation Caribbean and in Sierra Leone, and British antislavery activists, like Thomas Fowell Buxton, agreed. Since the 1820s, Buxton had become a leading antislavery member of Parliament, and he would later call for cotton cultivation in Africa as a means to undermine slavery in the British Caribbean and the United States.[45]

Of course, Delany would soon learn that the complexities of Atlantic world commerce and the sweet talk of British benevolence masked the interest of British merchants and investors who sought to extract the raw materials that greased the financial engine of capitalist expansion upon which the British empire depended. By the time of Delany's trip to Africa in the late 1850s, slavery was dead in the British empire. Yet, the exploitation of Indian laborers on cotton plantations in India, and the "coolie trade" to the Caribbean, provided some post-emancipation islands with a new population to exploit.[46] Nevertheless, Delany believed British philanthropists would support his efforts to purchase land in the Aku country north of Lagos, in the British-controlled section of West Africa, for a Black American–led nation. Specifically, Delany chose Abeokuta in Yorubaland in the Niger River Valley for his exploratory mission to find a place to create a nation that might exploit African natural resources without exploiting his "African brothers" as Europeans had done for nearly two hundred years. After the disruption caused by the Atlantic slave trade, Delany centered this mission on the notion of the regeneration of Africa as a means to a broader race redemption mission.[47]

Delany's decision to establish a Black nation within the British rather than American imperial network was primarily a feature of his long-standing view that the one place in Africa where U.S. citizens had any interest, Liberia, remained controlled by anti-Black slaveholders who had only one desire: mass deportation of free Blacks to make slavery more secure. Of course, Black people who joined the colonization movement and left for Liberia had, time and time again, rebuffed this anti-colonization rhetoric. And some of the most outspoken anti-colonizationists who attended the emigration conventions of the 1850s, such as James Holly, drifted from this anti-colonization position by the time Delany inaugurated his emigration movement in 1859. Even the previously anti-colonizationist editor Mary Ann Shadd Cary came out in support of Pennsylvania colonizationist Benjamin Coates's plan to create an African Civilization Society in the United States to promote Black resettlement in Africa. Delany actually respected Coates for leaving the ACS. As Delany explained, "One thing we do know is that he left the Colonization Society, because he could not conscientiously subscribe to its measures." Yet, Delany continued to search for funding and support from Black leaders and sympathetic whites who did not have any affiliation with the colonization movement.[48]

Due to illness, Delany's efforts stalled. In fact, he did not attend the 1856 emigration meeting in Chicago, Illinois, and it appeared his influence had waned. Having traveled within the abolitionists' network in the urban North, Midwest, and Canada in order to raise funds and gather supporters for his African emigration plan, it became apparent to Delany that those most invested in emigration viewed Africa, rather than Haiti, Canada, or Mexico, as the site for a future Black nation. Two years later, he traveled to Chatham, Canada, to recruit for his movement to Africa rather than the North American West or Latin America. He formed the Niger Valley Exploring Party at the third emigration convention in Chatham, and found a team of Black Americans to join his expedition. Robert Campbell, a respected chemist and science teacher at Philadelphia's Institute of Colored Youth, as well as J. W. Purnell, Robert Douglass, and Amos Aray composed the team.[49]

There were those, however, who did not understand why Delany refused to consider Liberia as a potential place to begin his movement. Black American expat and newspaper editor Henry Bibb encouraged Delany to start with Liberia rather than choose a new destination under British control. Bibb argued that "Liberia is still growing in importance, and is destined, by the Divine blessing, to stand as a great moral lighthouse to her heathen tribes."[50] After all, Liberia was already an independent nation even if the U.S. government did not recognize it as such. Even if Delany had denounced Liberia for more than twenty years, his previous beef with Black leaders might have been resolved given that former Black abolitionist allies, such as Alexander Crummell, had moved to Liberia to try to build it into a place Black Americans could look to with pride. After exhausting himself in his effort to raise funds and garner national support in the Black community, in ways that paralleled Paul Cuffe's previous efforts, Delany had no choice but to solicit funds from New York and Massachusetts colonizationists.[51] This meant he would have to negotiate this philanthropic terrain with a rival: Rev. Henry Highland Garnet, a Black abolitionist and emigrationist who had been recruited into the African cotton cultivation cause by Benjamin Coates. Coates believed if his mission was led by a Black man—Garnet—and the funding from the colonizationists was kept secret, those abolitionists and politicians who denounced the colonization movement in the United States and Britain would be more inclined to support his efforts to promote cotton cultivation in Africa.

Henry Highland Garnet's conversion to African colonization under the guise of cotton cultivation and civilization in Africa had been rooted in his transnationalism over the previous decade. Garnet had traveled widely in

Europe as one of the more prominent Black abolitionists in the early 1850s. He had been known as an impressive orator who held audiences rapt as he recounted the circumstances Black Americans found themselves in with the passage of the Fugitive Slave Law in 1850. Garnet believed that the African Civilization Society would "establish a grand center of Negro nationality from which shall flow the streams of commercial, intellectual and political power which shall make colored people respected everywhere."[52] This, of course, was nearly identical to Delany's plan. Despite Delany's competition with Garnet for funding, Delany agreed to share the Niger Valley Exploring Party's findings, as well as to give Liberia a chance. Thus, as a condition of accepting funding for his exploratory party from New York and Massachusetts colonization movement supporters, he agreed to visit and see Liberia for himself.[53]

What distinguished Delany's plan was that he imagined his proposed African nation would be closer to the Niger River than Sierra Leone or Liberia. This was, of course, intentional. Delany did not want his venture to be seen as an extension of the British colony of Sierra Leone or the independent Black American–led Liberia. However, neither Delany nor Robert Campbell, the only one of the original members of his exploratory party who still remained, were able to raise the funds necessary for either their exploratory mission or to purchase the land. They did not have Paul Cuffe's wealth, nor Cuffe's expertise as a ship captain. If Delany and Campbell were to make their Black nation a reality, they were dependent on British philanthropists for funds and the U.S. colonizationists for transportation to Africa.[54]

On May 24, 1859, Martin Delany boarded the *Mendi*, sponsored by the New York Colonization Society. On board was John D. Johnson as a representative of the Johnson, Turpin, and Dunbar mercantile firm with ambitions to fund regular trade from Liberia to the United States. On July 10, the *Mendi* docked in Monrovia. Delany's arrival in Liberia was an occasion for celebration and optimism. His arrival was marked by an event on the steps of the president's mansion at 11 A.M. President Stephen Allen Benson was away, but Vice President Beverly Yates and former president J. J. Roberts were joined by John Keys, the U.S. consul, as well as Edward Wilmot Blyden and other distinguished Liberians. A military company, the Young Guards, wore their new uniforms, blue pants with red stripes, and certainly felt the sense of importance. This was the first time they had worn them that year. Delany gave a few words and then the military led the procession of Delany and other distinguished citizens to the Methodist church for the formal part of the event.[55]

The trip must have been exhausting for Delany. On the day he left, he came down with "acclimating fever" despite taking a cocktail of "sulphate of quinia three times a day" and "two grain doses of Dover's Powder" when he first arrived in Liberia. Delany spent his first three days holed up in his room fighting the virus, and Crummell sent a letter inviting him to a "public interview" so they might "hear your views concerning the interest of our race in general, and of your mission in particular."[56]

Delany certainly had no interest in delaying his exploratory mission any longer than necessary. He might have considered his visit to Liberia as a token recognition of the republic as a noble, if flawed, venture. What Delany might not have been fully aware of was that white leaders of the New York and Massachusetts Colonization Societies and prominent Black leaders in Liberia hoped to persuade him to abandon his planned settlement in the Niger River Valley and join them in Liberia. Delany's response to Liberia when he arrived seemed to offer them hope. According to one white missionary, for example, Delany told her that "he could have wept when he came in sight of Cape Mount" at the "thought of so many lies he told about such a beautiful country" based on his "ignorance."[57] Edward Blyden, a Black editor, educator, and intellectual who came in Liberia from Jamaica in the early 1850s, wrote to Rev. John B. Pinney of the New York Colonization Society that Delany had been "disappointed, and most agreeably so, at the appearance of persons and things here." After having mocked Liberia and ridiculed those who joined the colonization movement for decades, Delany felt deceived now that he had seen Liberia firsthand. The African American republic had been "misrepresented," Delany said, and Blyden claimed Delany bemoaned that "a proper representation has never been made of Liberia to the free colored people of the United States." This caused Blyden to wonder: "Is Dr. Delany to be the Moses to lead in the exodus of his people from the house of bondage to a land flowing with milk and honey? He seems to have many qualifications for the task."[58]

After his stay in Monrovia, Delany embarked on the *Mendi* on August 4 to meet Alexander Crummell in Cape Palmas, the main coastal town in what was known as Maryland in Liberia.[59] Delany was too ill to attend a gathering Crummell had planned for him, but after a week, Delany finally addressed a "crowded assemblage" who had represented the "most respectable people of the Cape."[60] Delany told the audience how pleased he had been in Liberia and he would certainly tell those in America that his impressions based on previous commentary had been wrong. Delany appeared so pleased that one

Liberian wrote to the ACS in Washington exactly what they wanted to hear: "I should not be surprised should Dr. Delany recommend Liberia to the people of color as the fairest hope for themselves and their posterity."[61] How did his experience in Liberia change the way Delany viewed a Black nationality? Delany acknowledged that he had been misled about Liberia and believed white people had impeded Liberia's ability to become a site for the sort of authentic Black nation he had in mind. And he now agreed that Edward Blyden, Alexander Crummell, and others had shown him that Liberia did have potential for being the Black American nation he imagined.

Despite Delany's fond words about Liberia, he remained convinced that Liberia's ties to slaveholders undermined the nation's ability to become a symbol of a great Black nation. Delany walked a fine line when comparing Liberia and Abeokuta, inland from the city of Lagos, and thus chose to focus on what one might consider a scientific explanation for his choice of location rather than one rooted in the history of these two colonies. Delany explained that he "observed that all elevated places, as Monrovia and Freetown, subject to severe visitations of disease, are situated near mangrove swamps; consequently, from the rising of the malaria, they are more unhealthy than those in low plains, such as Lagos and many other places, above which the miasma generally rises for the most part passing off harmlessly."[62]

Martin Delany planned to meet Robert Campbell for a five-day journey through the Niger Valley to negotiate with African chiefs for land and support for an African American settlement. By this point, the Niger Valley had become the center of British imperial ambitions. The Egba people had established Abeokuta in the forest belt of the once powerful Oyo kingdom in the 1830s, and Delany focused his energy here for his settlement. Yoruba recaptives, known as the Aku in Sierra Leone, had remained Saros (from the term "sierra") in Yorubaland in the 1840s.[63] These two groups, as well as hundreds of other Yorubas who had been swallowed in the Atlantic slave trade and carried to labor in Brazil and Cuba, joined together in an exodus to Abeokuta in this period. While Delany had every intention of being one of the Black Americans who would lead this new nation, he most certainly had no intention of imposing on the Aku people imperial rule. Quite the contrary. And the Aku chiefs appeared enthusiastic about skilled African Americans settling among them. Delany argued "Africa for the Africans and Black men to rule them" in reference to the dominance of white missionaries and industrialists who were central cogs in the European and American imperial system. "With such prospects as these," Delany explained, "with such a people as the Yorubas and others of the best type, as a constituent industrial, social, and political element upon which to establish a national edifice, what is there to prevent success? Nothing in the world."[64] Here, then, Delany showed Black American imperial ambitions were rooted in the principles of liberty to establish an empire in opposition to the Atlantic world slave system that contributed to warfare and dispersal of Africans. Slavery bred racism, racism bred Black inferiority, and nothing short of establishing a new nation in Africa would show the world Black people's strength.[65]

What did Delany accomplish on his trip? First, he secured a treaty with "His Majesty, Okukenu, Alake," and other kings and chiefs that provided him and Campbell with "the right and privilege of settling in common with the Egba people, on any part of the territory belonging to Abeokuta, not otherwise occupied." Delany made clear that the "native chiefs" and those natives who were Christian missionaries affirmed his view that they sought "no heterogeneous nor promiscuous 'masses' or companies, but select and intelligent people of high moral as well as religious character were to be induced to go out."[66] Second, he gathered evidence—scientific and cultural—that reinforced his belief that this area was the best for such a venture. Finally, he found a complex and sophisticated African polity thriving within the British imperial system rather than in opposition. Of course, Delany did not stay long enough to witness the contradictions and the uneasy relations between various groups. On the surface, however, this area seemed stable and "civilized."

Some scholars, such as M. B. Akpan, have argued persuasively the deleterious effect Americo-Liberians had on Indigenous Liberians since the founding of Liberia, going so far as labeling them as "Black imperialists."[67] Yet, Delany's motives and the way he expressed a sense of respect toward native practices suggest he remained open to learning to appreciate the spirituality, customs, and practices of Africans he met in Liberia. He criticized the common missionary practice of renaming "native" children and those adults who lived in missionary settlements in Liberia. Delany might have decried the nakedness of those who served the white missionaries and Black American colonists in Liberia, yet he regarded Western civilized culture and ways of behaving in nonracial terms. Notions of "civilized society" were not white or European, but came to Europe from elsewhere, and then were passed to America and Africa via the spread of commerce and migration. Silverware, for example, came to Europe from China, and math, from North Africa. Not to mention, Delany pointed out, that there were those in Europe, Asia, and Latin America who had not been exposed to modern civilization and thus did not benefit from the scientific and technological achievements Delany and other Black Americans enjoyed. Even the Egba people believed learning the "ways of the white man" was valuable to survival in an ever-changing Atlantic world. Thus, Delany was not imposing modern civilized ways upon Africans, but, rather, promising to bring men of African descent from the United States who had the skills and felt a natural respect and kinship with them. The goal was not exploitation but harmony in service to a larger vision of African regeneration.

Furthermore, despite his elitism and ignorance of African culture, Delany did not represent the interests of an economically dominant class within the United States who sought to appropriate and expropriate land and people to further his individual interests. Quite the contrary. Capitalism, wealth accumulation, and free labor cotton cultivation would work toward, in Delany's imagination, the "greater good" of Africa and those African Americans writhing beneath the lash or huddled into ghettos in the North—people who were discriminated against regardless of how skilled they were in their trade. Delany's mission, then, was in service to an oppressed people rather than a few speculators who imagined West Africa as a site for their personal fortunes.

Ultimately, Delany's Black empire in the Niger River region remained only an illusion. Delany built upon the dreams of Paul Cuffe by reframing his notion of empire in ways that resembled the optimism of Thomas Jefferson, claiming a Black nation would actually foster a reclaiming of Africa. "Our only hope for the regeneration of our race from the curse and corrupting influences of our white American oppressors," Delany argued, must be "originated solely by ourselves" rather than "disinterested white societies in America, which interferingly came forward in a measure which was originated solely by ourselves (and that, too, but a few of us)."[68] Here Delany obliquely acknowledged Paul Cuffe's pioneering effort to bring Black people to Africa for the same reasons he did. However, a war among rival tribes in the region made any treaty he had signed irrelevant. Similarly, a civil war in the United States pulled Delany into the struggle to end U.S. slavery once and for all.

Although scholars rarely make such a clear connection between Paul Cuffe's and Martin Delany's emigration movements, both were centered on the regeneration of Africa through legitimate trade and commerce and stood apart from the missionary zeal and gradualist-deportationist philosophy of the ACS founders. Even though the ACS, and its state auxiliaries, specifically in Pennsylvania, Maryland, New York, and Massachusetts, supported Cuffe's and Delany's ideas about commerce, the driving force behind colonization was to create an asylum for free Blacks and to spread Christianity among the "heathen" and education in Africa. For Cuffe and Delany, by contrast, commerce and nation-building would provide not merely a refuge but a site to initiate the regeneration of Africa; proving Black people were equal to white people remained of secondary concern. If Liberia was to thrive it would be within the U.S. imperial system rather than as a beachhead for the building of a Black American empire of liberty and benevolence. These last two ambitions, though, were central to Paul Cuffe's and Martin Delany's agenda. Yet, to speculate about the circumstances that might have best facilitated this vision while Cuffe was alive or whether or not civil war—in both Yorubaland and the United States—halted Delany's plans is a lesson in futility.

Conclusion

Black abolitionists and emigrationists like Paul Cuffe and Martin Delany actually believed the establishment of a Black American empire in Africa would benefit African people on the continent and in the diaspora. The Atlantic slave trade that erased entire villages and exacerbated local tensions in Africa had caused death, dispersal, and the decline of African kingdoms that had reigned for centuries, such as the Oyo kingdom in the Niger Valley. Black emigrationists like Cuffe and Delany believed a Black settlement would end the slave trade, and thus cut down slavery at its roots rather than build an empire for the profit of a few, like the one Americans sought to establish as they pushed into the old Southwest and annexed Texas. U.S. empire in Africa, then, as Brandon Mills points out, was framed around the idea that African Americans were best suited to bring commerce, Christianity, and civilization to "benighted Africans" who were the victims of Atlantic world empire building because of the crucial role of the Atlantic slave trade.

To what degree were Delany's and Cuffe's missions an extension of U.S. imperial ambitions in Africa? On one hand, Paul Cuffe's effort to promote commerce in West Africa fit within the Atlantic world system, yet his primary goal was to foster legitimate trade and undermine slavery. For this reason, his emigration movement challenged one of the fundamental institutions that built European imperial fortunes: the Atlantic slave trade and slavery in the sugar and cotton plantations in North and South America, as well as the Caribbean. Even if the legal slave trade had been abolished by royal decree, Paul Cuffe imagined Sierra Leone as a beachhead for an "empire of liberty," one that would spread what he viewed as a constructive force for change in Africa rather than one that destroyed entire societies. In hindsight, Cuffe's emigration movement might appear paternalistic at best, and exploitative at worst. However, the ideas that underpinned his movement, as well as the personal capital he invested, speak to his commitment to something that contrasted with most wealthy white philanthropic types who championed abolition. Liberty for African people depended on the transformation of the West African political economy in ways that fostered alternative forms of commerce than those that promoted chattel slavery. Cuffe was one of the Black founders who composed a "moral community" of Americans who, as Bronwen Everill points out, believed "consumption and accumulation of wealth were possible" outside of the Atlantic slave system.[69]

Delany shared Cuffe's view about the association between capitalism and the rise of the Atlantic slave system. Yet, in an era defined by anti-Black state and federal laws, most notorious among them the Fugitive Slave Law, Delany's emigrationism sought to undermine European and American imperial ambitions even while utilizing them to serve his immediate need for funding. Even if Delany's views of the "natives" were chauvinistic, he hardly accepted the racist views perpetuated by white Americans and Europeans. Free Black Americans had been sapped of their "manhood" by living within a racist society. Regeneration of the race depended on leaving a racist environment in order to shed this inferiority and embrace one's authentic Africanness. Delany did believe African people had special racial traits, but he did not believe Africans were inferior because of these traits. In fact, he argued that white supremacy was an illusion and had been born out of two centuries of slavery. Delany was quick to point out that in ancient times, the Egyptian and Ethiopian empires were respected by those who claimed they were of Greek and Roman decent. While Delany did acknowledge European technology and modern medicine as superior to certain African traditional practices that lacked scientific verification, he never believed some racial characteristic led white Europeans or Americans to develop them. Of course, Delany's assessment was accurate, and the myth of white racial superiority rooted in innate biological traits would be shattered over the next century.[70]

Analyzing the early history of Black emigrationism reveals how Black American emigrationists were forced to reckon with a British and American Atlantic world system where Sierra Leone, Liberia, and the Gold Coast colony

provided both opportunity and obstacles to Paul Cuffe's and Martin Delany's Black American nation in Africa. Their vision overlapped and inter-
sected with both those who embraced the colonization movement to Liberia
that framed Liberia as homeland and a beacon of liberty for oppressed
people of African descent in North America, Africa, and the British West
Indies, as well as those critics who considered Liberia a tool for U.S. imperialism in Africa. This imagined homeland, then, had proven as illusionary
as Thomas Jefferson's desire to see the United States become an "empire of
liberty."[71]

PART III

The Ideologies of Empire

CHAPTER 11

Imperialism and the American Imagination

NICHOLAS GUYATT

When did Americans begin to see empire as un-American? The obvious answer would be the crisis of the 1760s and 1770s, when American patriots broke free from their oppressive imperial parent and founded a new nation on liberty. "To become aware of oneself as belonging to a subject people," Edward Said wrote, "is the founding insight of anti-imperialist nationalism." But a clear and coherent anti-imperialism took longer to emerge in the United States than we might imagine. "Empire" was a fluid concept in the late eighteenth and early nineteenth centuries. Americans carefully observed a number of empires—above all, Britain—and debated the meaning and morality of imperial dynamics as they considered their own national achievement. They flattered themselves with the belief that empire in the United States might look different to European models, which had ravaged Latin America and necessitated the War of American Independence. At the same time, as the new nation's white leaders looked greedily toward the vast American interior, they indulged "pathologies of colonization" (in Peter Onuf's phrase) that were all too familiar.[1]

This essay offers a sketch of the ways in which Americans talked and thought about empire from the 1760s to circa 1830. In the first section, I will suggest that the imperial crisis of the 1760s led not to a rejection of empire but to an embrace of what became known in the 1780s as an "empire of liberty." Separation from Britain did not convince Americans that empire was an illegitimate political formation. If anything, white American boosters of the new nation insisted that the United States could now become the empire Britain always should have been. But the idea of the "empire of liberty" led its American proponents into awkward engagement with Native Americans and African Americans, whose presence and resistance embarrassed claims that the United States had improved upon European templates.

In the second section, I will briefly trace American engagements with other people's empires from the 1780s to the 1820s. Although this was a period in which several anti-imperial struggles produced striking victories—in Haiti, Latin America, and Greece, for instance—Americans were slow to articulate a clear denunciation of empire. Partly this serves to remind us that our reflexive understanding of imperialism, grounded in coercive control over huge distances, owes much to the theorizing of imperialists and their opponents in the century between 1850 and 1950; during the preceding century, the language of expansion and control was considerably more fluid. In particular, Americans balanced sympathies for the victims of repression with an understanding—even an appreciation—of a key ambition of European empires: the desire to bring non-European areas into the commercial, religious, and legal ambit of Christian powers. In this respect, the belated emergence of American anti-imperialism owes something to the entanglement of internationalism and empire that underpinned new ideas about world order in the early nineteenth century.

The third and final section argues that it was people of color in the new United States who crafted the arguments that revealed the "empire of liberty" to be a contradiction in terms. Jeffrey Ostler has persuasively argued that Native Americans were key critics of emerging U.S. imperialism in the decades after 1783. Here I will focus on the debates over Black colonization from the 1780s to the 1820s. White proponents of Black colonies beyond the borders of the United States invited African Americans to imagine themselves as separate but equal, founding their own Jamestowns or Plymouths in the hinterlands of North America or on the coast of West Africa. Black critics broke through these analogies to grapple with the imperial logics that lay behind them. In the process, they proved themselves to be among the first genuinely anti-imperial thinkers in American history.[2]

*   *   *

At the outset we should acknowledge that imperial practices and imperial awareness were linked in complicated ways. Ann Laura Stoler has suggested that American imperialism was actively and consciously camouflaged by its practitioners: that U.S. historians have been misdirected on the empire question because "historical actors refused the term *empire* while practicing its tactics." Stoler also invokes W. E. B. Du Bois's suggestion that historians themselves became complicit in the concealment of empire, fostering an "educated ignorance" in which scholarship buries the facts of imperialism beneath layers of national history. But when did Americans come to think that empire was something they needed to hide? To give just one example, did Thomas Jefferson recognize the "empire of liberty" as an oxymoron, or convince himself that empire could be truly liberal? This essay leans toward the latter view, while acknowledging that some Americans became aware of the innately coercive dynamics of empire long before others.[3]

It is important to recognize that Americans could engage in imperial practices without a vocabulary or even an understanding of empire. Settlers who flooded into Kentucky or Ohio in the 1790s and 1800s brought with them a number of assumptions and ideologies—about religion, race, and improvement—but did not require a theory of empire to practice what we now call "settler colonialism." That phrase was only coined in the 1970s, initially in the context of white settler communities in southern Africa, but (as the work of Bethel Saler and others has demonstrated) it persuasively describes the processes of incorporating the North American interior in the decades after American independence. Conversely, opponents of settler colonialism and imperial expansion could critique these without explicitly identifying empire as their quarry. Cherokees in Georgia or Miamis in Indiana could take up arms against wildcat white settlements (and the state and federal troops that rushed to their defense) without denouncing empire, though many Native Americans thought deeply about the structural contexts that brought white people into their heartlands.[4]

I lean on this distinction between imperial thinking and practices to clarify that this essay focuses mostly on the former and does not pretend to encompass the full range of imperial and anti-imperial activities in the early United States. Instead, I will try to sketch the development of ideas about empire during the first half century of the American republic, with a focus both on the extension of U.S. sovereignty into the American interior and on the activities of other empires—British, French, Spanish, Ottoman, and so on—as witnessed or discussed by American commentators. I will try to explain why white Americans were slow to identify empire as a definitively malign phenomenon, and I will suggest that underlying structures of imperial coercion emerged with unusual clarity in the debates about Black colonization.

A Revolution Against Empire?

"There is something very absurd," wrote Thomas Paine, "in supposing a continent to be perpetually governed by an island." It is a truism of American history that 1776 represented a rejection of imperialism, but scholars have recently argued for a more nuanced understanding of the resistance that began in 1763. Justin du Rivage's *Revolution Against Empire* quickly complicates its bold title. Du Rivage argues that Americans and Britons found themselves arguing not over the legitimacy of empire but over different meanings of that term during the 1760s and 1770s. In the debates that divided commentators both within the metropole and in the colonies, one could find advocates of an empire of domination—rooted in the paramount sovereignty of the Westminster parliament and the king—and proponents of what du Rivage describes as a "federation of relative equals." It is important to recognize both models as imperial because their supporters presented them in precisely those terms.[5]

Take, for instance, the Massachusetts lawyer James Otis, whose pamphlets protesting the Westminster parliament's taxation of the colonies were among the most influential criticism of British authority in America. In *Rights of the British Colonies* (1764), Otis grounded the liberties of the colonists in their status as Britons and defended the (limited but distinct) sovereignty of colonial legislatures as entirely compatible with empire. The Spanish and French models of despotic empire were offensive to British principles, Otis insisted. As for the claim made by defenders of the Dutch empire that "the liberty of Dutchmen is confined to Holland" and "never intended for Provincials in America," Otis pointed out that by this logic the Dutch themselves would still be provincials within the Spanish empire. (By extension, British readers who imagined that they could treat Spain as a model for controlling North America might reflect on the successful Dutch revolt.) Otis disavowed any interest in independence, but queried whether Britons really understood the nature of their own empire. The American colonies were not "a parcel of little insignificant conquered islands" but instead "a very extensive settlement on the continent." This vast polity could be happily held within the empire, but only if British administrators recognized that Americans were "entitled to all the natural, essential, inherent and inseparable rights of our fellow subjects in Great Britain." The famous credo of "no taxation without representation" was a call for imperial reform before it became a cry for independence.[6]

The argument that Britain was simply mismanaging its empire became a commonplace among patriot critics during the 1760s and 1770s. Thomas Jefferson, in his 1774 *Summary View of the Rights of British America*, extended Otis's arguments into a full-blown theory of "well poised empire." The constituent parts would have their own legislatures making law for their section of the empire and would scrupulously respect the "rights and liberties of one another." Alexander Hamilton made the same point a year later: "The colony of New York may be a branch of the British Empire, though not subordinate to the legislative authority of Britain." Hamilton, unlike Jefferson, placed particular emphasis on the role of the monarch in making the "vast and complicated machine of government" run smoothly across huge distances. "The several parts of the empire, though otherwise independent [of] each other, will all be dependent on him."[7]

Was this cozy vision of federative empire a kind of trolling on the part of patriots? It certainly enraged American Tories and British conservatives: the Connecticut loyalist Samuel Seabury fulminated that "it is an impropriety of speech to talk of an independent colony." As Alison LaCroix has suggested, though, the patriots who wrote about colonial equality before 1776 proved reluctant to abandon their federal vision of empire on the other side of the Revolutionary War. One can see the continuity in Jefferson's and James Madison's conception of an "empire of liberty," and in Madison's embrace of a vast polity in the tenth number of the *Federalist*. Viewed through the lens of the decolonization wave of the twentieth century, the American Revolution seems an indelible renunciation of empire. Within the terms of the late eighteenth century, however, Madison and Jefferson could see the Revolution as a *defense* of empire. Hadn't the American colonists in the 1760s provided a clear route to reconciling equal political communities across vast distances? Weren't the colonists doing everything in their power to hold the British empire together? From this creative vantage point, it was the king and Parliament who had become (in Peter Onuf's phrase) "the real anti-imperialists."[8]

Rooting the "empire of liberty" in patriot thinking of the 1760s and early 1770s helps us to see American expansionism as a working out of the longer problem of federal union. It also deters us from concluding that initiatives like the equal footing doctrine (by which new states would come into the Union with the same rights as existing states) were dazzlingly new. According

to H. W. Brands, before the equal footing clause of the 1787 Northwest Ordinance, "the world history of geographical expansion" was "the history of
subjugation." ("What was the point of expansion," Brands breezily asks, "if
not exploitation?") In fact, Jefferson's emphasis on equal footing in the first
draft of the ordinance in 1784 built closely on patriots' idealized vision of the
British North American empire before the Seven Years' War. The lesson to
be learned from Britain was not that empire was bad, but that the new American empire should enshrine principles of balance and equality in its founding charters.[9]

Initially many eastern states were nervous that the equal footing principle would encourage a drain of power to the west; James Madison's attempt
to insert an equal footing clause into the federal Constitution in 1787 failed
dismally, with all but two of the states unwilling to tie the hands of Congress
on the question of how new territory would be governed. But the admission
of the first new states in the 1790s settled the principle along the lines Jefferson had originally envisaged. Federalists (and their political successors)
continued to fret about the effects of expansion long into the nineteenth
century, but Jeffersonians presented the Louisiana Purchase as triumph for
the principle of federative empire. According to David Ramsay of South Carolina, in an 1804 oration in Charleston, the "great empire" of the United
States could now improve on the corrupted and authoritarian models of previous ages. "When the Romans extended their dominions," Ramsay noted,
"the new members of their empire became the subjects of their old citizens."
To do the same in North America would be to transform Louisiana into a
"dependency" and to encourage western settlers to declare independence. But
since the United States had committed itself to the principle of equal rights
across vast distances, it had "nothing to fear from an extension of its boundaries." An expanding United States could escape the cycles of excess and de-
cay that had previously checked the civilizing power of empire.[10]

Ramsay's peroration was ecstatic: "All this country filled with freemen—
with citizens of the United States!" While Ramsay was silent on whether African Americans would be among their number, he presented the uplift and
integration of Native Americans as the inevitable consequence of the Louisiana Purchase. The numerous Indigenous inhabitants of the region would
welcome the United States because it worked on different principles from the
empires of Europe. The French and British had always seen Native people as
instruments to advance their own domination, or as proxy powers in an end-

less cycle of European wars. A U.S. monopoly over the interior would change all of this. "Those Indians are now all our own; included within our limits, and so far dependent on us that no other nation can interfere with them."[11]

Ramsay's thinking about "dependence" here amplified a view shared by Federalists and Republicans through the War of 1812: that the chief obstacle to securing Native "uplift" was the interference of European powers in the American interior. Jefferson himself ruefully told Alexander von Humboldt in 1813 that the benevolence of the federal government had foundered on the cynicism of European interlopers: "The interested and unprincipled policy of England has defeated all our labors for the salvation of these unfortunate people," and Britain's lamentable corruption of Native Americans "will oblige us now to pursue them to extermination, or drive them to new seats beyond our reach." But this lachrymose transference came a decade after the Louisiana Purchase, in the midst of another war. In 1804, as David Ramsay celebrated America's deal with Napoleon, it seemed that the United States had a "glorious field" for the "civilizing" of Indigenous people. The genius of the American empire, in Ramsay's exultant vision, was its aversion to domination.[12]

The idea of federative empire that had structured patriot critiques of British rule from the 1760s and 1770s survived the American Revolution to guide white American thinking about both political organization within the expanding nation and relations with people of color who lived within and beyond its borders. Carroll Smith-Rosenberg has suggested that the founders of the United States were Janus-faced: they sustained a liberal and republican vision as they looked east and an imperial and coercive vision as they looked west. In a similar vein, Robert Parkinson has argued that the founders carefully excluded Native Americans and African Americans from the "common cause" forged during the Revolution, racializing "all men are created equal" and drafting a blueprint for white supremacy. In fact, thinkers like Ramsay, Jefferson, and Madison declared that a federative empire might yet find ways to incorporate Native people without exposing them to the coercion or tyranny that Spain, France, and Britain had employed in their own management of distant spaces. As we will see later, they also nourished the hope that the "empire of liberty" might find ways to divest itself of enslaved people.[13]

But the danger that the United States might become identified with a more coercive form of empire was evident from the republic's earliest years. "It is a melancholy reflection," wrote the secretary of war Henry Knox to George Washington in 1794, "that our modes of population have been more destructive to the Indian natives than the conduct of the conquerors of Mexico and Peru." Running alongside the confidence of the founders that they could make a success of the "empire of liberty" was an awareness of the other variants of imperialism into which the United States might fall. "The favorable opinion and pity of the world is easily excited in favor of the oppressed," Knox warned one of his generals in 1793. But before white Americans looked for ways to conceal the exploitative nature of their national project, they told each other (and themselves) that liberty and empire could be mutually reinforcing.[14]

"Our Position in the World"

While the founders developed their "infant empire" at home, the half century following the Revolutionary War saw extraordinary challenges to empire in the Americas and the wider world. Britons thought deeply about the loss of the United States and experimented with different versions of empire in Canada, West Africa, and South and Southeast Asia. The French Revolution led to an uprising in Saint-Domingue and the emergence of an independent Haiti in 1804. The rapid ascent of Napoleon produced a speedily aggrandizing French state within and beyond Europe, which in turn bred fears among British and American observers of another "universal empire" to rival the despotisms of the early modern period. Napoleon's invasion of the Iberian Peninsula in 1807 triggered a cascade of insurgency across the Spanish and Portuguese empires in the Americas, with virtually the entire western hemisphere winning independence from Europe by the mid-1820s. The Greek uprising against the Ottoman empire, which began in 1821, produced a cognate struggle on the other side of the Atlantic.

While American politicians pondered the formal diplomatic response of the new United States to these convulsive events, thousands of Americans overseas—merchants, sailors, travelers, missionaries—gained a firsthand vantage on imperial governance and anti-imperial resistance. Beyond witnessing the struggles of European officials and armies to project power in distant places, "extraterritorial Americans" became close observers of non-European empires in the vast Ottoman regions of North Africa and the Middle East; in the Burmese empire, which maintained its independence from the East India Company until the 1820s; and in China, where imperial rule was deeply rooted. Generally speaking, Americans who witnessed or thought about other people's empires before 1830 were no more likely to isolate "imperialism" as a deleterious political formation than Madison or Jefferson had been after the American Revolution. Synthetic treatments of empire are hard to find in the written record of travelers or in the debates on foreign affairs in Congress. Instead, we are left with complex and contextual responses both to the continuation of European imperial ambition (after the setback of Britain's loss of the thirteen colonies) and to the progress of anti-imperial struggles across the world. Where was the grand unified theory of empire during this moment of American history?[15]

Part of the answer is that Americans did not assume that the American Revolution marked the beginning of a historical process by which nation-states would become the default political unit in world history. Scholars of imperialism caution against a teleology of political development that presents the nation-state as the natural successor to empire. The Spanish-American revolutions after 1807 may have been, in the words of John Quincy Adams, "a great revolution in world affairs," but in the first three decades of the nineteenth century Americans could observe the expansion and consolidation of European control over other world regions. (This was, after all, the moment of C. A. Bayly's "imperial meridian.") No coherent movement against imperialism had arisen in either Britain or France in the late eighteenth century, despite the skepticism about overseas coercion expressed by Diderot (in the *Histoire des Deux-Indes*) and by British commentators after the American Revolution. The weight of soul-searching within Britain over both the loss of the thirteen colonies and the excesses of the East India Company produced not a rejection of empire but a reformed sense of its place and purpose. The rise of Napoleon undermined anti-imperial critiques in Britain and France, and the emergence of the Holy Alliance at the end of the Napoleonic Wars gave Britons new confidence that their projection of power overseas was both justified and necessary.[16]

Americans were not oblivious to new obligations of nationhood in a world that was still dominated by coercive empires. In 1791, the Connecticut teacher (and future politician) Abraham Bishop wrote in a Boston newspaper that, since "freedom is the natural right of all human beings," the United States should throw its weight behind the uprising in Saint-Domingue: "Is not their cause as just as ours?" But did "all men are created equal" commit Americans to supporting anti-imperialism wherever it emerged? In a congressional debate in 1806, on the eve of the Spanish-American revolutions, the

Delaware senator Samuel White chastised his colleagues for not thinking clearly enough about the U.S. posture toward anti-imperial revolutions: "If gentlemen will look for a moment about them, will attend to our position in the world, and to the colonial establishments of the European nations around us, they cannot but be convinced, that cases similar to [Haiti] must often happen: the sooner, therefore, we take our ground, the better." Abraham Bishop had put the point with beguiling simplicity: "Let us be consistent Americans, and if we justify our own conduct in the late glorious Revolution, let us justify those who, in a cause like ours, fight with equal bravery." But consistency on the question of opposing empire proved elusive throughout the early republic.[17]

Three factors worked against the emergence of a consistent American approach to empire in the pell-mell of world affairs after 1783. First, empire seemed to many American observers a promising mechanism for bringing law, commerce, and religion to non-European places. In supporting the continuation of U.S. trade with Haiti in 1806, Samuel White of Delaware urged Americans to support anticolonial revolutions on the principle that neutrality should be the default assumption of international affairs: "A revolted colony or province," he told the U.S. Senate, "is to be treated by neutral nations as an independent people, without regarding the legality or illegality of their claim to such independence." This made sense in the context of anticolonial resistance, which might open new markets to U.S. commerce, especially in the western hemisphere. But in other regions of the world, the British empire could serve as a bulwark against both the excesses of other European nations (France, in particular) and the obstinacy of local powers (such as China).[18]

The realization that Britain might be a delivery mechanism for commerce and civilization took time to develop in the United States, not least due to the maddening British refusal before 1815 to respect the autonomy of American sailors and shipping. But the idea that American interests might be advanced by British imperialism had already occurred to evangelicals and moral reformers even before the War of 1812. A catalyst for this was the British commitment in 1807 to abolish the slave trade, which drove British law and power into non-European spaces under the rubric of humanitarianism. (As Padraic Scanlan has reminded us, British antislavery during the final decade of the Napoleonic Wars had a strikingly militaristic aspect.) British officials and writers became more evangelical in the promotion of "free trade" after 1815, and American statesmen and merchants could see advantage in riding on Britain's coattails into new regions and markets. Lauren Benton and Lisa Ford caution against assuming that the reach of British legal and commercial power was boundless in the first half of the nineteenth century. But the patchwork of control generated by the British "rage for order" after 1800 offered Americans opportunities to pursue their own reforming or reordering, both commercially and morally.[19]

Missionaries were key players in the construction of a kind of junior partnership between Americans overseas and British officials and institutions. The American Board of Commissioners for Foreign Missions (ABCFM) was founded in 1810, at a moment of growing tension between Britain and the United States. But in the decades after the War of 1812, the ABCFM and other missionary organizations were keenly aware of the power of the British empire to open distant spaces to American evangelism. Even in areas controlled by other imperial powers—most notably, within the Ottoman empire—American missionaries would share resources, strategies, and companionship with their British counterparts. The British empire offered a "cultural base" (in Emily Conroy-Krutz's phrase) for the working out of Americans' spiritual mission to the world.[20]

A vivid example of American missionaries' entanglement with Britain was supplied by Ann Judson, who along with her husband, Adoniram, was sent to India by the ABCFM in February 1812. Soon after their arrival in Calcutta, the Judsons chose to give up their Congregationalist faith and join the Baptist church, forfeiting their support from the ABCFM. British Baptist missionaries in Calcutta welcomed the couple, but then the Judsons were forced to flee from India by the news that the War of 1812 had begun. After briefly taking refuge in Mauritius, they settled in Rangoon, the flourishing center of the independent Burmese kingdom. Ann Judson initially assumed that U.S. missionaries would have an advantage in places like Burma, where "the British are suspected and feared, but not the Americans." During nearly a decade in Rangoon, the Judsons reassured Burmans that they were not part of the British imperial effort while continuing to socialize and strategize with British missionaries and imperial officials. But when the East India Company finally invaded in 1824, Adoniram was arrested by Burmese officials and charged with spying for the British. Ann placed her hopes in the invading British army, which eventually swept into Rangoon and secured both Adoniram's release and the permanent dismemberment of the Burmese kingdom. Elated by this turn of events, Ann declared that the prospects for American missionaries were now "bright indeed." Like many American missionaries,

Ann Judson came to realize that British control and influence provided a durable foundation for Christian imperialism.[21]

A second factor that prevented the emergence of a consistent American anti-imperialism was a widespread skepticism among white Americans about the ability of non-European peoples to govern themselves. Samuel White's spirited defense of U.S. trade with Haiti in 1806 was grounded on a basic principle: anti-imperial movements with enough momentum and expertise to form a provisional government were entitled to commercial relations with the United States. But the bulk of American commentary on Haiti was scornful of the political ability of its newly independent people, despite their extraordinary achievement of founding the first independent Black polity in the western hemisphere. "The blacks are wholly unacquainted with the arts of government," declared one Philadelphia magazine in 1804, predicting a "stern and sanguinary despotism" as the sequel to French rule. A similar skepticism in the United States met the bright predictions of Simón Bolívar that, after the anti-imperial revolutions of Spanish America, the entire western hemisphere could be rebuilt on the principles of self-rule; perhaps even as a gigantic "league" of American states. U.S. observers were doubtful of this and identified numerous sources of "degradation" among the citizens of the new American republics—from race mixing to Catholicism to a lack of political experience—which might cloud Bolívar's vision. While the pseudoscience of race was far from complete or authoritative in the early United States, a combination of racial assumptions and stadial arguments about civilizational progress worked to limit the revolutionary universalism that Abraham Bishop had briefly indulged by demanding that his compatriots be "consistent Americans."[22]

In the 1820s, the Greek uprising against the Ottoman empire reinforced an American belief that all subject peoples were not created equal. The outbreak of a holy war between Greek Orthodox Christians and Turkish Muslims in the spring of 1821 electrified observers in the United States and Europe. Thousands of volunteers (including hundreds from the United States) traveled to Greece to defend the supposed cradle of civilization; many more at home urged their governments to support the uprising. But, as Karine Walther has noted, American affinity with Greece was rooted in a specific narrative of whiteness and civilization rather than a dedication to universal principles of resistance. When Congress debated the proposal to send a diplomatic representative to the Greeks in 1824, Daniel Webster grounded his argument for American intervention not in a universal conception of human rights but in a Greek exceptionalism. "In the whole world," he declared, "no such oppression is felt as that which has crushed down the wretched Greeks." What of the other victims of empire? "In India, to be sure, it is bad enough in principle, but in the actual feeling of the oppression, it is not to be compared." The Greeks were "seven millions of civilized, enlightened Christian men, trampled into the very earth." In India, by contrast, "the oppressed natives are themselves as barbarous as their oppressors." The notion that some peoples were more deserving of liberation from empire than others drew on a long-standing cultural chauvinism (and an emerging racial science). But even Webster's narrow and bespoke appeal alarmed his colleagues in the House of Representatives. Several denied any meaningful correspondence between the peoples of the classical period and their modern successors. The Greeks were "the most degraded people of Europe," according to one congressman. Others, like the New York representative Silas Wood, trialed a new argument: "If a people possess the elements of freedom, they cannot be long held in slavery; and if they are destitute of these, no efforts they may make will terminate in the establishment of free institutions." Those peoples who could not emerge from imperial control on their own initiative were not fitted for nationhood.[23]

These ideas bring us to a third element that constrained the development of U.S. anti-imperialism: an anxiety that general opposition to empire would commit the United States to unending overseas interventions. In the debate over Greece, congressmen opposed to U.S. involvement invoked Washington's Farewell Address to insulate Americans from overseas commitments. Silas Wood presented interventionism as its own form of imperialism: the belief that "the United States are the guardians of liberty, and are bound to propagate it among all nations" was "the doctrine of the Pope, of Mahomet, and Bonaparte, and leads to universal war—to universal power." The South Carolina representative Joel Poinsett carefully distinguished between sympathy and statecraft: while the "heroic struggle for freedom" in Greece would win the admiration of every American, diplomatic or military intervention would set a dangerous precedent. Would the United States subsequently intervene if the Italians revolted against the Austrians, the Irish against the British, or the Poles against the Russians? Better by far that the United States serve as the refuge of liberty rather than its forward arsenal, Poinsett urged.[24]

Similar arguments about the perils of intervention were raised a year later in 1825, when Simón Bolívar proposed that the new American republics should convene in Panama for discussions on their political future. The

United States, admired by many Spanish American revolutionaries as the hemisphere's republican pioneer, received its own invitation to join the Panama Congress. Members of the Congress in Washington were scarcely more enthusiastic than they had been in the case of Greece. Some feared that a formal agreement with Spanish American states would drag the United States into a new set of conflicts. Others complained that Bolívar's plan amounted to its own form of federative empire in which the United States would play only a minor role. John Quincy Adams, who had been fiercely opposed to Greek intervention, was considerably more enthusiastic about involvement in the Panama Congress. As James Monroe's secretary of state, he had been the architect of the 1823 Monroe Doctrine, which channeled universal commitments to liberty toward U.S. hemispheric influence. In urging congressmen to approve a mission to Panama, Adams used the same trick Daniel Webster had tried during the Greek debate: representatives should recognize that the circumstances and geography of Latin American independence were exceptional. Washington's old advice, that the United States should avoid "distant or detached" affairs, was as solid as ever; but the states of Latin America were now "republics like ourselves . . . whose political principles and systems of government are congenial with our own." After a protracted debate, a lukewarm Congress eventually approved Adams's request.[25]

These three factors—the belief that other people's empires could advance civilization, a skepticism about the ability of non-Europeans to govern themselves, and a reluctance to commit the United States to intervention overseas—worked in tandem to limit U.S. anti-imperialism before 1830. Despite the commitment (rhetorical and sometimes material) of individual Americans to the cause of liberty overseas, the United States formally offered very little assistance to those struggling against empire during the half century after 1783. Samuel White's plea that the United States continue to trade with Haiti fell on deaf ears in 1806; Congress was persuaded by Thomas Jefferson to suspend commerce in the hopes of winning favor with Napoleon. Daniel Webster's paean to Greek civilization failed to persuade Congress in 1824 to support a mission to the rebels. John Quincy Adams's hopes that American delegates would attend the Panama Congress were delayed by months of congressional argument about what the United States might be signing up to through its participation. (In a beautifully concise metaphor for the rise of American anti-imperialism, one of the U.S. delegates arrived too late to take part, while the other died en route.) The pattern of these developments was clear: while the rhetoric of American liberty was powerful, and the aspirations of some of its proponents looked far beyond the borders of the United States, there was little to suggest that the American Revolution had established opposition to empire as a founding principle of the new republic.[26]

A Perfect Independence

Shadowing these debates about American values and overseas struggles for liberty was an inconvenient fact: peoples of color within the United States were themselves the victims of repression. African Americans and Native Americans had a unique vantage both on the limitations of white American commitments to equality and on the contradictions of federative empire. White patriots and founders, meanwhile, were uncomfortably aware that slavery and cruelty to Indigenous people could not easily be squared with their boasts of liberty. James Otis had insisted in 1764 that American colonists were "by the law of nature free born, as indeed all men are, white or black." But he also noted with frustration that the British public seemed to imagine that the North American colonies were principally sugar islands run by slaveholding tyrants. Concealing the presence of slavery throughout the mainland settlements, Otis urged his British readers to exempt the "the Northern Colonies" from their moral rebuke. He happily conceded that the "ferocity, cruelty and brutal barbarity" of Caribbean slaveholders disqualified them from membership of a liberal empire. "It is a clear truth," Otis concluded, "that those who every day barter away other men's liberty, will soon care little for their own." But the mainland, he insisted, looked very different from the islands.[27]

Otis anticipated by more than a decade Samuel Johnson's infamous jibe about the loudest yelps for liberty coming from the drivers of slaves, but he did so by condemning Caribbean planters and glossing over slavery's presence throughout the British North American colonies. On the other side of American independence, politicians found it considerably harder to contain the damage done by racial oppression to the flattering claims of liberal empire. In the 1780s and 1790s, George Washington fretted about slavery and liaised with his secretaries of war about how to avoid the formation of a new "black legend" surrounding U.S. treatment of Indigenous people. Jefferson shared his agonies on both fronts before, during, and after his presidency.

But with the logic of "all men are created equal" pointing toward racial integration and race-blind citizenship, a broad coalition of whites—from liberal
reformers to government officials—developed numerous schemes that would
allow a nominal acknowledgment of racial equality while ensuring physical
separation between African Americans, Native Americans, and white people.
These schemes vividly illuminate the halting development of white anti-
imperialism and reveal that people of color saw through the liberal cladding
of U.S. empire long before white people did.[28]

You could make a good case, for example, that one of the first anti-
imperialists in the history of the American republic was Anthony Taylor of
Newport, Rhode Island, president of the African Union Society (AUS)—the
first Black mutual aid society in the United States. In 1786, Taylor was introduced to William Thornton, an eccentric white reformer with grand ideas
about racial engineering. Thornton's parents owned a large plantation on the
British island of Tortola. During his education in Britain, Thornton embraced
the cause of antislavery and became convinced that he—the scion of
slaveholders—had a special role to play in effecting abolition. Having moved
permanently to the United States in 1785 to pursue his reforming ambitions,
Thornton heard from his British friends that they were planning to create a
settlement in West Africa for Black loyalists who had been brought to London after the Revolutionary War. Thornton imagined that a settlement along
these lines might persuade his parents to free the enslaved people on their
Tortola plantation. It might even convince enslavers on the American mainland to follow suit. Telling his antislavery correspondents in Britain that he
would test their idea on Black audiences, Thornton traveled up and down the
Eastern Seaboard with a simple question: Would African Americans have any
interest in a West African colony?[29]

Members of the AUS knew all about the idea of "resettling" Black Americans in Africa. It had been floated in 1776 by Samuel Hopkins, a white minister in Providence, as a way for white people to reconcile "all men are created
equal" with the "strong prejudices which have insensibly fixed on our minds."
In 1786, Taylor and other free Blacks in New England thought deeply about
colonization alongside the challenge of winning Black equality within the
United States. But as free people who lived within a nation that had failed to
keep its promises of equality, the African Americans of Providence would
only move to a new settlement with clear guarantees to land and self-
government. Thornton reported back to his English friends that Taylor and

the AUS were "very desirous of knowing whether they are to be considered as a colony of England, or perfectly independent." If the former, "none here will engage, for they think that they could alone be happy where there is perfect confidence in their lawgivers, and where their own voices are to be heard."[30]

The persistence of the AUS on the subject of self-determination is striking: "They have expressed a desire to have it represented that they would not embark without a perfect independence," Thornton told his British associates in subsequent letters. "If it be for a British settlement, the blacks of this country will not be disposed to go thither; if a free Negro settlement . . . *not meaning colony*, they will go in prodigious numbers." Thornton shared Anthony Taylor's demand with some of the most prominent members of the international antislavery movement: Thomas Clarkson, Jean-Jacques Brissot de Warville, and Granville Sharp, the architect of what became Sierra Leone in the spring of 1787. "The blacks of this country cannot be expected to form a colony for any European power," Thornton told Clarkson. They were "happily too much enlightened to ever submit to the dictates of any foreign usurper," he reminded Sharp. Taylor's rejection of imperial technologies seems to have rubbed off on Thornton himself: "I hate the word *colony*," he told a friend in 1788. "To colonize them it is still a species of slavery," he told another. Taylor and his free Black associates accepted Thornton's blandishments that they would not become the colonists of someone else's empire and resolved privately to encourage Thornton's "honest zeal." But they would not be "imposed upon" in the matter of colonization: if they were to leave the United States, it would be for a nation of their own.[31]

Anthony Taylor's suspicions about the British empire proved to be prescient. Sierra Leone's first settlers were quickly scattered by disease and bad weather. The colony was reestablished in 1792 by the Sierra Leone Company, a commercial venture presided over by leading British abolitionists. The company convinced another wave of Black loyalists (this time from Nova Scotia) to make the risky journey to West Africa; the company's agents and literature promised not only to provide economic opportunity but to perfect a free-labor model of tropical agriculture that would make the slave trade obsolete. In practice, the colony's white governors (and investors) reneged on their promises of economic and political opportunity, exactly as Anthony Taylor had feared they would. In 1806 Sierra Leone became a crown colony, and then the forward outpost of Britain's military campaign against the slave trade.

Whites continued to rule over what had been the "province of freedom," and thousands of "liberated Africans"—enslaved people who had been captured by the British in the Atlantic and taken to Sierra Leone—were placed under coercive "apprenticeships" throughout the colony.[32]

In the decades after Taylor's 1786 rejection of imperial citizenship, a kind of double discourse developed in the United States on the question of Black colonization. White reformers saw Black colonies as a happy alternative to the extremes of racial integration and racial subjugation: if African Americans could be resettled in the American West, the Caribbean, or Africa, they would expand the sphere of liberty without challenging white hang-ups over racial mixing. A racialized version of federative empire might relieve white Americans of both the moral imperative of integration and the moral embarrassment of racial oppression. In an 1804 tract celebrating the Louisiana Purchase, William Thornton excitedly urged the creation of racial homelands for the three major populations on the American continent: "Under the wings of the American Eagle, nations of white, red, and black men, all in peace, all in fraternity, all in happiness!" For African Americans, these schemes were as tantalizing as they were dangerous. While they might provide an opportunity to vindicate Black ability and facilitate self-determination, they relied on an idea that Black people within the United States were hopelessly degraded—a rhetoric that could only indulge the toxic prejudices of white Americans. Crucially, colonization schemes might only deliver African Americans from a familiar oppression at home to new forms of imperial subjugation beyond the United States.[33]

In the first three decades of the nineteenth century, African Americans either rejected colonization outright or drew the same careful distinction between independence and colonial subjection that Anthony Taylor had insisted upon in 1786. Virtually all African Americans who entertained the possibility of leaving the United States made Black self-rule a prerequisite. As William Thornton told Granville Sharp in 1789, "the blacks here are happily too much enlightened to ever submit to the dictates of any foreign usurper." Many were drawn to Haiti, where the fact of Black nationality was incontestable. Most rejected colonization outright, decrying the racial and imperial dynamics that informed schemes for Black resettlement. While white colonization boosters insisted that African Americans could relive the glories of Plymouth or Jamestown on the shores of Africa, Black critics (like the Baltimore schoolteacher William Watkins) offered a simple riposte: "Why this desire to be so remotely alienated from us?"[34]

But the idea of African Americans as the pioneers of American anti-imperialism needs to be hedged in two ways. First, Black leaders were considerably more critical of plans to settle under British or U.S. auspices in West Africa than to establish national projects in the American interior or the Caribbean. Black opponents of the American Colonization Society drew a clear distinction between resettlement in a slaveholder-created African colony and, in the words of a group of black Washingtonians in 1817, "a territory within the limits of our beloved Union." During the African American migration to Haiti in the 1820s, even the stalwart anti-colonizationist William Watkins recognized the power of Black nationality to demonstrate "that the descendants of Africa never were designated by their Creator to sustain an inferiority." While Haiti might give African Americans an opportunity to express their national ambitions without doing harm to Indigenous people, the same could not be said for plans to establish Black colonies in the distant West or, a little later in the nineteenth century, in Latin America. Second, African Americans were not completely immune to the idea that imperialism might promote Christianization and even "civilization" in non-European spaces. Paul Cuffe, the Massachusetts sea captain who promoted Black resettlement in Sierra Leone in the 1810s, viewed a Black colony as an instrument "to moralize and fraternize the inhabitants of Africa" and "attend greatly to the civilization of that country." Many Black critics of Liberia, meanwhile, acknowledged the need for a missionary invasion of Africa even as they questioned the intentions of the American Colonization Society.[35]

In the early nineteenth century, African Americans overwhelmingly rejected the offer of what Bronwen Everill calls "a represented citizenship within an imperial frame" in Sierra Leone or Liberia. But the assumptions of liberal imperial thought—rooted in ideas of uplift, religion, and order—crept into Black nationalist thinking in the middle decades of the century. So too did the notion that Black people might enjoy equality within the framework of federative empire—but this time within the British empire rather than an aggrandized United States. While Martin Delany and other black nationalists scoured Central and South America in search of a lasting home for African Americans, studying carefully the "fundamental principles of nationality" that had propelled white Europeans and Americans to greatness, Mary Ann Shadd Cary presented a simple alternative: African Americans should move to Canada or the West Indies and enjoy the protection of the British. "There would not be as in Africa, Mexico, or South America, hostile tribes to annoy the settler," she promised her African American readers. "The strong arm of

British power would summarily punish depredations made, of whatever character, and the emigrants would naturally assume the responsibility of British freemen." With some Black nationalists in the 1850s espousing imperial methods to create a Black nation in Latin America, and others urging African Americans to consider becoming British subjects in Canada or the Caribbean, it is clear that Anthony Taylor's pioneering anti-imperialism had not proved definitive. But Taylor had at least articulated a clear critique of empire during an era when, for the vast majority of white Americans, an anti-imperial epiphany was far in the future.[36]

*   *   *

According to Jane Burbank and Frederick Cooper, the difference between a nation-state and an empire is that the former "proclaims the commonality of its people" while the latter "declares the non-equivalence of multiple populations." Federative empire offered American colonists a route between nation-state and empire, promising initially to reconcile Britain and America and then to protect a vast American republic from the entropy of distance. When visionary plans for "civilizing" and integrating peoples of color led nowhere, federative empire seemed also to offer a solution to the problem of race: it might allow the rearrangement of Black and Indian populations into distant spaces in which their liberty could be squared with the racial squeamishness of white people. African Americans and Native Americans resisted this role: by refusing to consent to their expatriation, which turned colonization into removal (especially in the case of Native Americans) and exposed the illiberal foundations of these schemes; or by insisting, like Anthony Taylor, that a Black exodus from the United States must produce a truly independent Black nation.[37]

If we accept that the American Revolution was seen by the founders as a response to imperial mismanagement rather than a rejection of empire itself, it is easier to understand why so many Americans harbored imperial sensibilities after 1783. In the management of the vast western interior and in the project of advancing order and civilization in the wider world, empire retained both a liberal promise for white Americans and a normative status: it was the means by which Christian nations brought law, commerce, and religion to areas of the world that were despotic, savage, or both. Despite early hopes that federative empire might solve the race "problem" in America, the failure of the United States to recognize Black and Native peoples as equals left white Americans either to embrace racism openly or to indulge in new forms of uplift. "Despotism is a legitimate mode of government in dealing with barbarians," wrote John Stuart Mill in 1859, "provided the end be their improvement." In an American republic that would soon replace slavery with new forms of racial injustice, this imperial deception held sway long into the twentieth century.[38]

CHAPTER 12

Pax Americana?

The Imperial Ambivalence of American Peace Reformers

MARGOT MINARDI

In the year 84 C.E., standing at the far edge of the world he knew, a Caledonian military leader named Calgacus warned his men about the threat of imminent invasion to their Scottish homeland: "There are no more nations beyond us; nothing is there but waves and rocks, and the Romans, more deadly still than these—for in them is an arrogance which no submission or good behaviour can escape. Pillagers of the world, they have exhausted the land by their indiscriminate plunder, and now they ransack the sea. . . . To robbery, butchery, and rapine, they give the lying name of 'government'; they create a desolation and call it peace."[1] This speech, and even the speaker himself, might have been a figment of the imagination of Publius Cornelius Tacitus, the great historian of the Roman Empire who was also one of its most acerbic critics. But whether the speech came from the mouth of a Scottish warrior or the pen of an eloquent Roman, the conundrum it raised stuck. What was the relationship between imperial pacification—subduing a region and a people by force—and that pure, idyllic state of existence called peace? In a world dominated by imperial ambition and military might, whose prerogative was it to say whether a place was at peace or not? If peace was to signify something more than "desolation" (the Latin word has also been translated as "desert"), what sort of positive content could be attributed to that term? In short, did peace mean anything more than a lack of open warfare?[2]

Via Calgacus, Tacitus raised the possibility that "peace" was simply a pro-pagandistic term used by imperialists to tout pacification by conquest. His concern about the slipperiness of the term "peace" was not unknown in the nineteenth-century United States.[3] As Americans were chafing at the boundaries of their young nation, they provoked questions about the rela-tionship between expansionism and violence. Looking to Florida, Mex-ico, and beyond, those who devoted themselves to the cause of peace lambasted the use of war to extend American empire. But did this criticism of imperial warfare extend to a critique of imperialism itself? Peace reform-ers' idealization of "universal brotherhood" challenged one of the tenets of empire, the differential treatment and rule of different members of the pop-ulation.[4] Building on this belief in some kind of basic human equality, peace discourse invited white Americans to look on their own society through an outsider's gaze. This gesture enabled peace advocates to engage in critical reflection on their society's beliefs, such as the validity of imperial expansion.

Ultimately, however, peace reformers used such critical reflections and re-versals of conventional hierarchies to goad Euro-Americans into exercising their power more justly rather than to challenge imperial expansion itself. While peace reformers tended more than many of their contemporaries to value human equality, they nevertheless held on to ideas about cultural hierar-chy and racial difference that were common among white Americans in their day. Moreover, some contended that the expansion of American empire could at least theoretically be reconciled with pacifist goals. The incorporative di-mension of empire—its expansiveness, both territorially and in terms of population—appealed to many peace reformers, who envisioned bringing people together in increasingly large-scale confederations, alliances, and poli-ties as a means of reducing interstate warfare.[5] Some peace advocates even sug-gested that war was an impediment to successful expansion and colonization, and that by putting down arms, Americans would be better situated to fulfill their manifest destiny. Within such a framework, peace advocacy proved sur-prisingly easy to reconcile with imperial aspirations. This essay explores peace reformers' imperial ambivalence in two contexts: responses to frontier vio-lence during the early years of the organized peace movement (particularly during the First Seminole War) and critiques of the U.S.–Mexican War from 1846 to 1848.[6]

Toward a Benevolent Conquest: The Early Peace Movement's Critique of the First Seminole War

From its start, organized peace activism in the United States built upon the distinction between "barbarism" and "civilization" that undergirded many imperial projects. But whereas the common presumption among Europeans and Euro-Americans was that they were the agents of an imperial "civilizing mission," the first generation of American peace activists questioned which party to the colonial encounter should really be considered "civilized." The most influential exponent of this view was Noah Worcester, a founder of the Massachusetts Peace Society and one of the nascent peace movement's most influential voices in the late 1810s and 1820s. Worcester's pamphlet *A Solemn Review of the Custom of War*, published in the aftermath of the War of 1812 and the Napoleonic Wars, rallied its readers to sustain the newly secured peace. The core argument of *A Solemn Review* was that war was a barbaric custom, unsuited to people who called themselves rational, Christian, and republican. Worcester compared war to the practices of peoples whom most of his fellow Americans would have deemed as decidedly uncivilized. "We regard with horror the custom of the ancient heathens in offering their children in sacrifice to idols," he began, before grimly describing the horrifying practices of "the Hindoos," including into the supposed tossing of young children into the Ganges as offerings to the gods.[7]

And yet, Worcester asked, were these practices really any worse than the mass slaughter to which the peoples of Christendom had subjected themselves over centuries of brutal warfare? "What custom of the most barbarous nations is more repugnant to the feelings of piety, humanity and justice, than that of deciding controversies between nations by the edge of the sword, by powder and ball, or the point of the bayonet? What other savage custom has occasioned half the desolation and misery to the human race?"[8] The answer, in Worcester's view, was obvious. In his *Solemn Review* and other writings, Worcester, a Unitarian minister, held up a mirror to his audience of American Christians, asking them whether they were as worthy of the "civilized" label as they professed themselves to be. Worcester's tour de force in this vein was a set of letters he wrote from the fictional pen of one Lillian Ching, a visitor to the United States from the Loo Choo Islands (now the Ryukyu Islands). Inspired by the travel narratives of British sailors who insisted that the geographically isolated Loo Choo Islanders knew nothing of war, Worcester's "Letters of Lillian Ching" recounted the title character's shock at the many militaristic aspects of American culture, from Revolutionary War commemorations to children playing with toy guns. Ching, whose islands had never been visited by Christian missionaries, could not reconcile the pacific message he found in Jesus's life and teachings with the bloodthirst of the professed Christians he encountered in America. He concluded, "there is as much need of missionary exertions, to abolish human sacrifices in Christendom, as in Hindostan."[9]

With his pacifist writings, Worcester asked his American audience to step outside their own quotidian experience and look at their country from a detached perspective. Although neither his *Solemn Review of the Custom of War* nor the "Letters of Lillian Ching" constituted a direct indictment of imperialism, they did invite readers to assume a frame of mind that enabled questioning and even critique of imperialist presumptions. This move of getting an insider to step into the shoes of an outsider was the same that Tacitus had made in inventing the speech of Calgacus. It challenged readers to reevaluate their assumptions that their own societies were more civilized than those of barbarian (or "heathen") outsiders and to recognize that the practices they took for granted (like warfare) were not inevitable aspects of human experience but instead culturally conditioned. Worcester's critique invited a more rigorous definition of "civilization" and "barbarism." In his calculation, civilization was not whatever Europeans (or Euro-Americans) did. Instead, being civilized meant being ruled by reason, while indulging in warfare was fundamentally irrational, "the effect of popular delusion." But there was hope that such uncivilized delusions could be lifted. In the late eighteenth and nineteenth century, as revolutionaries across the Atlantic world deposed tyrants from the thrones of Europe, social reformers began to challenge the tyrannical customs that threatened human freedom and even human life itself: slavery, dueling, the consumption of alcohol. Worcester argued that war was a custom just like these, and he sought to capitalize on the successes of the antislavery, anti-dueling, and temperance causes in order to bolster his movement to end war.[10]

Worcester and other peace advocates were part of a nascent organized peace movement that crossed the Atlantic. The New York Peace Society formed first, in 1815, followed by Worcester's Massachusetts Peace Society that same year. Other state and local societies came together soon after, as did London's Society for the Promotion of Permanent and Universal Peace in 1816. These organizations were established not in the midst of war but at a moment that contemporaries perceived to be distinctively peaceable, with the recent cessation of the Napoleonic Wars and the War of 1812. Peace advocates sought to ensure that the peace of 1815 was a lasting one.[11]

Whether or not the years since 1815 actually qualified as years of peace depended on what one understood peace—and war—to be. Claiming that the United States had been at peace since 1815 meant overlooking the ongoing, often violent, struggles between white settlers and Native peoples that were part and parcel of the expansion of settler colonialism and U.S. sovereignty on the North American continent. While American peace advocates sometimes heralded the aftermath of 1815 as a peaceful period, they did not ignore the violence of American imperialism completely. In the peace movement's early years, American warfare against the Creeks and especially the Seminoles provoked particular anxiety among reformers because it challenged what Worcester and his cohort wanted the American nation to be. In critiquing the United States' incursions into Spanish Florida and its brutal treatment of Creeks and Seminoles there, Worcester was pushing back against a racialized distinction between "civilized" and "uncivilized" people that insisted that Indigenous people were not deserving of the protections of international law. As Deborah Rosen explains, in justifying the First Seminole War, "government officials and military officers [in the United States] relied on the principle that the law of nations applied only to 'civilized' people who were constituted as 'nations'"—a category that, in their view, did not include Native groups. While peace advocates generally wanted to end war entirely rather than render it more humane by subjecting it to a system of laws, their insistence that American incursions into Florida were unbefitting of a civilized, republican nation overlapped with broader critiques of the First Seminole War that emerged in Congress and in the media in the late 1810s. However, as Rosen shows, this critical take on the war in Florida ultimately constituted a minority perspective in the United States. Instead, the political debates over the First Seminole War helped pave the way for a more racially and culturally inflected approach to international law, abandoning the universalism championed by earlier thinkers, including Worcester.[12]

Noah Worcester's journal the *Friend of Peace* regularly commented on the First Seminole War as a particularly troubling example of how Americans failed to live up to civilized ideals. The *Friend* compared American involvement in Florida to other imperial engagements that the journal's readers were likely to perceive in a negative light, including British wars in India and Spanish conquest in the Americas. One unsigned piece (possibly by Worcester) argued that, in all these cases, imperial aggrandizement revealed the hollowness of arguments for "defensive war."[13] While nineteenth-century peace advocates agreed that offensive wars were wrong, they had persistent disagreements about whether or not a state could legitimately use violence in self-defense. This article, firmly arguing against defensive war, pointed out that any party to a conflict could manipulate the facts in order to claim that its use of violence was "defensive." Such was the case for the recent American war in Florida, which pitted "a great and powerful nation" (the United States) against "a small and feeble tribe" (the Seminoles). American observers disputed which side had provoked the conflict that would come to be known as the First Seminole War, but for the *Friend of Peace*, that disagreement was beside the point. Even if Seminoles living in Florida had initiated skirmishes across the border in Georgia, the more powerful U.S. government had no need to pursue a war in its (alleged) self-defense, the costs of which far outweighed the original offense. As "an aggressive war for plunder, for fame, for the acquisition of territory, or for improving its troops in the art of man-butchery," the Seminole War represented the arrogance of American power. The author reinforced this point by making a direct comparison with the recent war between the British and Marathas in India, another case in which imperialists had used the excuse of self-defense "to cover the crimes, and apologize for the calamities of war."[14]

By comparing American actions in Florida to British incursions in India, the *Friend of Peace* rejected the exceptionalist idea that American territorial expansion somehow set the United States apart from European colonial powers. This kind of critique-by-comparison recurred in peace discourse throughout the antebellum period and provides evidence for an anti-imperialist strand within early American pacifist ideology. As one peace reformer succinctly put it at the cusp of the U.S. war with Mexico, "Britain has an India; France an Algeria; young evangelical America, Mexico and the land of the Seminoles."[15] But this rejection of violent conquest did not necessarily constitute a repudiation of all imperial expansion. Repeatedly, items in the *Friend of Peace* (many of which were authored by Worcester himself) stressed the idea that the Seminoles, like other Indigenous people, could be subdued by peaceable means. "It is well known," one item announced, "that Indians are as capable of being 'conquered by beneficence' as 'by force.'"[16] Commenting on the First Seminole War, a report of the Massachusetts Peace Society (likely authored by Worcester) noted that diplomacy was a far more economical means of pacification—both in terms of money and lives—than warfare: "one half of the pecuniary expense of this war for a *single year*, would have been sufficient to attach the Seminoles to our government, and to have preserved peace with them for a *century*."[17]

The Massachusetts Peace Society's report drew on a logic common in peace reform literature that American Indians were willing to submit to colonial governance if it was extended peaceably. In this analysis, Native Americans were understood to be fundamentally peace-loving, and it was European and Euro-American brutality, not some kind of ingrained barbarity, that propelled Native people to use violence. The *Friend of Peace* drew on a range of sources to argue that American Indians had learned violence from their European conquerors: "We set them an example of violence, by burning their villages and laying waste their slender means of subsistence; and then wonder that savages will not show moderation and magnanimity towards men, who have left them nothing but mere existence and wretchedness."[18] This argument reinforced Worcester's claim that war was merely a custom—one peculiarly favored by Europeans and white Americans—and not a fundamental aspect of human nature. The peace advocates' arguments about Indians and frontier warfare thus simultaneously challenged and reinforced the logic of European and Euro-American imperialism. They called into question cultural presumptions that Indians were brutes motivated by violence rather than the rationality and benevolence that drove civilized people. At the same time, however, peace reformers insisted that if Native Americans *were* treated as reasonable people worthy of benevolence, they would uncomplainingly submit to Euro-American rule.

Peace advocates reinforced this argument by looking to colonial Pennsylvania, which Worcester and his cohort viewed as the best historical example of the superiority of conquest by beneficence over conquest by force. William Penn's policy of making treaties with Indians and paying them for their land was repeatedly cited in the *Friend of Peace* as a laudable means of securing land for Europeans and Euro-Americans without resorting to violence. One article rued the "contrast between the saving policy of William Penn, and the destroying policy pursued in the Seminole war!" This writer (very likely Worcester himself) thought that instead of sending an army to Florida, the U.S. government ought to have dispatched "a respectable number of Commissioners, well known as men of a pacific character, to inquire into the true state of things between the Seminoles and their white neighbors,—to hear the complaints and the testimonies on each side, and to employ their influence to effect a reconciliation." While not questioning the underlying logic of settler colonialism, this prescription for conflict resolution on the frontier acknowledged that both parties might have legitimate concerns.[19]

Similar hagiographies of William Penn appeared frequently in the *Friend of Peace*—and elsewhere. They were the basis, for instance, of some of Edward Hicks's "peaceable kingdom" paintings. Hicks, a Quaker, placed a vignette of Penn treating with Indians alongside biblical imagery of millennial peace (wild animals complacently lounging side by side with farm creatures, all watched over by little children). Representing in visual terms the arguments made in the same moment by peace advocates such as Worcester, Hicks's juxtaposition of these two scenes suggested that peace meant reconciling the "civilized" world with that which was "undomesticated," rather than using force to subject the latter to the former.[20] Not surprisingly, Hicks's benign view of English colonization in seventeenth-century Pennsylvania has been challenged by modern historiography; his "peaceable kingdom" represented the utopian vision of nineteenth-century reformers, not circumstances on the ground a century and a half before.[21]

From the case of William Penn in the past to the Seminoles of their own day, peace reformers in the 1810s and 1820s charted out a model for colonial relationships that eschewed force while emphasizing diplomacy and fair purchase. They applied this model to the various conflicts that emerged as American settlement pushed westward after the War of 1812. By the mid-1820s, peace reformers were joining the chorus of reform-minded Americans who opposed calls for Indian removal from the Southeast. The *Friend of Peace* criticized the injustices inflicted on Creeks and Cherokees by white settlers and the government entities that supported them. These ideas came through especially vividly in a poem written by one "M. C." for the *Friend of Peace*. The poem centered on a map of Creek land cessions, most likely depicting the land demarcations in the Treaty of Fort Jackson, in which Creeks, under duress, had ceded large swaths of territory in Georgia and Alabama to General Andrew Jackson.[22] In the poet's imagination, the "Speaking Map" had come to life in order to exhort legislators:

> If you desire to hold the land,
> The type of which I'm made to stand,
> Relinquish your *pretended* claim,
> Retract your wrongs with grief and shame;
> And then, by purchase fair and free,
> Display the love of probity,

Thus take from all the plundering crew,
Their plea *that they resemble you.*[23]

In pointed, if not especially artful, verse, the poem summarized peace reformers' position on American imperial expansionism. The use of force to
wear down Native people (and then to extort their land) was unacceptable;
legislators who supported such practices were no better than the gun-toting
frontiersmen who actually inflicted the violence. But redeeming the crimes
of Jackson and his ilk did not demand a wholesale rejection of settler colonialism itself but instead could be remedied simply "by purchase fair and
free" of the contested land.

The Lust of Conquest: Pacifist Opposition
to the U.S. Invasion of Mexico

The American invasion of Mexico in 1846 presented peace reformers with
both a crisis and an opportunity. If the ongoing violence along the nation's
frontiers (including in Florida) had not rallied the public to their movement,
the war with Mexico shattered the illusion of a thirty-year peace since the
close of the War of 1812.[24] For a peace movement that had grown up in what
was broadly understood to be peacetime, the outbreak of war presented novel
possibilities. Some had speculated that the movement had languished in the
1820s and 1830s precisely because it lacked significant opposition.[25] The invasion of Mexico gave peace advocates something big to oppose, and it allowed them to raise their cause's profile in the process. Arguments that
seemed abstract during peacetime acquired new and painful significance
during wartime, as the real costs of war in terms of money, lives, and morals
became increasingly palpable.[26] The U.S.–Mexican War invited peace reformers to renew their calls for peace with particular urgency—and, at times, to
couple them with more strident critiques of American imperialism.

Historians of the nineteenth century often discuss opposition to the
Mexican-American War in terms of antislavery politics. Abolitionists repeatedly mobilized against proslavery politicians' efforts to expand slavery into
new territories. They vigorously opposed the annexation of Texas, finalized
in 1845, which paved the way for the invasion of Mexico the next year. However, the peace and abolition movements did not overlap entirely, and discourse against the U.S.–Mexican War reveals the incongruities between them.

An abolitionist might have opposed the war with Mexico primarily, or even solely, because U.S. expansion was so tightly bound up with the spread of slavery. Such an activist's opposition to the war would have emerged out of the distinctive circumstances of 1846 and would not necessarily extend to opposition to the idea of war itself. This position left open the possibility of using the weapons of war to attack the institution of slavery, a stance that would become increasingly popular among antislavery activists in the coming decade. Those within the peace movement stood against the U.S.–Mexican War simply because it was a war. "The conflict in Mexico," rued American Peace Society leader Joshua Pollard Blanchard, "is but the latest scene of that martial tragedy which military despots have been for centuries enacting on this blood-stained earth."[27] Of course, many reform-minded Americans in the mid-nineteenth century supported both the antislavery and peace causes. But the distinctions between these different strands of opposition show that opposition to the U.S.–Mexican War did not stem solely from antislavery sentiment.

For many who spoke out against the war, the fact that the United States had invaded another sovereign nation, with the intention of annexing the land and subordinating the people, proved especially troubling. These anxieties about the imperialist orientation of U.S. policy in Mexico come through in American citizens' petitions to Congress, begging for a quick and peaceful resolution to the war. Primarily representing the reform strongholds of New England, upstate New York, and the Old Northwest, from 1846 to 1848 upwards of 17,000 Americans petitioned their senators and representatives to end the war in Mexico.[28] Most petitioners signed alongside groups of neighbors, with most of the petitions coming in from a particular town or county. Ranging from single voices of protest to groups of signatories in the hundreds or even thousands, some citizens attached their names to preprinted forms circulated by peace groups, while in other cases they articulated their opposition to the war in their own terms.[29] A petition form circulated in Ohio in 1847 and 1848 shows how the peace, antislavery, and anti-imperial causes all came together in protests against the war: "We wish there may be no more slave territory. We wish there may be no more war, nor cause of war. . . . We desire that our nation may never attempt to acquire or hold any territory upon a plea of conquest."[30]

As petitioners developed more specific critiques of this particular war, one argument that emerged frequently was that the war was invalid because Mexico was a "sister republic."[31] This argument worked in two directions. First, republican governance in the United States imposed on Americans the imperative that they rise above the aggressive imperialism that had marked the monarchies of the past. "The war which is waged against the Republic of Mexico, is purely a war of aggression," protested twenty-six men from Canfield County, Ohio, adding, "we believe that the President in erecting territorial government over foreign territory, declaring it to be part and parcel of the United States, has exercised *a power which ought not to be tolerated in a republic.*"[32] Second, republican governance in Mexico put that country on terms of equality with the United States, which meant it deserved the respect worthy of all sovereign nations. One popular petition form called the United States and Mexico "two Sister Republics"; the same form reinforced this vision of equality (though flipping the gendered language of siblinghood) by arguing that war threatened "the Spirit of Humanity which seeks to unite mankind in universal brotherhood."[33] Petitions also emphasized the mutuality of the relationship between the United States and Mexico by referring to the latter as a "neighbouring nation." Employing a convention in peace reform literature to analogize international and interpersonal relations, one petition compared the American invasion of Mexico to a man killing his neighbor and his neighbor's family and then taking possession of his property, all as a result of a petty dispute.[34]

By implying that the United States and Mexico were squabbling next-door neighbors, such arguments recognized that the two countries held equal standing in the world community. Moreover, references to Mexico as a "neighbor" invoked the ethics of everyday life, in which neighbors were to be treated with compassion and respect, thereby tying antiwar discourse to Christian virtue. Such reasoning was particularly important to the December 1847 petition of the American Peace Society, which drew on the Golden Rule to call for "an immediate, equitable and lasting Peace between these sister Republics."[35] In short, calling Mexico a "neighboring nation" or "sister republic" highlighted Mexico's national sovereignty. Erstwhile diplomat Albert Gallatin, in his magisterial pamphlet *Peace with Mexico*, identified the war with Mexico as only the third conflict "with civilized nations" that the United States had experienced since the end of the Revolutionary War. The previous two such conflicts were the Quasi-War with France in the 1790s and the War of 1812; the Mexican War had the dubious distinction, in Gallatin's view, of being the only one of the three conflicts to be unprovoked by aggression on the other side.[36] By speaking of the war with Mexico as a contest between civilized countries, Gallatin and other critics harkened back to the idea (prominent in Noah Worcester's earliest peace writings) that there was something peculiarly distasteful about two supposedly "civilized" parties going to war with one another. Further, in legitimating Mexico as a "civilized nation," this discourse differentiated the war in Mexico from other border disputes, including the ongoing conflict in Florida. Although critics of Indian wars, such as Noah Worcester, resisted conventional distinctions between "civilized" and "uncivilized," it remained easier for white Americans— including peace reformers—to recognize violence between European or Euro-American states as "war" and thus to see such violence as the legitimate object of pacifist critique. By contrast, violence against the Seminoles and many other Native people was understood as part of "a perpetual state of war against Indians," effectively blurring the boundaries between "peacetime" and "wartime" in the frontier context and making it harder for antiwar advocates to identify a discrete "war" to critique.[37]

Yet there was a flip side to the contention that the war with Mexico was unjust because it made adversaries of neighboring, civilized republics. Many protesters' opposition to the war was predicated on their sense of the superiority of the United States—morally, militarily, financially, politically, and even racially—vis-à-vis Mexico. Was the war problematic because it represented a dominant nation-state's abuse of power over a weaker rival, or because it pitted two equals against each other? Antiwar petitioners did not seem troubled by the tensions between these two lines of argumentation, as they freely intermingled them in their texts. More than two hundred voters from Ferrisburgh, Vermont, called for the "immediate termination" of what they termed "a war of conquest against a feeble and distracted sister republic." Like the Vermont petition, other critiques of the war emphasized Mexico's weakness. "Distracted," one of the most common terms to describe the present condition of Mexico, conjured up the country as divided against itself and troubled in mind.[38] The petitions sometimes paired the word "distracted" with adjectives such as "semi-barbarous" and "half civilized."[39] Besides suggesting racial inferiority, such formulations exposed the gendered implications of referring to Mexico as a "sister." In this usage, the language of feminine siblinghood connoted not a relationship of equals but a state of vulnerability. Drawing on a long tradition signifying conquest as an act of sexual domination, the radical Unitarian preacher Theodore Parker thundered about the causes and consequences of the war in 1848: "The Mexicans were as unprotected women, we, armed men. See how the lust of conquest will increase."[40]

Such arguments constructed Mexico and the Mexican people as suffering and vulnerable, deserving subjects of the benevolent aid of the United States, rather than an abusive show of American might. "As we would find mercy ourselves from the God of nations, it appears to us that we are bound to show mercy to the distracted & suffering Republic of Mexico," asserted a group of electors from DeWitt, New York.[41] While this petition begged legislators to show more restraint and humility, it did so in terms that analogized Americans to God. Other petitioners perceived the war as a contest "between our beloved and highly favored country—and our distracted and oppressed neighbor."[42] The many advantages the United States enjoyed imposed a moral obligation on Americans. Petitioners from Jackson Township, Ohio, reminded Congress that Americans "can afford to be magnanimous," before continuing: "let us now exhibit an example of American generosity and moderation, and teach the nations of the earth, that our Republic can be as just and liberal as our soldiers have been brave."[43] For such advocates of American exemplarism, showing restraint toward Mexico would actually enhance, not diminish, American greatness. These arguments resonated with those made against the First Seminole War in the *Friend of Peace* a generation earlier. In both cases, peace advocates found the idea of a more powerful entity overwhelming a weaker one with force to be both anti-republican and unchristian.

Such arguments stemmed from a fear that the war in Mexico would deprive the United States of its high moral standing on the international stage. Along with Theodore Parker, who equated aggressive imperialism with lust, many critics of the war worried about "that dangerous sentiment, the *love of conquest.*"[44] Again and again, petitioners railed against the Mexican War because it was motivated by a desire for "conquest" or "national aggrandizement."[45] American action in Mexico was especially distasteful because Americans were the aggressors, the invaders.[46] Even the few petitions to acknowledge that war might be acceptable in some instances made it clear that the conquest-driven war in Mexico was clearly not. Petitioners from Deerfield, Massachusetts, wrote, "all *invasive* wars, at least, are, & from the manner in which they are conducted, *must* be unjust & inhuman."[47] Those from Lower Merion Township, Pennsylvania, argued "that to prosecute the war with a view to conquer any portion of the territory of Mexico would be a departure from the objects which alone justify war."[48] Such critiques emanated from a sense that the nation ought to privilege justice and forbearance over acquisitiveness and aggression. These assertions about the proper course for American foreign affairs resonated with contemporary debates about the masculine ideal, which historian Amy Greenberg has identified as a struggle between "restrained manhood" and "martial manhood."[49] Without question, peace advocates came down on the side of restraint.

In early 1848, a group of nineteen "citizens of the US" brought together several common critiques of the U.S.–Mexican War when they implored Congress, "Regarding with deep sorrow & disapprobation the act of this government engaging in an aggressive War against any Nation, & especially one weaker than Herself, seriously petition you as you love all that is Holy & honorable to withdraw your armies from Mexico & offer to that afflicted Country, Peace on terms that this Nation would think just were the relative position of the two Nations reversed."[50] These concerned citizens invoked the widespread critique of aggression, as well as the idea that the strength of the United States relative to Mexico imposed a particular moral obligation on Americans. In calling on their representatives to think about what Americans would want were they in Mexico's position, the petitioners also stressed that the two neighboring countries were equal in moral terms, if not in terms of economics, population, political stability, or military might. In so doing, they harkened back to the spirit that had animated the first generation of peace reformers, like Noah Worcester, who called on fellow citizens to see themselves in the other and the other in themselves. Indeed, Theodore Parker explicitly referenced that earlier generation of peace activism when he invited his audience to imagine "a native of Loo Choo" witnessing with dismay how returning soldiers from the war in Mexico were hailed by their communities as heroes, despite having murdered and plundered the Mexican people. The outsider could see the ironies of American society that the insider took for granted.[51] In his ironically titled *The Triumphs of War*, Rev. Andrew P. Peabody pushed his American audience even further, imploring them to put themselves in the position of their supposed Mexican enemies. "Imagine the scene [of invasion] enacted among us," he beseeched them. "Suppose our whole population surrounded by the enginery of war,—our wives and children forbidden all egress,—witnessing day after day spectacles of the intensest agony, at the very thought of which the blood runs cold." The ravages of war offended basic human dignity, since, as Peabody reminded his audience, "Those Mexicans have human hearts. There are there as here fond parents and loving children. They have the same susceptibilities of suffering and anguish with ourselves."[52]

If the U.S.–Mexican War critics shared with early peace reformers a desire to look at American society from the outside, they also echoed the earlier generation's tendency to stop short of a wholesale critique of American empire itself. Peabody argued that had an army of benevolent Christian missionaries, rather than soldiers, crossed the Rio Grande, "the progress of that army would have been conquering and to conquer." Violence only served to alienate Mexico from the civilizing influence of Protestantism—which was both the just and expedient way to bring Mexico into the American orbit.[53] This pacifist vision resonated with a contemporary missionary view that Christianity would be willingly and gratefully accepted by those outside the Anglo-American sphere.[54] In his *Sermon of the Mexican War,* Theodore Parker betrayed even more confidence that Mexico would become annexed, one way or another, to the United States: "Before many years, all of this northern continent will doubtless be in the hands of the Anglo Saxon race." The crucial question was how this end would be achieved. Parker wished that Mexico could be conquered through trade and the "arts of peace."[55] By contrast, James K. Polk and Zachary Taylor had effected the conquest by the bloodiest, most acrimonious means.

In its December 1846 petition to end the war, the American Peace Society observed that the war was only turning Mexico away from diplomacy, which was the most promising means of American territorial expansion: "Every day of conflict is only rendering Mexico less able and less inclined to pay what she owes us, more and more desperate in defense of her soil, and less willing, for a just compensation, to part even with the well nigh useless outskirts of her vast territory. Were the sword sheathed at once, we might, by amicable negociation, obtain all the territory we can reasonably desire, for a mere fraction of what this war has already cost ourselves."[56] It is hard to tell whether the American Peace Society was actually advocating American annexation of Mexican territory here, or whether it was merely making the general point that negotiation tended to lead to better outcomes than war. What is notable, though, is that these peace reformers understood peace simply as a lack of warfare. For them, peace did not necessarily require the United States to curb its desire for territorial expansion. These critics endorsed or at least acquiesced to the eventual projection of U.S. sovereignty over Mexico, but they argued that such a power play was best achieved by softer means than war.

Conclusion: Imperial Ambivalence and the Quest for Peace

In Tacitus's telling, the Scottish general Calgacus revealed how empires used the language of peace and pacification to paper over the violence of conquest.

In the wake of the U.S.–Mexican War, one peace advocate explicitly invoked Calgacus's idea in an essay lambasting as absurd the notion of a "conquering peace": "You may indeed 'conquer' a people so near to extermination that you have the war all on your side, nay, make—as an ancient author said—'a desert and call it peace'; and your *peace* will be like the '*order*' which 'reigns in Warsaw,' like the unity of faith effected by Papal inquisition; but the only peace which ought to be desired by a civilized, a christian people—voluntary, reciprocal, cordial peace—can it ever be obtained by conquest?"[57] For this writer, peace was not the forced tranquility of a people worn down by war. "Conquest," when understood as the use of violence to bring a people into subjection, was antithetical to peace reform ideals; "conquering peace" was thus an oxymoron. But the rejection of violence on the part of nineteenth-century American peace reformers did not necessitate a simultaneous rejection of the imperialist vision that fueled many of their compatriots. In the context of both the First Seminole War and the U.S.–Mexican War, even as American peace reformers criticized the violence that white Americans and their government inflicted on people deemed outsiders, some of them also evinced great confidence that Native people and citizens of Mexico would, someday, willingly submit themselves to the sovereignty of the United States, the superiority of Anglo-American culture, and the blessings of Protestant Christianity. In the long run, they argued, peaceful means might just offer the best way of achieving imperial ends.

The willingness that peace reformers showed to embrace the concept of empire—even if they critiqued the use of war to attain it—might simply reflect the ubiquity of "imperializing" impulses in nineteenth-century Anglo-American thought.[58] Peace advocates sought to extricate war and other forms of militarism from American society, and they called into question some of the presumptions behind their own society's claims of "civilization" relative to supposedly "barbarous" others. But these critiques were designed more to hold Americans to their highest ideals of Christianity and republicanism—to live up to the superiority of their own religious and political systems—than to overturn the value system rooted in those ideals. In this respect, peace reformers were in line with other social reformers of their era. Yet the comfort that many peace advocates evinced with empire cannot simply be credited only to what scholars are increasingly recognizing as a widespread imperialist orientation in nineteenth-century American politics, society, and culture.[59] More specifically, the vision of "human brotherhood" that undergirded the reformers' vision of peace proved to be remarkably compatible with, and perhaps even dependent upon, the expansive reach of empire. Whether in accepting a fictional Ryukyu Islander as a credible critic of American society or in eliciting sympathy for beleaguered Mexico as a "sister republic," nineteenth-century American peace reformers showed their cosmopolitan inclinations, their willingness to see all fellow human beings as part of the same human family. But as recent scholars of nineteenth-century empires have pointed out, cosmopolitanism could harmonize quite effectively with empire.[60] Peace advocates recognized that war drove different branches of the human family apart, but a peacefully expanding American empire could be just the thing to bring them back together.

CHAPTER 13

Mercenary Ambivalence

Military Violence in Antebellum America's Wars of Empire

AMY S. GREENBERG

> My reader will be ready to ask why all this strife and
> bloodshed between the mercenaries of a great nation
> and one small tribe of Indians located in a wilderness so
> inaccessible to white men. All I can answer is that it is the
> natural heart of [the] white man filled with sin and craving
> for more than is good for him.
>
> —John Bemrose, *Reminiscences*
> *of the Second Seminole War*

No decade looms larger in histories of U.S. territorial expansion than the 1840s, when diplomacy with Great Britain and war with Mexico brought over a million square miles of new territory into the nation. The self-evident success of what boosters called "Manifest Destiny" makes it difficult to recognize the limits of territorial acquisition in the 1840s and the many individuals who lacked enthusiasm for the endeavor. One group in particular has escaped scrutiny in this regard: the soldiers who fought for the United States against the Seminoles in Florida from 1836 to 1842 and against Mexico from 1846 from 1848. This is surprising because disaffection within America's military helped bring both conflicts to an end. This chapter will look closely at the views of the men who took up arms under the American flag in the 1830s and 1840s to evaluate why enthusiasm for the military-expansionist project undertaken by the United States in the name of Manifest Destiny did not extend to many members of the military. Firsthand accounts of the wars in Florida and Mexico provided by common soldiers, officers, and observers reveal a previously unacknowledged level of anti-imperialist sentiment within the U.S. military in the heyday of empire building and suggest the power of these views to limit military expansionism itself.[1]

* * *

In 1836, the United States embarked upon a bloody and ruinously expensive war to uproot Seminole Indians who refused to leave their ancestral homelands in accordance with a fraudulent treaty. This was the final phase of a coordinated effort to remove the all the Indians of the American Southeast beyond the Mississippi River. Six years and 1,600 U.S. deaths later, the military pulled out of Florida, leaving the remaining Seminoles on an informal reservation.[2]

The Second Seminole War was largely a failure. It was also wildly unpopular among the frontline laborers of the conflict, soldiers in the U.S. Army. The posting provided neither honor nor acclaim, and combatants forced to fight a guerrilla war in the stifling Everglades resented it deeply. Widespread hostility between the military and white settlers in the region exacerbated soldier discontent. Desertion rates were high, as were the number of atrocities committed against the Seminoles, including the burning of villages and the desecration of corpses. As the conflict dragged on, officers voiced doubts about the purpose of the war and justness of removing the Seminoles.

Less than four years after pulling out of Florida, the United States embarked on its second imperial war of the decade, against the neighboring Republic of Mexico. Although initial enthusiasm for war against Mexico was dramatically higher than that for the war against the Seminoles, after a year, as common soldiers battled guerrilla partisans in an unfriendly climate, military enthusiasm waned. Once again, common soldiers committed atrocities against civilians that would have shocked their commanding officers, had not so many of those officers previously served in the Florida war.[3] The desertion rate in Mexico was the highest of any U.S. war, and the mortality rate a percentage point higher than in Florida: over 15 percent of American soldiers who served in Mexico died, for a total of 13,000 American lives lost.[4]

The differences between these two conflicts were dramatic: the Second Seminole War received little of the nationalist fervor, journalistic attention, or international acclaim garnered by the conflict with Mexico.[5] The impact of the war in Florida on national politics was limited; the one in Mexico over-turned the balance of power in Congress, crippled the Second Party System, and shaped presidential elections for a generation.[6] Despite the fact that it was the most costly Indian war in U.S. history (the official estimate at the time was $30 million), the Second Seminole War has barely figured in the nation's military history. The war with Mexico has been called both the "Forgotten War" and the United States' "first foreign war," but it is the war in Florida (against a "domestic dependent nation," as the Supreme Court defined In-dian tribes in 1831) that remains absent from many federal lists of U.S. wars.[7]

The rise of North American settler-colonial studies over the past decade has produced outstanding works revealing the role private citizen-settlers played in early nineteenth-century expansion, particularly in Florida. Lau-rel Clark Shire's work on gender and national expansion in Florida persua-sively argues that the settlement of white families in territorial Florida rationalized violence against the Native American owners of the territory and that "making homes in Florida was a political act carried out by white fami-lies supported by federal policies." In his study of the role of land policy in encouraging settler colonialism before the U.S. Civil War, Julius Wilm con-cludes that Florida was one of only two territories where the federal govern-ment was so dependent on settler violence to pacify Native American residents that legislators overcame their reluctance to give land away for free. C. S. Mo-naco, author of the first full-length academic study of the Second Seminole War in fifty years, asserts that in the 1830s and 1840s, "merely to be thought of as a patriotic American also required an unquestioned adherence to the often-contradictory tenets of settler-colonialism." And Paul Frymer has ar-gued that territorial expansion during the era of Manifest Destiny was so de-pendent on settler colonialism that it proceeded only as fast as settlement in adjacent counties was complete.[8]

Although settler colonialism helps explains certain aspects of American territorial expansion, there is a great deal it does not explain. Settler families were not the only ordinary Americans in Florida; during the war they were outnumbered by soldiers. And settlers played no role at all in the greatest an-tebellum land grab of all: the U.S.–Mexican War. The ordinary Americans in Mexico in the 1840s were almost exclusively soldiers or those providing aid to soldiers. Brian Rouleau's examination of the role of common sailors in the antebellum American empire has illuminated the significance of or-dinary men in foreign places to early American foreign relations, revealing the outsized role that thousands of these "informal diplomats" played in shaping perceptions of the United States abroad.[9] But with few exceptions, scholars of the early American republic have proven strangely uninterested in the views of U.S. soldiers when attempting to gauge attitudes toward American imperialism.[10]

This lacuna is particularly problematic when discussing the Second Seminole War and the U.S.–Mexican War, the only two major wars of the era of Manifest Destiny. America's antebellum wars of empire were bound by more than expansionist fervor and a troubling failure to count civilian casualties. Both conflicts were critiqued, and ultimately ended, by men on the front lines. After Colonel William Jenkins Worth, serving under the commanding general Winfield Scott, argued that diminishing returns made the Second Seminole War effectively unwinnable, Secretary of War John C. Spencer authorized the withdrawal of the army in 1842 and establishment of an informal Seminole reservation. Officer opposition to the continued occupation of central Mexico in the fall of 1847, and in particular the support offered to negotiator Nicholas Trist by General Winfield Scott, who was once again commanding the army, allowed for the successful negotiation of a treaty to end the war, one opposed by the president of the United States as too generous to Mexico. It is the contention of this essay that military service in Florida and Mexico led many soldiers to question American empire.[11]

"Imperialism," as Mark F. Proudman has illustrated, is a term notable for its "protean imprecision," and "anti-imperialism" is an equally slippery concept. "Empire," far from being monolithic, can perhaps best be understood as a complex set of unequal relations; not surprisingly the meaning and expression of "anti-imperialism" has also shifted over time. Anti-imperialism has been a political cause and a foreign policy, a form of language and a strain of political thought. Opposition to territorial expansion has been driven by complex and contradictory motivations, both conservative and radical, from the oppressed as well as the powerful. For the purposes of this chapter, I will define "anti-imperialism" as morally grounded opposition to wars of territorial expansionism.[12]

Recent scholarship has illuminated the power of anti-imperial sentiment within European imperial regimes, but relatively little has been written about opposition to expansion during the period of early growth of America's empire.[13] While there was no such thing as "anti-imperialism" in the first half of the nineteenth century, because the term did not yet exist, Peter Onuf has revealed a powerful strain of imperial opposition, born of the American Revolution, in the public discourse and political thought of the early American republic. Philip Foner and Richard C. Winchester's two-volume documentary history of anti-imperialism begins with the well-known opposition of abolitionists and Whigs to the U.S.–Mexican War, and John Nichols' recent collection on the same subject considers the origins of anti-imperialism in revolutionary thought, skipping from the Revolution to the late 1840s. Recent work by Margot Minardi and Sean P. Harvey has illuminated a wider extent of anti-imperial sentiments among American intellectuals in the 1840s.[14]

None of these works consider anti-expansionist attitudes within the antebellum army. One of the few scholars to address the issue in depth, Samuel Watson, argues against widespread anti-imperialism in the military. In his two-volume examination of the army officer class prior to 1846, Watson concludes, "It would be grossly inaccurate to portray the officer corps as a countercultural force resisting or hindering American territorial expansion."[15]

The officer corps in the era of Manifest Destiny may not have been "countercultural," but it is equally impossible to describe it as uniformly imperialistic. The curriculum of the U.S. Military Academy at West Point was steeped in Enlightenment ideals and "encouraged ethical distinction between just and unjust war." Where Indians fit in this dichotomy was left unspecified. The West Point curriculum made no mention of Indian war, nor did it offer instruction in irregular warfare. Cadets were instead required to read European works, including Emmerich de Vattel's 1758 *The Law of Nations*. Like other Enlightenment texts, *The Law of Nations* justified territorial expansion on the grounds that uncultivated lands should be considered "vacant," but also asserted that all people were justified in waging war in order to protect their homelands. Many popular West Point instructors, including the commander of cadets Ethan Allan Hitchcock, opposed the 1830 Indian Removal Act, and emphasized to their students that Indians were part of "the great human family."[16]

Conditions in Florida challenged these assumptions, and challenged, as well, the seemingly inexorable course of Manifest Destiny. When newly appointed federal judge Alfred Balch of Tennessee arrived in Tallahassee in April of 1840, he reported back to President Martin Van Buren that the "condition of affairs in this territory is deplorable" and that "violence is the order of the day." Balch gave up his judgeship and returned to Tennessee as quickly as possible.[17]

Soldiers in Florida had no such choice. Tennessee's volunteers threatened desertion when told they were headed to Florida at the very outset of the war in 1836, "cursing everything connected with" service in Florida. Three men disappeared before their commanding officer convinced the rest that desertion was dishonorable. By 1840, five years after Seminole Indians first ambushed two artillery companies and killed 105 U.S. soldiers in the precipitating event of the war, the "Dade Massacre," over 5,000 troops, half the strength of the entire army, were fighting a guerrilla war of attrition in Florida that was remarkably unpopular for a host of reasons that had little to do with ideology. While some soldiers enjoyed Florida's climate and landscape, most considered it "swampy, hammocky, low, excessively hot, sickly and repulsive in all its features." Troops had neither the food nor the supplies necessary for success; many were forced to eat their own horses. Others, without horses, came close to starving. "It was a melancholy sight . . . to see how miserably these troops were provided with the necessary equipments for a winter campaign, when, from the nature and geography of the country, they were to encounter great exposure and fatigue," one critic noted.[18]

Officers praised their men for "wading in water three days, with scanty food on their backs, destitute of blankets, without a murmur." But soldiers were demoralized by the bugs, snakes, and alligators that populated the Everglades, and even more so by the climate. Disease was rampant. In July 1841, nearly 50 percent of the 5,000 regular troops in Florida were out of service due to sickness. An enlisted hospital orderly recalled that he lost as many as five men daily to fever at one point, and that it was common for him "to be surrounded by the dead and dying." The commander of Tennessee's volunteer troops wondered, "with all these disadvantages what in the name of common sense can be expected of us?" Service in Florida was viewed as so undesirable that in 1836, alone, 18 percent of the officer corps resigned their commissions.[19]

But a close examination of the writings of officers and enlisted men reveals that service in Florida led some in the army to sympathize with the Seminoles. Contrasting the Seminoles' "persistence, patriotism, and fighting qualities and the greed, carping, and [according to officers] cowardice of white Floridians," officers in the Second Seminole War openly praised the Seminole for "the justice of his causes, and his abiding consciousness of moral right." Captain Nathaniel Hunter, a recent West Point graduate from Georgia, was among the most eloquent of those who struggled with the justice of the war. He recorded in his diary, "I've tried every argument to still my conscience, but this restless imp will not be quiet. . . . Have God and justice no claims upon you prior and paramount to a government that incites you to the commission of a crime? . . . Enforce a treaty, a compact begot in fraud and brought forth in the blackest villainy and now in process of condemnation aided by the vilest machinations man or demon could invent? Is not every act of the Indians sanctioned by the practice of civilized nations?" This critique of the morality of the war was so widespread that John Sprague, author of one of the earliest histories of the war, apologized in his introduction that the official papers of the time made it clear just how "discreditable and pernicious" the "state of affairs" in Florida was.[20]

Major Ethan Allen Hitchcock of Vermont, previously commander of cadets at West Point, was also vocal in his opposition to the morality of the Second Seminole War. He wrote that it was the United States "government [that] is in the wrong, and this is the chief cause of the persevering opposition of the Indians, who have nobly defended their country against our attempt to enforce a fraudulent treaty. The natives used every means to avoid a war, but were forced into it by the tyranny of our government."[21]

Even officers who were initially supportive of the war effort and felt no compunction about fighting a possibly "unjust war" lost faith in Manifest Destiny. The diary of twenty-three-year-old Henry Prince, a brevet second lieutenant from Eastport, Maine, is instructive in this regard. When Lieutenant Prince graduated from West Point in 1835, he, like the rest of his class, was assigned to duty in Florida.[22] Observant and thoughtful, Prince seems to have had no qualms with slavery, or with the war that brought him to what he immediately dubbed the "Land of Flowers." During his first months in Florida he burned Indian villages without compunction, and suffered hunger and mosquitoes without complaint, noting only that the volunteers "threatened to go home" because they were "disappointed the fighting was not what it was cracked up to be."[23]

There is little question that Prince initially understood his mission in Florida in grand terms. When he first stumbled upon the "sublime" vision of Tampa Bay during a thunderstorm, he expressed his feelings about "the free forms of nature" in transcendental terms: "The feeling of sublimity," he wrote, "alleviates itself in a serious exultation resembling internal laughter." Noting the "brilliant grouping of planets" that evening, and particularly "the moon, Jupiter, and Venus all huddled together about the Twins," Prince fell into a reverie about Manifest Destiny. Referring to the revolution underway in Texas, Prince asked himself, "Are not Texas & Florida twins, they are alike in nature and from heathen darkness are being brought to light—at the same time—and the same mother is laboring with both."[24]

But the reality of service in Florida tested the view that he was helping lead Florida from heathen darkness to light. It was challenged, early on, when he witnessed the departure of the "friendly Indians" who agreed to leave Florida for Indian Territory in April of 1836. Prince felt sympathy when one departing Indian "made a farewell speech to his hereditary home" and noted without judgment that another changed his mind about leaving. Repeated suicides, and particularly one by a fellow junior officer, drove him to ask if "the Great Spirit [is] on the side of the Seminole?"[25]

Ultimately, exposure to white settlers—whom Prince excoriated as "dirty foot, slipshod, but never knew a stocking, the unwashed face; ropy hair, the swearing, lazy, idle, slut! . . . drinking, drawling, boasting, cowardly sluggards"— drove him to reject the likelihood that heathen Florida would be birthed into light by America's Manifest Destiny.[26] By the close of his service, Florida had become, instead, the "Vile Country" where settlers, and not Indians, were the heathens. "Vile Country! I have risked my life three years for you!" he wrote in his diary. "As the worst—most unwelcome—occurrence that could happen to your heartless population, I wish that your Indian War may speedily terminate! And you left to work your bread out of the soils with neither Uncle Sam or the Indians in the way of your plundering hand!"[27]

The views of common soldiers are somewhat harder to ascertain. The vast majority of enlisted men in the peacetime regular army in the 1830s and 1840s were uneducated and unskilled. Of the enlistees, 36 to 40 percent were recently arrived immigrants (many not yet naturalized), and between 35 and 45 percent could not sign their name. Their average age was twenty-five. Service in the army was neither particularly remunerative nor honorable; in a democratic culture that upheld freedom and independence as precious American rights, soldiers were considered overly servile. They were subjected to harsh corporal punishment, including whipping, and forced to labor under conditions they considered degrading, often alongside slaves. There were no promised land bounties for soldiers in either Florida or Mexico—a fact that no doubt tempered any enthusiasm for these wars of expansion.[28]

Most men who enlisted in the regular army did so because they had no better options in the sluggish and unpredictable economy in the decade following the Panic of 1837. Even those poorly paid jobs open to unskilled laborers, like digging ditches and canals or hauling coal, were hard to come by. Service in the Seminole War paid a paltry six to seven dollars a month, while privates in the U.S.–Mexican War made between ten and a half and fifteen and a half dollars. These poverty-level wages were more than they could make back home. In the words of one enlisted man in Florida, "there is no human being in the civilized world that moves in so degraded a sphere as the U.S. enlisted soldier. The slave is the property of his owner and consequently he has an interest in studying his comfort and happiness . . . not so the American soldier, his officer has no interest in him no farther than if he could cheat him out of a part of his ration." Given their low rates of literacy, common soldiers were far less likely to leave written accounts of their military service than were officers.[29]

Several critical accounts of the Second Seminole War credited to "soldiers" (although possibly written by officers) appeared in U.S. newspapers between 1836 and 1842. "Who does not love his own country, the land of his fathers?" asked a self-described "subaltern" (likely a junior officer) writing in in the *Army and Navy Chronicle* in 1836. "People may laugh at the idea of a Seminole feeling an affection for his own country. Why sir even Scythians who inhabited sands and rocks, loved those sands and rocks, as much, too, as you love the hills and dales on the banks of the Potomac." He declared the Florida campaign a "humbug" and admitted, "It makes me sick" that "for the last six months . . . the Indians have been trying to hide themselves, and to live on roots, rather than to desert the home of their fathers. No wonder the army should have been become disgusted with this thankless . . . unholy war." Another, writing in the *North American* in 1840, concluded that "there was never a better theater for land piracy than poor Florida is now" and that the government should "hang the squad of pale-faces, who infest this country, much more to its detriment than a troop of redskins." He wrote of his regiment, "we are worn out and disheartened; and all our glorious anticipations consist of being sent out with broken down constitutions on sick leaves, or finding a grave in the wilderness."[30]

Secondhand accounts also suggest the extent of disaffection. Contemplating the lethargy and ambivalence of his Georgia troops in Florida, Captain Nathaniel Hunter concluded, "Little romance sprang from charging a village to snatch a few terrified children couched in the weeds or kidnapping old squaws begging for mercy."[31] When a detachment of soldiers, numbering about twenty, stopped at the home of a settler named Daniel H. Wiggins, en route from St. Marks to Deadman's Bay, Wiggins had the opportunity to talk with some of them. He recorded in his diary that "they say they have seen tuff times."[32] The unregulated trade in liquor resulted in regular drunken clashes between common soldiers and the Florida settlers whom they were supposed to protect but grew to loathe. Violence between soldiers and settlers,

whom they dismissively referred to as "crackers," grew so extreme that Florida's territorial governor speculated that when faced with the Hobson's
choice of Seminole and soldier, many of the settlers "prefer the Seminole."[33]

Surviving accounts of the Seminole War written by enlisted men offer
ample evidence that anti-expansion sentiment was not limited to officers in
the 1830s and suggest why service in Florida produced atrocities against the
Seminoles. John Bemrose ran away from an apothecary apprenticeship in a
small town in England and booked passage to the United States in August of
1831. Two months later the eighteen-year-old enlisted in the army, with hopes
of serving in the artillery. He was instead sent to St. Augustine as a hospital
steward. His views of the Seminoles were mixed. He described them as "savages" but noted, "where I stood amongst a group of them watching our men
at target practice, I could not help but see they [the Indians] knew and felt
their superiority. Also, when the [white] men were drilling in the woods at
Indian fighting, their [the Indians'] faces would express to each other a sense
of the ridiculous, intuitively conveying to me their knowledge of our inferiority if opposed to them in the native wilds."[34]

His views of the war and territorial expansion however were not mixed.
"My reader will be ready to ask why all this strife and bloodshed between the
mercenaries of a great nation and one small tribe of Indians located in a wilderness so inaccessible to white men. All I can answer is that it is the natural
heart of [the] white man filled with sin and craving for more than is good for
him." Territorial expansion was, in essence, theft. And it was the common
men of the army who had to "suffer hunger, thirst, wounds, and death for
the sins of others." This might seem unfair, since it was the "citizens and
squatters" as well as the "Government of the United States" that were to blame,
but Bemrose considered the hell of service in Florida as just punishment for
joining the army in the first place. "We were the shepherds of the earth, we
first bartered our liberty for pay, we became mercenaries, we sold our birthright, hence, as Esau, we are wanderers on the face of the earth."[35]

Sympathy for the Seminoles among army officers and regulars should not
blind us to the brutality of either the aims or the conduct of this war. Seminole scholar Susan A. Miller argues that the army withdrew once the United
States deemed the "ethnic cleansing" of Florida to be complete. Soldiers in
Florida embraced scalping and skull collecting as a natural part of battle, and
some wrote openly about burning down Seminole villages. Tribal oral histories recount widespread brutality by common soldiers. One elder recounted
what happened to his grandfather's village when the men were away:

The women, the children, the sick, and the old ages started scattering, but they were too late. Here came the soldiers on their horses, throwing burning torches at the thatched huts. They caught on fire like lightning. They were the brave, courageous soldiers. Courageous, all right! Fighting helpless women and children and the old people. They started shooting down the villagers like cattle sent to the slaughter. One could see chips of bone flying in the air, and the fresh smell of blood, enticing the vultures of the air. These vicious men would not stop with two or three shots. They would stand over the spread-out bodies and pour bullets into each corpse. They either would slit the throats or plunge the bayonets into the heart of the dying men. This was the way they destroyed one village. I'm sure many more villages were destroyed in the same way, but this particular village was the village of my grandfather, he was just a small boy when he saw all this.[36]

War in Florida left generational scars on its victims, but it was not the only war in the 1840s that did so. Mexicans actively commemorate a war that cost them half their territory.[37] Although the U.S.–Mexican War was initially greeted with widespread enthusiasm within the United States, the volunteers who chose to fight in Mexico were more likely to commit atrocities against civilians than were regular soldiers in Florida. They also became more vocal opponents of American imperialism.

Major Hitchcock, a critic of the Second Seminole War, was hardly more enthusiastic about matters when President James K. Polk ordered the army, under the command of another veteran of the Florida campaign, General Zachary Taylor, into disputed territory between Texas and Mexico in 1846. Polk had won the nomination of the Democratic Party by appealing to America's Manifest Destiny, and Hitchcock understood the troop movement for what it was. Hitchcock wrote in his diary: "We have not one particle of right to be here. . . . It looks as if the government sent a small force on purpose to bring on a war, so as to have a pretext for taking California and as much of this country as it chooses." Polk's designs on Mexico astounded Hitchcock. "It is enough to make atheists of us all to see such wickedness in the world, whether punished or unpunished," he wrote in his diary. Ulysses S. Grant, at the time a young lieutenant, agreed with Hitchcock about the morality of the "wicked" war they were soon both fighting.[38] Their commanding officer Zachary Taylor shared the misgivings of the younger officers, as did his replacement, Winfield Scott, who opposed taking central Mexico, and counseled Trist in 1847 to sign a treaty as soon as possible because "too much blood has already been shed in this unnatural war."[39]

Although some historians have attributed antiwar sentiment among officers in the U.S.–Mexican War to partisanship within the largely Whig officer class, Lieutenant Grant was hardly a Whig stalwart. He cast his first vote, in 1856, for the Democratic candidate, James Buchanan. And some Democratic officers who were initially enthusiastic supporters of both the war and Manifest Destiny, like Colonel John Hardin of Illinois, underwent a process of disillusionment once in Mexico. As I have written elsewhere, within one year of service in Mexico, Hardin no longer believed that Mexico was part of America's Manifest Destiny and wrote privately to friends that the United States would be better off without the "worthless" country or a population that he considered racially inferior and unfit for citizenship.[40]

It is not as easy to determine the view of Manifest Destiny among the rank and file, but letters expressing open opposition to both the war and America's Manifest Destiny in Mexico became common in American newspapers once the war entered its second year and no clear route to peace was apparent. Many veterans from the Northeast and Midwest, like Private Orlando John Hodge of Ohio, also made their views on expansionism clear by joining the young Free Soil Party, which upheld the Wilmot Proviso banning slavery from any territory gained from Mexico. Hodge, who prior to enlistment had shown little interest in politics, embraced the Free Soil platform after being "sickened" by the atrocities committed by his comrades in Mexico.[41] One common soldier (who made clear his fear that officers would confiscate his letter) wrote to workingman's advocate and New York State assemblyman Mike Walsh from La Paz, Mexico, in 1847. He and the rest of his regiment believed (rightly) that the army intended to leave them in California in order to help stabilize U.S. control of the Mexican territory. "This country has been represented to us . . . in a false light, as being a land flowing with Milk and honey," but "there is not 50 men in the regiment who will remain in the country after we are disbanded," he told Walsh. He was having none of it. "We frequently hear of the regulars deserting, and honestly I cannot blame them, for it is enough to give any man the horrors to live in this country."[42]

Perhaps the best evidence for opposition to the war on moral grounds is provided by those soldiers who chose to fight against, rather than for, the United States. A significant proportion of immigrants in the army were Catholic, while the officers, for the most part, were Protestant. The army reflected the virulent anti-Catholicism of American society in the 1840s, so much so

that one scholar has recently called the U.S.–Mexican War a "religious war."
While there were many Protestant soldiers who understood the war as "favored by the Almighty, because it will be the means of eradicating Papacy,
and extending the benefits of Protestantism," Catholic immigrants found it
difficult to abide by some of the army's rules. Soldiers of all faiths were advised, or compelled, to attend the Protestant services offered by the army
chaplain. They were often banned from attending Catholic mass. Not surprisingly they had trouble justifying a war waged on fellow Catholics. As Peter
Guardino has illustrated, Mexican authorities made ideological appeals to
American soldiers to desert, issuing handbills that described the U.S. war as
an "aggressive land grab that sought to enslave Mexico." Several hundred men
joined a Mexican battalion of U.S deserters: the San Patricios.[43]

Nor was opposition to the war limited to deserters. One Prussian soldier
who volunteered from Ohio, Otto Zirckel, noted in his diary that "the
Founding Fathers of the [American] Republic were right to . . . recommend
the strongest neutrality in all world affairs to their grandsons; but these
grandsons thought themselves wiser, and now there is talk of uniting the entire continent of North and South America into one enormous state." While
anyone who had traveled through Europe "can very well see the madness of
these plans," in the United States "the majority of the people . . . do not
doubt the possibility of the undertaking, and are supported . . . by countless demagogues."[44]

There are several reasons why the extent of anti-imperial sentiment among
antebellum America's soldiers has failed to receive attention from historians.
Many enlisted men were illiterate, others literate in languages other than English. And like other ordinary Americans, their papers are more frequently
lost than preserved. It is also the case that soldiers are expected to follow
orders and not pass judgment: as John Bemrose recognized, many of their
contemporaries believed that enlisted men in the Second Seminole War had
"sold their birthright."[45]

But we should also recognize the role of historians in perpetuating the
view that soldiers were willing participants in the growth of American empire. The "New Military History" and "War and Society" schools promised
to bring the methodologies of social and cultural history to the study of wars
and armies, and to recognize that "armies did not spring into being at the
whim of politicians, and generals could not manipulate troops as if they
were chess pieces devoid of ideas or attitudes." But most published histories
relating to the military continue to focus on generals and battles. Neither the

introduction nor the index to the edited edition of Lieutenant Henry Prince's diary, published in 1998, offers any clue that Prince experienced a change of heart while in Florida, or that he wrote anything about the justness of the war or about Manifest Destiny.[46]

Written records clearly suggest at least some anti-imperial sentiment among those charged with the work of Manifest Destiny, both in Florida and in Mexico. While some soldiers in Mexico made their opposition to war clear by fighting for the enemy, antiwar sentiment did not always stem from a sense of identification with the enemy. It seems appropriate to close with the experiences of Samuel Chamberlain of Vermont, a vehement nativist and common soldier who wrote a celebratory memoir about his adventures in Mexico, in a war against what he called the "greasers" of "greaserdom." For Chamberlain, violence ultimately offered a path to understanding. After witnessing "all manners of outrages" and atrocities committed by the volunteers across Mexico, including rape, torture, and the slaughter of massed civilians, Chamberlain concluded that "the conflict was no longer war but murder, and a disgrace to any nation calling themselves Christians."[47]

NOTES

Introduction

1. Thomas Hutchins, *An Historical Narrative and Topographical Description of Louisiana, and West-Florida* (Philadelphia: R. Aitken, 1784), 93–94.

2. "An Estimate for Exploring the Country Westward of the Sources of the River Mississippi, Towards the Pacific Ocean, or South Sea," n.d., box 2, folder 30, Thomas Hutchins Papers, Historical Society of Pennsylvania; Thomas Hutchins, November 28, 1788, quoted in Anna M. Quattrocchi, "Thomas Hutchins, 1730–1789" (Ph.D. diss., University of Pittsburgh, 1944), 284; Thomas Hutchins to Daniel Clark, December 20, 1788, quoted in David C. Narrett, *Adventurism and Empire: The Struggle for Mastery in the Louisiana-Florida Borderlands* (Chapel Hill: University of North Carolina Press, 2015), 183; Joseph G. Tregle, Jr., introduction to Hutchins, *An Historical Narrative and Topographical Description of Louisiana, and West-Florida* (reprint, Gainesville: University of Florida Press, 1968).

3. John Filson, *The Discovery, Settlement, and Present State of Kentucke* (Wilmington, Del.: James Adams, 1784), 107–8; Thomas Jefferson to George Rogers Clark, December 25, 1780, *The Papers of Thomas Jefferson*, ed. Julian P. Boyd et al., 44 vols. (Princeton, N.J.: Princeton University Press, 1950–), 4:237.

4. George Washington, speech to the Officers of the Army, March 15, 1783; George Washington to Elias Boudinot, April 18, 1783; George Washington to Antoine-Charles du Houx, Baron de Vioménil, June 11, 1783; George Washington to Philippe de Noailles, Duc de Mouchy, October 15, 1783; in *Founders Online: Early Access*, http://founders.archives.gov.

5. For a recent synthesis that continues to frame 1898 as the beginning of U.S. empire—and interprets the early republic as an era of continued (albeit informal) British imperialism rather than the origins of U.S. imperialism—see A. G. Hopkins, *American Empire: A Global History* (Princeton, N.J.: Princeton University Press, 2018).

6. William Appleman Williams, *The Tragedy of U.S. Diplomacy* (New York: W. W. Norton, 1959).

7. For examples of the new imperial history, see Antoinette Burton, ed., *After the Imperial Turn: Thinking With and Through the Nation* (Durham, N.C.: Duke University Press, 2003); Catherine Hall and Sonya Rose, *At Home with the Empire: Metropolitan Culture and the Imperial World* (New York: Cambridge University Press, 2011); Kathleen Wilson, ed. *A New Imperial History: Culture, Identity, and Modernity in Britain and the Empire, 1660–1840* (New York: Cambridge University Press, 2004); Catherine Hall, ed., *Cultures of Empire: Colonizers in Britain and the Empire in the Nineteenth and Twentieth Centuries* (New York: Routledge, 2000); Nupur Chaudhuri and Margaret Strobel, eds., *Western Women and Imperialism: Complicity and Resistance* (Bloomington: Indiana University Press, 1992). For perspectives on U.S. empire from the vantage of American studies, see Amy Kaplan and Donald E. Pease, eds., *Cultures of United States Imperialism* (Durham, N.C.: Duke University Press, 1994); Amy Kaplan, *The Anarchy of Empire*

in the Making of U.S. Culture (Cambridge, Mass.: Harvard University Press, 2005). For the concept of settler colonialism and its critiques, see notes 20 and 21 below.

8. Jane Burbank and Frederick Cooper, *Empires in World History: Power and the Politics of Difference* (Princeton, N.J.: Princeton University Press, 2010).

9. On the first and second British empires, see P. J. Marshall, "The First British Empire," and C. A. Bayly, "The Second British Empire," in *Oxford History of the British Empire*, vol. 5, *Historiography*, ed. Robin Winks and William Roger Louis (New York: Oxford University Press, 1999); C. A. Bayly, *Imperial Meridian: The British Empire and the World, 1780–1830* (New York: Routledge, 1989).

10. Historians of the British empire working on the American Revolution and its aftermath have been particularly illuminating on this theme. See P. J. Marshall, *The Making and Unmaking of Empires: Britain, India, and America, c. 1750–1783* (New York: Oxford University Press, 2005); Christopher Brown, *Moral Capital: Foundations of British Abolitionism* (Chapel Hill: University of North Carolina Press, 2006); Maya Jasanoff, *Liberty's Exiles: American Loyalists in the Revolutionary World* (New York: Knopf, 2011).

11. See Paul A. Kramer, "Power and Connection: Imperial Histories of the United States in the World," *American Historical Review* 116, no. 5 (December 2011): 1348–91. While Daniel Immerwahr's survey of American empire does include pre-1898 material, only three of the book's twenty-two chapters examine the nineteenth century. Immerwahr, *How to Hide an Empire: A History of the Greater United States* (New York: Farrar, Straus and Giroux, 2019).

12. Our thinking about scholarly ambivalence toward analyzing the early republic in imperial terms is indebted to Kramer, "Power and Connection."

13. See Joyce E. Chaplin, "Expansion and Exceptionalism in Early American History," *Journal of American History* 89, no. 4 (March 2003): 1431–55. "As distinct and largely disconnected subfields," Walter Hixson writes, diplomatic historians and historians of Native America "are just now beginning to address systematically the connections between continental Indian removal and twentieth-century overseas empire." Walter L. Hixson, *American Settler Colonialism: A History* (New York: Palgrave Macmillan, 2013), 17.

14. For new approaches to the early U.S. state, see, for example, William J. Novak, "The Myth of the Weak American State," *American Historical Review* 113, no. 3 (June 2008): 752–72; Max Edling, *A Revolution in Favor of Government: Origins of the U.S. Constitution and the Making of the American State* (New York: Oxford University Press, 2003), 10 ("inconspicuous"); Brian Balogh, *A Government Out of Sight: The Mystery of National Authority in Nineteenth-Century America* (New York: Cambridge University Press, 2009); essays by Ariel Ron, Gautham Rao, Hannah Farber, Ryan A. Quintana, Rachel St. John, Stephen Skowronek, and Richard R. John, in "Taking Stock of the State in Nineteenth-Century America," *Journal of the Early Republic* 38, no. 1 (Spring 2018): 61–118; Lindsay Schakenbach Regele, *Manufacturing Advantage: War, the State, and the Origins of American Industry* (Baltimore: Johns Hopkins University Press, 2019); Hannah Farber, *Underwriters of the United States: How Insurance Shaped the American Founding* (Chapel Hill: University of North Carolina Press, 2021). For contributions to this historiography that frame the new republic as an empire, see Paul Frymer, *Building an American Empire: The Era of Territorial and Political Expansion* (Princeton, N.J.: Princeton University Press, 2017); as well as the promising agenda outlined in Gautham Rao, "The New Historiography of the Early Federal Government: Institutions, Contexts, and the Imperial State," *William and Mary Quarterly* 77, no. 1 (January 2020): 97–128. It is noteworthy that most of this scholarship has focused on the U.S. state in domestic or continental contexts, rather than overseas. For an example of the traditional emphasis on the weakness of the U.S. state and its influence on American diplomacy in this era, see Bradford Perkins, *The Cambridge History of American Foreign Relations*, vol. 1, *The Creation of a Republican Empire, 1776–1865* (New York: Cambridge University Press, 1993), 73–77.

15. Immerwahr, *How to Hide an Empire*. The classic statement of the tensions between empire and republicanism in eighteenth-century Anglo-American thought is J. G. A. Pocock, *The Machiavellian Moment: Florentine Political Thought and the Atlantic Republican Tradition* (Princeton, N.J.: Princeton University Press, 1975), esp. 506–52.

16. Brian DeLay, "Indian Polities, Empire, and the History of American Foreign Relations," *Diplomatic History* 39, no. 5 (November 2015): 927–42.

17. Rosemarie Zagarri, "The Significance of the 'Global Turn' for the Early American Republic: Globalization in the Age of Nation-Building," *Journal of the Early Republic* 31, no. 1 (Spring 2011): 1–37.

18. Johann N. Neem, "From Polity to Exchange: The Fate of Democracy in the Changing Fields of Early American Historiography," *Modern Intellectual History* 17, no. 3 (September 2020): 867–88. This dichotomy and the plot it outlines feature prominently in scholarship ranging from Richard White's classic, *The Middle Ground: Indians, Empires, and Republics in the Great Lakes Region, 1650–1815* (New York: Cambridge University Press, 1991); to Jeremy Adelman and Stephen Aron's landmark essay, "From Borderlands to Borders: Empires, Nation-States, and the Peoples in Between in North American History," *American Historical Review* 104, no. 3 (June 1999): 814–41; to recent prize-winning books by Kathleen DuVal, *Independence Lost: Lives on the Edge of the American Revolution* (New York: Random House, 2015); and Tiya Miles, *The Dawn of Detroit: A Chronicle of Slavery and Freedom in the City of the Straits* (New York: New Press, 2017). For a darker view of imperial borderlands, see James H. Merrell, *Into the American Woods: Negotiators on the Pennsylvania Frontier* (New York: W. W. Norton, 1999). For an essay that casts doubt on the notion that European empires offered Native people greater opportunities than they faced with the rise of the U.S. republic, see Gregory Evans Dowd, "Indigenous Peoples Without the Republic," *Journal of American History* 104, no. 1 (June 2017): 19–41. On legal pluralism and imperial rule, see Lauren Benton, *Law and Colonial Cultures: Legal Regimes in World History, 1400–1900* (New York: Cambridge University Press, 2001); Lauren Benton and Richard J. Ross, eds., *Legal Pluralism and Empires, 1500–1850* (New York: New York University Press, 2013). On plural versus unitary sovereignty and the creation of the American republic, see Gregory Ablavsky, "Empire States: The Coming of Dual Federalism," *Yale Law Journal* 128, no. 7 (May 2019): 1792–868.

19. On the tensions between Atlantic and continental frameworks, see Elizabeth A. Fenn, "Whither the Rest of the Continent?," *Journal of the Early Republic* 24, no. 2 (Summer 2004): 167–75; François Furstenberg, "The Significance of the Trans-Appalachian Frontier in Atlantic History," *American Historical Review* 113, no. 3 (June 2008): 647–77. On "vast" conceptions of early American history as a way to reconcile Atlantic and continental approaches and to reframe the history of the early United States, see Karin Wulf, "Vast Early America: Three Simple Words for a Complex Reality," *Humanities* 40, no. 1 (Winter 2019), http://neh.gov/article/vast-early-america; "Forum: Situating the United States in Vast Early America," *William and Mary Quarterly* 78, no. 2 (April 2021): 187–280.

20. Patrick Wolfe, "Settler Colonialism and the Elimination of the Native," *Journal of Genocide Research* 8, no. 4 (December 2006): 387 (quotation). See also Lorenzo Veracini, *Settler Colonialism: A Theoretical Overview* (New York: Palgrave Macmillan, 2010); Hixson, *American Settler Colonialism*. For one example of a comparative approach, see Lisa Ford, *Settler Sovereignty: Jurisdiction and Indigenous People in America and Australia, 1788–1836* (Cambridge, Mass.: Harvard University Press, 2010).

21. For these critiques, see Daniel K. Richter, "His Own, Their Own: Settler Colonialism, Native Peoples, and Imperial Balances of Power in Eastern North America, 1660–1715," in *The World of Colonial America: An Atlantic Handbook*, ed. Ignacio Gallup-Díaz (New York: Routledge, 2017), 209–233; as well as the essays by Jeffrey Ostler, Nancy Shoemaker, Susanah Shaw Romney, Allan Greer, Michael Witgen, Ashley Glassburn, Stephanie E. Smallwood, Tiya Miles,

Jennifer M. Spear, and Samuel Truett in "Forum: Settler Colonialism in Early American History," *William and Mary Quarterly* 76, no. 3 (July 2019): 361–450. For other reflections on U.S. expansion in North America as a form of colonialism, see Jack P. Greene, "Colonial History and National History: Reflections on a Continuing Problem," *William and Mary Quarterly* 64, no. 2 (April 2007): 235–50; Eric Hinderaker, *Elusive Empires: Constructing Colonialism in the Ohio Valley, 1673–1800* (New York: Cambridge University Press, 1997).

22. See Kariann Akemi Yokota, *Unbecoming British: How Revolutionary America Became a Post-Colonial Nation* (New York: Oxford University Press, 2014); Eliga Gould, "Independence and Interdependence: The American Revolution and the Problem of Postcolonial Nationhood, Circa 1802," *William and Mary Quarterly* 74, no. 4 (October 2017): 729–52. In a collection that brought together Americanists to respond to Ann Laura Stoler's call to think with postcolonial theory, few essays focused on the nineteenth century: Stoler, ed., *Haunted by Empire: Geographies of Intimacy in North American History* (Durham, N.C.: Duke University Press, 2006). On colonial intimacies, see Ann Laura Stoler, "Tense and Tender Ties: The Politics of Comparison in North American History and (Post) Colonial Studies," in *Haunted by Empire*, 23–70.

23. On U.S. presence in spaces of Native sovereignty, see Kathleen DuVal, *The Native Ground: Indians and Colonists in the Heart of the Continent* (Philadelphia: University of Pennsylvania Press, 2006); Brian DeLay, *War of a Thousand Deserts: Indian Raids and the U.S.–Mexican War* (New Haven, Conn.: Yale University Press, 2008); Pekka Hämäläinen, *The Comanche Empire* (New Haven, Conn.: Yale University Press, 2008); Michael Witgen, *An Infinity of Nations: How the Native New World Shaped Early North America* (Philadelphia: University of Pennsylvania Press, 2012); Noelani Arista, *The Kingdom and the Republic: Sovereign Hawai'i and the Early United States* (Philadelphia: University of Pennsylvania Press, 2019); Pekka Hämäläinen, *Lakota America: A New History of Indigenous Power* (New Haven, Conn.: Yale University Press, 2019); Jacob F. Lee, *Masters of the Middle Waters: Indian Nations and Colonial Ambitions Along the Mississippi* (Cambridge, Mass.: Harvard University Press, 2019). On the guano islands, see Christina Duffy Burnett, "The Edges of Empire and the Limits of Sovereignty: American Guano Islands," *American Quarterly* 57, no. 3 (September 2005): 779–803; Immerwahr, *How to Hide an Empire*, chap. 3.

24. Zagarri, "Significance of the 'Global Turn.'" See the essays by Konstantin Dierks, Emily Conroy-Krutz, Nancy Shoemaker, Rachel Tamar Van, and Courtney Fullilove in "Forum: Globalizing the Early American Republic," *Diplomatic History* 42, no. 1 (January 2018). Representative works in this body of scholarship include Emily Conroy-Krutz, *Christian Imperialism: Converting the World in the Early American Republic* (Ithaca, N.Y.: Cornell University Press, 2015); Caitlin Fitz, *Our Sister Republics: The United States in an Age of American Revolutions* (New York: W. W. Norton, 2016); Eliga Gould, *Among the Powers of the Earth: The American Revolution and the Making of a New World Empire* (Cambridge, Mass.: Harvard University Press, 2012); Walter Johnson, *River of Dark Dreams: Slavery and Empire in the Cotton Kingdom* (Cambridge, Mass.: Harvard University Press, 2013); Matthew Karp, *This Vast Southern Empire: Slaveholders at the Helm of American Foreign Policy* (Cambridge, Mass.: Harvard University Press, 2016); Brandon Mills, *The World Colonization Made: The Racial Geography of Early American Empire* (Philadelphia: University of Pennsylvania Press, 2020); Brian Rouleau, *With Sails Whitening Every Sea: Mariners and the Making of American Maritime Empire* (Ithaca, N.Y.: Cornell University Press, 2014); Bethel Saler, *The Settlers' Empire: Colonialism and State Formation in America's Old Northwest* (Philadelphia: University of Pennsylvania Press, 2015); Michael Verney, *A Great and Rising Nation: Naval Exploration and Global Empire in the Early US Republic* (Chicago: University of Chicago Press, 2022); Yokota, *Unbecoming British*.

25. On U.S. imperialism and nineteenth-century Hawai'i, see Arista, *The Kingdom and the Republic*; Eric T. L. Love, *Race over Empire: Racism and U.S. Imperialism, 1865–1900* (Chapel Hill: University of North Carolina Press, 2004); Joy Schulz, *Hawaiian by Birth: Missionary Children, Bicultural Identity, and U.S. Colonialism in the Pacific* (Lincoln: University of Ne-

braska Press, 2018); Jennifer Thigpen, *Island Queens and Mission Wives: How Gender and Empire Remade Hawai'i's Pacific World* (Chapel Hill: University of North Carolina Press, 2014).

26. On the colonization movement more broadly, see Eric Burin, *Slavery and the Peculiar Solution: A History of the American Colonization Society* (Gainesville: University Press of Florida, 2008); Conroy-Krutz, *Christian Imperialism*, chap. 6; Nicholas Guyatt, *Bind Us Apart: How Enlightened Americans Invented Racial Segregation* (New York: Basic Books, 2016); Mills, *The World Colonization Made*; Ousmane K. Power-Greene, *Against Wind and Tide: The African American Struggle Against the Colonization Movement* (New York: New York University Press, 2014); Beverly Tomek, *Colonization and Its Discontents: Emancipation, Emigration, and Antislavery in Antebellum Pennsylvania* (New York: New York University Press, 2011); Beverly Tomek and Matthew Hetrick, eds., *New Directions in the Study of African American Recolonization* (Gainesville: University Press of Florida, 2017).

27. For discussions of the global as distinctive from the imperial, see Nancy Shoemaker, "The Extraterritorial United States to 1860," *Diplomatic History* 42, no. 1 (January 2018): 36–54; Nancy Shoemaker, *Pursuing Respect in the Cannibal Isles: Americans in Nineteenth-Century Fiji* (Ithaca, N.Y.: Cornell University Press, 2020).

28. On imperial fragility, see Linda Colley, *Captives: Britain, Empire, and the World, 1600–1850* (New York: Pantheon Books, 2002); and Antoinette Burton, *The Trouble with Empire: Challenges to Modern British Imperialism* (New York: Oxford University Press, 2015).

29. For a discussion of these two images in a different context, see Kathryn Gin Lum, *Heathen: Religion and Race in American History* (Cambridge, Mass.: Harvard University Press, 2022), 21–24.

30. Kramer, "Power and Connection."

31. On the revolutionary-era origins of the notion of a North American "continent," see James D. Drake, *The Nation's Nature: How Continental Presumptions Gave Rise to the United States of America* (Charlottesville: University of Virginia Press, 2011).

32. Jodi A. Byrd writes, "All too rarely outside American Indian and indigenous studies are American Indians theorized as the field through which U.S. empire became possible at all." See Byrd, *The Transit of Empire: Indigenous Critiques of Colonialism* (Minneapolis: University of Minnesota Press, 2011), xv–38, quotation on xx.

33. Lauren Benton, *A Search for Sovereignty: Law and Geography in European Empires, 1400–1900* (Cambridge: Cambridge University Press, 2010), 10. See also Samuel Truett, "Settler Colonialism and the Borderlands of Early America," *William and Mary Quarterly* 76, no. 3 (July 2019): 435–42.

34. On languages of (anti-)imperialism and (anti-)colonialism, see also Peter S. Onuf, *Jefferson's Empire: The Language of American Nationhood* (Charlottesville: University Press of Virginia, 2000); Jay Sexton, *The Monroe Doctrine: Empire and Nation in Nineteenth-Century America* (New York: Hill and Wang, 2011); Ian Tyrrell and Jay Sexton, eds., *Empire's Twin: U.S. Anti-Imperialism from the Founding Era to the Age of Terrorism* (Ithaca, N.Y.: Cornell University Press, 2015).

Chapter 1

Acknowledgments: This essay comes from a larger body of research on U.S. expansion along the Indian boundary line in which Mark Peterson and Brian DeLay played essential roles. I would also like to thank the participants in the "Making a Republic Imperial" conference for comments and encouragement, the editors of this volume for criticism and guidance, and the anonymous reviewers for saving me from errors. Any that remain are my own.

1. "The Royal Proclamation—October 7, 1763," http://avalon.law.yale.edu/18th_century /procl763.asp; "An Act to Regulate Trade and Intercourse with the Indian Tribes, and to Preserve Peace on the Frontiers" (1796), http://avalon.law.yale.edu/18th_century/na030.asp.

2. The end of treaty-making is the best known of these developments. See Francis Paul Prucha, *American Indian Treaties: The History of a Political Anomaly* (Berkeley: University of California

Press, 1997), 289–310; Colin G. Calloway, *Pen and Ink Witchcraft: Treaties and Treaty Making in American Indian History* (Oxford: Oxford University Press, 2013), 226–44. For the elimination of the nonintercourse line, compare the Trade and Intercourse Act of 1834 to statutes for the "Government of Indian Country" in the *Revised Statutes of the United States* (Washington, D.C.: U.S. Government Printing Office, 1875), 373–77; "An Act to Regulate Trade and Intercourse with the Indian Tribes, and to Preserve Peace on the Frontiers," June 30, 1834, chap. 161, 4 Stat. 729. On the end of the superintendencies, see Edward E. Hill, *The Office of Indian Affairs, 1824–1880: Historical Sketches* (New York: Clearwater, 1974).

3. For understandings of empire building in the American context in this era, see A. G. Hopkins, *American Empire: A Global History* (Princeton, N.J.: Princeton University Press, 2018), 21–25, quotation on 22; Richard H. Immerman, *Empire for Liberty: A History of American Imperialism from Benjamin Franklin to Paul Wolfowitz* (Princeton, N.J.: Princeton University Press, 2010), 1–58.

4. Verner Crane, *The Southern Frontier, 1670–1732* (Durham, N.C.: Duke University Press, 1929), 137 (quotation); Francis Paul Prucha, *American Indian Policy in the Formative Years: The Indian Trade and Intercourse Acts, 1790–1834* (Cambridge, Mass.: Harvard University Press, 1962), 286 (quotation); S. Max Edelson, *The New Map of Empire: How Britain Imagined America Before Independence* (Cambridge, Mass.: Harvard University Press, 2017), 144 (quotation). The most useful overviews of the mid-eighteenth-century imperialization of Indian affairs are Francis Paul Prucha, *The Great Father: The United States Government and the American Indians*, 2 vols. (Lincoln: University of Nebraska Press, 1984), 1:21–28; Prucha, *American Indian Policy in the Formative Years*, 5–25.

5. Prucha, *The Great Father*; Ronald N. Satz, *American Indian Policy in the Jacksonian Era* (Lincoln: University of Nebraska Press, 1974); Reginald Horsman, *Expansion and American Indian Policy, 1783–1812* (Norman: University of Oklahoma Press, 1967); Bernard W. Sheehan, "The Indian Problem in the Northwest: From Conquest to Philanthropy," in *Launching the "Extended Republic": The Federalist Era*, ed. Ronald Hoffman and Peter J. Albert (Charlottesville: University Press of Virginia, 1996), 190–222; Reginald Horsman, "The Indian Policy of an 'Empire for Liberty,'" in *Native Americans and the Early Republic*, ed. Frederick E. Hoxie, Ronald Hoffman, and Peter J. Albert (Charlottesville: University Press of Virginia, 1999), 37–61.

6. This is most evident in recent overview essays. See David A. Nichols, "US Indian Policy, 1783–1830," *Oxford Research Encyclopedia of American History*, October 5, 2015, https://doi.org /10.1093/acrefore/9780199329175.013.42; Elspeth Martini, "Toward a 'New Indian History' of Foreign Relations: U.S.–American Indian Diplomacy from Greenville to Wounded Knee, 1795–1890," in *A Companion to U.S. Foreign Relations: Colonial Era to the Present*, ed. Christopher R. W. Dietrich, vol. 1 (Hoboken, N.J.: Wiley, 2020), 114. Also see Dorothy V. Jones, *License for Empire: Colonialism by Treaty in Early America* (Chicago: University of Chicago Press, 1982); Paula Mitchell Marks, *In a Barren Land: American Indian Dispossession and Survival* (New York: William Morrow, 1998); Stuart Banner, *How the Indians Lost Their Land: Law and Power on the Frontier* (Cambridge, Mass.: Harvard University Press, 2005); Robert M. Owens, *Mr. Jefferson's Hammer: William Henry Harrison and the Origins of American Indian Policy* (Norman: University of Oklahoma Press, 2007); David Andrew Nichols, *Red Gentlemen and White Savages: Indians, Federalists, and the Search for Order on the American Frontier* (Charlottesville: University of Virginia Press, 2008); Stephen J. Rockwell, *Indian Affairs and the Administrative State in the Nineteenth Century* (New York: Cambridge University Press, 2010); Roxanne Dunbar-Ortiz, *An Indigenous Peoples' History of the United States* (Boston: Beacon Press, 2014); Paul Frymer, *Building an American Empire: The Era of Territorial and Political Expansion* (Princeton, N.J.: Princeton University Press, 2017).

7. For other works emphasizing continities in the revolutionary era, see Joyce E. Chaplin, "Expansion and Exceptionalism in Early American History," *Journal of American History* 89,

no. 4 (March 2003): 1431–55; Jack P. Greene, "Colonial History and National History: Reflections on a Continuing Problem," *William and Mary Quarterly* 64, no. 2 (2007): 235–50; Trevor Burnard, "Empire Matters? The Historiography of Imperialism in Early America, 1492–1830," *History of European Ideas* 33, no. 1 (2007): 87–107; François Furstenberg, "The Significance of the Trans-Appalachian Frontier in Atlantic History," *American Historical Review* 113, no. 3 (2008): 647–77; Paul A. Kramer, "Power and Connection: Imperial Histories of the United States in the World," *American Historical Review* 116, no. 5 (December 2011): 1348–91; David Prior, "After the Revolution: An Alternative Future for Atlantic History," *History Compass* 12, no. 3 (March 2014): 300–309; Adam Rothman, "The Paracolonial Republic and War of 1812," in *1812 in the Americas*, ed. Jean-Marc Serme (Newcastle upon Tyne: Cambridge Scholars, 2015), 1–11; Alan Taylor, "Introduction: Expand or Die: The Revolution's New Empire," *William and Mary Quarterly* 74, no. 4 (October 2017): 619–32; Jessica Choppin Roney, "1776, Viewed from the West," *Journal of the Early Republic* 37, no. 4 (Winter 2017): 655–700.

8. Craig Bryan Yirush, "Claiming the New World: Empire, Law, and Indigenous Rights in the Mohegan Case, 1704–1743," *Law and History Review* 29, no. 2 (May 2011): 333–73.

9. *Historical Statistics of the United States, Colonial Times to 1970*, 2 vols. (Washington, D.C.: U.S. Department of Commerce, Bureau of the Census, 1975), 2:1168.

10. Robert N. Clinton, "The Proclamation of 1763: Colonial Prelude to Two Centuries of Federal State Management of Indian Affairs," *Boston University Law Review* 69 (1989): 344; Georgianna C. Nammack, *Fraud, Politics, and the Dispossession of the Indians: The Iroquois Land Frontier in the Colonial Period* (Norman: University of Oklahoma Press, 1969), 86–106.

11. The Albany Congress proceedings and related documents appear in E. B. O'Callaghan, ed., *Documents Relative to the Colonial History of the State of New York*, 11 vols. ([Albany, N.Y.], 1853–61), 6:850–92 (hereafter cited as O'Callaghan, ed., *Documents*).

12. Timothy J. Shannon, *Indians and Colonists at the Crossroads of Empire: The Albany Congress of 1754* (Ithaca, N.Y.: Cornell University Press, 2000), esp. 72–76; Alison Gilbert Olson, "The British Government and Colonial Union, 1754," *William and Mary Quarterly* 17, no. 1 (January 1960): 22–34.

13. George Clinton to Duke of Newcastle, December 9, 1746, O'Callaghan, ed., *Documents*, 7:313–14; Archibald Kennedy, *The Importance of Gaining and Preserving the Friendship of the Indians to the British Interest, Considered* (New York, 1751), 13 (quotation, emphasis in original).

14. "Plan of General Concert," in O'Callaghan, ed., *Documents*, 6:901–3; John Pownall, "Considerations Towards a General Plan of Measures for the Colonies," O'Callaghan, ed., *Documents*, 6:893–97; John R. Alden, "The Albany Congress and the Creation of the Indian Superintendencies," *Mississippi Valley Historical Review* 27, no. 2 (September 1940): 193–210.

15. Kennedy, *Importance of Gaining and Preserving the Friendship*, 13; O'Callaghan, ed., *Documents*, 6:961–63; "Representation to the King on the Proceedings of the Congress at Albany," O'Callaghan, ed., *Documents*, 6:918; "Commission from Edward Braddock," April 15, 1755, in *The Papers of Sir William Johnson*, vol. 1, ed. James Sullivan (Albany: University of the State of New York, 1921), 466.

16. Roger L. Nichols, *Indians in the United States and Canada: A Comparative History* (Lincoln: University of Nebraska Press, 1998), 122–50, esp. 138; Robert S. Allen, *His Majesty's Indian Allies: British Indian Policy in the Defence of Canada, 1774–1815* (Toronto: Dundurn Press, 1992). On powers returned to colonial officials, see Peter Marshall, "Colonial Protest and Imperial Retrenchment: Indian Policy 1764–1768," *Journal of American Studies* 5, no. 1 (1971): 1–17.

17. Alden, "The Albany Congress and the Creation of the Indian Superintendencies," 193–210; Prucha, *American Indian Policy in the Formative Years*, 5–25; Prucha, *The Great Father*, 21–22; Wilbur R. Jacobs, "Edmond Atkin's Plan for Imperial Indian Control," *Journal of Southern History* 19, no. 3 (August 1953): 313 (quotation); Wilbur R. Jacobs, ed., *The Appalachian Indian Frontier: The Edmond Atkin Report and Plan of 1755* (Lincoln: University of Nebraska Press, 1967).

18. Lords of Trade to Sir Danvers Osborne, September 18, 1753, quoted in Prucha, *American Indian Policy in the Formative Years*, 12.

19. O'Callaghan, ed., *Documents*, 7:3, 86–91; 6:1027. For additional detail on these incidents of Johnson wrangling for authority with colonial governors, see Clinton, "The Proclamation of 1763," 349–51.

20. David Andrew Nichols, *Red Gentlemen and White Savages*.

21. Edelson, *The New Map of Empire*, 144–59, quotation 151–52; Clinton, "The Proclamation of 1763," 351–53.

22. Verner Crane, ed., "Hints Relative to the Division and Government of the Conquered and Newly Acquired Countries in America," *Mississippi Valley Historical Review* 8, no. 4 (1922): 371; Thomas C. Barrow, "A Project for Imperial Reform: 'Hints Respecting the Settlement for Our American Provinces,' 1763," *William and Mary Quarterly* 24, no. 1 (January 1967): 114–15; Edward J. Cashin, *Governor Henry Ellis and the Transformation of British North America* (Athens: University of Georgia Press, 1994), 185–86; O'Callaghan, ed., *Documents* 7:377 (quotation); Edelson, *The New Map of Empire*, 154–55.

23. "Report on Acquisitions in America," in *Documents Relating to the Constitutional History of Canada, 1759–1791*, ed. Adam Shortt and Arthur G. Doughty, 2nd ed. (Ottawa, 1918), 132–47; R. A. Humphreys, "Lord Shelburne and the Proclamation of 1763," *English Historical Review* 49, no. 194 (1934): appendix, 259–61.

24. It also ordered unsanctioned settlers to relocate and announced a trade licensing system. "The Royal Proclamation—October 7, 1763," http://avalon.law.yale.edu/18th_century/proc1763.asp.

25. The language itself echoed calls to "fix upon some Line for a Western Boundary to our ancient provinces, beyond which our People should not *at present* be permitted to settle" (Crane, "Hints Relative to the Division and Government," 371; emphasis added).

26. Edelson, *The New Map of Empire*, 141–95. For other statements on the impermanence of the line, see Prucha, *American Indian Policy in the Formative Years*, 16; Max Farrand, "The Indian Boundary Line," *American Historical Review* 10, no. 4 (July 1905): 783.

27. On the plan's failure, see Daniel Richter, "The Plan of 1764: Native Americans and a British Empire That Never Was," in *Trade, Land, Power: The Struggle for Eastern North America* (Philadelphia: University of Pennsylvania Press, 2013), 177–201.

28. Edelson, *The New Map of Empire*, 159–91; "The Regulation of Indian Affairs, July 10–September 30, 1764," *Collections of the Illinois State Historical Library* (Illinois State Historical Library, 1915), 10:273–81.

29. "The Regulation of Indian Affairs, July 10–September 30, 1764," 280.

30. Figures tabulated from David H. DeJong, *American Indian Treaties: A Guide to Ratified and Unratified Colonial, United States, State, Foreign, and Intertribal Treaties and Agreements, 1607–1911* (Salt Lake City: University of Utah Press, 2015).

31. Jeremiah Dummer, *A Defence of the New-England Charters* (London, 1721), 14 (quotation, emphasis in original); Paul Gerard McHugh, "The Aboriginal Rights of the New Zealand Maori at Common Law" (Ph.D. diss., University of Cambridge, 1988), 200–203; Francis Jennings, *The Invasion of America: Indians, Colonialism, and the Cant of Conquest* (New York: W. W. Norton, 1976), 128; "Regulation of Indian Affairs, July 10–September 30, 1764," 280.

32. Although the Revolution eliminated the proclamation's legal effect in what became the United States, it continued to influence Indian policy in Canada. See Terry Fenge and Jim Aldridge, eds., *Keeping Promises: The Royal Proclamation of 1763, Aboriginal Rights, and Treaties in Canada* (Montreal: McGill-Queen's University Press, 2015).

33. *Journals of the Continental Congress, 1774–1789*, ed. Worthington C. Ford et al., 34 vols. (Washington, D.C.: Government Printing Office, 1904–37), 2:175–77.

34. James Madison would denounce this arrangement as "obscure and contradictory." "Articles of Confederation: March 1, 1781," http://avalon.law.yale.edu/18th_century/artconf.asp; James Madison, "The Federalist Papers: No. 42," http://avalon.law.yale.edu/18th_century/fed42.asp.

35. Clinton, "The Proclamation of 1763," 369 n. 177; Robert J. Miller, *Native America, Discovered and Conquered: Thomas Jefferson, Lewis and Clark, and Manifest Destiny* (Westport, Conn.: Praeger, 2006), 45.

36. Figures tabulated from DeJong, *American Indian Treaties*.

37. Brian DeLay, "Indian Polities, Empire, and the History of American Foreign Relations," *Diplomatic History* 39, no. 5 (November 2015): 927–42; Michael A. Blaakman, "'Haughty Republicans,' Native Land, and the Promise of Preemption," *William and Mary Quarterly* 78, no. 2 (April 2021): 243–50.

38. Eliga Gould, *Among the Powers of the Earth: The American Revolution and the Making of a New World Empire* (Cambridge, Mass.: Harvard University Press, 2012); Leonard J. Sadosky, *Revolutionary Negotiations: Indians, Empires, and Diplomats in the Founding of America* (Charlottesville: University of Virginia Press, 2010).

39. Reginald Horsman, "American Indian Policy in the Old Northwest, 1783–1812," *William and Mary Quarterly* 18, no. 1 (January 1961): 35–53.

40. *Journals of the Continental Congress*, 25:686.

41. *Report on Indians Taxed and Indians Not Taxed (Except Alaska) at the Eleventh Census: 1890* (Washington, D.C.: Government Printing Office, 1894), 641.

42. *Laws of the United States of America, from the 4th of March, 1789, to the 4th of March, 1815*, 5 vols. (Philadelphia: John Bioren and W. John Duane; Washington City: R. C. Weightman, 1815), 1:614–16.

43. *Journals of the Continental Congress*, 32:66–69, esp. 68.

44. The spare phrasing of the commerce clause strengthened federal control over Indian affairs in theory while leaving its scope open-ended in practice. "U.S. Constitution: Article I," http://avalon.law.yale.edu/18th_century/art1.asp; Gregory Ablavsky, "Beyond the Indian Commerce Clause," *Yale Law Journal* 124, no. 4 (January–February 2015): 1022–24.

45. "An Act for Establishing the Salaries of the Executive Officers of Government, with Their Assistants and Clerks," September 11, 1789, chap. 13, 1 Stat. 67.

46. John R. Alden, *John Stuart and the Southern Colonial Frontier: A Study of Indian Relations, War, Trade, and Land Problems in the Southern Wilderness, 1754–1775* (Ann Arbor: University of Michigan Press, 1944), 139–55. Figures on the U.S. system were compiled from Hill, *The Office of Indian Affairs, 1824–1880*.

47. Of course, there were exceptions to this arrangement, such as when the secretary of war saw a need for a superintendent to oversee ongoing Indian relations in regions where territories had graduated to statehood.

48. For a useful study focused on how this conflict of interest manifested in the Montana Superintendency, see William Howard Roche, "The Territorial Governor as *Ex-Officio* Superintendent of Indian Affairs and the Decline of American-Indian Relations" (M.A. thesis, University of Montana, 1991).

49. William Henry Harrison to Jonathan Dayton, October 29, 1804, box 1, folder 10, William Henry Harrison Papers and Documents, 1791–1864, Indiana Historical Society, Indianapolis.

50. "An Act to Regulate Trade and Intercourse with the Indian Tribes, and to Preserve Peace on the Frontiers" (1796), http://avalon.law.yale.edu/18th_century/na030.asp.

51. "An Act to Regulate Trade and Intercourse with the Indian Tribes, and to Preserve Peace on the Frontiers," June 30, 1834, ch. 161, 4 Stat. 729.

52. Yirush, "Claiming the New World," 333–73.

53. DeLay, "Indian Polities, Empire, and the History of American Foreign Relations," 927–42.

54. Felix Cohen, "How We Bought the United States," *Collier's*, January 19, 1946, 62.

55. See, for example, Richard White, *The Roots of Dependency: Subsistence, Environment, and Social Change Among the Choctaws, Pawnees, and Navajos* (Lincoln: University of Nebraska Press, 1983).

Chapter 2

Acknowledgments: I would like to thank the editors for including me and the Library Company of Philadelphia for supporting my work.

1. Although a few texts offer a description of the duel, they say little about either its cause or about Hunt, who remains largely obscure. Most accounts say that the duel was the result of strong partisan differences between the staunchly Federalist Hunt and the devoted Democratic-Republican Poindexter. See, for instance, Robert V. Haynes, *The Mississippi Territory and the Southwest Frontier, 1795–1817* (Lexington: University Press of Kentucky, 2010), 212; J. F. H. Claiborne, *Mississippi, as a Province, Territory, and State: With Biographical Notices of Eminent Citizens* (Jackson, Miss.: Power and Barksdale, 1880), 1:371–73; Mack Buckley Swearingen, "The Early Life of George Poindexter: A Story of the First Southwest" (Ph.D. diss., University of Chicago, 1932), 114–16.

2. D. Clayton James, *Antebellum Natchez* (Baton Rouge: Louisiana State University Press, 1968), 157–58.

3. James A. Ramage's dissertation and book on John Wesley Hunt of Kentucky have been invaluable in piecing together the story of Abijah Hunt. Ramage, "The Hunts and Morgans: A Study of a Prominent Kentucky Family" (Ph.D. diss., University of Kentucky, 1972); Ramage, *John Wesley Hunt, Pioneer Merchant, Manufacturer, and Financier* (Lexington: University Press of Kentucky, 1974).

4. Jeremy Adelman and Stephen Aron, "From Borderlands to Borders: Empires, Nation-States, and the Peoples in Between in North American History," *American Historical Review* 104, no. 3 (June 1999): 814–41. On transformations, see Stephen Aron, *How the West Was Lost: The Transformation of Kentucky from Daniel Boone to Henry Clay* (Baltimore: Johns Hopkins University Press, 1996); John Reda, *From Furs to Farms: The Transformation of the Mississippi Valley, 1762–1825* (DeKalb: Northern Illinois University Press, 2016).

5. For works that emphasize connections between Euro-American traders and the Osages, see Jay Gitlin, *The Bourgeois Frontier: French Towns, French Traders, and American Expansion* (New Haven, Conn.: Yale University Press, 2010); Anne Farrar Hyde, *Empires, Nations, and Families: A History of the North American West, 1800–1860* (Lincoln: University of Nebraska Press, 2011); Jacob F. Lee, *Masters of the Middle Waters: Indian Nations and Colonial Ambitions Along the Mississippi* (Cambridge, Mass.: Harvard University Press, 2019).

6. Recent interest in the new history of capitalism focuses on coastal cities, especially in the case of finance. See, for instance, Stephen Mihm, "Follow the Money: The Return of Finance in the Early Republic," *Journal of the Early Republic* 36, no. 4 (2016): 783–804; Jessica M. Lepler, *The Many Panics of 1837: People, Politics, and the Creation of a Transatlantic Financial Crisis* (New York: Cambridge University Press, 2013); Brian Phillips Murphy, *Building the Empire State: Political Economy in the Early Republic* (Philadelphia: University of Pennsylvania Press, 2015); Gautham Rao, *National Duties: Custom Houses and the Making of the American State* (Chicago: University of Chicago Press, 2016). The central exception to this rule is studies of the relationship between slavery and capitalism; see Walter Johnson, *River of Dark Dreams: Slavery and Empire in the Cotton Kingdom* (Cambridge, Mass.: Belknap Press of Harvard University Press, 2013); Edward E. Baptist, *The Half Has Never Been Told: Slavery and the Making of American Capitalism* (New York: Basic Books, 2014); Sven Beckert, *Empire of Cotton: A Global History* (New York: Alfred A. Knopf, 2014); Daina Ramey Berry, *The Price for Their Pound of Flesh: The Value of the Enslaved, from Womb to Grave, in the Building of a Nation* (Boston: Beacon Press, 2017); Caitlin Rosenthal, *Accounting for Slavery: Masters and Management* (Cambridge, Mass.: Harvard University Press, 2018). For studies that emphasize the role of merchants in western development,

see Kim M. Gruenwald, *River of Enterprise: The Commercial Origins of Regional Identity in the Ohio Valley, 1790–1850* (Bloomington: Indiana University Press, 2002); Catherine Cangany, *Frontier Seaport: Detroit's Transformation into an Atlantic Entrepôt* (Chicago: University of Chicago Press, 2014); Lawrence B. A. Hatter, *Citizens of Convenience: The Imperial Origins of American Nationhood on the U.S.-Canadian Border* (Charlottesville: University of Virginia Press, 2017).

7. See Claudio Saunt, "Financing Dispossession: Stocks, Bonds, and the Deportation of Native Peoples in the Antebellum United States," *Journal of American History* 106, no. 2 (2019): 315–37; Emilie Connolly, "Panic, State Power, and Chickasaw Dispossession," *Journal of the Early Republic* 40, no. 4 (2020): 683–89.

8. Several scholars have emphasized the role of the army in injecting money into the trans-Appalachian West; they have done less to illustrate the movement of money into and through the region. See Andrew R. L. Cayton, "'Separate Interests' and the Nation-State: The Washington Administration and the Origins of Regionalism in the Trans-Appalachian West," *Journal of American History* 79, no. 1 (June 1992): 39–67; William H. Bergmann, "A 'Commercial View of This Unfortunate War': Economic Roots of an American National State in the Ohio Valley, 1775–1795," *Early American Studies: An Interdisciplinary Journal* 6, no. 1 (2008): 137–64; Bergmann, *The American National State and the Early West* (New York: Cambridge University Press, 2012).

9. Charles Frederic Goss, *Cincinnati, the Queen City, 1788–1912* (Cincinnati: S. J. Clarke, 1912), 483; John Cleves Symmes to Jonathan Dayton, Esq., July 17, 1789, in *The Correspondence of John Cleves Symmes, Founder of the Miami Purchase, Chiefly from the Collection of Peter G. Thomson* (New York: Macmillan, 1926), 106–7.

10. David Andrew Nichols, *Red Gentlemen and White Savages: Indians, Federalists, and the Search for Order on the American Frontier* (Charlottesville: University of Virginia Press, 2008), 42.

11. Nichols, *Red Gentlemen and White Savages*, 116.

12. Bergmann, *The American National State and the Early West*, 134.

13. David Michael Delo, *Peddlers and Post Traders: The Army Sutler on the Frontier* (Salt Lake City: University of Utah Press, 1992), 1.

14. Delo, *Peddlers and Post Traders*, 16.

15. Woody Holton, *Unruly Americans and the Origins of the Constitution* (New York: Hill and Wang, 2007); Terry Bouton, *Taming Democracy: "The People," the Founders, and the Troubled Ending of the American Revolution* (New York: Oxford University Press, 2007).

16. Nichols, *Red Gentlemen and White Savages*, 164.

17. While the Battle of Fallen Timbers itself was relatively minor, lasting less than an hour and resulting in only about forty fatalities for the Indigenous forces, when the fleeing Indians attempted to claim British aid by retreating to Fort Miami, the British barred their doors against them, effectively ending nearly a decade of aid. The loss of British support was crucial to the Northwest Confederacy's decision to not continue the war after this battle. Nichols, *Red Gentlemen and White Savages*, 165.

18. General Wayne's Orderly Book, June 10, 1795, in *Michigan Historical Collections*, vol. 34 (Lansing, Mich.: Wynkoop Hallenbeck Crawford, 1905), 618.

19. Delo, *Peddlers and Post Traders*, 19.

20. Delo, *Peddlers and Post Traders*, 22; General Wayne's Orderly Book, *Michigan Historical Collections*, 34:615.

21. Abijah Hunt to John W. Hunt, April 30, 1795, John Wesley Hunt Papers (subsequently cited as JWHP), Filson Historical Society, Louisville, Kentucky (subsequently cited as FHS).

22. Ramage, "The Hunts and Morgans," 43.

23. Abijah Hunt to John W. Hunt, April 30, 1795, JWHP, FHS.

24. Abijah Hunt to John W. Hunt, April 30, 1795, JWHP, FHS.

25. Ramage, "The Hunts and Morgans," 25.

26. "Invoice, Philadelphia, May 11, 1795," Whelan & Miller; "Philadelphia, May 18th, 1795," Taylor & Newbold, John Wesley Hunt (Morgan) Collection (subsequently cited as JWHM), FHS; Ramage, "The Hunts and Morgans," 25.

27. Ramage, "The Hunts and Morgans," 26.

28. *Kentucky Gazette* (Lexington), July 25, 1795; Ramage, "The Hunts and Morgans," 27.

29. Abijah Hunt to John Hunt, April 30, 1795, JWHP, FHS.

30. Elizabeth A. Perkins, "The Consumer Frontier: Household Consumption in Early Kentucky," *Journal of American History* 78, no. 2 (September 1991): 493.

31. Perkins, "The Consumer Frontier," 499. Much of Perkins's article focuses on a sampling of the 541 transactions recorded in the Hunt's daybook. James A. Ramage's dissertation and book also focus on the operations of this store.

32. Ramage, "The Hunts and Morgans," 24.

33. According to Stephen Aron, in examining the account of one Kentucky merchant firm from 1790–91, only one in twenty transactions was paid for in cash. Aron, *How the West Was Lost*, 131.

34. Abraham Hunt to John Wesley Hunt, March 20, 1796, Hunt-Morgan Family Papers, University of Kentucky Library, Special Collections Research Center, Lexington (subsequently cited as HMFP, UK).

35. Jeremiah Hunt to John W. Hunt, March 11, 1796, HMFP, UK; General Wayne's Orderly Book, February 27 and 29, 1796, *Michigan Historical Collections*, 34:679–80; Delo, *Peddlers and Post Traders*, 21; Ramage, *John Wesley Hunt*, 27.

36. Jeremiah Hunt to John W. Hunt, March 11, 1796, HMFP, UK.

37. The role of the army in injecting specie and providing a market outlet for the West has been discussed by numerous authors, among them Bergmann, *The American National State and the Early West*; Cayton, "'Separate Interests' and the Nation-State," 53; Randolph C. Downes, "Trade in Frontier Ohio," *Mississippi Valley Historical Review* 16, no. 4 (1930): 477.

38. *Centinel of the North-Western Territory* (Cincinnati), January 9, 1796; Bill of Exchange, Greenville, June 26, 1796, HMFP, UK. See also Downes, "Trade in Frontier Ohio," 478.

39. Edward D. Mansfield, *Memoirs of the Life and Services of Daniel Drake, M.D.* (Cincinnati, 1855), as quoted in Downes, "Trade in Frontier Ohio," 478.

40. Bill of Exchange, Greenville, June 26, 1796, HMFP, UK; Bergmann, *The American National State and the Early West*, 135.

41. Bergmann, *The American National State and the Early West*, 135.

42. Bergmann, *The American National State and the Early West*, 134.

43. Ramage, "The Hunts and Morgans," 40.

44. Petition to James McHenry, February 27, 1798, Marietta College Collection, Hildreth Papers, Ohio Historical Society (subsequently cited as MCCHP), MIC 48, reel 3, item 90.

45. "The Petition of the Subscribers Merchants & Traders in the Territory of the United States Norwest [*sic*] of the River Ohio" to Congress, n.d., MCCHP, MIC 48, reel 3, item 92.

46. Petition to James McHenry, Esq., February 27, 1798, MCCHP.

47. "Petition of the Subscribers Merchants & Traders," MCCHP.

48. Treaty of San Lorenzo, art. 22, available at "Treaty of Friendship, Limits, and Navigation Between Spain and the United States; October 27, 1795," Avalon Project at Yale Law School, Lillian Goldman Law Library, http://avalon.law.yale.edu/18th_century/sp1795.asp.

49. "Petition of the Subscribers Merchants & Traders," MCCHP.

50. Alexander Hamilton to James Gunn, December 22, 1798, in *The Papers of Alexander Hamilton*, ed. Harold C. Syrett (New York: Columbia University Press, 1975), 22:388–90; Francis Paul Prucha, *The Sword of the Republic: The United States Army on the Frontier, 1783–1846* (New York: Macmillan, 1968), 54.

51. Although Abijah Hunt visited Detroit, for instance, in 1795, the firm did very little if any business with the new fort. Bergmann, *The American National State and the Early West*, 137; on northern origins of supplies to the posts received from the British, see 137–51.

52. Deposition of Andrew Burd, Abijah Hunt Papers, Dolph Briscoe Center for American History, University of Texas. The date marked on this deposition is 1809, but it seems like that date is likely for a further deposition given several years after the original. All of the other depositions in this case were given in 1803; there is an addendum in a very different handwriting, and it seems likely that only that deposition was gathered in 1809.

53. Winthrop Sargent to Timothy Pickering, December 11, 1798, and November 1, 1799, in *The Mississippi Territorial Archives, 1798–1803* (Nashville, Tenn.: Brandon Printing, 1905), 1:93–94 and 183.

54. Ramage, *John Wesley Hunt,* 35–36.

55. Winthrop Sargent to Agents of the United States, February 28, 1800, in *Mississippi Territorial Archives, 1798–1803,* 1:209–10; Ramage, *John Wesley Hunt,* 41. In becoming a postmaster, Abijah Hunt followed in John Wesley Hunt's footsteps; John had been appointed the postmaster of Lexington, Kentucky, in 1798.

56. James, *Antebellum Natchez,* 157.

57. Abijah Hunt to J. W. Hunt, February 28, 1800, JWHP, FHS.

58. Jack D. L. Holmes, *Gayoso: The Life of a Spanish Governor in the Mississippi Valley, 1789–1799* (Baton Rouge: Louisiana State University Press, [1965]), 100; John Craig Hammond, *Slavery, Freedom, and Expansion in the Early American West* (Charlottesville: University of Virginia Press, 2007), 18.

59. William Dunbar to Dinah Clark Dunbar, June 6, 1798, in *Records of Ante-Bellum Southern Plantations from the Revolution Through the Civil War,* ed. Kenneth Stampp (Frederick, Md.: University Publications of America, 1985–), microfilm, series N, reel 10, image 147.

60. Although it is impossible to be sure, it is highly likely the Hunts were among the first Americans to import large numbers of enslaved people to Natchez for sale. By the 1820s, the business of slave trading came to be dominated by firms that focused solely on supplying enslaved laborers to the expanding cotton frontier. Walter Johnson, *Soul by Soul: Life Inside the Antebellum Slave Market* (Cambridge, Mass.: Harvard University Press, 1999); Baptist, *The Half Has Never Been Told,* 179–80.

61. Pen Bogert, "Sold for My Account: The Early Slave Trade Between Kentucky and the Lower Mississippi Valley," *Ohio Valley History* 2, no. 1 (2002): 6.

62. Ramage, *John Wesley Hunt,* 37.

63. John helped Jeremiah purchase twelve enslaved men and women from General John Adair—another wealthy early Kentucky slave trader; John Adair to John W. Hunt, December 17, 1800, HMFP, UK.

64. "Diary of Captain Philip Buckner," *William and Mary Quarterly* 6, no. 3 (1926): 179.

65. Philip Buckner, receipt, February 23, 1801, JWHM, FHS.

66. "Diary of Captain Philip Buckner," 185.

67. Deposition of Benjamin Simmons, April 26, 1803, Abijah Hunt Papers, Dolph Briscoe Center for American History, University of Texas.

68. Ramage, *John Wesley Hunt,* 39.

69. Claiborne, *Mississippi, as a Province, Territory, and State,* 1:371.

70. "The proprietor [of a public gin] gave the planter a receipt specifying the amount of cotton delivered, and these receipts, by usage at first, and afterwards by law, became the paper currency of the country, and were received in payment of all dues" (Claiborne, *Mississippi, as a Province, Territory, and State,* 1:143).

71. Note: this information is located in the finding aid of the Abijah Hunt Papers in the Briscoe Center for American History at the University of Texas at Austin. Some corroborating

evidence can be found in William K. Thurston to Abijah Hunt, New York, March 17, 1804, and Jesse Hunt to Jeremiah Hunt, Cincinnati, June 29, 1809, both in Hunt (David and Abijah) Papers, box 1, folder 1, Mississippi Department of Archives and History, Jackson.

72. Caleb Hunt is sometimes referred to as Kaleb Hunt.

73. Abijah Hunt to John W. Hunt, n.d., JWHM, FHS; James Ramage, "The Hunts and Morgans," 91.

74. Ramage, *John Wesley Hunt*, 1.

Chapter 3

Acknowledgments: For their comments and advice, the author thanks Brooke Bauer, Brandon Bayne, Maggie Blackhawk, Ned Blackhawk, Megan Cherry, Patricia Dawson, Carolyn Eastman, Elizabeth Ellis, Jonathan Hancock, Reeve Huston, Malinda Maynor Lowery, Tim Marr, Warren Milteer, Jocelyn Olcott, Philip Otterness, Bethel Saler, Cynthia Radding, and Karin Wulf, as well as the editors and other contributors to this volume and the original conference.

1. John Dunn Hunter, *Manners and Customs of Several Indian Tribes Located West of the Mississippi* (Philadelphia, 1823), 53–56; John Sugden, *Tecumseh: A Life* (New York: Holt, 1997), 253–55; Pierre Chouteau to John Armstrong, March 5, 1813, *The Territorial Papers of the United States*, ed. Clarence E. Carter (Washington, D.C.: U.S. Government Printing Office, 1934–62), 14:640; William Clark to the Secretary of War, September 18, 1814, *Territorial Papers*, 14:787; William Henry Harrison to the Secretary of War, August 6, 1811, *Messages and Letters of William Henry Harrison*, ed. Logan Esarey (Indianapolis: Indiana Historical Commission, 1922), 1:545. John Hunter, a white captive raised among the Osages, recalled these words as those of Tecumseh, but the speaker could instead have been one of the movement's other emissaries. However, other sources agree that Tecumseh visited the Osages in 1811. It's not clear that Hunter's use of "red children" is an accurate translation of what Tecumseh said in Shawnee, translated not only through Osage into English but also Hunter's memory, but "red" was a term that southeastern Native people used for themselves by this point. See Nancy Shoemaker, "How Indians Got to Be Red," *American Historical Review* 102 (1997): 625–44.

2. There is a growing historiography on how Native people preserved their nationhood in the nineteenth century and twentieth centuries. See, for example, Julie L. Reed, *Serving the Nation: Cherokee Sovereignty and Social Welfare, 1800–1907* (Norman: University of Oklahoma Press, 2016).

3. Harrison to the Secretary of War, August 7, 1811, *Messages and Letters*, 1:548; Benjamin Hawkins to William Eustis, January 13, 1812, *Letters, Journals and Writings of Benjamin Hawkins*, ed. Charles L. Grant (Savannah, Ga.: Beehive Press, 1980), 2:601; R. David Edmunds, *The Shawnee Prophet* (Lincoln: University of Nebraska Press, 1983), 28–31; Angela Pulley Hudson, *Creek Paths and Federal Roads: Indians, Settlers, and Slaves and the Making of the American South* (Chapel Hill: University of North Carolina Press, 2010), 88–89.

4. Edmunds, *Shawnee Prophet*, 33–37.

5. Shawnee speech, 1803, in *Indian Biography; or, An Historical Account of Those Individuals Who Have Been Distinguished Among the North American Natives as Orators, Warriors, Statesmen, and Other Remarkable Characters*, ed. B. B. Thatcher (New York: J. & J. Harper, 1832), 190; "Shauwonoa Traditions—Black Hoof's Account," undated (1825?), in *Shawnese Traditions: C. C. Trowbridge's Account*, ed. Vernon Kinietz and Erminie Wheeler-Voegelin, Occasional Contributions from the Museum of Anthropology of the University of Michigan, no. 9 (Ann Arbor: University of Michigan Press, 1939), 61; Edmunds, *Shawnee Prophet*, 25–26. See also *Folk-Lore and Legends, Oriental and North American Indian* (London: Gibbings, 1894), 192.

6. George Bluejacket, "A Story of the Shawanoes," October 29, 1829, ed. John Allen Raynor, http://www.ohiohistorycentral.org/w/A_Story_of_the_Shawanoes.

7. "Diary of the Little Indian Congregation on the White River for the Year 1805," December 3, 1805, *Indiana Historical Collections* 23 (1939): 392; Edmunds, *Shawnee Prophet*, 34–35.

8. David Andrew Nichols, *Red Gentlemen and White Savages: Indians, Federalists, and the Search for Order on the American Frontier* (Charlottesville: University of Virginia Press, 2008), 199.

9. Stephen Warren and Randolph Noe, "'The Greatest Travelers in America': Shawnee Survival in the Shatter Zone," in *Mapping the Mississippian Shatter Zone: The Colonial Indian Slave Trade and Regional Instability in the American South*, ed. Robbie Ethridge and Sheri M. Shuck-Hall (Lincoln: University of Nebraska Press, 2009), 167; Alyssa Mt. Pleasant, "Independence for Whom? Expansion and Conflict in the Northeast and Northwest," in *The World of the Revolutionary American Republic: Land, Labor, and the Conflict for a Continent*, ed. Andrew Shankman (New York: Routledge, 2014), 123; Michael Witgen, *An Infinity of Nations: How the Native New World Shaped Early North America* (Philadelphia: University of Pennsylvania Press, 2012); Michael N. McConnell, *A Country Between: The Upper Ohio Valley and Its Peoples, 1724–1774* (Lincoln: University of Nebraska Press, 1992), 209–10; Richard White, *The Middle Ground: Indians, Empires, and Republics in the Great Lakes Region, 1650–1815* (New York: Cambridge University Press, 1991).

10. Bluejacket, "A Story of the Shawanoes."

11. Stephen Warren, *The Shawnees and Their Neighbors, 1795–1870* (Urbana: University of Illinois Press, 2005); Sami Lakomäki, *Gathering Together: The Shawnee People Through Diaspora and Nationhood, 1600–1870* (New Haven, Conn.: Yale University Press, 2014); Laura Keenan Spero, "'Stout, Bold, Cunning and the Greatest Travellers in America': The Colonial Shawnee Diaspora" (Ph.D. diss., University of Pennsylvania, 2010).

12. Warren, *Shawnees and Their Neighbors*, 15, 19, 26; Susan Sleeper-Smith, *Indigenous Prosperity and American Conquest: Indian Women of the Ohio River Valley, 1690–1792* (Chapel Hill: University of North Carolina Press, 2018), 203–9, 285, 317; Lakomäki, *Gathering Together*, 132–43.

13. "Diary of the Little Indian Congregation on the White River," December 3, 1805, 392; Black Hawk, *Life of Ma-Ka-Tai-Me-She-Kia-Kiak, or Black Hawk* (Boston, 1834; repr., Iowa City: State Historical Society of Iowa, 1932), 51; Richard M'Nemar, *The Kentucky Revival; or, A Short History of the Late Extraordinary Outpouring of the Spirit of God in the Western States of America* (New York: Edward O. Jenkins, 1846), 123–32; Edmunds, *Shawnee Prophet*, 54, 57, 59–61; Gregory E. Dowd, "Thinking and Believing: Nativism and Unity in the Ages of Pontiac and Tecumseh," *American Indian Quarterly* 16 (1992): 311.

14. Gregory Evans Dowd, *A Spirited Resistance: The North American Indian Struggle for Unity, 1745–1815* (Baltimore: Johns Hopkins University Press, 1992), 145.

15. The Trout, Speech to Various Tribes, May 4, 1807, *Michigan Historical Collections* 40 (1929): 127–33; J. Dunham to William Hull, May 20, 1807, *Michigan Historical Collections* 40 (1929): 123–27; Dowd, "Thinking and Believing," 321.

16. The Five Nations, Hurons, Ottawas, Twichtwees, Shawanese, Chippewas, Cherokees, Delawares, Powtewatimies, and the Wabash Confederates, "Speech of the United Indian Nations at Their Confederate Council," 1786, *American State Papers: Indian Affairs*, ed. Walter Lowrie and Matthew St. Clair Clarke (Washington, D.C.: Gales and Seaton, 1832), 1:8–9; Dowd, *Spirited Resistance*, 140–41.

17. Tenskwatawa to Harrison, August 1, 1808, *Messages and Letters*, 1:300; Adam Jortner, *The Gods of Prophetstown: The Battle of Tippecanoe and the Holy War for the American Frontier* (New York: Oxford University Press, 2012), 151–52.

18. William Wells to Henry Dearborn, April 22, 1808, *Territorial Papers*, 7:559.

19. Harrison to the War Department, May 19, 1808, in *American State Papers: Indian Affairs*, 1:798; Clark to the War Department, April 5, 1809, in *American State Papers: Indian Affairs*, 1:798.

20. Thomas Forsythe to Clark, December 23, 1812, transcribed in Lucy Trumbull Brown, "The Writings of Thomas Forsyth on the Sauk and Fox Indians, 1812–1832" (M.A. thesis, College of

William and Mary, 1982), 67; Sleeper-Smith, *Indigenous Prosperity,* 317; Gregory A. Waselkov, *A Conquering Spirit: Fort Mims and the Redstick War of 1813–1814* (Tuscaloosa: University of Alabama Press, 2006), 75–76. Also see Sarah M. S. Pearsall, *Polygamy: An Early American History* (New Haven, Conn.: Yale University Press, 2019).

21. R. David Edmunds, "Forgotten Allies: The Loyal Shawnees and the War of 1812," in *The Sixty Years' War for the Great Lakes, 1754–1814,* ed. D. C. Skaggs and L. L. Nelson (East Lansing: Michigan State University Press, 2001), 338–39; Lakomäki, *Gathering Together,* 143; Warren, *Shawnees and Their Neighbors,* 13–42; Robert J. Miller, "Treaties between the Eastern Shawnee Tribe and the United States: Contracts between Sovereign Governments," in *The Eastern Shawnee Tribe of Oklahoma: Resilience through Adversity,* ed. Stephen Warren in collaboration with the Eastern Shawnee Tribe of Oklahoma (Norman: University of Oklahoma Press, 2017), 149.

22. Treaty of Greenville, 1795, *Indian Affairs: Laws and Treaties,* vol. 2 (Treaties), ed. Charles J. Kappler (Washington, D.C.: U.S. Government Printing Office, 1904), 41–42; Edmunds, "Forgotten Allies," 340; Warren, *Shawnees and Their Neighbors,* 20–22, 26; Dowd, "Thinking and Believing," 317. For Native use of annuities as economic security as the fur trade declined, see Michael John Witgen, *Seeing Red: Indigenous Land, American Expansion, and the Political Economy of Plunder in North America* (Chapel Hill: University of North Carolina Press, 2022). On a similar Catawba use of land title, see Brooke Bauer's chapter in this book.

23. Wells to Dearborn, April 22, 1808, *Territorial Papers,* 7:560; Sleeper-Smith, *Indigenous Prosperity,* 315–16; Dowd, *Spirited Resistance,* 138.

24. Jonathan Todd Hancock, "Widening the Scope on the Indians' Old Northwest," in *Warring for America: Cultural Contests in the Era of 1812,* ed. Nicole Eustace and Fredrika J. Teute (Chapel Hill: University of North Carolina Press, 2017), 374–75; Dowd, "Thinking and Believing," 319–20; Lakomäki, *Gathering Together,* 147.

25. Harrison to the Secretary of War, August 22, 1810, *Messages and Letters,* 1:460; Treaty of Fort Wayne, *Indian Affairs: Laws and Treaties,* 2:101–2; Edmunds, *Shawnee Prophet,* 80–83.

26. Tecumseh's speech to Harrison, August 20, 1810, *Messages and Letters,* 1:465–66; Harrison to the War Department, June 26, 1810, in *American State Papers: Indian Affairs,* 1:799.

27. Edmunds, "Forgotten Allies," 338; Warren, *Shawnees and Their Neighbors,* 26; Hancock, "Widening the Scope," 373.

28. Edmunds, "Forgotten Allies," 338; Warren, *Shawnees and Their Neighbors,* 27; Kathleen DuVal, *The Native Ground: Indians and Colonists in the Heart of the Continent* (Philadelphia: University of Pennsylvania Press, 2006), 208–9.

29. Nehemiah Matson, "Sketch of Shaubena, Pottowattamie Chief," *Collections of the State Historical Society of Wisconsin* 7 (1876): 416; Sugden, *Tecumseh,* 205–7, 210, 253.

30. Bethel Saler, *The Settlers' Empire: Colonialism and State Formation in America's Old Northwest* (Philadelphia: University of Pennsylvania Press, 2015), 196; Warren, *Shawnees and Their Neighbors,* 15, 19.

31. Harrison to the Secretary of War, August 7, 1811, *Messages and Letters,* 1:549.

32. Erastus Granger, April 18, 1812, in *American State Papers: Indian Affairs,* 1:807; Mt. Pleasant, "Independence for Whom?," 124; Lisa Brooks, *The Common Pot: The Recovery of Native Space in the Northeast* (Minneapolis: University of Minnesota Press, 2008), 121–62.

33. Young King of the Six Nations, speech, May 21, 1791, *American State Papers: Indian Affairs,* 1:165.

34. Hendrick Aupaumut to Sergeant, January 3, 1809, cited in Jonathan Todd Hancock, *Convulsed States: Earthquakes, Prophecy, and the Remaking of Early America* (Chapel Hill: University of North Carolina Press, 2021), 1; Hancock, *Convulsed States,* 82–83; Jortner, *Gods of Prophetstown,* 194–99.

35. Wells to Dearborn, April 22, 1808, *Territorial Papers,* 7:559; James W. Biddle, "Recollections of Green Bay in 1816–17," *Collections of the State Historical Society of Wisconsin, for the*

Year 1854 1 (1855): 53–54; Matson, "Sketch of Shaubena," 416; Nehemiah Matson, *Pioneers of Illinois, Containing a Series of Sketches Relating to Events That Occurred Previous to 1813* (Chicago, 1882), 231–32; Sugden, *Tecumseh*, 205.

36. Forsythe to Clark, December 23, 1812, transcribed in Brown, "Writings of Thomas Forsyth," 68; Hancock, "Widening the Scope," 369–70; Sleeper-Smith, *Indigenous Prosperity*, 141, 316; Edmunds, *Shawnee Prophet*, 68; R. David Edmunds, "Main Poc: Potawatomi Wabeno," *American Indian Quarterly* 9 (1985): 259, 265.

37. William H. Keating, *Narrative of an Expedition to the Source of St. Peter's River, Lake Winnepeek, Lake of the Woods, &c. &c., Performed in the Year 1823* (Philadelphia: H. C. Carey and I. Lea, 1824), 1:229–30.

38. Forsyth to Clark, January 15, 1827, quoted in Edmunds, "Main Poc," 262.

39. Edmunds, *Shawnee Prophet*, 63–64, 68.

40. Harrison to the Secretary of War, July 4, 1810, *Messages and Letters*, 1:439.

41. Jacob F. Lee, *Masters of the Middle Waters: Indian Nations and Colonial Ambitions Along the Mississippi* (Cambridge, Mass.: Harvard University Press, 2019), 135.

42. Hawkins to Eustis, September 21, 1811, *Letters, Journals and Writings of Benjamin Hawkins*, 2:591; Hawkins to Eustis, January 13, 1812, *Letters, Journals and Writings of Benjamin Hawkins*, 2:601; Dowd, *Spirited Resistance*, 93–94, 144–45; Sugden, *Tecumseh*, 240, 243; Hudson, *Creek Paths*, 88–89; Kathleen DuVal, *Independence Lost: Lives on the Edge of the American Revolution* (New York: Random House, 2016), 300.

43. Harrison to the Secretary of War, May 15, 1810, *Messages and Letters*, 1:421; Harrison to the Secretary of War, August 6, 1811, *Messages and Letters*, 1:545; Harrison to the Secretary of War, August 7, 1811, *Messages and Letters*, 1:548; John Gordon to the War Department, September 10, 1811, *American State Papers: Indian Affairs*, 1:801; Matson, "Sketch of Shaubena," 416; Henry S. Halbert and T. H. Ball, *Creek War of 1813 and 1814*, ed. Frank L. Owsley, Jr. (Tuscaloosa: University of Alabama Press, 1969), 40, 63; George Stiggins, "A Historical Narration of the Genealogy Traditions and Downfall of the Ispocaga or Creek Tribe of Indians, Written by One of the Tribe," part 2, transcribed in Theron A. Nunez, Jr., "Creek Nativism and the Creek War of 1813–1814," *Ethnohistory* 5 (1958): 145; Thomas S. Woodward, *Woodward's Reminiscences of the Creek, or Muscogee Indians, Contained in Letters to Friends in Georgia and Alabama* (Montgomery, Ala.: Barrett & Wimbish, 1859), 94; Sugden, *Tecumseh*, 237; Dowd, "Thinking and Believing," 328; Frank L. Owsley, Jr., "Prophet of War: Josiah Francis and the Creek War," *American Indian Quarterly* 9 (1985): 277; Dowd, *Spirited Resistance*, 144–45.

44. Alexander McGillivray for the Chiefs of the Creek, Chickasaw, and Cherokee Nations, July 10, 1785, *McGillivray of the Creeks*, ed. John Walton Caughey, 2nd ed. (Columbia: University of South Carolina Press, 2007), 90–93; DuVal, *Independence Lost*, 295–309, 324–32.

45. Halbert and Ball, *Creek War*, 40; Stiggins "Historical Narration," part 2, 146–47; Woodward, *Woodward's Reminiscences*, 36; Sugden, *Tecumseh*, 237, 247; Dowd, *Spirited Resistance*, 146; Waselkov, *Conquering Spirit*, 78, 296.

46. Stiggins, "Historical Narration," part 2, 146–47; Tustunnuggee Hopoie, paraphrased in Hawkins to Eustis, January 13, 1812, *Letters, Journals and Writings of Benjamin Hawkins*, 2:601; Hawkins to Big Warrior, Little Prince, and other Creek Chiefs, June 16, 1814, *Letters, Journals and Writings*, 2:687; Hawkins to Eustis, September 21, 1811, *Letters, Journals and Writings*, 2:591; James Robertson to the War Department, September 9, 1811, *American State Papers: Indian Affairs*, 1:801; J. Neilly to War Department, November 29, 1811, *American State Papers: Indian Affairs*, 1:802; Woodward, *Woodward's Reminiscences*, 95; Thomas McKenney, *Memoirs, Official and Personal; with Sketches of Travels Among the Northern and Southern Indians* (New York: Paine and Burgess, 1846), 164–65; Hudson, *Creek Paths*, 94; *Dictionary of Creek/Muskogee*, ed. Jack B. Martin and Margaret McKane Mauldin (Lincoln: University of Nebraska Press, 2000), 46–47; Halbert and Ball, *Creek War*, 41–52; Dowd, *Spirited Resistance*, 148; Sugden, *Tecumseh*, 244–46.

47. Stiggins, "Historical Narration," part 2, pp. 151–52; Hunter, *Manners and Customs*, 151; *Dictionary of Creek/Muskogee*, 46–47, 49; Woodward, *Woodward's Reminiscences*, 36, 95; Edmunds, *Tecumseh*, 148–51; Waselkov, *Conquering Spirit*, 82–86; Sugden, *Tecumseh*, 247–48; Dowd, *Spirited Resistance*, 169; Nunez, "Creek Nativism," part 1, pp. 8–12.

48. McGillivray to William Leslie, November 20, 1788, *McGillivray of the Creeks*, 206–8.

49. Chulustamastabe speech at Mobile Congress, April 2, 1765, *Mississippi Provincial Archives: English Dominion*, ed. Dunbar Rowland (Nashville: Press of Brandon Print. Co., 1911), 244; Greg O'Brien, "Quieting the Ghosts: How the Choctaws and Chickasaws Stopped Fighting," in *The Native South: New Histories and Enduring Legacies*, ed. Tim Alan Garrison and Greg O'Brien (Lincoln: University of Nebraska Press, 2017), 47–69; Wendy Barbara St. Jean, "Trading Paths: Chickasaw Diplomacy in the Greater Southeast, 1690s–1790s" (Ph.D. diss., University of Connecticut, 2004), 126–52.

50. Francisco Cruzat to Esteban Miró, March 19, 1782, in *The Spanish Régime in Missouri: A Collection of Papers and Documents Relating to Upper Louisiana*, ed. Louis Houck (New York: Arno Press, 1971), 1:209–10.

51. Cruzat to Miró, August 23, 1784, *Spain in the Mississippi Valley, 1765–1794*, ed. and trans. Lawrence Kinnaird (Washington, D.C.: U.S. Government Printing Office, 1946–49), 2:117–19; Dowd, *Spirited Resistance*, 93.

52. Arturo O'Neill to Miró, August 3, 1787, "Papers from the Spanish Archives Relating to Tennessee and the Old Southwest," ed. and trans. D. C. Corbitt and Roberta Corbitt, *East Tennessee Historical Society's Publications* 11 (1939): 91; Piomingo to Joseph Martin, February 15, 1787, *Early American Indian Documents: Treaties and Laws, 1607–1789*, vol. 18, *Revolution and Confederation*, ed. Colin G. Calloway, gen. ed. Alden T. Vaughan (Bethesda, Md.: University Publications of America, 1994), 443; Arrell M. Gibson, *The Chickasaws* (Norman: University of Oklahoma Press, 1971), 80–81; Samuel Cole Williams, *History of the Lost State of Franklin* (New York: Press of the Pioneers, 1933), 141–42; McGillivray to Miró, July 25, 1787, "Papers from the Spanish Archives Relating to Tennessee and the Old Southwest," 88–89; McGillivray to O'Neill, July 25, 1787, *McGillivray of the Creeks*, 159; Carlos de Grande-Pré to Miró, October 26, 1787, *Spain in the Mississippi Valley*, 2:236–37; John Doughty, "Up the Tennessee in 1790: The Report of Major John Doughty to the Secretary of War," ed. Colton Storm, *East Tennessee Historical Society's Publications* 17 (1945): 125–26.

53. R. David Edmunds, *Tecumseh and the Quest for Indian Leadership* (Boston: Little, Brown, 1984), 146–47, 150–51.

54. Samuel S. M. Manac, deposition, August 2, 1813, in Halbert and Ball, *Creek War of 1813 and 1814*, 92–93; Waselkov, *Conquering Spirit*, 98.

55. Edmunds, *Tecumseh*, 152; Nichols, *Red Gentlemen and White Savages*, 198.

56. Clark to the War Department (extract), March 22, 1812, *American State Papers: Indian Affairs*, 1:807; Sleeper-Smith, *Indigenous Prosperity*, 302.

57. Some U.S. officials claimed that Hunter did not live with the Osages at all, but John Sugden and other scholars have noted that U.S. officials at the time were trying to discredit him as a critic of U.S. Indian policies. Hunter, *Manners and Customs*, 51–56; Sugden, *Tecumseh*, 253–55.

58. Thomas Jefferson to Albert Gallatin, July 12, 1804, Series 1: General Correspondence. 1651–1827, Thomas Jefferson Papers, Library of Congress, available at https://www.loc.gov/resource/mtj1.030_1054_1054/; Tai S. Edwards, *Osage Women and Empire: Gender and Power* (Lawrence: University Press of Kansas, 2018), 51–52; DuVal, *Native Ground*, chap. 4.

59. Edwards, *Osage Women and Empire*, 51–52.

60. Hunter, *Manners and Customs*, 51.

61. Hunter, *Manners and Customs*, 56; Willard Hughes Rollings, *Unaffected by the Gospel: Osage Resistance to the Christian Invasion, 1673–1906: A Cultural Victory* (Albuquerque: University of New Mexico Press, 2004).

62. Josiah Francis, the Old King, Old Interpreter, and Mougceweihche to Governor González Manrique, August 1813, quoted in Waselkov, *Conquering Spirit*, 92–93, 146.

63. Waselkov, *Conquering Spirit*, 173.

Chapter 4

1. Colin G. Calloway, *The Indian World of George Washington: The First President, the First Americans, and the Birth of the Nation* (New York: Oxford University Press, 2018), 284.

2. I use the term "landholder" when referring to Catawba ownership of the land because they did not view themselves as "owning" the land in the European/Anglo-American way. Instead, they believed the Creator gifted them the land, allowing them to hold the land in common for all Catawba people, past, present, and future.

3. For a discussion of land use and dispossession among New England Natives, see Jean M. O'Brien, *Dispossession by Degrees: Indian Land and Identity in Natick, Massachusetts, 1650–1790* (New York: Cambridge University Press, 1997), 20–26, 66–67. For a similar discussion of Indigenous land and community, see Lisa Brooks, *The Common Pot: The Recovery of Native Space in the Northeast* (Minneapolis: University of Minnesota Press, 2008), xxxvii.

4. "Newburgh Address: George Washington to Officers of the Army, March 15, 1783," George Washington's Mount Vernon, https://www.mountvernon.org/education/primary-sources-2/article /newburgh-address-george-washington-to-officers-of-the-army-march-15-1783/; George Washington to Lafayette, August 15, 1786, *The Papers of George Washington*, Confederation Series, vol. 4, *2 April 1786–31 January 1787*, ed. W. W. Abbot (Charlottesville: University Press of Virginia, 1995), 214–16; Alexander Hamilton, John Jay, and James Madison, *The Federalist: A Commentary on the Constitution of the United States* (London: M. Walter Dunne, 1901), 94. Thomas Jefferson to George Rogers Clark, December 25, 1780, *The Papers of Thomas Jefferson*, vol. 4, ed. Julian P. Boyd (Princeton, N.J.: Princeton University Press, 1951), 233–38 (quotation). For further reading on Jefferson's ideology of the "empire of liberty," see Gordon S. Wood, *Empire of Liberty: History of the Early Republic, 1789–1815* (New York: Oxford University Press, 2009); Robert W. Tucker and David C. Hendrickson, *Empire of Liberty: The Statecraft of Thomas Jefferson* (New York: Oxford University Press, 1990). See also *Superintendents of the Catawba Nation, Plat and Lease Book, 1810–1825*, microfilm, South Carolina Department of Archives and History, Columbia, part 3, pp. 13, 51.

5. Ian Saxine, *Properties of Empire: Indians, Colonists, and Land Speculators on the New England Frontier* (New York: New York University Press, 2019), 2–3.

6. For a comprehensive treatment of Native American and European and Anglo-American perspectives of owning land, see Stuart Banner, *How the Indians Lost Their Land: Law and Power on the Frontier* (Cambridge, Mass.: Harvard University Press, 2005).

7. For more on Catawba land leasing before the American Revolution, see Brooke M. Bauer, *Becoming Catawba: Catawba Women and Nation-Building, 1540–1840* (Tuscaloosa: University of Alabama Press, 2022).

8. "Orders in Council on the 24th February 1771 concerning appointments to the councils of South Carolina, West Florida and Antigua," Order, National Archives, Kew, CO 5/27 1771/02/24; Keith Krawczynski, *William Henry Drayton: South Carolina Revolutionary Patriot* (Baton Rouge: Louisiana State University Press, 2007), 22–25.

9. *South Carolina Council Journal (SCCJ)*, December 1, 1772, *Records of the States of the United States (RSUS)*, S.C. E.1p, 10/6, 247, January 20, 1773, 11/1, 29 ("improper"); Stuart to the Catawbas, February 18, 1773, Joseph Brevard Kershaw Papers; *SCCJ*, October 30, 1773, *RSUS*, S.C. E.1p, 11/2, 2 ("they would not part").

10. Richard Winn, "General Richard Winn's Notes, 1780," *South Carolina Historical and Genealogical Magazine* 44, no. 1 (1943): 7; James H. Merrell, *The Indians' New World: The Catawbas and Their Neighbors from European Contact Through the Era of Removal* (Chapel Hill: University of North Carolina Press, 2009), 215–16.

11. Michael C. Scoggins, *The Day It Rained Militia: Huck's Defeat and the Revolution in the South Carolina Backcountry, May–July 1780* (Charleston, S.C.: History Press, 2005), 41–50; Colin G. Calloway, *The American Revolution in Indian Country: Crisis and Diversity in Native American Communities* (New York: Cambridge University Press, 1995); Frank G. Speck, "Catawba Religious Beliefs, Mortuary Customs, and Dances," *Primitive Man* 12, no. 2 (April 1939): 42; Charles L. Heath, "Catawba Militarism: Ethnohistorical Archaeological Overview," *North Carolina Archaeology* 53 (2004): 103–4. Rumor speculates the Catawbas fled to Virginia and sought refuge with the Pamunkeys. There is no evidence to support this claim and it is unlikely that Catawba men would move their families from one place of combat to a similarly dangerous space. I suspect the families took shelter in the mountains near the North Carolina–Virginia state line after passing the Moravian settlement of Bethabara. The region provided the perfect terrain for hiding and protecting Catawba families.

12. James Mooney, *Siouan Tribes of the East* (Washington, D.C.: U.S. Government Printing Office, 1894), 73–74; *Register of the Debates in Congress*, vol. 6 (Washington, D.C.: Gales and Seaton, 1830), 1083 (quotation).

13. South Carolina did not cede its western territory until August of 1787; see Charles E. Little, *Cyclopedia of Classified Dates, with an Exhaustive Index* (New York: Funk & Wagnalls, 1900), 99; William Robertson Garrett, *History of the South Carolina Cession, and the Northern Boundary of Tennessee* (Nashville: Southern Methodist Publishing House, 1884), 3.

14. Calloway, *Indian World of George Washington*, 264, 304–5.

15. Lark Emerson Adams and Rosa Stoney Lumpkin, eds., *Journals of the House of Representatives, 1785–1786* (Columbia: University of South Carolina Press for the South Carolina Department of Archives and History, 1979), 97 (quotations).

16. Ballard C. Campbell, "1785 Economic Crisis," in *Disasters, Accidents, and Crises in American History: A Reference Guide to the Nation's Most Catastrophic Events* (New York: Facts on File, 2008), 43–46; Rachel N. Klein, *Unification of a Slave State: The Rise of the Planter Class in the South Carolina Backcountry, 1760–1808* (Chapel Hill: University of North Carolina Press, 1990), 126–28; Thomas Jefferson to George Rogers Clark, December 25, 1780, *The Papers of Thomas Jefferson*, vol. 4, ed. Julian P. Boyd (Princeton, N.J.: Princeton University Press, 1951), 233–38 (quotation).

17. Adams and Lumpkin, *Journals of the House of Representatives, 1785–1786*, 97 ("Suffered"), 133 ("inexpedient"); Nathan Bailey, *An Universal Etymological English Dictionary* (London, 1731), s.v. "inexpedient."

18. Louise Pettus, *Leasing Away a Nation: The Legacy of Catawba Indian Land Leases* (Columbia, S.C.: Palmetto Conservation Foundation, 2007), 29; Alexander Sutton et al. v. John Jackson, 1830, Court of Equity, York County, No. 60, File 1, 1830, Historical Center of York, York, S.C. (regarding the Samuel Knox Estate).

19. Michael E. Stevens and Christine M. Allen, eds., *Journals of the House of Representatives, 1791* (Columbia: University of South Carolina Press, 1985), 212–13 (quotation).

20. Author's personal and family knowledge as a Catawba Nation citizen. The methodology of "upstreaming" aids in the understanding of the Catawba past by working our way back from the present society's historical knowledge, such as oral tradition. Upstreaming demonstrates that major societal patterns and practices changed slowly, if at all.

21. Michael E. Stevens, ed., *Journals of the House of Representatives, 1792–1794* (Columbia: University of South Carolina Press, 1988), 77–78 (quotation). For rent payments, see Ian Watson, *Catawba Indian Genealogy* (Geneseo: Geneseo Foundation and the Department of Anthropology, State University of New York at Geneseo, 1995).

22. Timothy Silver, *A New Face on the Countryside: Indians, Colonists, and Slaves in South Atlantic Forests, 1500–1800* (New York: Cambridge University Press, 1990), 110–11, 115 ("attack all the timber"); John Drayton, *A View of South Carolina: As Respects Her Natural and Civil Concerns* (Charleston, S.C.: W. P. Young, 1802), 32, 114. For similar environmental change in

New England, see William Cronon, *Changes in the Land: Indians, Colonists, and the Ecology of New England* (New York: Hill and Wang, 2003).

23. "Distroy" quotation in Stevens, *Journals of the House of Representatives, 1792–1794*, 77.

24. Land Indenture, Lancaster County Courthouse, South Carolina, Deed Book G, 166. For log cabins, see Henrietta Liston, *Tour to the Southern States: Virginia, North & South Carolina's* [*sic*], *Journal of Lady Henrietta (Mrs. Robert Liston), 1797*, Wilson Library, University of North Carolina (original at the National Library of Scotland). The description of this meeting is based on personal knowledge about Catawba politics. For an example of a similar council, see Walter Clark, ed., "Minutes of the Southern Congress at Augusta, Georgia: Georgia; North Carolina; Cherokee Indian Nation; Catawba Indian Nation; et al., October 01, 1763–November 21, 1763," in *The Colonial Records of North Carolina*, vol. 11 (Winston, N.C.: M. I. & J. C. Stewart, Printers to the State, 1895), 156–207.

25. Land Indenture, Lancaster County Courthouse. The absence of the names of "other women" became an issue after Sally's death in 1821 because unnamed persons could not legally receive the deeded land. Instead, the deed was transferred to Sally's niece, who may have been coerced by her brother to sell the land; see Douglas Summers Brown, *The Catawba Indians: The People of the River* (Columbia: University of South Carolina Press, 1966), 320. For earlier documentation of the matrilineal custom among Catawba ancestors, see Charles M. Hudson, *The Southeastern Indians* (Knoxville: University of Tennessee Press, 1976), 185–91; Charles Lanman, "Origin of the Catawba Indians," in *Adventures in the Wilds of the United States and British American Provinces*, vol. 2 (Philadelphia: John W. Moore, 1856), 410–11; Merrell, *The Indians' New World*, 236.

26. Clark, "Minutes of the Southern Congress," 156–207; Samuel Wyly, Surveyor, "Plat of land of the Catawba Indians, February 22, 1764, surveyed pursuant to treaty of Augusta," map fragment, South Carolina Department of Archives and History, Columbia, http://e-archives.sc .gov/record/sdb%3AdeliverableUnit%7C0b7931e8-03e3-47ea-9ca2-8ea5b78992dc/.

27. The rent book contains three sections: plats, renter's names, and rent payments; see *Superintendents of the Catawba Nation, Plat and Lease Book, 1810–1825*, parts 1, 2, 3. Unfortunately, Catawbas lost the five hundred acres reserved for their towns, homes, and burial grounds in 1822. James Kegg, who claimed to be a nephew to Sally New River, secretly leased this land to John Hutchison for an initial eight-hundred-dollar bounty, agreeing to a three dollar annual payment for ninety-nine years. By 1838, acting chief William Harris and his wife Sally Ayers sold Kings Bottom out from under the Catawbas. See Merrell, *The Indians' New World*, 247–48.

28. *Superintendents of the Catawba Nation, Plat and Lease Book, 1810–1825*, part 3, 13, 51.

29. "An Act to Ascertain the Manner and Form of Electing Members to Represent the Inhabitants of This Province in the Commons House of Assembly, and to Appoint Who Shall Be Deemed and Adjudged Capable of Choosing or Being Chosen Members of the Said House," 1719, in *The Statutes at Large of South Carolina*, ed. Thomas Cooper, vol. 3, no. 394 (Columbia, S.C.: Printed by A. S. Johnston, 1838), 50; "The Constitution of South Carolina, 19th March 1778," in *The Statutes at Large of South Carolina*, ed. Thomas Cooper, vol. 1 (Columbia, S.C.: Printed by A. S. Johnston, 1836), 137–45. For the 1790 state constitution, see Cole Blease Graham, Jr., *The South Carolina State Constitution* (New York: Oxford University Press, 2011), 21–23.

30. Mikaela M. Adams, *Who Belongs? Race, Resources, and Tribal Citizenship in the Native South* (New York: Oxford University Press, 2016), 61–95.

31. Personal knowledge of author.

Chapter 5

1. Robert Lee, "Accounting for Conquest: The Price of the Louisiana Purchase of Indian Country," *Journal of American History* 103, no. 4 (2017): 921.

2. Gregory Ablavsky, *Federal Ground: Governing Property and Violence in the First U.S. Territories* (Oxford: Oxford University Press, 2020); Allan Greer, "Dispossession in a Commercial

Idiom: From Indian Deeds to Land Cession Treaties," in *Contested Spaces of Early America*, ed. Juliana Barr and Edward Countryman (Philadelphia: University of Pennsylvania Press, 2014), 69–92; Stuart Banner, *How the Indians Lost Their Land: Law and Power on the Frontier* (Cambridge, Mass.: Harvard University Press, 2005); Paul Frymer, *Building an American Empire: The Era of Territorial and Political Expansion* (Princeton, N.J.: Princeton University Press, 2017); Bethel Saler, *The Settlers' Empire: Colonialism and State Formation in America's Old Northwest* (Philadelphia: University of Pennsylvania Press, 2015); Alan Taylor, *The Divided Ground: Indians, Settlers and the Northern Borderland of the American Revolution* (New York: Alfred A. Knopf, 2006).

3. Louisiana Purchase Treaty, April 30, 1803, Perfected Treaties, 1778–1945, General Records of the United States Government, Record Group 11, National Archives, Washington D.C.; "Statement exhibiting the quantity of public land purchased by the United States in each State and Territory," 1826, *American State Papers: Documents, Legislative and Executive, of the Congress of the United States*, class 8, *Public Lands*, vol. 4, pp. 912–16 (hereafter cited as *ASP* with relevant class title, volume, and page numbers), https://memory.loc.gov/ammem/amlaw/lwsplink.html; Peter J. Kastor, *The Nation's Crucible: The Louisiana Purchase and the Creation of America* (New Haven, Conn.: Yale University Press, 2004); Ory Poret, *History of Land Titles in the State of Louisiana* (Baton Rouge: Louisiana Department of Natural Resources, 1973); Paul Gates, *History of Public Land Law Development* (Washington, D.C.: U.S. Government Printing Office, 1968).

4. Anthony Pagden, *Lords of All the World: Ideologies of Empire in Spain, Britain and France c. 1500–c. 1800* (New Haven, Conn.: Yale University Press, 1995); Allan Greer, *Property and Dispossession: Natives, Empires and Land in Early Modern North America* (Cambridge: Cambridge University Press, 2017); Lauren Benton, *A Search for Sovereignty: Law and Geography in European Empires, 1400–1900* (Cambridge: Cambridge University Press, 2010).

5. Jeremy Adelman and Stephen Aron, "From Borderlands to Borders: Empires, Nation-States, and the Peoples in Between in North American History," *American Historical Review* 104 (1999): 814–41. On Louisiana Indigenous history, see Elizabeth N. Ellis, *The Great Power of Small Nations: Indigenous Diplomacy in the Gulf South* (Philadelphia: University of Pennsylvania Press, 2022); Daniel Usner, *American Indians in the Lower Mississippi Valley: Social and Economic Histories* (Lincoln: University of Nebraska Press, 1998); Brian Klopotek, *Recognition Odysseys: Indigeneity, Race, and Federal Tribal Recognition Policy in Three Louisiana Indian Communities* (Durham, N.C.: Duke University Press, 2011); Mark Edwin Miller, *Forgotten Tribes: Unrecognized Indians and the Federal Acknowledgment Process* (Lincoln: University of Nebraska Press, 2004); F. Todd Smith, *From Dominance to Disappearance: The Indians of Texas and the Near Southwest, 1786–1859* (Lincoln: University of Nebraska Press, 2005); Fred B. Kniffen, Hiram F. Gregory, and George A. Stokes, *The Historic Indian Tribes of Louisiana: From 1542 to the Present* (Baton Rouge: Louisiana State University Press, 1987); Sheri Shuck-Hall, *Journey to the West: The Alabama and Coushatta Indians* (Norman: University of Oklahoma Press, 2008).

6. Banner, *How the Indians Lost Their Land*; Lindsay Gordon Robertson, *Conquest by Law: How the Discovery of America Dispossessed Indigenous Peoples of Their Lands* (New York: Oxford University Press, 2005).

7. John Sibley, "Historical Sketches of the Several Indian Tribes in Louisiana, South of the Arkansas River, and Between the Mississippi and River Grande," in *ASP: Indian Affairs*, 1:721–31; Usner, *American Indians in the Lower Mississippi Valley*; Ellis, *Great Power of Small Nations*, 214–16, 202–3; Smith, *From Dominance to Disappearance*; Kniffen, Gregory, and Stokes, *Historic Indian Tribes of Louisiana*; Lauren C. Post, "Some Notes on the Attakapas Indians of Southwest Louisiana," *Louisiana History* 3, no. 3 (1962): 221–42.

8. Thomas Jefferson, "Notes on John Sibley's Account of the Indians in the Louisiana Territory, 5 April 1805," *Founders Online*, National Archives, https://founders.archives.gov/documents/Jefferson/99-01-02-1500.

9. William C. C. Claiborne et al., *Official Letter Books of W. C. C. Claiborne, 1801–1816* (Jackson, Miss.: State Dept. of Archives and History, 1917), 2:148; Daniel H. Usner, Jr., "American Indians in Colonial New Orleans," in *Powhatan's Mantle: Indians in the Colonial Southeast,* rev. ed., ed. Gregory A. Waselkov, Peter H. Wood, and Tom Hatley (Lincoln: University of Nebraska Press, 2006), 172.

10. Claiborne et al., *Official Letter Books,* 4:237–39; *ASP: Indian Affairs,* 1:755–56; Shuck-Hall, *Journey to the West,* 133.

11. Claiborne et al., *Official Letter Books,* 4:236–39; "An Act for the Relief of Certain Alibama and Wyandott Indians," February 28, 1809, 10 Cong., 2 Sess., chap. 23, in *The Public Statutes at Large of the United States of America from the Organization of the Government in 1789, to March 3, 1845* (Boston: Charles C. Little and James Brown, 1845), 527; Joyce Purser, "The Administration of Indian Affairs in Louisiana, 1803–1820," *Louisiana History* 5, no. 4 (1964): 410–15.

12. "Statement exhibiting the quantity of public land purchased," 1826, *ASP: Public Lands,* 4:916; Kniffen, Gregory, and Stokes, *Historic Indian Tribes of Louisiana,* 76.

13. Sibley, "Historical Sketches," *ASP: Indian Affairs,* 1:721–31.

14. Thomas Freeman, Peter Custis, and United States War Office, *An Account of the Red River in Louisiana* (Washington, D.C., 1807), 9–10.

15. "Secretary of the Treasury to Isaac Briggs," 1805, *ASP: Public Lands,* 1:537.

16. "General Land Office," 1824, *ASP: Public Lands,* 4:32.

17. Malcolm J. Rohrbough, *The Land Office Business: The Settlement and Administration of American Public Lands, 1789–1837* (New York: Oxford University Press, 1968), 161–64, 211; William Garrard obituary, *Opelousas Gazette,* November 24, 1838.

18. "Land Titles in the Territory of Orleans," 1805, *ASP: Public Lands,* 1:233; Kastor, *The Nation's Crucible,* 81–85.

19. David E. Narrett, *Adventurism and Empire: The Struggle for Mastery in the Louisiana-Florida Borderlands, 1762–1803* (Chapel Hill: University of North Carolina Press, 2015), 147–48; Gilbert C. Din, "The Immigration Policy of Governor Esteban Miró in Spanish Louisiana," *Southwestern Historical Quarterly* 73, no. 2 (1969): 155–75.

20. Marcel Giraud, *A History of French Louisiana: The Reign of Louis XIV, 1698–1715* (Baton Rouge: Louisiana State University Press, 1974), 31, 183–84; W. B. Knipmeyer, "Settlement Succession in Eastern French Louisiana" (Ph.D. diss., Louisiana State University, 1956), 19; Kathleen DuVal, "Interconnectedness and Diversity in 'French Louisiana,'" in Waselkov, Wood, and Hatley, *Powhatan's Mantle,* 139; Sylvia Hilton, "Spanish Louisiana in Atlantic Contexts: Nexus of Imperial Transactions and International Relations," in *Louisiana: Crossroads of the Atlantic World,* ed. Cécile Vidal (Philadelphia: University of Pennsylvania Press, 2014), 72.

21. "Digest of the Laws of Louisiana" (Alexander O'Reilly, 1770), in *ASP: Miscellaneous,* 1:376–77; Edward T. Price, *Dividing the Land: Early American Beginnings of Our Private Property Mosaic* (Chicago: University of Chicago Press, 1995), 297–301.

22. "Land Titles in the Territory of Orleans," 1805, *ASP: Public Lands,* 1:232–33.

23. Gates, *History of Public Land Law Development,* 94–111; Harry L. Coles, "Applicability of the Public Land System to Louisiana," *Mississippi Valley Historical Review* 43, no. 1 (1956): 55.

24. Elizabeth Ellis describes patterns of multinational settlement as fundamental to Petites Nations' survival, especially during difficult eras of war and colonization. For the significance of this pattern, see Ellis, *Great Power,* 5–6.

25. Ellis, *Great Power,* 222–24; Smith, *From Dominance to Disappearance,* 63–64.

26. "Land Claims in Louisiana," 1813, *ASP: Public Lands,* 2:648–50.

27. De Blanc to Miró, August 11, 1789, in *Spain in the Mississippi Valley, 1765–1794,* part 2, *Post War Decade, 1782–1791,* ed. Lawrence Kinnaird (Washington, D.C.: U.S. Government Printing Office, 1946), 278–79.

28. "Land Claims in Louisiana," 1813, *ASP: Public Lands,* 2:648–50.

29. "Land Claims in Louisiana," 1813, *ASP: Public Lands*, 2:648–50.

30. Amos Stoddard, *Sketches, Historical and Descriptive, of Louisiana* (Philadelphia: Mathew Carey, 1812), 248.

31. Smith, *From Dominance to Disappearance*, 63–64.

32. "Land Claims in Louisiana," 1813, *ASP: Public Lands*, 2:655.

33. "Land Claims in Louisiana," 658.

34. "Copy of a Letter from Doctor T. Sibley," 1806, *ASP: Public Lands*, 2:666.

35. "Land Claims in Louisiana," 1813, *ASP: Public Lands*, 2:661.

36. "Land Claims in Louisiana," 660.

37. "Land Claims in Louisiana," 661.

38. "Monthly Return of Certificates Issued by the Commissioners of the Western District," August 1811, *ASP: Public Lands*, 2:701; Gustavus Myers, *History of the Supreme Court of the United States* (Chicago: C. H. Kerr, 1912), 319–20.

39. "Balances Against Receivers of Public Moneys," 1835, *ASP: Public Lands*, 7:561. The suit was dismissed in 1830 but then renewed. Garrard died in 1838.

40. Post, "Some Notes on the Attakapas Indians," 230–34; Kniffen, Gregory, and Stokes, *Historic Indian Tribes of Louisiana*, 47; Smith, *From Dominance to Disappearance*, 40.

41. "Claims in Attakapas," 1816, *ASP: Public Lands*, 3:124.

42. "Claims in Attakapas," 90–91.

43. "Claims in Opelousas," 1816, *ASP: Public Lands*, 3:86.

44. "Claims in Attakapas," 129.

45. "Claims in Opelousas," 86–88 (quotation at 88; emphasis in original); Eric Kades, "The Dark Side of Efficiency: *Johnson v. M'Intosh* and the Expropriation of American Indian Lands," *University of Pennsylvania Law Review* 148, no. 4 (April 2000): 1065–190; Robertson, *Conquest by Law*.

46. "Claims in Opelousas," 86 (quotation).

47. Ellis, *Great Power*, 196–213.

48. "Claims in Western Louisiana, Twelfth Class," 1816, *ASP: Public Lands*, 3:212–13.

49. United States Department of the Interior, Bureau of Indian Affairs, "Recommendation and Summary of Evidence for Proposed Finding for Federal Acknowledgment of the Tunica-Biloxi Indian Tribe of Louisiana Pursuant to 25 CFR 54," December 4, 1980, 4; Corinne L. Saucier, *History of Avoyelles Parish, Louisiana* (New Orleans: Pelican, 1943); Jeffrey P. Brain, "Archaeology of the Tunicas," in *The Tunica-Biloxi Tribe: Its Culture and People*, ed. Brian Klopotek, John D. Barbry, Donna M. Pierite, and Elisabeth Pierite-Mora (Marksville, La.: Tunica-Biloxi Tribe of Louisiana, 2017), 7.

50. "Claims in Western Louisiana, Twelfth Class," 1816, *ASP: Public Lands*, 3:213.

51. Miller, *Forgotten Tribes*, 161–64.

52. "Claims in Eastern Louisiana," *ASP: Public Lands*, 3:231–32.

53. "Claims in Eastern Louisiana," 232.

54. "Report of the register of the land office at Opelousas," in "Claims in Louisiana," 1826, *ASP: Public Lands*, 4:497–98.

55. "Land Office at Opelousas," 498.

56. Ablavsky, *Federal Ground*, 7–14.

57. Daniel H. Usner, *Weaving Alliances with Other Women: Chitimacha Indian Work in the New South* (Athens: University of Georgia Press, 2015), 3; "Tribal History," Chitimacha Tribe of Louisiana, accessed April 11, 2022, http://www.chitimacha.gov/history-culture/tribal-history.

58. Klopotek, *Recognition Odysseys*, 44; Miller, *Forgotten Tribes*, 197–98.

59. Miller, *Forgotten Tribes*, 166.

Chapter 6

Acknowledgments: I would like to thank Emily Conroy-Krutz and Michael Blaakman for the invitation to join this volume and for their generous and substantive feedback, the anonymous reviewers whose suggestions made this essay better, and Brooks Winfree for his keen editorial eye.

1. "A Slave State in Embryo," *New York Evening Post*, November 21, 1850.

2. Ibid.

3. 1860 U.S. Federal Census—Slave Schedules, *Ancestry.com*.

4. "A Slave State in Embryo."

5. On the westward expansion of slavery and Manifest Destiny, see Michael A. Morrison, *Slavery and the American West: The Eclipse of Manifest Destiny and the Coming of the Civil War* (Chapel Hill: University of North Carolina Press, 1999); Amy S. Greenberg, *Manifest Manhood: Manifest Destiny and the Antebellum American Empire* (New York: Cambridge University Press, 2005); Stephen Aron, *How the West Was Lost: The Transformation of Kentucky from Daniel Boone to Henry Clay* (Bloomington: University of Indiana Press, 2009); Walter Johnson, *River of Dark Dreams: Slavery and Empire in the Cotton Kingdom* (Cambridge, Mass.: Harvard University Press, 2013). One of the few historians to discuss Indian Territory in the political crisis of the 1850s was Anne Heloise Abel in her book *The American Indian as Slaveholder and Secessionist: An Omitted Chapter in the Diplomatic History of the Southern Confederacy* (Cleveland, Ohio: Arthur H. Clark, 1915), chaps. 1 and 2. Barbara Krauthamer briefly discusses the role of the Choctaw and Chickasaw nations during this time period in her monograph *Black Slaves, Indian Masters: Slavery, Emancipation, and Citizenship in the Native American South* (Chapel Hill: University of North Carolina Press, 2013), chap. 3. See also Reginald Horsman, *Race and Manifest Destiny: The Origins of American Racial Anglo-Saxonism* (Cambridge, Mass.: Harvard University Press, 1981); Adam Rothman, *Slave Country: American Expansion and the Origins of the Deep South* (Cambridge, Mass.: Harvard University Press, 2005); Claudio Saunt, *Unworthy Republic: The Dispossession of Native Americans and the Road to Indian Territory* (New York: W. W. Norton, 2020).

6. For U.S. slaveholders' expansionist ambitions, see Matthew Karp, *This Vast Southern Empire: Slaveholders at the Helm of American Foreign Policy* (Cambridge, Mass.: Harvard University Press, 2016).

7. Robert F. Berkhofer, Jr., *The White Man's Indian: Images of the American Indian from Columbus to the Present* (New York: Vintage Books, 1979), 134.

8. Krauthamer, *Black Slaves, Indian Masters*, 25. For more on the Civilization Program among the Five Tribes, see Ronald N. Satz, *American Indian Policy in the Jacksonian Era* (Lincoln: University of Nebraska Press, 1974); William G. McLoughlin, *Cherokee Renascence in the New Republic* (Princeton, N.J.: Princeton University Press, 1986); Francis Paul Prucha, *The Great Father: The United States Government and the American Indians* (Lincoln: University of Nebraska Press, 1995); Theda Perdue, *"Mixed Blood Indians": Racial Construction in the Early South* (Athens: University of Georgia Press, 2003); Colin G. Calloway, *The Indian World of George Washington: The First President, the First Americans, and the Birth of the Nation* (New York: Oxford University Press, 2018).

9. *Laws of the Cherokee Nation Adopted by the Council at Various Periods: Printed for the Benefit of the Nation* (Tahlequah, Cherokee Nation: Cherokee Advocate Office, 1852), 120–21. For foundational texts about slavery and the law in the Cherokee Nation before removal, see R. Halliburton, Jr., *Red Over Black: Black Slavery Among the Cherokee Indians* (Westport, Conn.: Greenwood Press, 1977); Theda Perdue, *Slavery and the Evolution of Cherokee Society* (Knoxville: University of Tennessee Press, 1979); Tiya Miles, *Ties That Bind: The Story of an Afro-Cherokee Family in Slavery and Freedom* (Berkeley: University of California Press, 2005). Celia E. Naylor's book, *African Cherokees in Indian Territory: From Chattel to Citizens* (Chapel Hill: University of North Carolina Press, 2008), looks at slave codes in the Cherokee Nation in the West.

10. Krauthamer, *Black Slaves, Indian Masters*, 83.

11. Grant Foreman, *Indian Removal* (Norman: University of Oklahoma Press, 1934); Saunt, *Unworthy Republic*.

12. Claudio Saunt, Barbara Krauthamer, Tiya Miles, Celia E. Naylor, and Circe Sturm, "Rethinking Race and Culture in the Early South," *Ethnohistory* 53, no. 2 (2006): 399.

13. James P. Ronda, "'We Have a Country': Race, Geography, and the Invention of Indian Territory," *Journal of the Early Republic* 19, no. 4 (Winter 1999), 741.

14. Arthur DeRosier, *The Removal of the Choctaw Indians* (Knoxville: University of Tennessee Press, 1970), 44.

15. John Calhoun, "Report on the System of Indian Trade," December 8, 1818, in *The Works of John C. Calhoun*, vol. 5, *Reports and Public Letters*, ed. Richard K. Crallé (New York: D. Appleton, 1854), Google Books.

16. Charles Kappler, ed., *Indian Affairs: Laws and Treaties*, vol. 2 (Treaties) (Washington, D.C: U.S. Government Printing Office, 1904), 311.

17. Ibid.

18. Tiya Miles, *The House on Diamond Hill: A Cherokee Plantation Story* (Chapel Hill: University of North Carolina Press, 2010), 181.

19. Rothman, *Slave Country*, 168.

20. Susan Colbert interview, Indian Pioneer Papers, University of Oklahoma Western History Collection, accessed May 10, 2020, https://digital.libraries.ou.edu/cdm/ref/collection/indianpp/id/7135 (hereafter cited as IPP).

21. Krauthamer, *Black Slaves, Indian Masters*, 41.

22. *Annual Report of the Commissioner of Indian Affairs, 1836* (Washington, D.C.: U.S. Office of Indian Affairs, 1836), 14.

23. Ibid.

24. Ibid.

25. Waterman L. Ormsby, *The Butterfield Overland Mail*, ed. Lyle H. Wright and Josephine M. Bynum (San Marino, Calif.: Huntington Library, 1955), 26.

26. Ibid, 34.

27. Ibid.

28. Ibid, 35.

29. Krauthamer, *Black Slaves, Indian Masters*, 81.

30. *Annual Report of the Commissioner of Indian Affairs, 1839* (Washington, D.C.: U.S. Office of Indian Affairs, 1839), 149.

31. Eliza Hardrick interview, IPP, accessed May 10, 2020, https://digital.libraries.ou.edu/cdm/singleitem/collection/indianpp/id/1963/rec/1.

32. General E. P. Gaines to Arbuckle and Rose, April 5, 1836, Headquarters Western Department, Letter Book 8, 298, quoted in Grant Foreman, *Advancing the Frontier, 1830–1860* (Norman: University of Oklahoma Press, 1933), 156.

33. "Correspondence Between the U.S. and Mexico," *Telegraph and Texas Register*, September 6, 1836.

34. Foreman, *Advancing the Frontier*, 156.

35. Ibid., 157.

36. Ibid., 154.

37. Ibid., 155.

38. Ibid.

39. Ibid.

40. For more information about the life of Pierre Juzan and his time at the Choctaw Academy in Kentucky, see Christina Snyder, *Great Crossings: Indians, Settlers, and Slaves in the Age of Jackson* (New York: Oxford University Press, 2017).

41. Foreman, *Advancing the Frontier*, 156.

42. William Armstrong to Crawford, February 4, 1839, Office of Indian Affairs, Western Superintendency, File A 120, quoted in Foreman, *Advancing the Frontier*, 157.

43. Ibid.

44. Ibid., 158.

45. Ibid.

46. Pierre Juzan to William Armstrong, March 8, 1839, Letters Received by the Office of Indian Affairs, Choctaw Agency, 1824–78, microfilm series 234, roll 171, National Archives, Washington, D.C.

47. Ibid.

48. Ibid.

49. Ibid.

50. "600 Dollars (States' Money) Reward," April 25, 1840, *Austin City Gazette*, Texas Runaway Slave Project, accessed May 5, 2020, https://digital.sfasu.edu/digital/collection/RSP/id /13791/rec/1.

51. Isaac Folsom, May 1842, Choctaw Agency, roll 171.

52. Scrapbook, folder 3, Cooke County History Collection, 1843–1967, Dolph Briscoe Center for American History, The University of Texas at Austin.

53. Jonathan Martin, *Divided Mastery: Slave Hiring in the Antebellum South* (Cambridge, Mass.: Harvard University Press, 2004), 96–97.

54. Andrew Torget, *Seeds of Empire: Cotton, Slavery, and the Transformation of the Texas Borderlands, 1800–1850* (Chapel Hill: University of North Carolina Press, 2015), 12.

55. Randolph Campbell, *An Empire for Slavery: The Peculiar Institution in Texas, 1821–1865* (Baton Rouge: Louisiana State University Press, 1989), 56.

56. Petition of Overton Love and John Guest, Reports of Committee, 33rd Cong., 1st Sess., Rep. Com., No. 295, S. Doc. 1.

57. Ibid.

58. Ibid.

59. Ibid.

60. Krauthamer, *Black Slaves, Indian Masters*, 92.

61. "Address of the Southern Convention," *Texas State Gazette*, July 13, 1850; the Compromise of 1850 resolved Texas's ambitious territorial visions (encompassing most of modern New Mexico) by fixing the borders of that state to its contemporary boundaries. See David M. Potter, *The Impending Crisis: America Before the Civil War, 1848–1861* (New York: Harper Perennial, 1976), 99.

62. "Address of the Southern Convention," *Texas State Gazette*.

63. "Our Indian Neighbors," *Southern Intelligencer*, December 30, 1857.

64. "Indian Policy," *Daily Picayune*, December 29, 1858.

65. "The Indian States," *Annapolis Gazette*, December 30, 1858.

66. "Chickasaw and Choctaw Indians," *San Antonio Ledger*, June 1, 1861.

67. For an example of this language, see Resolution of the Choctaw Nation, February 7, 1861, in *The War of the Rebellion: A Compilation of the Official Records of the Union and Confederate Armies*, series 1, vol. 1 (Washington, D.C.: U.S. Government Printing Office, 1880), 682.

Chapter 7

Acknowledgments: Many thanks to Seth Archer and Carys Brown for reading versions of this essay and offering helpful comments, as well as to the editors and the anonymous reviewers.

1. Haunani-Kay Trask, *From a Native Daughter: Colonialism and Sovereignty in Hawai'i*, rev. ed. (Honolulu: University of Hawai'i Press, 1999), 6; Houston Wood, *Displacing Natives: The Rhetorical Production of Hawai'i* (Lanham, Md.: Rowman & Littlefield, 1999), 37, 136. For more

on the ways in which Congregationalist Christianity distanced Native Hawaiians from their history and culture, see Kealani Cook, *Return to Kahiki: Native Hawaiians in Oceania* (New York: Cambridge University Press, 2018), chaps. 1-2.

2. Emily Conroy-Krutz, *Christian Imperialism: Converting the World in the Early Republic* (Ithaca, N.Y.: Cornell University Press, 2015), 5, 104, 129. For detailed portraits of the ABCFM's Hawaiian mission, see Patricia Grimshaw, *Paths of Duty: American Missionary Wives in Nineteenth-Century Hawaii* (Honolulu: University of Hawai'i Press, 1989); Clifford Putney, *Missionaries in Hawai'i: The Lives of Peter and Fanny Gulick, 1797-1883* (Amherst: University of Massachusetts Press, 2010); Jennifer Thigpen, *Island Queens and Mission Wives: How Gender and Empire Remade Hawai'i's Island World* (Honolulu: University of Hawai'i Press, 2014).

3. Seth Archer, "Remedial Agents: Missionary Physicians and the Depopulation of Hawai'i," *Pacific Historical Review* 79, no. 4 (November 2010): 515.

4. Jennifer Fish Kashay, "Agents of Imperialism: Missionaries and Merchants in Early-Nineteenth-Century Hawaii," *New England Quarterly* 80, no. 2 (June 2007): 296; Joy Schulz, *Hawaiian by Birth: Missionary Children, Bicultural Identity, and U.S. Colonialism in the Pacific* (Lincoln: University of Nebraska Press, 2017), 44.

5. Schulz, *Hawaiian by Birth*, 142; Wood, *Displacing Natives*, 37-41.

6. "Proceedings at Annual Meeting of the Board," *Missionary Herald*, November 1840, 445; Sally Engle Merry, *Colonizing Hawai'i: The Cultural Power of Law* (Princeton, N.J.: Princeton University Press, 2000), 28.

7. Noelani Arista, *The Kingdom and the Republic: Sovereign Hawai'i and the Early United States* (Philadelphia: University of Pennsylvania Press, 2018), 3.

8. Lilikalā Kame'eleihiwa, *Native Land and Foreign Desires: Pehea lā e pono ai?* (Honolulu: University of Hawai'i Press, 1992), 79-82.

9. Seth Archer, *Sharks upon the Land: Colonialism, Indigenous Health, and Culture in Hawai'i, 1778-1855* (New York: Cambridge University Press, 2018), 10.

10. Arista, *Kingdom*, 3, 226; Jennifer Fish Kashay, "Savages, Sinners, and Saints: The Hawaiian Kingdom and the Imperial Contest, 1778-1839" (Ph.D. diss., University of Arizona, 2002), 315-16.

11. Arista, *Kingdom*, 138-39.

12. Kashay, "Savages," 303-6.

13. Kashay, "Savages," 295; Jennifer Fish Kashay, "Native, Foreigner, Missionary, Priest: Western Imperialism and Religious Conflict in Early 19th-Century Hawaii," *Cercles* 5 (2002): 3-10.

14. David Sehat, *The Myth of American Religious Freedom* (New York: Oxford University Press, 2011), 4-5.

15. Tisa Wenger, *Religious Freedom: The Contested History of an American Ideal* (Chapel Hill: University of North Carolina Press, 2017), 1-2.

16. Hokulani K. Aikau, *A Chosen People, a Promised Land: Mormonism and Race in Hawai'i* (Minneapolis: University of Minnesota Press, 2012), 3; Gavan Daws, *Shoal of Time: A History of the Hawaiian Islands* (Honolulu: University of Hawai'i Press, 1968), 292; Noenoe K. Silva, *Aloha Betrayed: Native Hawaiian Resistance to American Colonialism* (Durham, N.C.: Duke University Press, 2004), 48; Rob Wilson, *Be Always Converting, Be Always Converted: An American Poetics* (Cambridge, Mass.: Harvard University Press, 2009), 27.

17. Ronald C. Williams, Jr., "To Raise a Voice in Praise: The Revivalist Mission of John Henry Wise, 1889-1896," *Hawaiian Journal of History* 46 (2012): 3, 29.

18. "The Missionary Herald," *Missionary Herald*, January 1827, 11; Conroy-Krutz, *Christian Imperialism*, 4.

19. "The Missionary Herald," *Missionary Herald*, January 1827, 11.

20. On other ABCFM publications, see "Publications of the Board," *Missionary Herald*, May 1833, 182-83; "American Board of Commissioners for Foreign Missions," *Missionary Herald*, November 1843, 415.

21. "American Board of Commissioners for Foreign Missions," *Missionary Herald*, November 1841, 446.

22. "American Board of Foreign Missions," *Missionary Herald*, January 1828, 5–6. On the flourishing of religious publishing in this era, see David Paul Nord, *Faith in Reading: Religious Publishing and the Birth of Mass Media in America* (New York: Oxford University Press, 2004).

23. "American Board of Commissioners for Foreign Missions," *Missionary Herald*, October 1846, 331.

24. "American Board of Commissioners for Foreign Missions," *Missionary Herald*, November 1843, 415.

25. "The Missionary Herald," *Missionary Herald*, January 1827, 11; Conroy-Krutz, *Christian Imperialism*, 4–5.

26. Kashay, "Savages," 296; Ralph Simpson Kuykendall, *The Hawaiian Kingdom*, vol. 1, *1778-1854, Foundation and Transformation* (Honolulu: University of Hawai'i Press, 1938), 139.

27. Kashay, "Savages," 297–98.

28. Kashay, "Savages," 303–5; Reginald Yzendoorn, *History of the Catholic Mission in the Hawaiian Islands* (Honolulu: Honolulu Star-Bulletin, 1927), 43.

29. Jay P. Dolan, *In Search of an American Catholicism: A History of Religion and Culture in Tension* (New York: Oxford University Press, 2002), 54–57.

30. Conroy-Krutz, *Christian Imperialism*, 124–26; Kashay, "Agents," 292; Kashay, "Savages," 300.

31. Cook, *Return to Kahiki*, 53; Hiram Bingham to Jeremiah Evarts, July 19, 1828, Papers of the American Board of Commissioners for Foreign Missions, Houghton Library, Harvard University, Cambridge, Mass. (hereafter cited as ABC), ser. 19.1, vol. 2, no. 17; Hiram Bingham, Ephraim Clark, and Levi Chamberlain to Jeremiah Evarts, January 1, 1829, ABC 19.1, vol. 3, no. 265; Ephraim Clark, Hiram Bingham, and Lorrin Andrews to Jeremiah Evarts, February 20, 1830, ABC 19.1, vol. 3, no. 269; Ephraim Clark, Levi Chamberlain, Gerrit P. Judd, and Stephen Shepard to Jeremiah Evarts, September 20, 1830, ABC 19.1, vol. 4, no. 4; Levi Chamberlain to ABCFM, August 16, 1830, ABC 19.1, vol. 6, no. 148.

32. Kashay, "Savages," 306–8.

33. Levi Chamberlain to ABCFM, August 16, 1830, ABC 19.1, vol. 6, no. 148.

34. Minutes of a General Meeting of the Sandwich Island Mission, January 1830, ABC 19.1, vol. 3, no. 273.

35. Ephraim Clark, Levi Chamberlain, Gerrit P. Judd, and Stephen Shepard to Jeremiah Evarts, September 20, 1830, ABC 19.1, vol. 4, no. 4; Ephraim Clark to Rufus Anderson, November 10, 1830, ABC 19.1, vol. 5, no. 137.

36. Ephraim Clark, Hiram Bingham, and Lorrin Andrews to Jeremiah Evarts, February 20, 1830, ABC 19.1, vol. 3, no. 269; Ephraim Clark, Levi Chamberlain, Gerrit P. Judd, and Stephen Shepard to Jeremiah Evarts, September 20, 1830, ABC 19.1, vol. 4, no. 4; Hiram Bingham to Jeremiah Evarts, June 28, 1831, ABC 19.1, vol. 4, no. 8; Ephraim Clark to Rufus Anderson, November 10, 1830, ABC 19.1, vol. 5, no. 137; Ephraim Clark to Jeremiah Evarts, September 14, 1831, ABC 19.1, vol. 5, no. 140; Kashay, "Savages," 306.

37. "Sandwich Islands," *Missionary Herald*, October 1830, 313–18.

38. For an example of the *Herald*'s complaints about Catholicism in other ABCFM mission fields, see "Mediterranean," *Missionary Herald*, June 1830, 177–78.

39. "Sandwich Islands," *Missionary Herald*, September 1827, 271–75.

40. "Art. V," *Quarterly Review*, March 1827, 423–24. This story is further affirmed in Sheldon Dibble, *A History of the Sandwich Islands* (Lahainaluna: Press of the Mission Seminary, 1843), 356–57; Thigpen, *Island Queens*, 56–61; Yzendoorn, *History*, 18–20.

41. "Art. V," *Quarterly Review*, March 1827, 439–41.

42. Levi Chamberlain to Jeremiah Evarts, November 1, 1827, ABC 19.1, vol. 2, no. 71; William Richards to ABCFM, December 6, 1827, ABC 19.1, vol. 3, no. 138.

43. "Sandwich Islands," *Missionary Herald*, February 1827, 41.

44. Arista, *Kingdom*, 1–2.

45. Ephraim Clark to David Greene, September 16, 1829, ABC 19.1, vol. 3, no. 158; "Sandwich Islands," *Missionary Herald*, January 1829, 27–31.

46. Kashay, "Savages," 308–13.

47. Hiram Bingham to Jeremiah Evarts, February 6, 1832, ABC 19.1, vol. 5, no. 9. On missionaries' discomfort with the persecution of Native Hawaiians, see Hiram Bingham to Rufus Anderson, June 23, 1832, ABC 19.1, vol. 4, no. 22; Dibble, *History*, 95; Kuykendall, *Hawaiian Kingdom*, 1:141.

48. Hiram Bingham to Rufus Anderson, February 16, 1832, ABC 19.1, vol. 5, no. 6.

49. Hiram Bingham to Jeremiah Evarts, June 23, 1832, ABC 19.1, vol. 4, no. 22; Kuykendall, *Hawaiian Kingdom*, 1:143.

50. Hiram Bingham, Ephraim Clark, Joseph Goodrich, Levi Chamberlain, Andrew Johnstone, and Gerrit P. Judd to Jeremiah Evarts, January 17, 1832, ABC 19.1, vol. 4, no. 15.

51. "Sandwich Islands," *Missionary Herald*, November 1832, 351; Schulz, *Hawaiian by Birth*, 17, 124.

52. "Sandwich Islands," *Missionary Herald*, November 1832, 351–52. For a later and more direct published defense of missionaries' actions respecting the removal of the priests, see Dibble, *History*, 386–90.

53. Levi Chamberlain to Rufus Anderson, February 6, 1832, ABC 19.1, vol. 6, no. 159; Kashay, "Savages," 313–14.

54. "Sandwich Islands," *Missionary Herald*, November 1832, 352; Kashay, "Savages," 299.

55. "Sandwich Islands," *Missionary Herald*, November 1832, 352–53.

56. "Sandwich Islands," *Missionary Herald*, November 1832, 352.

57. Kashay, "Savages," 333.

58. Kashay, "Savages," 336; Kameʻeleihiwa, *Native Land*, 176; Kuykendall, *Hawaiian Kingdom*, 1:164–65.

59. "Sandwich Islands," *Missionary Herald*, March 1840, 96–97.

60. Kashay, "Savages," 315, 321, 337.

61. Kuykendall, *Hawaiian Kingdom*, 1:105.

62. "Sandwich Islands," *Missionary Herald*, March 1840, 95.

63. "Sandwich Islands," *Missionary Herald*, March 1840, 96–97.

64. Hiram Bingham to Rufus Anderson, November 18, 1839, ABC 19.1, vol. 9, no. 11; Sandwich Island Missionaries to U.S. House of Representatives, July 11, 1839, ABC 19.1, vol. 8, no. 46.

65. "Sandwich Islands," *Missionary Herald*, March 1840, 99; Kashay, "Savages," 339.

66. "Sandwich Islands," *Missionary Herald*, March 1840, 95.

67. "Sandwich Islands," *Missionary Herald*, March 1840, 99; Kashay, "Savages," 325.

68. "Sandwich Islands," *Missionary Herald*, March 1840, 98–101.

69. "Proceedings at Annual Meeting of the Board," *Missionary Herald*, November 1840, 444–45.

70. "Proceedings at Annual Meeting of the Board," *Missionary Herald*, November 1840, 445.

71. Joseph Tracy, *Refutation of the Charges Brought by the Roman Catholics Against the American Missionaries at the Sandwich Islands* (Boston: T. R. Marvin, 1843), 7, 21; Hiram Bingham to Rufus Anderson, May 15, 1839, ABC 19.1, vol. 9, no. 9.

72. "Proceedings at Annual Meeting of the Board," *Missionary Herald*, November 1840, 446.

73. Kashay, "Native, Foreigner," 8.

74. Daws, *Shoal*, 89; Kuykendall, *Hawaiian Kingdom*, 1:143; Yzendoorn, *History*, 49, 74–75.

75. Hiram Bingham, Ephraim Clark, Joseph Goodrich, Levi Chamberlain, Andrew Johnstone, and Gerrit P. Judd to Jeremiah Evarts, January 17, 1832, ABC 19.1, vol. 4, no. 15.

76. Ephraim Clark to Rufus Anderson, November 10, 1830, ABC 19.1, vol. 5, no. 137.

77. Daws, *Shoal*, 94–96; Kashay, "Savages," 316–34; Kuykendall, *Hawaiian Kingdom*, 1:141–50; Yzendoorn, *History*, 93–112.

78. "Twenty-Fourth Annual Report of the Board," *Missionary Herald*, December 1833, 454.

79. "Twenty-Fourth Annual Report of the Board," *Missionary Herald*, December 1833, 458.

80. "Sandwich Islands," *Missionary Herald*, January 1838, 34.

81. "Sandwich Islands," *Missionary Herald*, October 1836, 384–85.

82. Archer, "Remedial Agents," 544; Patrick Brantlinger, *Dark Vanishings: Discourse on the Extinction of Primitive Races, 1800–1930* (Ithaca, N.Y.: Cornell University Press, 2003), 2; Brian W. Dippie, *The Vanishing American: White Attitudes and U.S. Indian Policy* (Middletown, Conn.: Wesleyan University Press, 1982); Virginia Metaxas, "'Licentiousness Has Slain Its Hundreds of Thousands': The Missionary Discourse of Sex, Death, and Disease in Nineteenth-Century Hawai'i," in *Gender and Globalization in Asia and the Pacific: Method, Practice, Theory*, ed. Kathy E. Ferguson and Monique Mironesco (Honolulu: University of Hawai'i Press, 2008).

83. William Richards to Rufus Anderson, December 7, 1832, ABC 19.1, vol. 5, no. 80.

84. "VI. Sandwich Islands," *Missionary Herald*, January 1833, 21.

85. "Twenty-Fourth Annual Report of the Board," *Missionary Herald*, December 1833, 455.

86. "Sandwich Islands," *Missionary Herald*, March 1840, 99.

87. "Sandwich Islands," *Missionary Herald*, March 1840, 95.

88. "Proceedings at Annual Meeting of the Board," *Missionary Herald*, November 1840, 445–46.

89. "Sandwich Islands," *Missionary Herald*, September 1840, 371–76; "Sandwich Islands," *Missionary Herald*, June 1841, 271; "Sandwich Islands," *Missionary Herald*, March 1842, 95–96; "Sandwich Islands," *Missionary Herald*, February 1843, 53–54; "Sandwich Islands," *Missionary Herald*, May 1843, 199; "Sandwich Islands," *Missionary Herald*, June 1848, 182; Kashay, "Native, Foreigner," 6; Kashay, "Savages," 295.

90. "Sandwich Islands," *Missionary Herald*, June 1841, 271; "Sandwich Islands," *Missionary Herald*, March 1842, 95.

91. "Sandwich Islands," *Missionary Herald*, September 1840, 375; "Sandwich Islands," *Missionary Herald*, June 1841, 268; "Sandwich Islands," *Missionary Herald*, March 1842, 96; "Sandwich Islands," *Missionary Herald*, June 1842, 249; "Sandwich Islands," *Missionary Herald*, December 1842, 472; "Sandwich Islands," *Missionary Herald*, November 1845, 363; "Sandwich Islands," *Missionary Herald*, March 1847, 97–98; "Sandwich Islands," *Missionary Herald*, January 1849, 18.

92. "Sandwich Islands," *Missionary Herald*, December 1842, 471.

93. "Sandwich Islands," *Missionary Herald*, March 1843, 128–29; "Miscellanies," *Missionary Herald*, July 1843, 291–94.

94. "Sandwich Islands," *Missionary Herald*, February 1850, 61–66; Daws, *Shoal*, 118–19.

95. "Sandwich Islands," *Missionary Herald*, June 1844, 187–89; "Miscellanies," *Missionary Herald*, May 1845, 173–75; "Sandwich Islands," *Missionary Herald*, May 1846, 147–48; "Sandwich Islands," *Missionary Herald*, February 1850, 66–67.

96. "Foreign Department," *Missionary Herald*, January 1841, 13; "Sandwich Islands," *Missionary Herald*, March 1842, 96; "Annual Survey of the Missions of the Board," *Missionary Herald*, January 1844, 10; "Sandwich Islands," *Missionary Herald*, November 1845, 363.

97. "Sandwich Islands," *Missionary Herald*, April 1842, 159; "Sandwich Islands," *Missionary Herald*, December 1842, 470.

98. Paul William Harris, *Nothing but Christ: Rufus Anderson and the Ideology of Protestant Foreign Missions* (New York: Oxford University Press, 1999), 79.

99. Rufus Anderson to Sandwich Islands Mission, October 27, 1852, *General Letter to the Sandwich Islands Mission*, Rare Book and Special Collections Division, Library of Congress, Washington, D.C.; Elias Bond to N. G. Clark, December 8, 1880, ABC 19.1, vol. 22, no. 156.

100. Arista, *Kingdom*, 176; Kashay, "Savages," 341–42; Merry, *Colonizing Hawai'i*, 4; Jonathan Kay Kamakawiwo'ole Osorio, *Dismembering Lāhui: A History of the Hawaiian Nation to 1887* (Honolulu: University of Hawai'i Press, 2002), 23.

101. Nathaniel Bright Emerson, "A Page from Hawaiian History!," 1893, Nathaniel Bright Emerson Papers, Huntington Library, San Marino, Calif., box 3, EMR 80.

102. Amy Kaplan, *The Anarchy of Empire in the Making of U.S. Culture* (Cambridge, Mass.: Harvard University Press, 2002), 1–3; Paul A. Kramer, *The Blood of Government: Race, Empire, the United States, & the Philippines* (Chapel Hill: University of North Carolina Press, 2006), 109–10, 162–63; Owen J. Lynch, "The U.S. Constitution and Philippine Colonialism: An Enduring and Unfortunate Legacy," in *Colonial Crucible: Empire in the Making of the Modern American State*, ed. Alfred W. McCoy and Francisco A. Scarano (Madison: University of Wisconsin Press, 2009), 360–63; Gerald L. Neuman and Tomiko Brown-Nagin, eds., *Reconsidering the Insular Cases: The Past and Future of American Empire* (Cambridge, Mass.: Harvard University Press, 2015); Bartholomew H. Sparrow, *The Insular Cases and the Emergence of American Empire* (Lawrence: University of Kansas Press, 2006).

Chapter 8

1. On federative empire, see Nicholas Guyatt's chapter in this volume.

2. Eugene S. Van Sickle, "Reluctant Imperialists: The U.S. Navy and Liberia, 1819–1845," *Journal of the Early Republic* 31, no. 4 (Spring 2011): 107–34; Bronwen Everill, "British West Africa or 'The United States of Africa'? Imperial Pressures on the Transatlantic Anti-Slavery Movement, 1839–1842," *Journal of Transatlantic Studies* 9, no. 2 (June 2011): 135–50; Brandon Mills, "Situating African Colonization Within the History of U.S. Expansion," and Bronwen Everill, "Experiments in Colonial Citizenship in Sierra Leone and Liberia," both in *New Directions in the Study of African American Recolonization*, ed. Beverly C. Tomek and Matthew J. Hetrick (Gainesville: University Press of Florida, 2017), 166–83, 184–205.

3. P. J. Staudenraus, *The African Colonization Movement, 1816–1860* (New York: Columbia University Press, 1961), 37–47; Kevin G. Lowther, *The African American Odyssey of John Kizell: A South Carolina Slave Returns to Fight the Slave Trade in His African Homeland* (Columbia: University of South Carolina Press, 2011).

4. Douglas R. Egerton, "'Its Origins Are Not a Little Curious': A New Look at the American Colonization Society," *Journal of the Early Republic* 5 (Winter 1985): 463–80; Eric Burin, "The Slave Trade Act of 1819: A New Look at Colonization and the Politics of Slavery," *American Nineteenth Century History* 12, no. 1 (2012): 1–14; *Memoirs of John Quincy Adams: Comprising Portions of His Diary from 1795 to 1848*, ed. Charles Francis Adams, 12 vols. (Philadelphia: Lippincott, 1874–77), 4:294.

5. James Sidbury, *Becoming African in America: Race and Nation in the Early Black Atlantic* (New York: Oxford University Press, 2007), 170–79.

6. William Lloyd Garrison, *Thoughts on Colonization* (Boston: Garrison and Knapp, 1832), 63; Sidbury, *Becoming African in America*, 183.

7. Padriac X. Scanlan, "The Colonial Rebirth of British Anti-Slavery: The Liberated African Villages of Sierra Leone, 1815–1824," *American Historical Review* 121, no. 4 (October 2016): 1085–113.

8. Charles Henry Huberich, *The Political and Legislative History of Liberia* (New York: Central Book Company, 1947), 163, 172.

9. Eric Burin, "The Cape Mesurado Contract: A Reconsideration," in Tomek and Hetrick, *New Directions*, 234–36.

10. Christian Wiltberger Journal, May 30, 1821, July 28, 1821, October 28, 1821, and December 21, 1821, Earnest Edward Ells Papers, Amistad Research Center, Tulane University (hereafter ARC, TU).

11. Huberich, *Political and Legislative History of Liberia*, 196, 274.

12. Christian Wiltberger Journal, December 22, 1821, ARC, TU; Huberich, *Political and Legislative History of Liberia*, 225–26.

13. Huberich, *Political and Legislative History of Liberia*, 205–8.

14. Huberich, *Political and Legislative History of Liberia*, 209–10, 212.

15. Huberich, *Political and Legislative History of Liberia*, 218.

16. Ralph Randolph Gurley, *Life of Jehudi Ashmun, Late Colonial Agent in Liberia* (Washington, D.C.: James C. Dunn, 1835), 119; Huberich, *Political and Legislative History*, 279.

17. Miles Mark Fisher, "Lott Cary, the Colonizing Missionary," *Journal of Negro History* 7, no. 4 (October 1922): 394–95.

18. Huberich, *Political and Legislative History of Liberia*, 284–85.

19. Huberich, *Political and Legislative History of Liberia*, 286–89.

20. Huberich, *Political and Legislative History of Liberia*, 286–89.

21. Gurley, *Life of Jehudi Ashmun*, 133–49.

22. Eli Ayres to Smith Thompson, January 15, February 24, and April 6, 1823, in Reel 177B, Records of the American Colonization Society, Library of Congress; Huberich, *Political and Legislative History of Liberia*, 224, 290–91.

23. D. Elwood Dunn, Amos J. Beyan, and Carl Patrick Burrows, eds., *Historical Dictionary of Liberia*, 2nd ed. (Lanham, Md.: Scarecrow Press, 2001), 31.

24. Marie Tyler-McGraw, "Harriet Graves Waring: Reluctant Founding Mother," May 1, 2008, *Virginia Emigrants to Liberia*, www.vcdh.virginia.edu/liberia/index.php?page=Stories&section =Harriet+Waring.

25. In 1831, Curtis was accused of financial improprieties, and three years later, as his wife left for British Accra, Curtis took up residence in Grand Cape Mount, which was then beyond Liberia's borders. There, he became the brother-in-law of an influential Indigenous leader, Prince George Cain. Marie Tyler-McGraw, "Augustus Curtis: Liberia and the Slave Trade," May 1, 2008, *Virginia Emigrants to Liberia*, www.vcdh.virginia.edu/liberia/index.php?page =Stories&section=Augustus+Curtis.

26. *Sixth Annual Report of the American Society for the Colonizing of the Free People of Colour of the United States* (Washington, D.C.: Davis and Force, 1823), 160–61; Gurley, *Life of Jehudi Ashmun*, 167.

27. Huberich, *Political and Legislative History of Liberia*, 145–48.

28. Huberich, *Political and Legislative History of Liberia*, 205, 221, 290, 314, 316.

29. Gurley, *Life of Jehudi Ashmun*, 172.

30. Gurley, *Life of Jehudi Ashmun*, 184.

31. Huberich, *Political and Legislative History of Liberia*, 300–7.

32. Gurley, *Life of Jehudi Ashmun*, 186.

33. Gurley, *Life of Jehudi Ashmun*, 186–87. Elijah Johnson was "Commissary of Stores" in August 1822 but it is unclear if he was still serving in that capacity in December 1823. Huberich, *Political and Legislative History of Liberia*, 281.

34. *Roll of Emigrants That Have Been Sent to the Colony of Liberia*, 28th Cong., 2d sess., S. Doc. 150; Gurley, *Life of Jehudi Ashmun*, 190–91.

35. Gurley, *Life of Jehudi Ashmun*, 190, 195.

36. Gurley, *Life of Jehudi Ashmun*, 209–11.

37. Huberich, *Political and Legislative History of Liberia*, 295–96, 308.

38. Huberich, *Political and Legislative History of Liberia*, 300–11, 319, 1265.

39. Gurley, *Life of Jehudi Ashmun*, 391; James Barnett Taylor, *Biography of Elder Lott Cary, Late Missionary to Africa* (Baltimore: Armstrong and Strong, 1837), 93.

40. Huberich, *Political and Legislative History of Liberia*, 373. Additionally, several independently operated state colonization societies maintained settlements that were later absorbed into

Liberia, the largest being Maryland in Africa, which in 1843 had a population of 624. 1843 Cape Palmas Census, Records of the Maryland State Colonization Society, Maryland Historical Society.

41. Eric Burin, *Slavery and the Peculiar Solution: A History of the American Colonization Society* (Gainesville: University Press of Florida, 2005), 150–54; Brandon Mills, "'The United States of Africa': Liberian Independence and the Contested Meaning of a Black Republic," *Journal of the Early Republic* 34, no. 1 (Spring 2014): 79–107; Marie Tyler-McGraw, "Roberts Family," May 1, 2008, *Virginia Emigrants to Liberia*, www.vcdh.virginia.edu/liberia/index.php?page =Stories&section=The+Roberts+Family.

42. Mills, "'The United States of Africa,'" 107.

Chapter 9

Acknowledgments: Research for this chapter was possible thanks to the Library Company of Philadelphia's NEH Fellowship. Any views, findings, conclusions, or recommendations expressed in this chapter do not necessarily reflect those of the NEH. Further research was made possible thanks to funding from the Provost Research Award and the Arts and Humanities Award from the University of Miami. Thank you to Sarah L. H. Gronningsater, Isadora Mota, Nathan Perl-Rosenthal, Honor Sachs, Molly Warsh, and Kim Welch for their comments on drafts.

1. Arthur Lynn to Earl of Clarendon, British Consulate, Galveston, June 13, 1854, Foreign Office Records for the Suppression of the Slave Trade, Class 84, vol. 1027, The National Archives, Kew, England (hereafter FO 84/vol. no., TNA).

2. This has become a standard interpretation such that one recent scholar observed that "the sin of slavery and anti-Black racism must be paired with the legacy of land theft and Indigenous dispossession." See Michael John Witgen, *Seeing Red: Indigenous Land, American Expansion, and the Political Economy of Plunder in North America* (Chapel Hill: University of North Carolina Press, 2022), 324. On the connection between slavery and U.S. expansion into the Deep South in recent literature, see Ira Berlin, *Generations of Captivity: A History of African American Slaves* (Cambridge, Mass.: Harvard University Press, 2003), 159–243; Adam Rothman, *Slave Country: American Expansion and the Origins of the Deep South* (Cambridge, Mass.: Harvard University Press, 2005); Steven Deley, *Carry Me Back: The Domestic Slave Trade in American Life* (New York: Oxford University Press, 2005); Andrew Torget, *Seeds of Empire: Cotton, Slavery, and the Transformation of the Texas Borderland, 1800–1850* (Chapel Hill: University of North Carolina Press, 2015); Walter Johnson, *River of Dark Dreams: Slavery and Empire in the Cotton Kingdom* (Cambridge, Mass.: Harvard University Press, 2015). On slave labor camps, see Edward Baptist, *The Half Has Never Been Told: Slavery and the Making of American Capitalism* (New York: Basic Books, 2015). On the formulation of turning blood into gold, see John Clegg, "Capitalism and Slavery," *Critical Historical Studies* 2, no. 2 (Fall 2015): 281–304.

3. This borrows from the concept of "confined cosmopolitanism" in Rashauna Johnson, *Slavery's Metropolis: Unfree Labor in New Orleans During the Age of Revolutions* (New York: Cambridge University Press, 2016), esp. 3–5; and from Jane Landers, *Atlantic Creoles in the Age of Revolutions* (Cambridge, Mass.: Harvard University Press, 2015), esp. 13–15.

4. Arthur Lynn to Earl of Clarendon, British Consulate, Galveston, June 13, 1854, FO 84/1027, TNA.

5. James Willie to the Governor of the State of Texas, Attorney General Office, Austin, June 22, 1857, FO 84/1027, TNA. Although a resident of St. Thomas, his parents were British subjects, affording him status to claim the consul's protection. In light of the fact that he worked out of Trinidad during his childhood, he may have relocated, or been relocated, shortly after birth.

6. "Kidnapping" was a term of art that had a contested and incredibly elastic meaning over the nineteenth century. In this essay it refers to people of African descent who were free subjects of the British or U.S. state taken into a foreign jurisdiction, either voluntarily or through force, and turned into slaves.

7. The transatlantic slave trade, as well as the regional trade in the hemispheric Caribbean, commands an impressive literature, but certain gaps still remain in our understanding. Notably, comparatively little work exists on the nineteenth-century slave trade in the North Atlantic, and the trade falls out of major U.S history syntheses, frequently not even meriting a mention after its abolition in 1808. For instance it receives only passing mentions in Steven Hahn's *A Nation Without Borders: The United States and Its World in an Age of Civil Wars, 1830–1910* (New York: Penguin, 2017), 45–46; Berlin, *Generations of Captivity*, 45, 60, 79; Manisha Sinha, *The Slave's Cause: A History of Abolition* (New Haven, Conn.: Yale University Press, 2016), 66, 90; David Brion Davis, *Inhuman Bondage: The Rise and Fall of Slavery in the New World* (New York: Oxford University Press, 2006), 142. Most of these discussions focus on its abolition, and how that set the stage for a domestic trade. Important new work correcting this trend includes John Harris, *The Last Slave Ships: New York and the End of the Middle Passage* (New Haven, Conn.: Yale University Press, 2020); Sharla Fett, *Recaptured Africans: Surviving Slave Ships and Dislocation in the Final Years of the Slave Trade* (Chapel Hill: University of North Carolina Press, 2016); Leonardo Marques, *The United States and the Transatlantic Slave Trade to the Americas, 1776–1876* (New Haven, Conn.: Yale University Press, 2016).

8. On imperial competition, see François Furstenberg, "The Significance of the Trans-Appalachian Frontier in Atlantic History," *American Historical Review* 113, no. 3 (June 2008): 647–77. See also Patrick Griffin, *American Leviathan: Empire, Nation, and Revolutionary Frontier* (New York: Hill and Wang, 2008); and Witgen, *Seeing Red*, 41–73.

9. For more on approaching the history of empire as repertories of imperialism, see Jane Burbank and Frederick Cooper, *Empires in World History: Power and the Politics of Difference* (Princeton, N.J.: Princeton University Press, 2010), introduction. It shares much in common with the process-oriented approach to empire advocated in Konstantin Dierks, "Americans Overseas in the Early American Republic," *Diplomatic History* 42, no.1 (January 2018): 17–35.

10. The turn to study the "second slavery" has generated enormous amounts of scholarship in the past ten years. On this framework, see Dale Tomich, *Through the Prism of Slavery: Labor, Capital, and World Economy* (New York: Oxford University Press, 2004); and Dale Tomich and Michael Zeuske, "Introduction, the Second Slavery: Mass Slavery, World-Economy, and Comparative Microhistories," *Review (Fernand Braudel Center)* 31, no. 2 (2008): 91–100. A useful overview appears in Anthony E. Kaye, "The Second Slavery: Modernity in the Nineteenth-Century South and the Atlantic World," *Journal of Southern History* 75, no. 3 (August 2009): 627–50; and more recently, Dale Tomich, ed., *The Politics of the Second Slavery* (Albany: State University of New York Press, 2016).

11. Robert Thorpe, *A View of the Present Increase of the Slave Trade* (London: Longman, Hurst, Rees, Orme, and Brown, 1818), 16 ("The number"; "so greatly"), Library Company of Philadelphia (hereafter cited as LCP); *Third Annual Report of the American Society for Colonizing the Free People of Colour of the United States* (Washington, D.C.: Davis and Force, 1820), 12 ("enhanced price"), LCP.

12. *Fifth Annual Report of the American Society for Colonizing the Free People of Colour of the United States* (Washington, D.C.: Davis and Force, 1822), 33, LCP.

13. On the broad contours of this, see Seymour Drescher, *Abolition: A History of Slavery and Anti-Slavery* (New York: Cambridge University Press, 2009), 205–41; Ryan Espersen, "Fifty Shades of Trade: Privateering, Piracy, and Illegal Slave Trading in St. Thomas, Early Nineteenth Century," *New West Indian Guide* 93, no. 2 (Summer 2019): 41–68; Nicholas Radburn and David Eltis, "Visualizing the Middle Passage: The Brooks and the Reality of Ship Crowding in the Transatlantic Slave Trade," *Journal of Interdisciplinary History* 49, no. 4 (2019): 533–65.

14. Marques, *The United States and the Transatlantic Slave Trade*, 23–28, and, on the taxation provision, see 49–50; Padraig Riley, *Slavery and the Democratic Conscience: Political Life in Jeffersonian America* (Philadelphia: University of Pennsylvania Press, 2016), 119–28; David Head,

"Slave Smuggling by Foreign Privateers: The Illegal Slave Trade and the Geopolitics of the Early Republic," *Journal of the Early Republic* 33, no. 3 (Fall 2013): 433.

15. *Fifth Annual Report of the American Society for Colonizing the Free People of Colour,* 29.

16. Testimony of William Kril in the District Court of the United States, in and for Pennsylvania, August 15, 1805, box 3b, folder 10, Papers of the Pennsylvania Abolition Society, Historical Society of Pennsylvania, Philadelphia (hereafter cited as PAS, HSP).

17. On internationalization, see Marques, *The United States and the Transatlantic Slave Trade,* 136.

18. Richard Huzzey, *Freedom Burning: Anti-Slavery and Empire in Victorian Britain* (Ithaca, N.Y.: Cornell University Press, 2012); Drescher, *Abolition,* 181–204.

19. Hugh Thomas, *The Slave Trade: The Story of the Atlantic Slave Trade, 1440–1870* (New York: Simon and Schuster, 2013), 585, see also 449–537; Jenny S. Martinez, *The Slave Trade and the Origins of International Human Rights Law* (New York: Oxford University Press, 2012), 32–33.

20. David Eltis, *Economic Growth and the Ending of the Transatlantic Slave Trade* (New York: Oxford University Press, 1987), 47–61; Martinez, *The Slave Trade,* 67–98.

21. Randy J. Sparks, "Blind Justice: The United States's Failure to Curb the Illegal Slave Trade," *Law and History Review* 35, no. 1 (2017): 53–70; Harris, *The Last Slave Ships,* 19; Craig B. Hollander, "Underground on the High Seas: Commerce, Character, and Complicity in the Illegal Slave Trade," in *Capitalism by Gaslight: Illuminating the Economy of Nineteenth-Century America,* ed. Brian P. Luskey and Wendy A. Woloson (Philadelphia: University of Pennsylvania Press, 2015), 127–49.

22. *Sixth Annual Report of the American Society for Colonizing the Free People of Colour of the United States* (Washington, D.C.: Davis and Force, 1823), 60, LCP. See more generally Radburn and Eltis, "Visualizing the Middle Passage," 533–65.

23. Henry Fox to John Forsyth, Washington, October 29, 1839, FO 84/296, TNA. On these trends, see Harris, *The Last Slave Ships,* 114–24.

24. On these developments generally, see Rafael Marquese, Tâmis Parron, and Márcia Berbel, *Slavery and Politics: Brazil and Cuba, 1790–1850,* trans. Leonardo Marques (Albuquerque: University of New Mexico Press, 2016); João José Reis, Flávio dos Santos Gomes, and Marcus J. M. de Carvalho, *The Story of Rufino: Slavery, Freedom, and Islam in the Black Atlantic,* trans. H. Sabrina Gledhill (New York: Oxford University Press, 2020); Torget, *Seeds of Empire.*

25. Thorpe, *View of the Present Increase,* 17.

26. John Forsyth to Henry Fox, Washington, Department of State, February 12, 1840, FO 84/332, TNA.

27. The *Mary Ann,* 21 U.S. 380 (1823); Paul Finkelman, *Supreme Injustice: Slavery in the Nation's Highest Court* (Cambridge, Mass.: Harvard University Press, 2018), 87–89; Hendrik Hartog, *The Trouble with Minna: A Case of Slavery and Emancipation in the Antebellum North* (Chapel Hill: University of North Carolina Press, 2018), 76–77; James J. Gigantino II, "Trading in Jersey Souls: New Jersey and the Interstate Slave Trade," *Pennsylvania History* 77, no. 3 (Summer 2010): 281–302; Priya Khangura, "A 'Law-Bound Conspiracy': How Forty-Five Men, Women, and Children Were Sailed into Slavery Aboard the Brig *Mary Ann*" (forthcoming). My thanks to Priya Khangura for her help with this chapter, both connected to the *Mary Ann* and the larger stakes of the piece.

28. *Fifth Annual Report of the American Society for Colonizing the Free People of Colour,* 39.

29. Marques, *The United States and the Transatlantic Slave Trade,* 91–101.

30. Mary Wills, "At War with the 'Detestable Traffic': The Royal Navy's Anti-Slavery Cause in the Atlantic Ocean," in *The Royal Navy and the British Atlantic World, c. 1750–1820,* ed. John McAleer and Christer Petley (London: Palgrave Macmillan, 2016), 123–46; John Broich, *Squadron: Ending the African Slave Trade* (New York: Peter Mayer, 2017); Martinez, *The Slave Trade,* 67–99; Marika Sherwood, *After Abolition: Britain and the Slave Trade Since 1807* (New

York: Tauris, 2007); Lamin Sanneh, *Abolitionists Abroad: American Blacks and the Making of a Modern West Africa* (Cambridge, Mass.: Harvard University Press, 2009).

31. For a summary of the policy, see Richard Rush to John Quincy Adams, London, March 15, 1824; on the amendments and failure to ratify, see George Canning to Richard Rush, Foreign Office, August 2, 1824, both in Despatches from United States Ministers to Great Britain, 1791–1906, M-30, vol. 31, Record Group 59, U.S. State Department Records, National Archives and Records Administration, College Park, Md. (hereafter cited as RG 59, NARA).

32. This key gap in the international force alarmed activists at the time. As one report on the slave trade noted, the coasts along West Africa and in the Americas were "indented, by too many inlets for smuggling to be successfully watched by a few revenue cutters." *Third Annual Report of the American Society for Colonizing the Free People of Colour*, 13. See also Harris, *The Last Slave Ships*, esp. 15–41.

33. Matthew Karp, *This Vast Southern Empire: Slaveholders at the Helm of American Foreign Policy* (Cambridge, Mass.: Harvard University Press, 2016). On U.S. participation in the slave trade, especially to Cuba, see Ada Ferrer, *Cuba: An American History* (New York: Scrivener, 2022), 85–86.

34. *Fifth Annual Report of the American Society for Colonizing the Free People of Colour*, 33.

35. Ernest Obadele-Starks, *Freebooters and Smugglers: The Foreign Slave Trade in the United States After 1808* (Fayetteville: University of Arkansas Press, 2007); Gerald Horne, *Deepest South: The United States, Brazil, and the African Slave Trade* (New York: New York University Press, 2008); Martin Ohman, "A Convergence of Crises: The Expansion of Slavery, Geopolitical Realignment, and Economic Depression in the Post-Napoleonic World," *Diplomatic History* 37, no. 3 (June 2013): 419–45.

36. On northern Florida in this era, see Deborah A. Rosen, *Border Law: The First Seminole War and American Nationhood* (Cambridge, Mass.: Harvard University Press, 2015); and Matthew J. Clavin, *The Battle of the Negro Fort: The Rise and Fall of a Fugitive Slave Community* (New York: New York University Press, 2019). On its later transformation into a slave society, see Edward E. Baptist, *Creating an Old South: Middle Florida's Plantation Frontier Before the Civil War* (Chapel Hill: University of North Carolina Press, 2002).

37. James G. Cusick, *The Other War of 1812: The Patriot War and the American Invasion of Spanish East Florida* (Athens: University of Georgia Press, 2007).

38. Craig B. Hollander, "Against a Sea of Troubles: Slave Trade Suppressionism During the Early Republic" (Ph.D. diss., Johns Hopkins University, 2013), 50–86. For an account of the slave trade in this era and place, see Jonathan M. Bryant, *Dark Places of the Earth: The Voyage of the Slave Ship* Antelope (New York: Norton, 2015).

39. Obadele-Starks, *Freebooters and Smugglers*, 75–109.

40. Torget, *Seeds of Empire*, 19–57; Juliana Barr, *Peace Came in the Form of a Woman: Indians and Spaniards in the Texas Borderlands* (Chapel Hill: University of North Carolina Press, 2007), 247–87; Pekka Hämäläinen, *The Comanche Empire* (New Haven, Conn.: Yale University Press, 2008), esp. 191–238; Brian DeLay, *War of a Thousand Deserts: Indian Raids and the U.S.-Mexican War* (New Haven, Conn.: Yale University Press, 2009).

41. "Extract of a letter from Captain Charles Morris to the Secretary of the Navy, dated U.S. Frigate Congress, off the Balize, 10th June, 1817" ("most of the goods"); "Extract of a letter from Lieutenant Commander John Porter, to the Secretary of the Navy, dated U. S. Brig Boxer, off the Balize June 28th, 1817" ("off the Sabine") both in *Third Annual Report of the American Society for Colonizing the Free People of Colour*, 50.

42. Ibid. Still others noted that even without new laws, more officials would be necessary to win verdicts against the owners of ships suspected of engaging in the slave trade. As one observer stressed, "Vast numbers of slaves will be introduced to an alarming extent, unless prompt and effectual measures are adopted by the general government." Ibid., 55.

43. Copy of Report of Vice Consul Crawford on the Traffic in Slaves between Cuba and Texas September 18, 1837, enclosure in John Parkinson to Viscount Palmerston, British Consulate, Mexico, October 3, 1837, FO 84/225, TNA.

44. Richard Madden to Richard Pakenham, Havana, April 4, 1837, enclosure in Richard Pakenham to Viscount Palmerston, Mexico, May 1, 1837, FO 84/225, TNA.

45. Ibid.

46. Nicholas P. Trist to John Forsyth, Havana, February 12, 1836, Despatches from U.S. Consuls in Havana, Cuba, 1783–1906 (M-899), vol. 7, RG 59, NARA.

47. Ibid.

48. Nicholas P. Trist to John Forsyth, March 10, 1840, Havana, Enclosure No. 2, November 29, 1839, M-899, vol. 13, RG 59, NARA.

49. Copy of Report of Vice Consul Crawford on the Traffic in Slaves between Cuba and Texas, September 18, 1837, enclosure in John Parkinson to Viscount Palmerston, British Consulate, Mexico, October 3, 1837, FO 84/225, TNA.

50. William Metcalf to John Russell, Jamaica, King's House, December 6, 1840, Colonial Office and Predecessors: Jamaica, Original Correspondence, Class 137, vol. 250, CO 137/250, TNA ("that the slaves"); Metcalf to John Russell, Kingston, December 2, 1840, CO 137/250, TNA ("there is much") (hereafter CO 137/vol. no., TNA).

51. William Metcalf to John Russell, Jamaica, King's House, December 6, 1840, CO 137/250, TNA.

52. William Metcalf to John Russell, Kingston, December 2, 1840, CO 137/250, TNA.

53. William Metcalf to John Russell, Jamaica, King's House, December 6, 1840, CO 137/250, TNA.

54. Daniel Hershenzon, *The Captive Sea: Slavery, Communication, and Commerce in Early Modern Spain and the Mediterranean* (Philadelphia: University of Pennsylvania Press, 2018); Gillian Weiss, *Captives and Corsairs: France and Slavery in the Early Modern Mediterranean* (Stanford, Calif.: Stanford University Press, 2011), 2, 6, 29, 92, 116–19; Ellen G. Friedman, *Spanish Captives in North Africa in the Early Modern Age* (Madison: University of Wisconsin Press, 1983), esp. a discussion of ransom agencies on 112–14.

55. See Nathan Perl-Rosenthal, *Citizen Sailors: Becoming American in the Age of Revolution* (Cambridge, Mass.: Harvard University Press, 2015). See also Linda Colley, *Captives: Britain, Empire, and the World, 1600–1850* (New York: Anchor Books, 2002), esp. 56–65, 90–92.

56. For more on the British empire in Sierra Leone, see Padraic X. Scanlan, *Freedom's Debtors: British Antislavery in Sierra Leone in the Age of Revolution* (New Haven, Conn.: Yale University Press, 2017); Bronwen Everill, *Abolition and Empire in Sierra Leone and Liberia* (New York: Palgrave Macmillan, 2013); Kenneth Morgan, *Slavery and the British Empire: From Africa to America* (New York: Oxford University Press, 2007); Kristin Mann, *Slavery and the Birth of an African City: Lagos, 1760–1900* (Bloomington: Indiana University Press, 2007); James Walvin, *Black Ivory: Slavery in the British Empire*, 2nd ed. (Oxford: Blackwell, 2001).

57. All quotations in the preceding paragraph come from Thorpe, *View of the Present Increase*, 72–74.

58. Viscount Palmerston to Viscount Granville, Foreign Office, April 9, 1831, FO 84/123, TNA.

59. Ibid.

60. Viscount Palmerston to John Bloomfield, Foreign Office, December 12, 1835, FO 84/181, TNA; emphasis added.

61. Thorpe, *View of the Present Increase*, 74.

62. Thomas C. Holt, *The Problem of Freedom: Race, Labor, and Politics in Jamaica and Britain, 1832–1938* (Baltimore: Johns Hopkins University Press, 1992), 56.

63. Lord William Metcalf to Lord John Russell, Kingston, March 30, 1840, CO 137/248, TNA.

64. On the claim that the state took over new power to "enforce labor discipline" and liberation, see Diana Paton, *No Bond but the Law: Punishment, Race, and Gender in Jamaican State Formation, 1780–1870* (Durham, N.C.: Duke University Press, 2004), 54–58.

65. Sidney Mintz, "The Origins of Reconstituted Peasantries," in *Caribbean Freedom: Economy and Society from Emancipation to the Present,* ed. Hilary Beckles and Verene Shepherd (Kingston: Ian Randle Publishers, 1993), 94–98; on these themes more generally, see Natasha Lightfoot, *Troubling Freedom: Antigua and the Aftermath of British Emancipation* (Durham, N.C.: Duke University Press, 2015).

66. Caree A. Banton, *More Auspicious Shores: Barbadian Migration to Liberia, Blackness, and the Making of an African Republic* (New York: Cambridge University Press, 2019), 61.

67. On post-emancipation Barbados generally, see Melanie J. Newton, *The Children of Africa in the Colonies: Free People of Color in Barbados in the Age of Emancipation* (Baton Rouge: Louisiana State University Press, 2008); Hilary Beckles, *Afro-Caribbean Women and Resistance to Slavery in Barbados* (London: Karnak House, 1988); Robin Blackburn, *The American Crucible: Slavery, Emancipation and Human Rights* (London: Verso, 2011), 280–83.

68. I cannot firmly establish it as the same vessel, as I have not found a ship manifest. The *Mary Ann* in 1818 was a U.S. brig, while this ship had British ownership, indicating that the vessel was sold or that it was a different brig altogether. The presence of two brigs named *Mary Ann*, or the transfer of one vessel into a different set of hands, evokes elements of my argument that the rise of the Deep South had origins in the domestic slave trade *and* an international slave trade and that the two dimensions of U.S. expansion need to be seen in tandem.

69. John Crawford to Viscount Palmerston, New Orleans, September 25, 1839, Foreign Office: Political and Other Departments: General Correspondence before 1906, United States of America, series II, vol. 337, TNA (hereafter FO 5/vol. no., TNA). Further correspondence about this case is at John Crawford to Viscount Palmerston, New Orleans, December 15, 1838, FO 84/259, TNA.

70. James Chessher to John Crawford, Jasper County, Texas, March 2, 1839, FO 5/337, TNA. The observers noted that some were some captives taken to "the west bank of the Neches River, nine miles from the Sabine Lake." Others were "living at Arkansas near the mouth of Trinity River." Another man was at "Galveston Island or Brazonia," and the woman and one of her children "was taken to Atacapanla La. by a Scotchman who came with Taylor from Barbados."

71. Ibid.

72. Ibid.

73. John Murray McGregor to John Russell, Government House, Barbados, March 31, 1840, CO 28/133, TNA.

74. These questions can best be answered by working in the Barbadian archives and with local archivists and historians. However, due to global travel restrictions amid the coronavirus pandemic, I have not been to Barbados to research this case. As a result, the analysis is confined by the view from London and Washington, D.C., a metropolitan perspective on an event that had profound importance to formerly enslaved people, their families, and neighborhoods. Writing the history of the U.S. empire with State Department or Colonial Office sources alone obscures the many important dimensions of living under, and between, empires in the mid-nineteenth century.

75. On the case in Alabama, see Randy J. Sparks, *Africans in the Old South: Mapping Exceptional Lives Across the Atlantic World* (Cambridge, Mass.: Harvard University Press, 2016), 134–56.

76. John Crawford to Viscount Palmerston, British Consulate, New Orleans, September 25, 1839, FO 5/337, TNA.

77. Acting Committee Minutes, vol. 5, 1824–1842, p. 199, PAS, HSP.

78. Daniel Walker Howe, *What Hath God Wrought: The Transformation of America, 1815–1848* (New York: Oxford University Press, 2007), 658–71. See also Amy S. Greenberg, *A Wicked War: Polk, Clay, Lincoln, and the U.S. Invasion of Mexico* (New York: Vintage Books, 2013).

79. Alice L. Baumgartner, *South to Freedom: Runaway Slaves to Mexico and the Road to the Civil War* (New York: Basic Books, 2020), 66–70, 99–111. See also Andrew J. Torget, "The Saltillo Slavery Debates: Mexicans, Anglo-Americans, and Slavery's Future in Nineteenth-Century North America" in *Linking the Histories of Slavery: North America and Its Borderlands*, ed. Bonnie Martin and James F. Brooks (Santa Fe, N. Mex.: SAR Press, 2015): 171–96; and Sarah Cornell, "Citizens of Nowhere: Fugitive Slaves and Free African Americans in Mexico, 1833–1857," *Journal of American History* 100, no. 2 (September 2013): 351–74.

80. For an overview of Manifest Destiny platforms in this period, see Amy S. Greenberg, "Cuba and the Failure of Manifest Destiny," *Journal of the Early Republic* 41, no.1 (Spring 2022): 1–20, esp. 5–7 for a discussion of the Oregon Territory. For an overview of the border dispute in Oregon, see Hahn, *A Nation Without Borders*, esp. 121–22. For an on-the-ground analysis, see Anne F. Hyde, *Empires, Nations, and Families: A History of the North American West, 1800–1860* (Lincoln: University of Nebraska Press, 2012), esp. 142–43. On the Webster-Ashburton Treaty, see Howe, *What Hath God Wrought*, 673–75.

81. Thomas Morgan to Viscount Palmerston, Middlesex, March 6, 1841, FO 5/371, TNA.

82. Thomas Morgan to Viscount Palmerston, Middlesex, March 12, 1841, FO 5/371, TNA; emphasis in original.

83. Earl of Aberdeen to Richard Pakenham, Foreign Office, December 26, 1843, Foreign Office: Embassy and Consulates, United States of America: General Correspondence, Class 115, vol.83, TNA (hereafter FO 115/ vol. no., TNA).

84. House of Commons Debate, August 5, 1836, *Hansard Parliamentary Debates*, 3rd ser., vol. 35, col. 941.

85. Ferrer, *Cuba*, 94–95.

86. Richard Pakenham to Earl of Aberdeen, Washington, April 14, 1844, FO 5/404.

87. The literature on the post-1848 sectional debate over slavery is too substantial to cite. But see, for instance, Hahn, *A Nation Without Borders*, 114–92; Richard Blackett, *The Captive's Quest for Freedom* (New York: Cambridge University Press, 2018).

88. William Mure to Viscount Palmerston, British Consulate, New Orleans, January 16, 1852, FO 84/885, TNA.

89. Karp, *This Vast Southern Empire*, 70–103.

90. Here I draw heavily on the insights of Alexander X. Byrd, *Captives and Voyagers: Black Migrants Across the Eighteenth-Century British Atlantic World* (Baton Rouge: Louisiana State University Press, 2008), introduction. As he convincingly shows, the uneven scale of migration does not invalidate the comparison between the slave trade and the emigration to Liberia. See also Tiffany Ruby Patterson and Robin D. G. Kelley, "Unfinished Migrations: Reflections on the African Diaspora and the Making of the Modern World," *African Studies Review* 43, no. 1 (April 2000): 13. This point is echoed by Gregory E. O'Malley in *Final Passages: The Intercolonial Slave Trade of British America, 1619–1807* (Chapel Hill: University of North Carolina Press, 2014), where he shows that the smaller inter-American slave trade still was a driving force in the wider Atlantic. In this case as well, the relatively smaller scope of black kidnapping does not undermine what this method of analysis can tell us about the hemispheric Caribbean.

91. On this framing, see Paul Kramer, "Power and Connection: Imperial Histories of the United States in the World," *American Historical Review* 116, no. 5 (December 2011): 1348–91. See also Ann Laura Stoler and Frederick Cooper, "Between Metropole and Colony: Rethinking a Research Agenda," in *Tensions of Empire: Colonial Cultures in a Bourgeois World*, ed. Frederick Cooper and Ann Laura Stoler (Berkeley: University of California Press, 1997), 1–56.

Chapter 10

1. Robert S. Levine, *Martin Delany, Frederick Douglass, and the Politics of Representative Identity* (Chapel Hill: University of North Carolina Press, 1997), 11–12.

2. Eddie S. Glaude, Jr., *Exodus! Religion, Race, and Nation in Early Nineteenth-Century Black America* (Chicago: University of Chicago Press, 2000), 19–20.

3. For more on Paul Cuffe, see Sheldon H. Harris, *Paul Cuffe: Black America and the African Return* (New York: Simon and Schuster, 1972); Lamont D. Thomas, *Rise to Be a People: A Biography of Paul Cuffe* (Urbana: University of Illinois Press, 1986), 45; Rosalind Cobb Wiggins, *Captain Paul Cuffe's Logs and Letters, 1808–1817: A Black Quaker's "Voice from Within the Veil"* (Washington, D.C.: Howard University Press, 1996); Paul Cuffe, *A Brief Account of the Settlement and Present Situation of the Colony of Sierra Leone, in Africa* (New York, 1812; repr., Nendeln: Kraus, 1970), 3.

4. Cassandra Mark-Thiesen and Moritz Mihatsch, "Liberia an(d) Empire? Sovereignty, 'Civilisation' and Commerce in Nineteenth-Century West Africa," *Journal of Imperial and Commonwealth History* 47, no. 5 (September 2019): 884–911; Christine Whyte, "Between Empire and Colony: American Imperialism and Pan-African Colonialism in Liberia, 1810–2003," *National Identities* 18, no. 1 (2016): 71–88; Brandon Mills, *The World Colonization Made: The Racial Geography of Early American Empire* (Philadelphia: University of Pennsylvania Press, 2019), 44.

5. Drew R. McCoy, *The Elusive Republic: Political Economy in Jeffersonian America* (Chapel Hill: University of North Carolina Press, 1980), 174; Peter S. Onuf, *Jefferson's Empire: The Language of Nationhood* (Charlottesville: University of Virginia Press, 2000), 182; Don E. Fehrenbacher, *The Slaveholding Republic: An Account of the United States Government's Relations to Slavery*, completed and ed. Ward M. McAfee (Oxford: Oxford University Press, 2001), 113–14; Paul Finkelman, *Slavery and the Founders: Race and Liberty in the Age of Jefferson* (Armonk, N.Y.: M. E. Sharpe, 1996), 133–35.

6. Harris, *Paul Cuffe*, 38–39.

7. For a history of Liberia, see Tom W. Shick, *Behold the Promised Land: A History of Afro-American Settler Society in Nineteenth-Century Liberia* (Baltimore: Johns Hopkins University Press, 1980); Bronwen Everill, *Abolition and Empire in Sierra Leone and Liberia* (New York: Palgrave Macmillan, 2013); Carl Patrick Burrowes, *Power and Press Freedom in Liberia, 1830–1970: The Impact of Globalization and Civil Society on Media-Government Relations* (Trenton, N.J.: Africa World Press, 2004).

8. Harris, *Paul Cuffe*, 68–69.

9. Cuffe, *A Brief Account*, 3; Cuffe's ideas expressed in his journal were published after and reprinted. Also see Wiggins, *Captain Paul Cuffe's Logs*.

10. Martha S. Jones, *Birthright Citizens: A History of Race and Rights in Antebellum America* (New York: Cambridge University Press, 2018), 23.

11. William H. Robinson, ed., *The Proceedings of the Free African Union Society and the African Benevolent Society: Newport, Rhode Island, 1780–1824* (Providence: Urban League of Rhode Island, 1976), 111–15.

12. Fernando Fairfax, "Plan for Liberating the Negroes Within the United States," *American Museum, or, Universal Magazine* (December 1, 1790), 285–87.

13. Thomas, *Rise to Be a People*, 45.

14. Suzanne Schwartz, "From Company Administration to Crown Control: Experimentation and Adaptation in Sierra Leone in the Late Eighteenth and Early Nineteenth Centuries," in *Slavery, Abolition and the Transition to Colonialism in Sierra Leone*, ed. Paul E. Lovejoy and Suzanne Schwartz (Trenton, N.J.: Africa World Press, 2014), 175.

15. Cuffe, *A Brief Account*, 10.

16. Harris, *Paul Cuffe*, 50; James Sidbury, *Becoming African in America: Race and Nation in the Early Black Atlantic* (New York: Oxford University Press 2007), 148. For more on the role of

British Quakers in the abolition movement, see Christopher Leslie Brown, *Moral Capital: Foundations of British Abolitionism* (Chapel Hill: University of North Carolina Press, 2006), 407.

17. Harvey Amani Whitfield, *Blacks on the Border: The Black Refugees in British North America, 1815–1860* (Burlington: University of Vermont Press, 2006), 18–19.

18. Everill, *Abolition and Empire*, 23–24.

19. Thomas, *Rise to Be a People*, 51; Sidbury, *Becoming African in America*, 151.

20. Harris, *Paul Cuffe*, 51.

21. Ibid., 53.

22. Thomas, *Rise to Be a People*, 64.

23. Harris, *Paul Cuffe*, 57; Floyd J. Miller, *The Search for a Black Nationality: Black Emigration and Colonization, 1787–1863* (Urbana: University of Illinois Press, 1975), 31.

24. Harris, *Paul Cuffe*, 57–60.

25. Miller, *Search for a Black Nationality*, 44.

26. Paul Cuffe to James Forten, March 1, 1817, in Harris, *Paul Cuffe*, 249.

27. Nicholas Guyatt, "'The Outskirts of Our Happiness': Race and the Lure of Colonization in the Early Republic," *Journal of American History* 95, no. 4 (March 2009): 996.

28. Guyatt, "'Outskirts of Our Happiness,'" 996; Nicholas Guyatt, *Providence and the Invention of the United States, 1607–1876* (New York: Cambridge University Press, 2007), 174.

29. Nikki M. Taylor, *Frontiers of Freedom: Cincinnati's Black Community, 1802–1868* (Athens: Ohio University Press, 2005).

30. Paul Frymer, *Building an American Empire: The Era of Territorial and Political Expansion* (Princeton, N.J.: Princeton University Press, 2017), 226. For racial violence and Black emigration to Canada in the 1830s, see Taylor, *Frontiers of Freedom*.

31. Alvin B. Tillery, Jr., *Between Homeland and Motherland: Africa, U.S. Foreign Policy, and Black Leadership in America* (Ithaca, N.Y.: Cornell University Press, 2011), 16–17; Harris, *Paul Cuffe*, 63.

32. "Catalogue of the families on board the Brig. *Traveller* going from America for Sierra Leone in Africa sailed 12 month 10 1815 from Westport," in *Apropos of Africa: Afro-American Leaders and the Romance of Africa*, ed. Adelaide Cromwell Hill and Martin Kilson (Garden City, N.Y.: Doubleday, 1971), 23.

33. Harris, *Paul Cuffe*, 64–65.

34. Sidbury, *Becoming African in America*, 178–79.

35. Manisha Sinha, *The Slave's Cause: A History of Abolition* (New Haven, Conn.: Yale University Press, 2016), 340–41.

36. Samantha Seeley, *Race, Removal, and the Right to Remain: Migration and the Making of the United States* (Chapel Hill: University of North Carolina Press, 2021), 306–8.

37. Augustus Washington, "African Colonization," *African Repository* 27, no. 9 (1851): 259–65; Okon Edet Uya, ed., *Black Brotherhood: Afro-Americans and Africa* (Lexington, Mass.: Heath, 1970), 38.

38. William E. Allen, "Rethinking the History of Settler Agriculture in Nineteenth-Century Liberia," *International Journal of African Historical Studies* 37, no. 3 (2004): 435–62.

39. Robert S. Levine, ed., *Martin R. Delany: A Documentary Reader* (Chapel Hill: University of North Carolina Press, 2003), 183.

40. Martin Robison Delany, *The Condition, Elevation, Emigration, and Destiny of the Colored People of the United States* (New York: Arno Press and the New York Times, 1969), 91.

41. Sebastian N. Page, *Black Resettlement and the American Civil War* (New York: Cambridge University Press, 2018), 141.

42. Jason M. Colby, *The Business of Empire: United Fruit, Race, and U.S. Expansion in Central America* (Ithaca, N.Y.: Cornell University Press, 2011), 20–22.

43. Delany, *Condition*, 212.

44. Martin R. Delany, *The Origins of Races and Color* (Baltimore: Black Classic Press, 1991; orig. pub. 1879), 94.

45. Thomas F. Buxton, *The African Slave Trade and Its Remedy* (London: John Murray, 1840), 336–37.

46. Scholars have debated the financial costs of emancipation. For an influential early history of one British colony, Guiana, see Michael Moohr, "The Economic Impact of Slave Emancipation in British Guiana, 1832–1852," *Economic History Review* 25, no. 4 (November 1972): 588–607.

47. Victor Ullman, *Martin R. Delany: The Beginning of Black Nationalism* (Boston: Beacon Press, 1971), 225–27.

48. Delany, *Condition*, 35; Beverly C. Tomek, *Colonization and Its Discontents: Emancipation, Emigration, and Antislavery in Antebellum Pennsylvania* (New York: New York University Press, 2011), 209. Delany was wrong about Coates. True, Coates had distanced himself from the Colonization Society, but he would be the chief architect of the African Civilization Society, an organization funded by New York and other colonizationists. Emma J. Lapsansky-Werner and Margaret Hope Bacon, eds., *Back to Africa: Benjamin Coates and the Colonization Movement in America, 1848–1880* (University Park: Pennsylvania State University Press, 2010), 41–42.

49. Ullman, *Martin R. Delany*, 220–21; Martin Delany, "Official Report of the Niger Valley Exploring Party," in M. R. Delany and Robert Campbell, *Search for a Place: Black Separatism and Africa, 1860* (Ann Arbor: University of Michigan Press, 1969), 43.

50. "Liberia," *Voice of the Fugitive*, April 22, 1852, Black Abolitionists Archive, University of Detroit Mercy.

51. "Niger Valley Exploring Party," *African Repository* 35, no. 10 (October 1859), 29.

52. *Weekly Anglo-African*, September 3, 1859. As it turned out, the Scottish church had needed a person to work in the Caribbean islands and Garnet took a commission from the United Presbyterian Church of Scotland to work as a missionary in Jamaica. He returned to the United States in 1855, having spent three years away. See Anna Mae Duane, *Educated for Freedom: The Incredible Story of Two Fugitive Schoolboys Who Grew Up to Change a Nation* (New York: New York University Press, 2022), 147.

53. *North American and U.S. Gazette*, December 3, 1858, p. 1; Richard Blackett, "Martin R. Delany and Robert Campbell: Black Americans in Search of an African Colony," *Journal of Negro History* 62, no. 1 (January 1977): 7–8.

54. Blackett, "Martin R. Delany and Robert Campbell," 7.

55. From the Liberia *Star*, July 27, 1859, reprinted in *African Repository* 35, no. 10 (October 1859): 299.

56. Delany, "Official Report of the Niger Valley Exploring Party," 51.

57. Letter from Miss Kilpatrick, Methodist School at White Plains, August 20, 1859, in *African Repository* 35, no. 11 (November 1859): 329.

58. E. W. Blyden to Rev. John B. Pinney, Monrovia, July 29, 1859, in *African Repository* 35, no. 10 (October 1859): 299.

59. Ronald Fox, "The Reverend Alexander Crummell: An Apostle of Black Culture" (Ph.D. diss., General Theological Seminary, 1969); Kathleen O'Mara Wahle, "Alexander Crummell: Black Evangelist and Pan-Negro Nationalist," *Phylon* 29, no. 4 (1968): 388–95; Luckson Ejofodomi, "The Missionary Career of Alexander Crummell in Liberia, 1853–1873" (Ph.D. diss., Boston University, 1974).

60. Delany, "Official Report of the Niger Valley Exploring Party," 52.

61. Dr. H. J. Roberts, writing from Monrovia, July 28, 1859, *African Repository* 35, no. 10 (October 1859): 290.

62. Delany, "Official Report of the Niger Valley Exploring Party," 67.

63. Olufemi Vaughan, *Religion and the Making of Nigeria* (Durham, N.C.: Duke University Press, 2016), 26–29.

64. Delany, "Official Report of the Niger Valley Exploring Party," 67.

65. Ullman, *Martin Delany*, 222–24.

66. Delany, "Official Report of the Niger Valley Exploring Party," 77.

67. M. B Akpan, "Black Imperialism: Americo-Liberian Rule over the African Peoples of Liberia, 1841–1964," *Canadian Journal of African Studies* 7, no. 2 (1973): 217–36; Tunde Adeleke, *UnAfrican Americans: Nineteenth-Century Black Nationalists and the Civilizing Mission* (Lexington: University Press of Kentucky, 1998); Tunde Adeleke, *Without Regard to Race: The Other Martin Delany* (Jackson: University of Mississippi Press, 2003).

68. Delany, "Official Report of the Niger Valley Exploring Party," 77.

69. Bronwen Everill, *Not Made By Slaves: Ethical Capitalism in the Age of Abolition* (Cambridge, Mass.: Harvard University Press, 2020), 54.

70. Ibram X. Kendi, *Stamped from the Beginning: A History of Racist Ideas in America* (New York: Nation Books, 2016), 198–99.

71. Onuf, *Jefferson's Empire*, 148–50.

Chapter 11

Acknowledgments: The author is deeply grateful to the editors for the opportunity to contribute to this collection, to the other contributors and participants in the 2019 McNeil Center workshop from which these essays emerged, and to the anonymous readers for their extremely helpful comments and suggestions.

1. Edward W. Said, *Culture and Imperialism* (London: Chatto & Windus, 1993), 258; Peter S. Onuf, "Imperialism and Nationalism in the Early American Republic," in *Empire's Twin: U.S. Anti-Imperialism from the Founding Era to the Age of Terrorism*, ed. Ian Tyrrell and Jay Sexton (Ithaca, N.Y.: Cornell University Press, 2015), 21–40, 38.

2. Jeffrey Ostler, "Native Americans Against Empire and Colonial Rule," in Tyrrell and Sexton, *Empire's Twin*, 41–58. See also Samantha Seeley, *Race, Removal, and the Right to Remain: Migration and the Making of the United States* (Chapel Hill: University of North Carolina Press, 2021).

3. Ann Laura Stoler, "Intimidations of Empire: Predicaments of the Tactile and Unseen," in *Haunted By Empire: Geographies of Intimacy in North American History*, ed. Stoler (Durham, N.C.: Duke University Press, 2006), 1–22, quotation on 10. The problem of conceptualizing "empire" in the early United States is taken up by Patrick Griffin in two essays: "Imagining an American Imperial-Revolutionary History," in *Experiencing Empire: Power, People, and Revolution in Early America*, ed. Griffin (Charlottesville: University of Virginia Press, 2017), 1–24; and "Imperial Confusion: America's Post-Colonial and Post-Revolutionary Empire," *Journal of Imperial and Commonwealth History* 49, no. 3 (2021): 414–30. See also Gautham Rao, "The New Historiography of the Early Federal Government: Institutions, Contexts, and the Imperial State," *William and Mary Quarterly* 77, no. 1 (2020): 97–128; and Emily Conroy-Krutz, "Empire and the Early Republic," H-Diplo Essay No. 133 (September 2015), http://tiny.cc/E133.

4. Lorenzo Veracini, "Settler Colonialism: Career of a Concept," *Journal of Imperial and Commonwealth History* 41, no. 2 (2013): 313–33; Bethel Saler, *The Settlers' Empire: Colonialism and State Formation in America's Old Northwest* (Philadelphia: University of Pennsylvania Press, 2015); Walter L. Hixson, *American Settler Colonialism: A History* (New York: Palgrave, 2013); Ostler, "Native Americans Against Empire."

5. Thomas Paine, *Common Sense: Addressed to the Inhabitants of America* (Philadelphia: R. Bell, 1776), 25; Justin du Rivage, *Revolution Against Empire: Taxes, Politics, and the Origins of American Independence* (New Haven, Conn.: Yale University Press, 2017), 5. See also Jack P. Greene, *Evaluating Empire and Confronting Colonialism in Eighteenth-Century Britain* (Cambridge: Cambridge University Press, 2013). On the question of continuity between "colonial" and "early national" American history, see Eliga Gould, "Independence and Interdependence:

The American Revolution and the Problem of Postcolonial Nationhood, Circa 1802," *William and Mary Quarterly* 74, no. 4 (2017): 729–52; Serena R. Zabin, "Writing To and From the Revolution," *William and Mary Quarterly* 74, no. 4 (2017): 753–64; and Alan Taylor, "Expand or Die: The Revolution's New Empire," *Journal of the Early Republic* 37, no. 4 (2017): 599–614.

6. James Otis, *The Rights of the British Colonies Asserted and Proved* (London: J. Almon, 1764), 58, 52.

7. Thomas Jefferson, *A Summary View of the Rights of British America* (London: G. Kearsly, 1774), 20; Alexander Hamilton, *The Farmer Refuted; or, A More Impartial and Comprehensive View of the Dispute Between Great Britain and the Colonies* (New York: James Rivington, 1775), 21, 17.

8. Samuel Seabury, *A View of the Controversy Between Great-Britain and Her Colonies* (New York: James Rivington, 1774), 9; Alison L. LaCroix, *The Ideological Origins of American Federalism* (Cambridge, Mass.: Harvard University Press, 2010), 105–31; Onuf, "Imperialism and Nationalism," 22.

9. H. W. Brands, "The Golden Death of Jefferson's Dream: California and the Sectional Crisis," in *The Louisiana Purchase and American Expansion, 1803–1898*, ed. Sanford Levinson and Bartholomew H. Sparrow (Lanham, Md.: Rowman & Littlefield, 2005), 129–38, quotation on 132. On the ambiguity over whether "equal footing" gave new states the right to determine for themselves whether to allow or prohibit slavery, see George William Van Cleve, *A Slaveholders' Union: Slavery, Politics, and the Constitution in the Early American Republic* (Chicago: University of Chicago Press, 2010), 154–56. On the longer history of federalism in North America, see Andrew Shankman, "Toward a Social History of Federalism: The State and Capitalism To and From the American Revolution," *Journal of the Early Republic* 37, no. 4 (2017): 615–53.

10. Gaillard Hunt, ed., *The Debates in the Federal Convention of 1787* (New York: Oxford University Press, 1920), 2:487–88; David Ramsay, *An Oration on the Cession of Louisiana to the United States* (Newport, R.I.: Oliver Farnsworth, 1804), 20–21. On the confident contortions of federative expansionism, see Peter S. Onuf, *Jefferson's Empire: The Language of American Nationhood* (Charlottesville: University Press of Virginia, 2000); and Paul Frymer, *Building an American Empire: The Era of Territorial and Political Expansion* (Princeton, N.J.: Princeton University Press, 2017).

11. Ramsay, *Oration*, 21.

12. "Thomas Jefferson to Alexander von Humboldt, 6 December 1813," *Founders Online*, National Archives, https://founders.archives.gov/documents/Jefferson/03-07-02-0011; Ramsay, *Oration*, 13–14.

13. Carroll Smith-Rosenberg, *This Violent Empire: The Birth of an American National Identity* (Chapel Hill: University of North Carolina Press, 2010), 6; Robert G. Parkinson, *The Common Cause: Creating Race and Nation in the American Revolution* (Chapel Hill: University of North Carolina Press, 2016). See also Aziz Rana, *The Two Faces of American Freedom* (Cambridge, Mass.: Harvard University Press, 2010).

14. Henry Knox to George Washington, "Report on Indian Affairs," December 29, 1794, *Papers of George Washington, Digital Edition*, ed. Theodore J. Crackel et al. (Charlottesville: University of Virginia Press, Rotunda, 2008); Knox to Anthony Wayne, January 5, 1793, in *Anthony Wayne: A Name in Arms; Soldier, Diplomat, Defender of Expansion Westward of a Nation*, ed. Richard C. Knopf (Pittsburgh: University of Pittsburgh Press, 1960), 165.

15. Nancy Shoemaker, "The Extraterritorial United States to 1860," *Diplomatic History* 42, no. 1 (2018): 36–54.

16. John Quincy Adams, "Message to the House of Representatives," March 25, 1825, *Appendix to the Register of Debates*, 19th Cong., 1st sess., 69; C. A. Bayly, *Imperial Meridian: The British Empire and the World, 1780–1830* (London: Longman, 1989); Nicholas B. Dirks, *The Scandal of Empire: India and the Creation of Imperial Britain* (Cambridge, Mass.: Harvard University Press, 2006); Greene, *Evaluating Empire*, 341–61; Jennifer Pitts, *A Turn to Empire: The Rise of Imperial*

Liberalism in Britain and France (Princeton, N.J.: Princeton University Press, 2005); Lisa Lowe, *The Intimacies of Four Continents* (Durham, N.C.: Duke University Press, 2015).

17. Abraham Bishop, "The Rights of Black Men," ed. Tim Matthewson, *Journal of Negro History* 67, no. 2 (1982): 148–54, quotation on 151; Samuel White statement, *Annals of Congress*, Senate, 9th Cong., 1st sess., February 20, 1806, 118.

18. White statement, *Annals*, 129.

19. On the connections between imperialism and the development of international law and commercial orders, see Antony Anghie, *Imperialism, Sovereignty and the Making of International Law* (Cambridge: Cambridge University Press, 2005); Lauren Benton, *A Search for Sovereignty: Law and Geography in European Empires, 1400–1900* (Cambridge: Cambridge University Press, 2010); Jennifer Pitts, *Boundaries of the International: Law and Empire* (Cambridge, Mass.: Harvard University Press, 2018); Padraic X. Scanlan, *Freedom's Debtors: British Antislavery in Sierra Leone in the Age of Revolution* (New Haven, Conn.: Yale University Press, 2017); Lauren Benton and Lisa Ford, *Rage for Order: The British Empire and the Origins of International Law, 1800–1850* (Cambridge, Mass.: Harvard University Press, 2016). On British–U.S. missionary collaboration, see Emily Conroy-Krutz, "'Engaged in the Same Glorious Cause': Anglo-American Connections in the American Missionary Entrance into India, 1790–1815," *Journal of the Early Republic* 34, no. 1 (2014): 21–44; and Christine Leigh Heyrman, *American Apostles: When Evangelicals Entered the World of Islam* (New York: Hill and Wang, 2015). On U.S. ties more broadly with emerging imperial world orders after the War of 1812, see Ian Tyrrell, "Inter-Imperial Entanglements in the Age of Imperial Globalization," in *The Cambridge History of America and the World*, vol. 2, *1820–1900*, ed. Kristin L. Hoganson and Jay Sexton (Cambridge: Cambridge University Press, 2022), 716–37.

20. Emily Conroy-Krutz, *Christian Imperialism: Converting the World in the Early American Republic* (Ithaca, N.Y.: Cornell University Press, 2015), 211.

21. Ann H. Judson, *A Particular Relation of the American Baptist Mission to the Burman Empire* (Washington, D.C.: John S. Meehan, 1823), 99–100; James D. Knowles, *Memoir of Mrs. Ann H. Judson* (London: Wightman and Cramp, 1829), 231, 233, 260.

22. *Literary Magazine and American Register* (Philadelphia), December 1804, 655–56. On American attempts to deny the legitimacy of Haiti's nationhood after 1804, see James Alexander Dun, *Dangerous Neighbors: Making the Haitian Revolution in Early America* (Philadelphia: University of Pennsylvania Press, 2016), 225–31. On "degradation" and Latin America, see Paul D. Naish, *Slavery and Silence: Latin America and the U.S. Slave Debate* (Philadelphia: University of Pennsylvania Press, 2017), 29–63.

23. *Annals of Congress*, House of Representatives, 18th Cong., 1st sess., January 19, 1824, 1094. For the claim that the Greeks were "degraded" and "cannot be identified with the people who produced Aristides and Socrates," see ibid., January 26, 1824 (Alexander Smyth), 1210; see also January 21, 1824 (Silas Wood), 1134. On the U.S. debate over the Greek independence struggle in the 1820s, see Karine V. Walther, *Sacred Interests: The United States and the Islamic World, 1821–1921* (Chapel Hill: University of North Carolina Press, 2015), 33–67; David Mayers, *Dissenting Voices in America's Rise to Power* (Cambridge: Cambridge University Press, 2007), 56–79; and Maureen Connors Santelli, *The Greek Fire: American-Ottoman Relations and Democratic Fervor in the Age of Revolutions* (Ithaca, N.Y.: Cornell University Press, 2020).

24. *Annals of Congress*, House of Representatives, 18th Cong., 1st sess., January 21, 1824, 1132; and January 20, 1824, 1105–6.

25. Adams, "Message to the House of Representatives"; Caitlin Fitz, *Our Sister Republics: The United States in an Age of American Revolutions* (New York: W. W. Norton, 2016), 194–239; Jay Sexton, "An American System: The North American Union and Latin America in the 1820s," in *Connections After Colonialism: Europe and Latin America in the 1820s*, ed. Matthew Brown and Gabriel Paquette (Tuscaloosa: University of Alabama Press, 2013), 139–59.

26. Fitz, *Our Sister Republics*, 226.

27. Otis, *Rights of the British Colonies*, 43–44.

28. Nicholas Guyatt, *Bind Us Apart: How Enlightened Americans Invented Racial Segregation* (New York: Basic Books, 2016).

29. C. M. Harris, "Introduction," *Papers of William Thornton*, vol. 1, *1781–1802*, ed. C. M. Harris (Charlottesville: University Press of Virginia, 1995), xxxi–lix; James Sidbury, *Becoming African in America: Race and Nation in the Early Black Atlantic* (New York: Oxford University Press, 2007), 78–79; Christy Clark-Pujara, *Dark Work: The Business of Slavery in Rhode Island* (New York: New York University Press, 2018), 117–19; Guyatt, *Bind Us Apart*, 211–14.

30. Anthony Taylor to William Thornton, January 24, 1787; Thornton to John Coakley Lettsom, February 15, 1787; Thornton to the Elders and Members of the [African] Union Society, March 6, 1787; all in Harris, *Papers of William Thornton*, 41–42, 43–47, 48–49.

31. Thornton to Lettsom, May 20, 1787; Thornton to Lettsom, July 26, 1788; Thornton to Thomas Clarkson, November 13, 1789; Thornton to Granville Sharp, November 13, 1789; all in Harris, *Papers of William Thornton*, 55–57, 71, 110–12, 113–14; and Anthony Taylor and Salmar Nubia to Samuel Stevens and the African Company at Boston, October 4, 1787, in *The Proceedings of the Free African Union Society and the African Benevolent Society, Newport, Rhode Island, 1780–1824*, ed. William Henry Robinson (Providence: Urban League of Rhode Island, 1976), 18.

32. On Sharp, see Deirdre Coleman, *Romantic Colonization and British Anti-Slavery* (Cambridge: Cambridge University Press, 2005), 85–86; and Guyatt, *Bind Us Apart*, 203–5. On the difficulties experienced by Black loyalists who made their way to Sierra Leone (often via Nova Scotia), see Cassandra Pybus, *Epic Journeys of Freedom: Runaway Slaves of the American Revolution and Their Global Quest for Liberty* (Boston: Beacon Press, 2006), 139–55, 183–202; and A. G. Hopkins, *American Empire: A Global History* (Princeton, N.J.: Princeton University Press, 2018), 95–96. On "liberated Africans" in Sierra Leone, see Richard Anderson, "The Diaspora of Sierra Leone's Liberated Africans: Enlistment, Forced Migration, and 'Liberation' at Freetown, 1808–1863," *African Economic History* 41 (2013): 101–38; and Padraic X. Scanlan, "The Colonial Rebirth of British Anti-Slavery: The Liberated African Villages of Sierra Leone, 1815–1824," *American Historical Review* 121, no. 1 (2016): 1085–113.

33. William Thornton, *Political Economy: Founded in Justice and Humanity, in a Letter to a Friend* (Washington, D.C.: Samuel Harrison Smith, 1804), 23. On the range of colonization schemes and proposals beyond the American Colonization Society, see Samantha Seeley, "Beyond the American Colonization Society," *History Compass* 14, no. 3 (2016): 93–104; and Guyatt, *Bind Us Apart*, 197–224, 247–62,

34. Thornton to Sharp, November 13, 1789, 114. [William Watkins], "A Coloured Baltimorean," *Freedom's Journal*, July 6, 1827, 66. On African American emigration to Haiti, see Sara Fanning, *Caribbean Crossing: African Americans and the Haitian Emigration Movement* (New York: New York University Press, 2015).

35. "At a Meeting of Free People of Color," *Philadelphia Daily Advertiser*, January 10, 1817, 3; "Address to a Meeting of Colored People in Camden Street, Baltimore," *Genius of Universal Emancipation* 4, no. 11 (August 1825): 168–70, quotation on 171; Paul Cuffe to Cato Sawyer, February 17, 1814, in *Captain Paul Cuffe's Logs and Letters, 1808–1817: A Black Quaker's "Voice from Within the Veil,"* ed. Rosalind Cobb Wiggins (Washington, D.C.: Howard University Press, 1996), 271–72.

36. Bronwen Everill, "Experiments in Colonial Citizenship in Sierra Leone and Liberia," in *New Directions in the Study of African American Recolonization*, ed. Beverly C. Tomek and Matthew J. Hetrick (Gainesville: University Press of Florida, 2017), 184–205; Martin R. Delany et al., "Political Destiny of the Colored Race," in *Proceedings of the National Emigration Convention of Colored People* (Pittsburgh: A. A. Anderson 1854), 33–70, 38–39; Mary Ann Shadd Cary, *A Plea for Emigration; or, Notes of Canada West* (Detroit: George W. Pattison 1852), 44.

37. Jane Burbank and Frederick Cooper, *Empires in World History: Power and the Politics of Difference* (Princeton, N.J.: Princeton University Press, 2010), 8.

38. John Stuart Mill, *On Liberty* (London: John W. Parker, 1859), 23.

Chapter 12

Acknowledgments: The author thanks Ray Self, Sarah Wagner-McCoy, the members of the Pacific Northwest Early Americanist Group, and the organizers and attendees of the 2019 "Making a Republic Imperial" conference, as well as the editors and reviewers of this volume.

1. Tacitus, *The Agricola and the Germania*, trans. Harold Mattingly (New York: Penguin, 1970), 80–81.

2. Mark Bradley, "Tacitus' *Agricola* and the Conquest of Britain: Representations of Empire in Victorian and Edwardian Britain," in *Classics and Imperialism in the British Empire*, ed. Bradley (New York: Oxford University Press, 2010), 124–25.

3. See, for instance, Yardley Warner, "Conquest of Peace," in *An Appeal for Peace, Addressed to Those Concerned in Making and Administering the Laws* (Philadelphia: Kite & Walton, 1848), 7; essay by John Bolles in *Prize Essays on a Congress of Nations* (Boston: Whipple & Damrell, 1840), 86. A twist on the Calgacus quotation is the basis for the epigraph (and title) to Brian DeLay, *War of a Thousand Deserts: Indian Raids and the U.S.–Mexican War* (New Haven, Conn.: Yale University Press, 2009), vii.

4. The idea of "universal brotherhood" is particularly associated with Elihu Burritt, the leading American peace activist of the mid-nineteenth century; Peter Tolis, *Elihu Burritt: Crusader for Brotherhood* (Hamden, Conn.: Archon Books, 1968). On empire and differentiation, see Jane Burbank and Frederick Cooper, *Empires in World History: Power and the Politics of Difference* (Princeton, N.J.: Princeton University Press, 2010), 8–13.

5. Burbank and Cooper, *Empires in World History*, 8–13.

6. Most works concentrating on nineteenth-century peace reform are decades old. See Merle Eugene Curti, *The American Peace Crusade, 1815–1860* (1929; repr., New York: Octagon Books, 1973); Peter Brock, *Radical Pacifists in Antebellum America* (Princeton, N.J.: Princeton University Press, 1968); Charles DeBenedetti, *The Peace Reform in American History* (Bloomington: Indiana University Press, 1980). For more recent work on particular dimensions of the peace movement, see Valarie H. Ziegler, *The Advocates of Peace in Antebellum America* (Bloomington: Indiana University Press, 1992); Carolyn Eastman, "Fight Like a Man: Gender and Rhetoric in the Early Nineteenth-Century American Peace Movement," *American Nineteenth Century History* 10, no. 3 (September 2009): 247–71.

7. Philo Pacificus [Noah Worcester], *A Solemn Review of the Custom of War; Showing That War Is the Effect of Popular Delusion, and Proposing a Remedy* (Cambridge, Mass.: Hilliard and Metcalf, 1816), 3.

8. Worcester, *Solemn Review*, 3–4.

9. "Letters of Lillian Ching, to His Brethren in the Island of Loo Choo, Written During His Residence in the United States," *Friend of Peace* 4, no. 13 (1827): 385–409, quotation on 409; Margot Minardi, "The Lessons of Loo Choo: The Historical Vision of American Peace Reformers, 1815–1837," in *The Specter of Peace: Rethinking Violence and Power in the Colonial Atlantic*, ed. Michael Goode and John Smolenski (Leiden: Brill, 2018), 216–51.

10. Worcester, *Solemn Review*, title page; Minardi, "The Lessons of Loo Choo," 224–27.

11. Brock, *Radical Pacifists*, chap. 1.

12. Deborah Rosen, *Border Law: The First Seminole War and American Nationhood* (Cambridge, Mass.: Harvard University Press, 2015), chaps. 3–5 (quotation on p. 123).

13. "Review of Modern Defensive War," *Friend of Peace* 2, no. 4 (1819): 24.

14. "Review of Modern Defensive War," 21–23; S. Doc. No. 100, at 1–2 (1819).

15. "The Christian Alliance," *Bond of Brotherhood* 2 (September 1846).

16. "Proceedings at which Humanity Shudders," *Friend of Peace* 2, no. 7 (1820): 25.

17. "Third Annual Report of the Mass. Peace Society," *Friend of Peace* 2, no. 13 (1819): 7.

18. "Testimonies Relating to the American Indians," *Friend of Peace* 2, no. 4 (1819): 17.

19. "Review of Alarming Facts—No. 1," *Friend of Peace* 2, no. 5 (1819): 17–18.

20. On the Quaker background for Hicks's paintings, see David Tatham, "Edward Hicks, Elias Hicks and John Comly: Perspectives on the Peaceable Kingdom Theme," *American Art Journal* 13, no. 2 (1981): 40–47.

21. Stephen Craig Harper, *Promised Land: Penn's Holy Experiment, the Walking Purchase, and the Dispossession of the Delawares* (Bethlehem, Pa.: Lehigh University Press, 2006), esp. chap. 4; and Fred Anderson and Andrew Cayton, *The Dominion of War: Empire and Liberty in North America, 1500–2000* (New York: Viking, 2004), chap. 2.

22. The Treaty of Fort Jackson exemplified the language and logic that peace reformers sought to undercut. Making a clear distinction between the civilized United States and the barbaric Indian, the 1814 treaty presented the conflict it purported to resolve as "an unprovoked, inhuman, and sanguinary war, waged by the hostile Creeks against the United States," while claiming that the United States had exemplified "principles of national justice" and "humanity"; "Treaty of Fort Jackson, 1814," in Alan Axelrod, *Political History of America's Wars* (Washington, D.C.: CQ Press, 2007), 89.

23. M. C., "The Speaking Map," *Friend of Peace* 4, no. 1 (ca. 1824): 23.

24. While the Seminole Wars are commonly periodized as three distinct episodes (the First, Second, and Third Seminole Wars), William S. Belko argues that they ought to be considered as a century of violent struggle; see *America's Hundred Years' War: U.S. Expansion to the Gulf Coast and the Fate of the Seminole, 1763–1858*, ed. William S. Belko (Gainesville: University Press of Florida, 2011), introduction.

25. "Peace and Peace Societies," *Christian Examiner and General Review*, May 1839, 180.

26. See, for instance, the comments of Ezra Stiles Gannett in A. D., "Peace Meeting in Park St. Church," *Christian Register*, April 7, 1849, 55.

27. J. P. Blanchard, "Criminality and Injury of War," in *Communications on Peace* (Boston: Moody, 1848), 33. See also "Eighteenth Anniversary of the American Peace Society," *Advocate of Peace and Universal Brotherhood*, June 1846, 131; *Facts and Considerations Relating to War* (n.p., ca. 1847), 9, Swarthmore College Peace Collection, Swarthmore, Pa.

28. The data in this and the following paragraphs come from 187 petitions against the U.S. war with Mexico in the Records of the U.S. House of Representatives, Record Group 233, National Archives Building, Washington, D.C. All petitions discussed in this chapter come from this record group; in what follows, all references include the folder number where the relevant petitions are stored.

29. The median number of signatories was sixty-two.

30. Over 530 people affixed their names to eight petitions bearing this text, representing communities in Trumbull, Ashtabula, and Lake Counties, Ohio. All these petitions can be found in HR30A-G6.2.

31. References to Mexico as a "sister republic" appear in at least sixteen petitions, representing communities ranging from Ferrisburgh, Vt., to Lorain County, Ohio, and religious groups from a Quaker meeting in Richmond, Ind., to Unitarians in Massachusetts. See HR29A-G5.3; HR30A-G6.2. For the roots of this language as applied to other newly independent Latin American nations, see Caitlin Fitz, *Our Sister Republics: The United States in an Age of American Revolutions* (New York: W. W. Norton, 2016). Many other petitions made a similar point more subtly by referring to Mexico as "the Republic of Mexico."

32. Petition of electors of Canfield County, Ohio, January 28, 1847, in HR29A-H1.3 (emphasis added). For a similar expression of the obligations of republicanism, see the resolutions adopted at a meeting at White Hall, Lower Merion Township, Pa., February 7, 1848, in HR30A-G6.2.

Unless otherwise noted, dates listed for petitions reflect when they were tabled or sent to committee.

33. For examples of this form and variations on it, see the petitions of Massachusetts Unitarian ministers and laymen; Syracuse, N.Y.; Cambridge, Mass.; Billerica and other towns, Mass.; Springport, Ohio; Lorain County, Ohio; and twenty-four "daughters of America"; all in HR30A-G6.2.

34. Memorial and protest of the York Springs [Pennsylvania] Anti-Slavery Society, signed July 10, 1846, in HR29A-G5.3; petition of Michael H. Barton and other citizens of Jerusalem, N.Y., signed December 30, 1847, in HR30A-G6.2.

35. Petition of the American Peace Society, signed December 1847, HR30A-G6.2.

36. Albert Gallatin, *Peace with Mexico* (New York: Bartlett & Welford, 1847), 12.

37. On the idea that there were "no boundaries to wartime" in American violence against Indians, see Rosen, *Border Law*, 149 (quotation). On the protracted nature of conflict with Indians during "peacetime," see Edward M. Coffman, *The Old Army: A Portrait of the American Army in Peacetime, 1784–1898* (New York: Oxford University Press, 1986), 42–50.

38. Petition of Ferrisburgh, Vt., and vicinity, April 11, 1848, in HR30A-G6.2. Mexican commentators themselves worried about their country's vulnerability to foreign invasion given the weakness of political institutions and the lack of a sense of national unity in this period; Michael C. Meyer, William L. Sherman, and Susan M. Deeds, *The Course of Mexican History*, 7th ed. (New York: Oxford University Press, 2003), chaps. 19–20; Christon I. Archer, "Fashioning a New Nation," in *The Oxford History of Mexico*, ed. Michael C. Meyer and William H. Beezley (New York: Oxford University Press, 2000), 301–37; Josefina Zoraida Vázquez, "War and Peace with the United States," trans. Michael M. Brescia, in Meyer and Beezley, *Oxford History of Mexico*, 339–69.

39. Frederick A. Farley, *Military Glory. A Sermon Preached at the Church of the Saviour, Brooklyn, New York* (New York, 1848), 3; petition of legal voters of North Brookfield, Mass., January 25, 1847, in HR29A-G5.3.

40. Theodore Parker, *A Sermon of the Mexican War* (Boston: Coolidge and Wiley, 1848), 43. Amy S. Greenberg explores this gendered and sexualized discourse of American imperialism in Latin America in *Manifest Manhood and the Antebellum American Empire* (New York: Cambridge University Press, 2005), esp. chap. 3.

41. Petition of electors of DeWitt, N.Y., December 20, 1847, in HR30A-G6.2.

42. This language was part of a printed petition form. Signed copies from Ohio and New York can be found in HR29A-G5.3.

43. Petition of Jackson Township, Ohio, January 24, 1848, in HR30A-G6.2.

44. Samuel Harris, *The Mexican War: A Sermon Delivered on the Annual Thanksgiving at Conway, Mass., November 26, 1846* (Greenfield, Mass.: Merriam and Mirick, 1847), 14.

45. On "conquest," see petitions of Baltimore Yearly Meeting, December 19, 1846, in HR29A-G5.3; Jackson Township; Muskingum County, Ohio, December 20, 1847; Newton Falls, Ohio, February 3, 1848; Danvers, Mass., January 17, 1848; New York State, signed February 28, 1848, all in HR30A-G6.2. On "national aggrandizement," see petitions of DeWitt; Lysander, N.Y., December 16, 1847; Syracuse, N.Y., January 10; 1848; all in HR30A-G6.2.

46. Petitions of Jerusalem, New York; Cleveland, January 18, 1848, in HR30A-G6.2; petition of Northborough, Mass., signed December 9, 1847, in HR30A-G6.3.

47. Petition of Deerfield, Mass., December 30, 1847, in HR30A-G6.2.

48. Petition of Lower Merion Township.

49. Greenberg, *Manifest Manhood*, introduction, quotation on 11.

50. Petition of "citizens of the US," January 25, 1848, in HR30A-G6.2.

51. Parker, *Sermon of the Mexican War*, 49–50.

52. Andrew P. Peabody, *The Triumphs of War* (Portsmouth, N.H.: John W. Foster, 1847), 9–10.

53. Peabody, *The Triumphs of War*, 6. On the relationship between missionaries and empire in this period, see William R. Hutchison, *Errand to the World: American Protestant Thought and Foreign Missions* (Chicago: University of Chicago Press, 1987), chaps. 2–3.

54. See the editors' discussion of Figure I.2 in the introduction to this volume. For more on the relationship between peace reform and mission movements, see Minardi, "The Lessons of Loo Choo," 227–32.

55. Parker, *Sermon of the Mexican War*, 54.

56. American Peace Society, "Petition for Peace," December 7, 1846, in HR29A-G5.3.

57. Warner, "Conquest of Peace," 7.

58. I take the useful term "imperializing," connoting empire as a formative process rather than a completed state, from Konstantin Dierks, "Americans Overseas in the Early American Republic," *Diplomatic History* 42, no. 1 (2018): 32.

59. Beyond the essays in the current volume, this trend, and scholarship relating to it, is discussed in the forum on "Globalizing the Early American Republic," in *Diplomatic History* 42, no. 1 (2018): 17–108, particularly the contributions by Dierks ("Americans Overseas") and Emily Conroy-Krutz ("The Hierarchy of Heathenism: Missionaries Map the Globe"), as well as in Kristin L. Hoganson and Jay Sexton, introduction to *Crossing Empires: Taking U.S. History into Transimperial Terrain*, ed. Hoganson and Sexton (Durham, N.C.: Duke University Press, 2020), 1–22.

60. Valeska Huber and Jan C. Jansen, "Dealing with Difference: Cosmopolitanism in the Nineteenth-Century World of Empires," *Humanity* 12, no. 1 (2021): 39–46.

Chapter 13

Acknowledgments: The author thanks the University of Pennsylvania Press's anonymous readers and the editors of this volume, particularly Emily Conroy-Krutz, for their helpful critiques on earlier versions of this essay.

1. On Manifest Destiny and the limits of territorial acquisition in the 1840s, see Amy S. Greenberg, "Cuba and the Failure of Manifest Destiny," *Journal of the Early Republic* 42, no. 1 (Spring 2022): 1–20.

2. On the Second Seminole War, see C. S. Monaco, *The Second Seminole War and the Limits of American Aggression* (Baltimore: Johns Hopkins University Press, 2018); Susan A. Miller, *Coacoochee's Bones: A Seminole Saga* (Lawrence: University of Kansas Press 2003); Daniel Scallet, "This Inglorious War: The Second Seminole War, the Ad Hoc Origins of American Imperialism, and the Silence of Slavery" (Ph.D. diss., Washington University in St. Louis, 2011); Laurel Clark Shire, *The Threshold of Manifest Destiny: Gender and National Expansion in Florida* (Philadelphia: University of Pennsylvania Press, 2016); John K. Mahon, *History of the Second Seminole War, 1835–1842* (Gainesville: University of Florida Press, 1967); J. T. Sprague, *The Origin, Progress, and Conclusion of the Florida War* (New York: D. Appleton, 1848); and John Missall and Mary Lou Missall, *The Seminole Wars: America's Longest Indian Conflict* (Gainesville: University of Florida Press, 2004).

3. On the U.S.–Mexican War, see Peter Guardino, *The Dead March: A History of the Mexican-American War* (Cambridge, Mass.: Harvard University Press, 2017); Amy S. Greenberg, *A Wicked War: Polk, Clay, Lincoln, and the 1846 U.S. Invasion of Mexico* (New York: Vintage Books, 2013); David A. Clary, *Eagles and Empire: The United States, Mexico, and the Struggle for a Continent* (New York: Bantam, 2009); Irving W. Levinson, *Wars Within War: Mexican Guerrillas, Domestic Elites, and the United States of America, 1846–1848* (Fort Worth, Tex.: TCU Press, 2005); Jesús Velasco Márquez, *La guerra del 47 y la opinión pública (1845–1848)* (Mexico City: Secretaría de Educación Pública, 1975).

4. Scott Sigmund Gartner, "Military Personnel and Casualties, by War and Branch of Service: 1775–1991," Table Ed1-5, in *Historical Statistics of the United States: Millennial Edition*, ed.

Susan Carter, Scott Sigmund Gartner, Michael Haines, Alan Olmsted, Richard Sutch, and Gavin Wright (Cambridge: Cambridge University Press, 2006), accessed September 24, 2018, http://hsus.cambridge.org/. The mortality rate in Florida was 14 percent.

5. C. S. Monaco emphasizes the importance of reporting to the public perception of the Florida conflict, but coverage of that war pales when compared to the role of imbedded journalists on shaping opinion about events in Mexico. See Monaco, *The Second Seminole War*, 64–65; Greenberg, *A Wicked War*; see also Robert W. Johannsen, *To the Halls of the Montezumas: The Mexican War in the American Imagination* (New York: Oxford University Press, 1985).

6. Monaco argues that criticism of the Florida war became a standard theme of the Whig Party (*The Second Seminole War*, 166–67).

7. See, for example, Gartner, "Military Personnel and Casualties," Table Ed1-5.

8. Shire, *Threshold of Manifest Destiny*, 2; Julius Wilm, *Settlers and Conquerors: Free Land Policy in Antebellum America* (Stuttgart: Franz Steiner Verlag, 2008); Monaco, *The Second Seminole War*, 7; Paul Frymer, *Building an American Empire: The Era of Territorial and Political Expansion* (Princeton, N.J.: Princeton University Press, 2017).

9. Brian Rouleau, *With Sails Whitening Every Sea: Mariners and the Making of an American Maritime Empire* (Ithaca, N.Y.: Cornell University Press, 2014).

10. Peter Guardino's *The Dead March* and this author's *A Wicked War* are notable exceptions.

11. John W. Hall, "'A Reckless Waste of Blood and Treasure': The Last Campaign of the Second Seminole War," in *Between War and Peace: How America Ends Its Wars*, ed. Matthew Moten (New York: Free Press, 2011), 64–84; Greenberg, *A Wicked War*, 222.

12. Mark F. Proudman, "Words for Scholars: The Semantics of 'Imperialism,'" *Journal of the Historical Society* 8, no. 3 (September 2008): 395–433, quotation on 395; Ian Tyrell and Jay Sexton, eds., *Empire's Twin: U.S. Anti-imperialism from the Founding Era to the Age of Terrorism* (Ithaca, N.Y.: Cornell University Press, 2015), 1–7; David Mayers, *Dissenting Voices in America's Rise to Power* (Cambridge: Cambridge University Press, 2007); John Nichols, *Against the Beast: A Documentary History of American Opposition to Empire* (New York: Thunder's Mouth Press/ Nation Books, 2003).

13. See, for example, Sankar Muthu, *Enlightenment Against Empire* (Princeton, N.J.: Princeton University Press, 2009); Gregory Claeys, *Imperial Sceptics: British Critics of Empire, 1850– 1920* (New York: Cambridge University Press, 2010); Richard Whatmore, *Against War and Empire: Geneva, Britain, and France in the Eighteenth Century* (New Haven, Conn.: Yale University Press, 2012).

14. Peter Onuf, "Imperialism and Nationalism in the Early American Republic," in Tyrell and Sexton, *Empire's Twin*, 21–40; Philip S. Foner and Richard C. Winchester, eds., *The Anti-Imperialist Reader: A Documentary History of Anti-Imperialism in the United States*, 2 vols. (New York: Holmes and Meier, 1984); Nichols, *Against the Beast*; Margot Minardi, "'Centripetal Attraction' in a Centrifugal World: The Pacifist Vision of Elihu Burritt," *Early American Studies* 1 (2013): 176–91; Sean Harvey, "Albert Gallatin and the Mobilization of Opposition to the U.S.– Mexican War," paper in possession of the author. See also Amanda B. Moniz, *From Empire to Humanity: The American Revolution and the Origins of Humanitarianism* (New York: Oxford University Press, 2016).

15. Watson admits that army officers in Florida expressed clear "distrust for the short-term consequences of territorial expansion," but contends that "personal inconvenience rather than political allegiance or ideology" led to officer opposition to the Second Seminole War. This chapter argues otherwise. Samuel J. Watson, *Peacekeepers and Conquerors: The Army Officer Corps on the American Frontier, 1821–1846* (Lawrence: University of Kansas Press, 2013), 179, 181.

16. Monaco, *The Second Seminole War*, 81–83; Pärtel Piirimäe, "Men, Monsters and the History of Mankind in Vattel's Law of Nations," in *The Law of Nations and Natural Law 1625–1800*, ed. Simone Zurbuchen (Leiden: Brill, 2019), 159–85.

17. Alfred Balch to Martin Van Buren, Tallahassee, April 3, 1840, in *The Territorial Papers of the United States*, vol. 26, *The Territory of Florida, 1839–1845*, ed. Clarence Edwin Carter (Washington, D.C.: U.S. Government Printing Office, 1962), 128; Amy Greenberg, *Lady First: The World of First Lady Sarah Polk* (New York: Knopf, 2019), 93–94.

18. Stanley F. Horn, "Tennessee Volunteers in the Seminole Campaign of 1836: The Diary of Henry Hollingsworth," *Tennessee Historical Quarterly* 1, no. 3 (September 1942): 271; Horn, "Tennessee Volunteers," *Tennessee Historical Quarterly* 1, no. 4 (December 1942): 351; M. M. Cohen, *Notices of Florida and the Campaigns* (Charleston, S.C.: Burges and Honor, 1836), 88.

19. Sprague, *Origin, Progress, and Conclusions*, 460; John Bemrose, *Reminiscences of the Second Seminole War*, ed. John K. Mahon (Gainesville: University of Florida Press, 1966), 98–99; Horn, "Tennessee Volunteers," *Tennessee Historical Quarterly* 1, no. 4 (December 1942): 360; Hall, "A Reckless Waste of Blood and Treasure," 69; Edward M. Coffman, *The Old Army: A Portrait of the American Army in Peacetime, 1784–1898* (New York: Oxford University Press, 1986), 50–52. On illness, see Watson, *Peacekeepers and Conquerors*, 187; Monaco, *The Second Seminole War*.

20. Watson, *Peacekeepers and Conquerors*, 202; Hunter diary, 28, quoted in Reynold M. Wik, "Captain Nathaniel Wyche Hunter and the Florida Indian Campaigns, 1837–1842," *Florida Historical Quarterly* 39 (June 1960): 74; Sprague, *Origin, Progress, and Conclusions*, 5.

21. Ethan Allen Hitchcock, *Fifty Years in Camp and Field*, ed. W. A. Croffut (New York: G. P. Putnam's Sons, 1909), 120.

22. Henry Prince, *Amidst a Storm of Bullets: The Diary of Lt. Henry Prince in Florida, 1836–1842*, ed. Frank Laumer (Tampa, Fla.: University of Tampa Press, 1998), xxiii–xxiv.

23. Prince, *Amidst a Storm of Bullets*, 11.

24. Prince, *Amidst a Storm of Bullets*, 48–49.

25. Prince, *Amidst a Storm of Bullets*, 39, 61.

26. Prince, *Amidst a Storm of Bullets*, 118.

27. Prince, *Amidst a Storm of Bullets*, 121–22.

28. Coffman, *The Old Army*, 141; Paul Foos, *A Short, Offhand, Killing Affair: Soldiers and Social Conflict During the Mexican-American War* (Chapel Hill: University of North Carolina Press, 2002), 23–25.

29. Felix P. McGaughy, Jr., "The Squaw Kissing War: Bartholomew M. Lynch's Journal of the Second Seminole War, 1836–1839" (M.S. thesis, Florida State University, 1965), 210; Samuel Bigger McCartney, "Illinois in the Mexican War" (M.A. thesis, Northwestern University, 1939), 29; Foos, *A Short, Offhand, Killing Affair*, 19. On unskilled labor options, see Seth Rockman, *Scraping By: Wage Labor, Slavery, and Survival in Early Baltimore* (Baltimore: Johns Hopkins University Press, 2008).

30. "Florida War, No. 4," *Army and Navy Chronicle*, April 4, 1839, 220; "The Florida War," *North American*, September 17, 1840.

31. Wik, "Captain Nathaniel Wyche Hunter," 68–69.

32. Daniel H. Wiggins, diaries, collection M-89-32, box 1, Florida State Library and Archives.

33. Bemrose, *Reminiscences of the Second Seminole War*, 86; James M. Denham, "'Some Prefer the Seminoles': Violence and Disorder Among Soldiers and Settlers in the Second Seminole War, 1835–1842," *Florida Historical Quarterly* 70 (July 1991): 38–54, quotation on 46. On ill will between soldiers and settlers, see also *Army and Navy Chronicle*, December 26, 1839, 408.

34. Bemrose, *Reminiscences of the Second Seminole War*, 49, 22, 25.

35. Bemrose, *Reminiscences of the Second Seminole War*, 53.

36. Miller, *Coacoochee's Bones*, 42; Jean Chaudhuri monologue (recollections of a conversation with a Seminole man she had seen carving out wood images), n.d., p. 1, Samuel Proctor Oral History Program Collection, P. K. Yonge Library of Florida History, University of Florida; Cameron Strang, "Violence, Ethnicity, and Human Remains During the Second Seminole War," *Journal*

of American History 100, no. 4 (2014): 973–94. On village burning, see, for example, James Barr, *A Correct and Authentic Narrative of the Indian War in Florida* (New York: J. Narine, 1836).

37. On historical memory, see, for example, Bradley Mueller and Alyssa Boge, eds., *Egmont Key: A Seminole Story* (Clewiston, Fla.: Seminole Tribe of Florida Tribal Historic Preservation Office, 2019); Helen Escobedo, *Mexican Monuments: Strange Encounters* (New York: Abbeville Press, 1989), 158.

38. Hitchcock, *Fifty Years in Camp and Field*, 213, 198; John Russell Young, *Around the World with General Grant* (New York: American News, 1879), 2:447–48.

39. Hitchcock, *Fifty Years in Camp and Field*, 200; Scott to Santa Anna, August 21, 1847, in *Diplomatic Correspondence of the United States*, vol. 8, ed. William R. Manning (Washington, D.C.: Carnegie Endowment for International Peace, 1937), 922. See also "Dinner to Gen. Scott at Sandusky," *Daily National Intelligencer*, October 15, 1852

40. William McFeely, *Grant: A Biography* (New York: Norton, 2002), 64; Greenberg, *A Wicked War*.

41. Greenberg, *A Wicked War*, 189–99; on Hodge, see Foos, *A Short, Offhand, Killing Affair*, 157–59.

42. Benjamin Ogden, Jr., to Mike Walsh, December 20, 1847, Benjamin Ogden File, New-York Historical Society.

43. John C. Pinheiro, *Missionaries of Republicanism: A Religious History of the Mexican-American War* (New York: Oxford University Press, 2014), 13; Harry E. Pratt, ed., *Illinois as Lincoln Knew It: A Boston Reporter's Record of a Trip in 1847* (Springfield, Ill.: Abraham Lincoln Association, 1938): 45; Guardino, *The Dead March*, 253.

44. Otto Zirckel, *Tagebuch geschrieben während der nordamerikanisch-mexikanischen Campagne in den Jahren 1847 und 1848 auf beiden Operationslinien* (Halle: H. W. Schmidt, 1849), 1–3. Translation by Peter van Lidth de Jeude.

45. Bemrose, *Reminiscences of the Second Seminole War*, 53.

46. Guardino, *The Dead March*, 5; Robert Citino, "Military Histories Old and New: A Reintroduction," *American Historical Review* 112, no. 4 (October 2007): 1070–90.

47. Samuel Chamberlain, *My Confession: Recollections of a Rogue*, ed. William H. Goetzmann (Austin: Texas State Historical Association, 1996), 130, 203.

CONTRIBUTORS

Noelani Arista (Kanaka Maoli) is director of the Indigenous Studies Program at McGill University and associate professor in history and classical studies. Her research interests include Hawaiian governance and law, Indigenous language archives, and knowledge organization systems. She is the author of *The Kingdom and the Republic: Sovereign Hawai'i and the Early United States* (University of Pennsylvania Press, 2019). Her current project seeks to apply artificial intelligence and machine learning solutions to Hawaiian language texts, supplying models applicable to other Indigenous language contexts. Her next book project focuses on the first Hawaiian constitutional period, 1839–45.

Brooke Bauer is a citizen of the Catawba Nation of South Carolina and assistant professor of history at the University of Tennessee Knoxville. She is the author of *Becoming Catawba: Catawba Women and Nation-Building, 1540–1840* (University of Alabama Press, 2022).

Michael A. Blaakman is an assistant professor of history and the David L. Rike University Preceptor at Princeton University. His first book, *Speculation Nation: Land Mania in the Revolutionary American Republic*, is forthcoming in 2023 from the University of Pennsylvania Press.

Eric Burin is a professor of history at the University of North Dakota. He is the author of *Slavery and the Peculiar Solution: A History of the American Colonization Society* (University Press of Florida, 2005) and editor of *Picking the President: Understanding the Electoral College* (The Digital Press at the University of North Dakota, 2017) and *Protesting on Bended Knee: Race, Dissent, and Patriotism in 21st Century America* (The Digital Press at the University of North Dakota, 2018).

Emily Conroy-Krutz is an associate professor of history at Michigan State University and the author of *Christian Imperialism: Converting the World in the Early American Republic* (Cornell University Press, 2015). Her writings can be found in the *Journal of the Early Republic, Early American Studies, Diplomatic History*, and several edited volumes. She is currently writing *Missionary Diplomacy: Religion and American Foreign Relations in the Nineteenth Century*.

Kathleen DuVal is a professor of history at the University of North Carolina, Chapel Hill. She is the author of *Independence Lost: Lives on the Edge of the American Revolution* (Random House, 2015) and *The Native Ground: Indians and Colonists in the Heart of the Continent* (University of Pennsylvania Press, 2006) and coeditor of *Interpreting a Continent: Voices from Colonial America* (Rowman & Littlefield, 2009). She is currently writing a book on Native dominance of North America from the eleventh to nineteenth centuries.

Amy S. Greenberg is George Winfree Professor of History at Penn State University and immediate past president of the Society for Historians of the Early American Republic. She is the author of five books, including *A Wicked War: Polk, Clay, Lincoln, and the 1846 U.S. Invasion of Mexico* (Knopf, 2012); *Manifest Manhood and the Antebellum American Empire* (Cambridge University Press, 2005); and, most recently, *Lady First: The World of First Lady Sarah Polk* (Knopf, 2019).

Nicholas Guyatt is a professor of North American history at the University of Cambridge. He is the author of many books including *Bind Us Apart: How Enlightened Americans Invented Racial Segregation* (Basic Books, 2016) and *The Hated Cage: An American Tragedy in Britain's Most Terrifying Prison* (Basic Books, 2022).

M. Scott Heerman is an associate professor of history at the University of Miami. He is the author of *The Alchemy of Slavery: Human Bondage and Emancipation in the Illinois Country, 1730–1865* (University of Pennsylvania Press, 2018).

Robert Lee is an assistant professor of American history and a fellow of Selwyn College at the University of Cambridge and a former junior fellow at the Harvard Society of Fellows. His articles and digital scholarship examining the relationship between Indigenous dispossession and U.S. state formation in the nineteenth century have received numerous history and journalism awards. He has a Ph.D. from the University of California, Berkeley, and an M.A. from the University of Heidelberg.

Julia Lewandoski is an assistant professor in the Department of History at California State University San Marcos. Her publications include "'The Same Force, Authority, and Effect': Formalizing Native Property and British Plurality in Lower Canada," *Quebec Studies Journal*, Winter 2015/16. She is at work on a book about nineteenth-century Indigenous land reclamation and imperial legal regimes, forthcoming from the University of Pennsylvania Press. Research for her chapter was supported by the Louisiana Historical Association and the American Society for Legal History.

Margot Minardi is a professor of history and humanities at Reed College. She is the author of *Making Slavery History: Abolitionism and the Politics of Memory in Massachusetts* (Oxford University Press, 2010). Her current project centers on ideas of nation, empire, and cosmopolitanism in the political imagination of nineteenth-century American peace reformers.

Nakia D. Parker is an assistant professor of history at Michigan State University. She is a scholar of slavery, African American history, and American Indian history. She is currently working on her first book, *Trails of Tears and Freedom: Black Life in Indian Slave Country, 1830–1866.*

Ousmane K. Power-Greene is an associate professor in the History Department at Clark University. Dr. Power-Greene's book *Against Wind and Tide: The African American Struggle Against the Colonization Movement* was published by NYU Press in 2014. He is also coeditor of *In Search of Liberty: African American Internationalism in the Nineteenth-Century Atlantic World* (University of Georgia Press, 2021).

Tom Smith is the Keasbey Research Fellow in American Studies at Selwyn College, University of Cambridge. He is currently working on a book manuscript examining the historical thinking of American Protestant missionaries in Hawai'i and the Philippines in the late nineteenth and early twentieth centuries. His previous work has been published in *Diplomatic History*, *Historical Journal*, and *American Nineteenth Century History*.

Susan Gaunt Stearns is an assistant professor of history at the University of Mississippi. She is a specialist in the history of capitalism and early national expansion, and she is currently at work on a manuscript on the significance of Pinckney's Treaty to the political economy of the early republic.

INDEX

EDITORS' ACKNOWLEDGMENTS

Our first thanks are to our contributors, for their dedication to this volume despite all the personal and professional challenges that the coronavirus pandemic has caused. We are so grateful to have had the opportunity to work with you.

This project began as a conference, "Making a Republic Imperial," which was cohosted by the McNeil Center for Early American Studies and the Library Company of Philadelphia in March 2019. We would like to thank the conference's sponsors: the McNeil Center, the Library Company's Program in Early American Economy and Society, the Institute for Thomas Paine Studies at Iona University, and the Department of History at Princeton University. The conference would not have been possible without the hard work and support of Amy Baxter-Bellamy, Kathleen Brown, Cathy Matson, Barbara Natello, Daniel Richter, Nicole Scalessa, and Laura Keenan Spero. Thanks also to the wonderful members of the program committee: Elizabeth Ellis, Rashauna Johnson, and Honor Sachs. We are grateful to all of the conference's participants and attendees for their lively discussion and deep engagement with the theme of empire in the early republic. As we prepared the volume, it has been a delight to welcome additional voices into this conversation.

For their thoughtful comments on the introduction, Michael and Emily would like to thank Jeremy Adelman, Konstantin Dierks, and Wendy Warren. We are grateful to Penn Press's anonymous reviewers for their thorough and insightful feedback on the volume as a whole, and to the Press's editorial team—especially Cheryl Hirsch and Jennifer Shenk—for ushering it across the finish line. The publication of this volume received generous support from the Humanities and Arts Research Program at Michigan State University.

At Penn Press, Robert Lockhart has been a steadfast and enthusiastic supporter of this project. We have appreciated his sensitivity and flexibility as the pandemic forced a shift in our expected timeline, as well as his keen editorial eye and general good cheer.